This is the last page.

In keeping with the original Japanese comic format, this book reads from right to left—so action, sound effects, and word balloons are completely reversed. This preserves the orientation of the original artwork—plus, it's fun! Check out the diagram shown here to get the hang of things, and then turn to the other side of the book to get started!

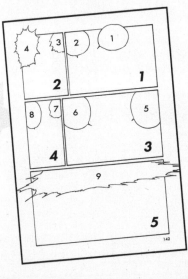

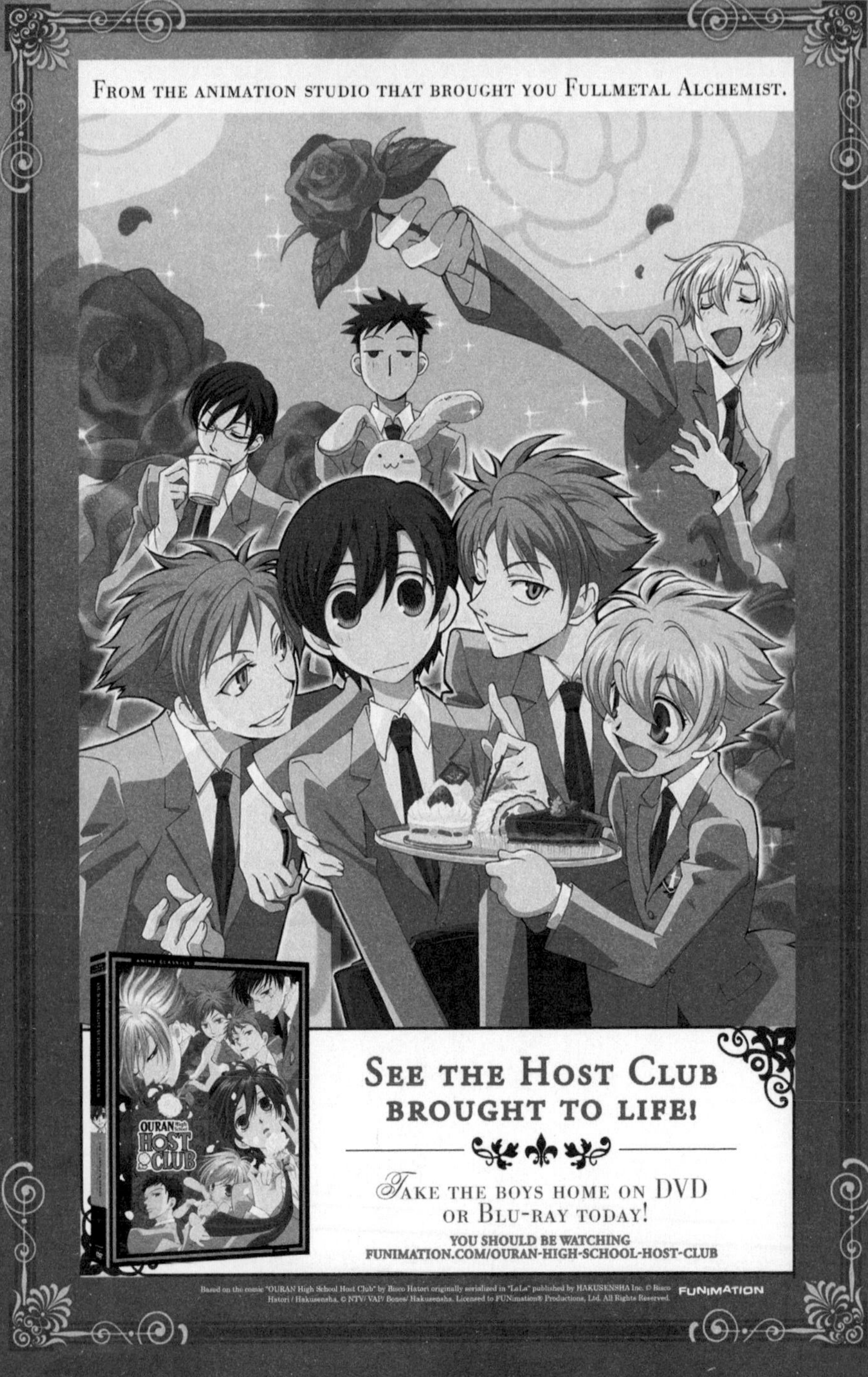

FROM THE ANIMATION STUDIO THAT BROUGHT YOU FULLMETAL ALCHEMIST.
OURAN High School HOST CLUB
SEE THE HOST CLUB BROUGHT TO LIFE!
TAKE THE BOYS HOME ON DVD OR BLU-RAY TODAY!
YOU SHOULD BE WATCHING
FUNIMATION.COM/OURAN-HIGH-SCHOOL-HOST-CLUB
Based on the comic "OURAN High School Host Club" by Bisco Hatori originally serialized in "LaLa" published by HAKUSENSHA Inc. © Bisco Hatori / Hakusensha. © NTV/ VAP/ Bones/ Hakusensha. Licensed to FUNimation® Productions, Ltd. All Rights Reserved.
FUNIMATION

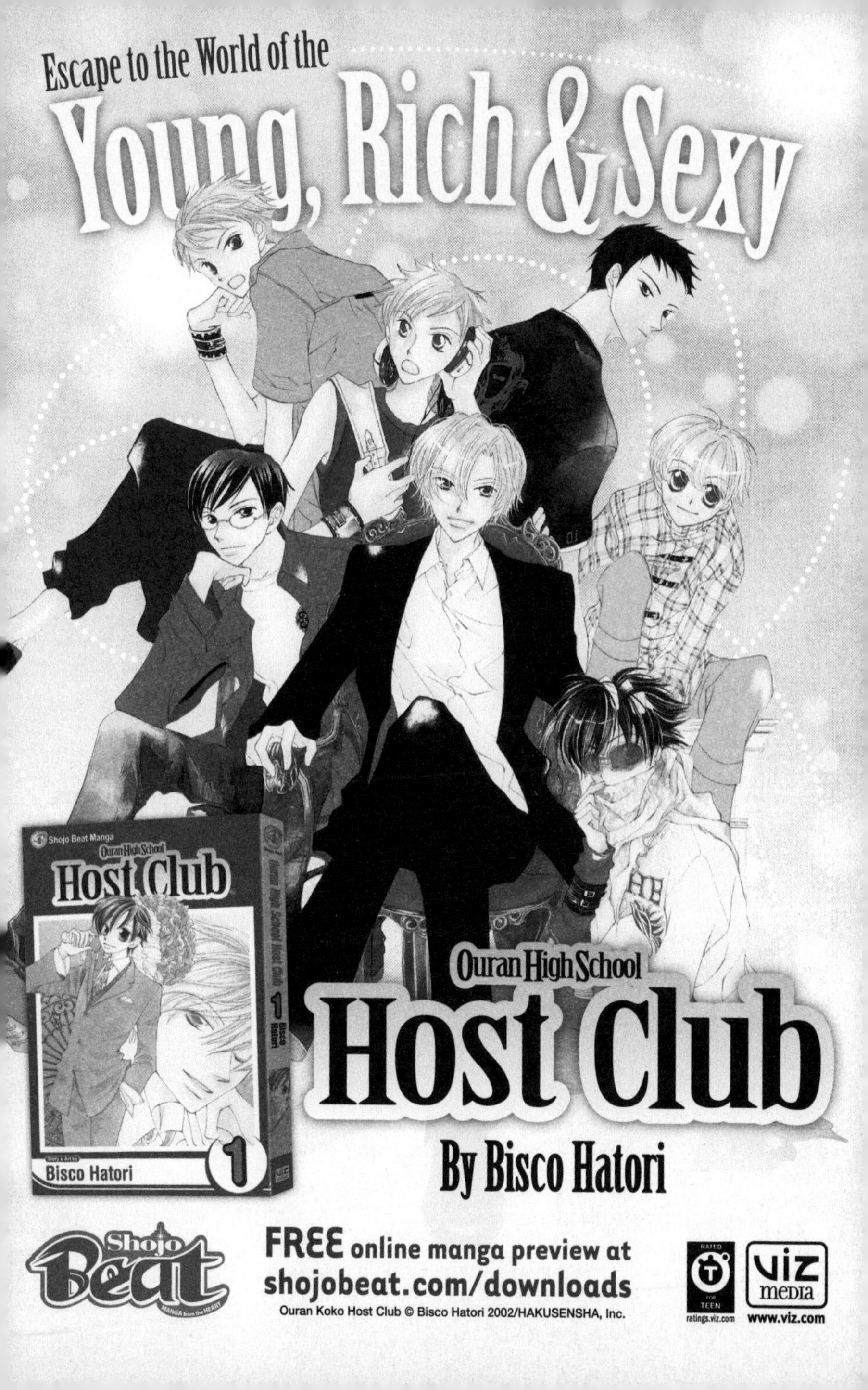
Escape to the World of the
Young, Rich & Sexy
Shojo Beat Manga
Ouran High School
Host Club
Story & Art by
Bisco Hatori
1
Ouran High School
Host Club
By Bisco Hatori
Shojo Beat
MANGA from the HEART
FREE online manga preview at
shojobeat.com/downloads
Ouran Koko Host Club © Bisco Hatori 2002/HAKUSENSHA, Inc.
RATED
T
FOR
TEEN
ratings.viz.com
VIZ media
www.viz.com

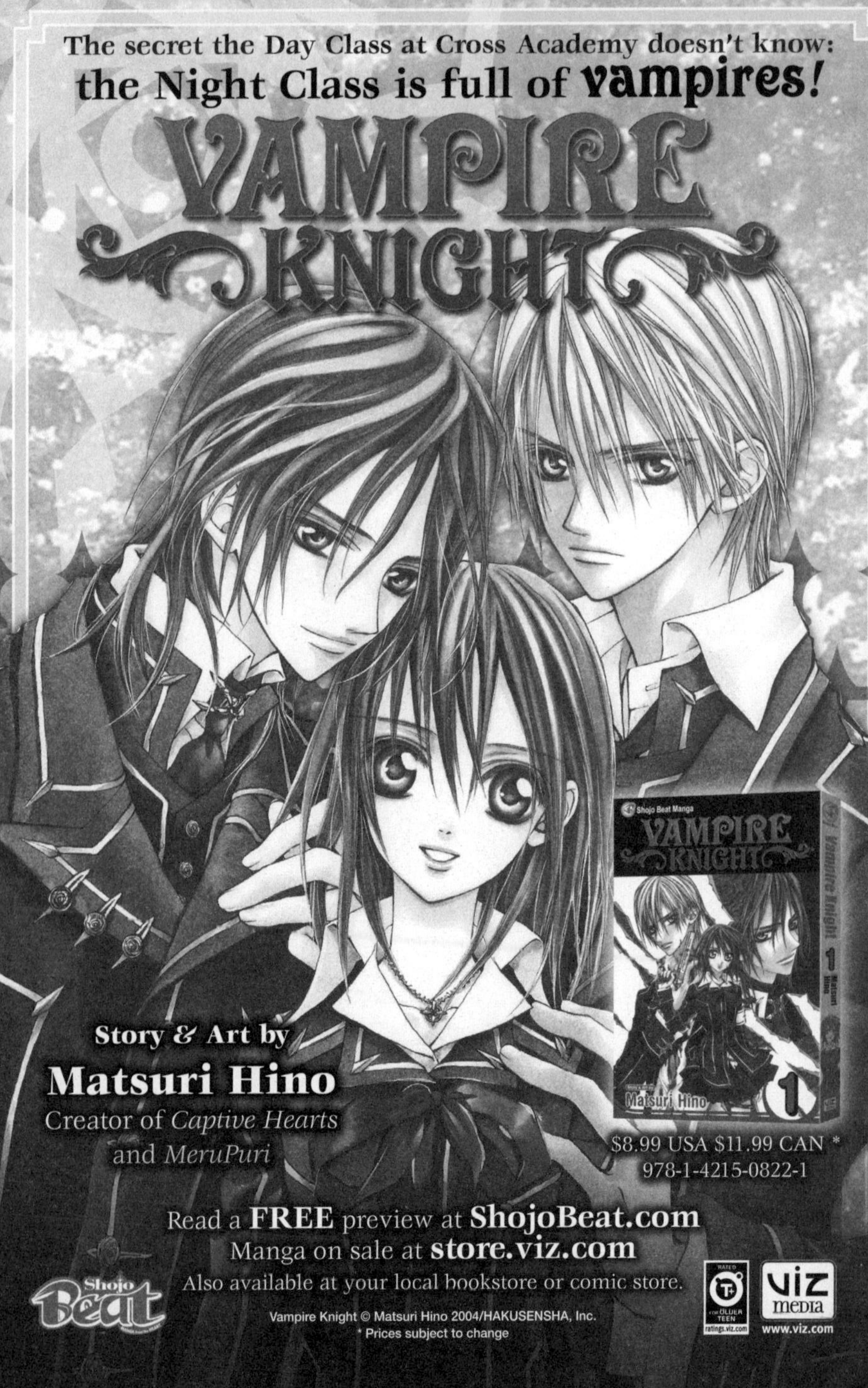
The secret the Day Class at Cross Academy doesn't know:
the Night Class is full of vampires!
VAMPIRE KNIGHT
Shojo Beat Manga
VAMPIRE KNIGHT
Vampire Knight 1 Matsuri Hino
Matsuri Hino
1
Story & Art by
Matsuri Hino
Creator of Captive Hearts
and MeruPuri
$8.99 USA $11.99 CAN *
978-1-4215-0822-1
Read a FREE preview at ShojoBeat.com
Manga on sale at store.viz.com
Also available at your local bookstore or comic store.
Shojo Beat
RATED T+ FOR OLDER TEEN ratings.viz.com
viz media
www.viz.com
Vampire Knight © Matsuri Hino 2004/HAKUSENSHA, Inc.
* Prices subject to change

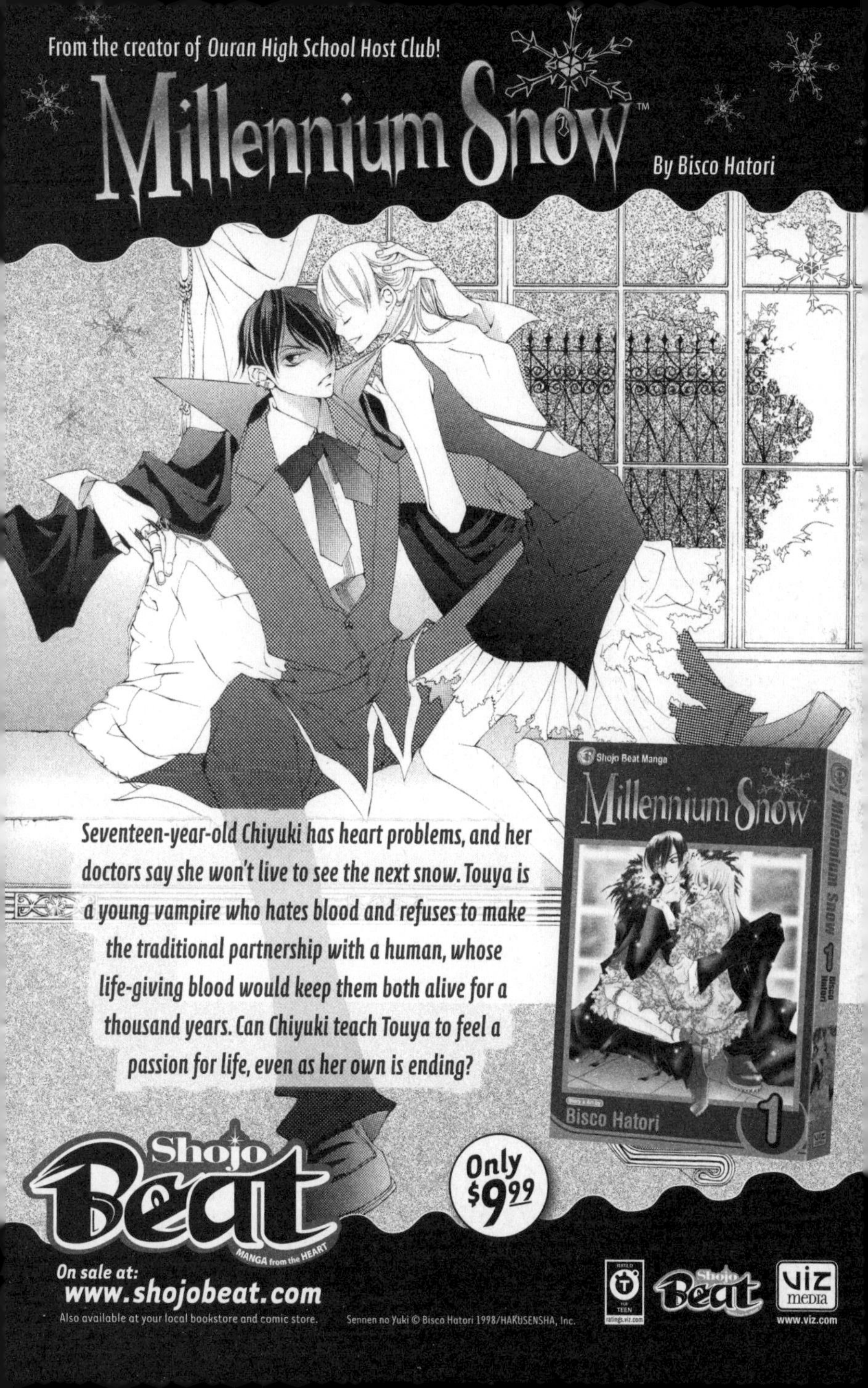
From the creator of Ouran High School Host Club!
Millennium Snow™
By Bisco Hatori
Seventeen-year-old Chiyuki has heart problems, and her doctors say she won't live to see the next snow. Touya is a young vampire who hates blood and refuses to make the traditional partnership with a human, whose life-giving blood would keep them both alive for a thousand years. Can Chiyuki teach Touya to feel a passion for life, even as her own is ending?
Shojo Beat Manga
Millennium Snow
1
Bisco Hatori
Shojo Beat
MANGA from the HEART
Only $9.99
On sale at:
www.shojobeat.com
Also available at your local bookstore and comic store.
Sennen no Yuki © Bisco Hatori 1998/HAKUSENSHA, Inc.
RATED T TEEN ratings.viz.com
Shojo Beat
viz media
www.viz.com

VOICE OVER!
SEIYU ACADEMY
VOL. 5
Shojo Beat Edition

STORY AND ART BY
MAKI MINAMI

TECHNICAL ADVISORS
Yoichi Kato, Kaori Kagami, Ayumi Hashidate,
Ayako Harino and Touko Fujitani

Special Thanks
81produce
Tokyo Animator College
Tokyo Animation College

English Translation & Adaptation/John Werry
Touch-up Art & Lettering/Sabrina Heep
Design/Yukiko Whitley
Editor/Pancha Diaz

SEIYU KA! by Maki Minami
© Maki Minami 2011
All rights reserved.
First published in Japan in 2011 by HAKUSENSHA, Inc., Tokyo.
English language translation rights arranged with
HAKUSENSHA, Inc., Tokyo.

Printed in the U.S.A.

Published by VIZ Media, LLC
P.O. Box 77010
San Francisco, CA 94107

10 9 8 7 6 5 4 3 2 1
First printing, June 2014

www.viz.com   www.shojobeat.com

Voice Over!
Seiyu Academy

5

Vol.**5**
Story & Art by
Maki Minami

TECHNICAL ADVISORS
Yoichi Kato, Kaori Kagami, Ayumi Hashidate,
Ayako Harino and Touko Fujitani

Voice Over! Seiyu Academy

Vol.5

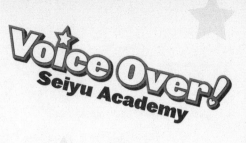

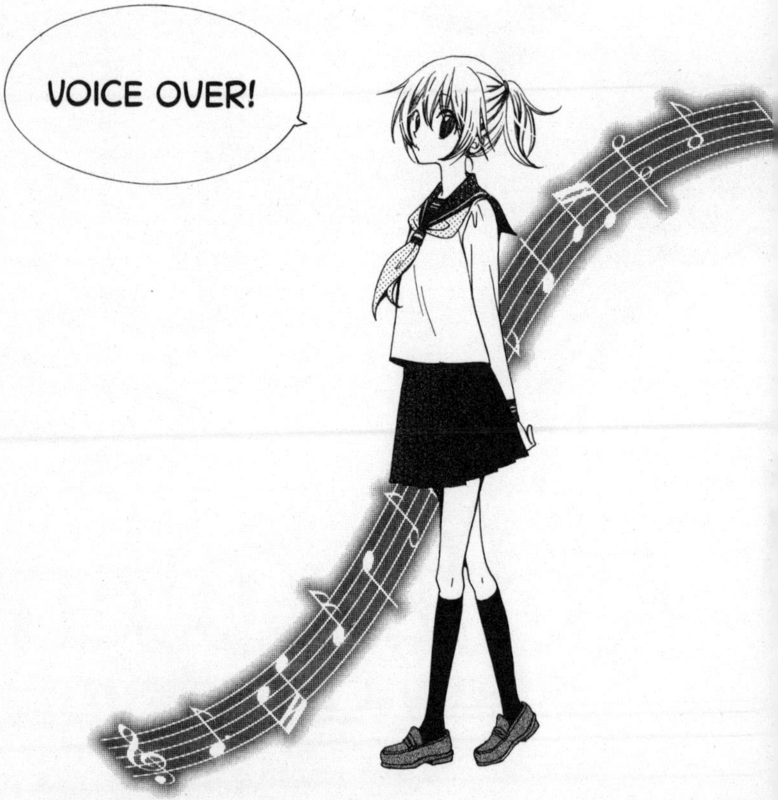
VOICE OVER!

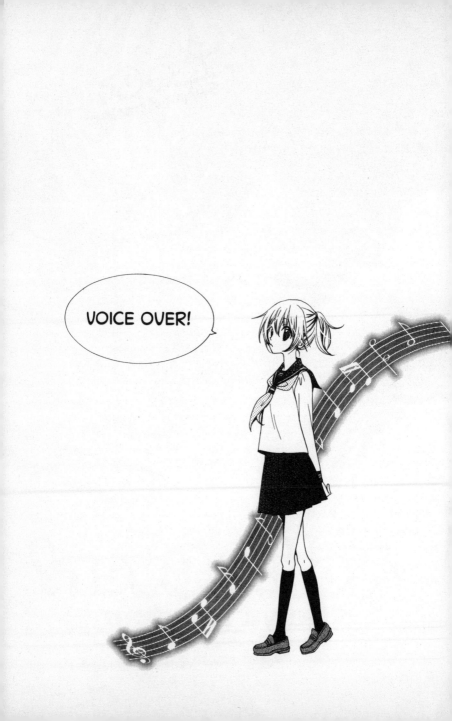

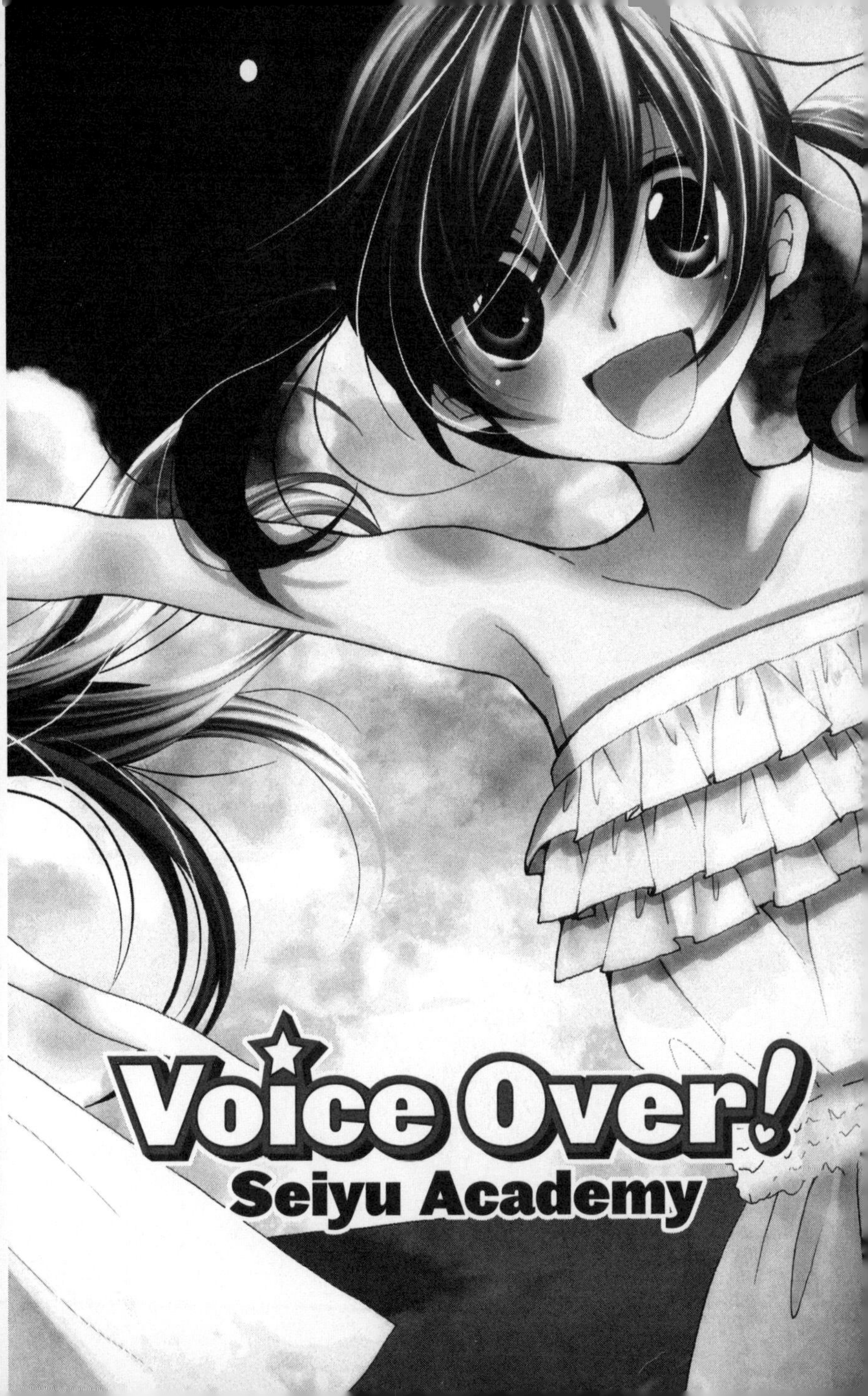
Voice Over!
Seiyu Academy

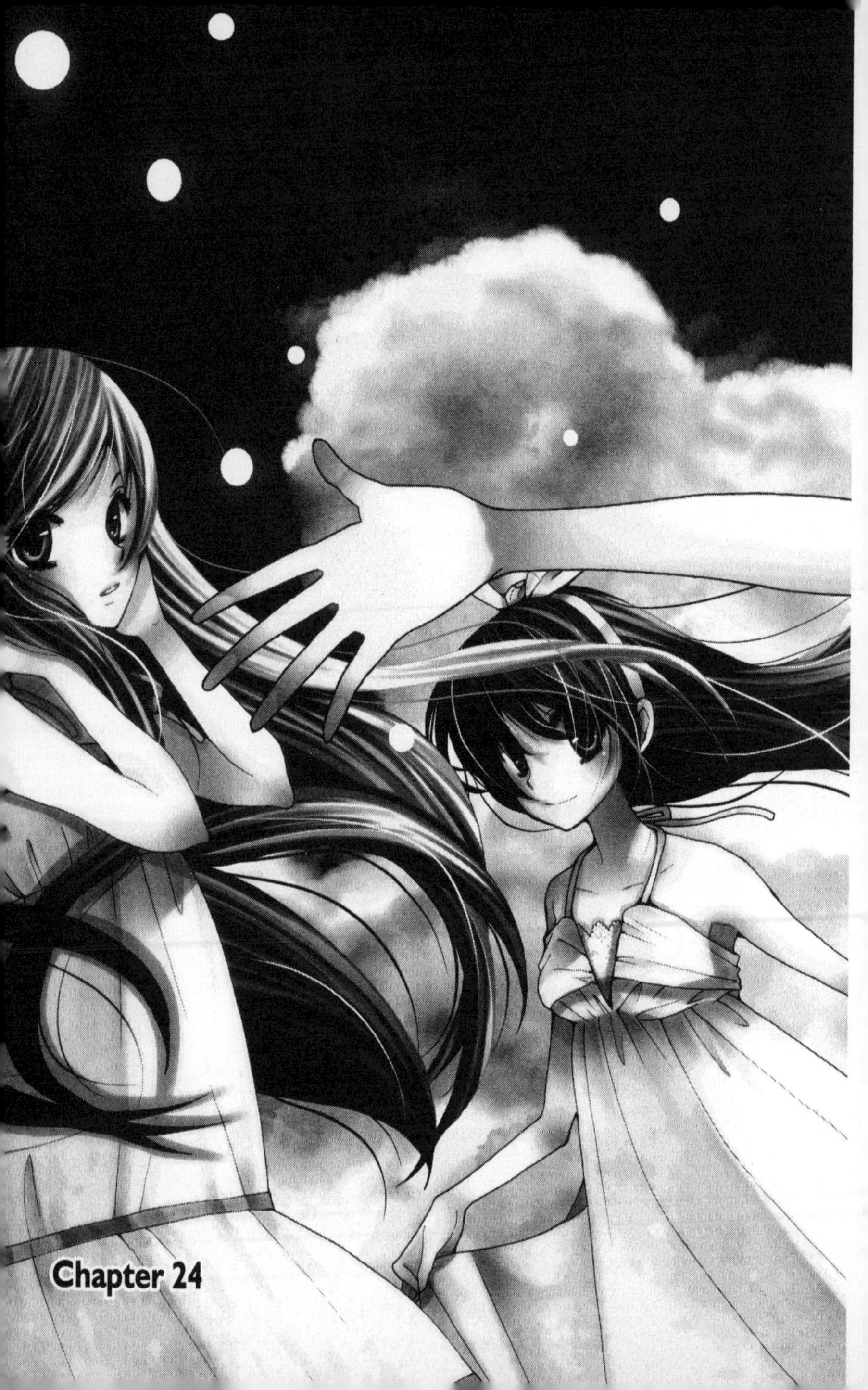
Chapter 24

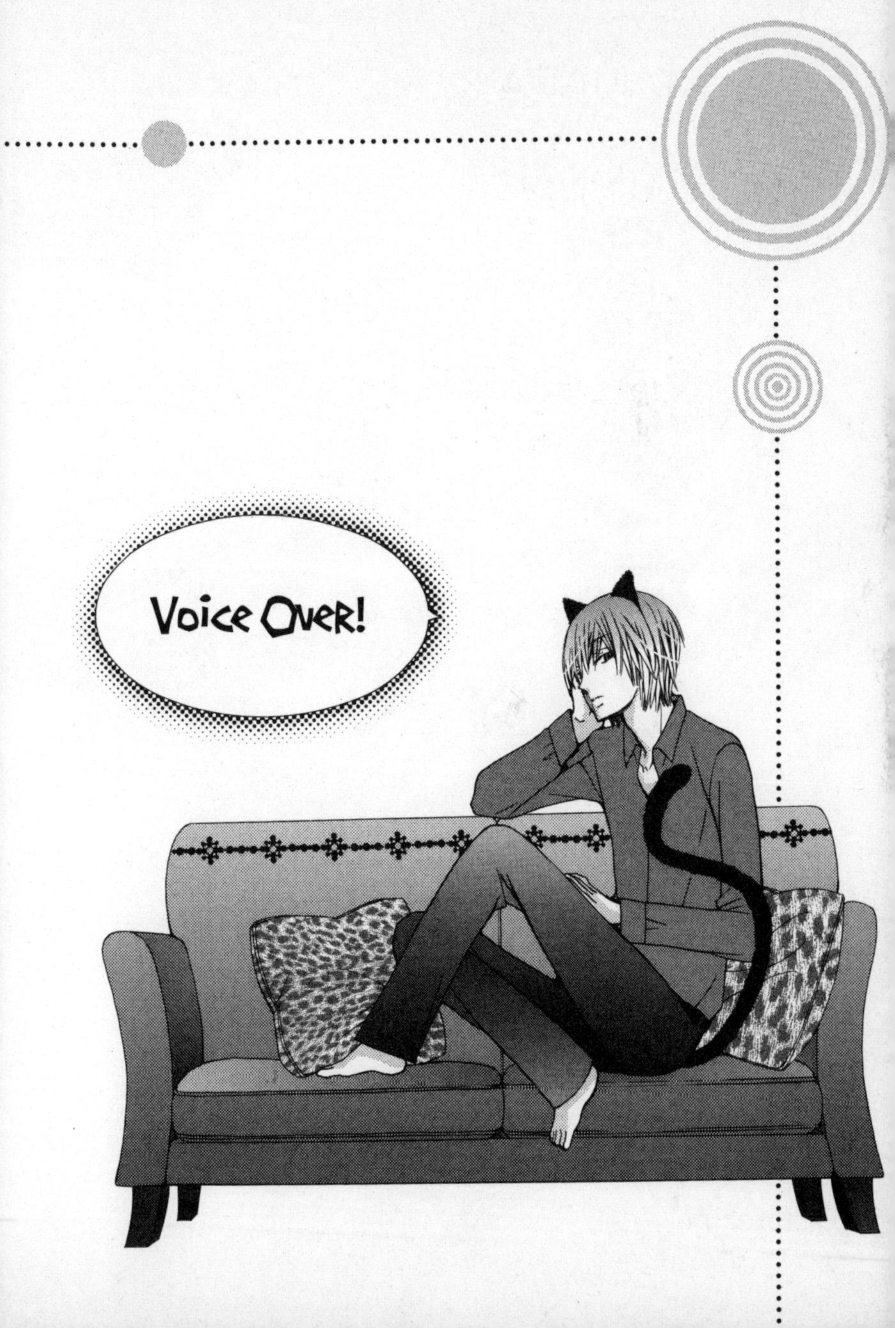
Voice Over!

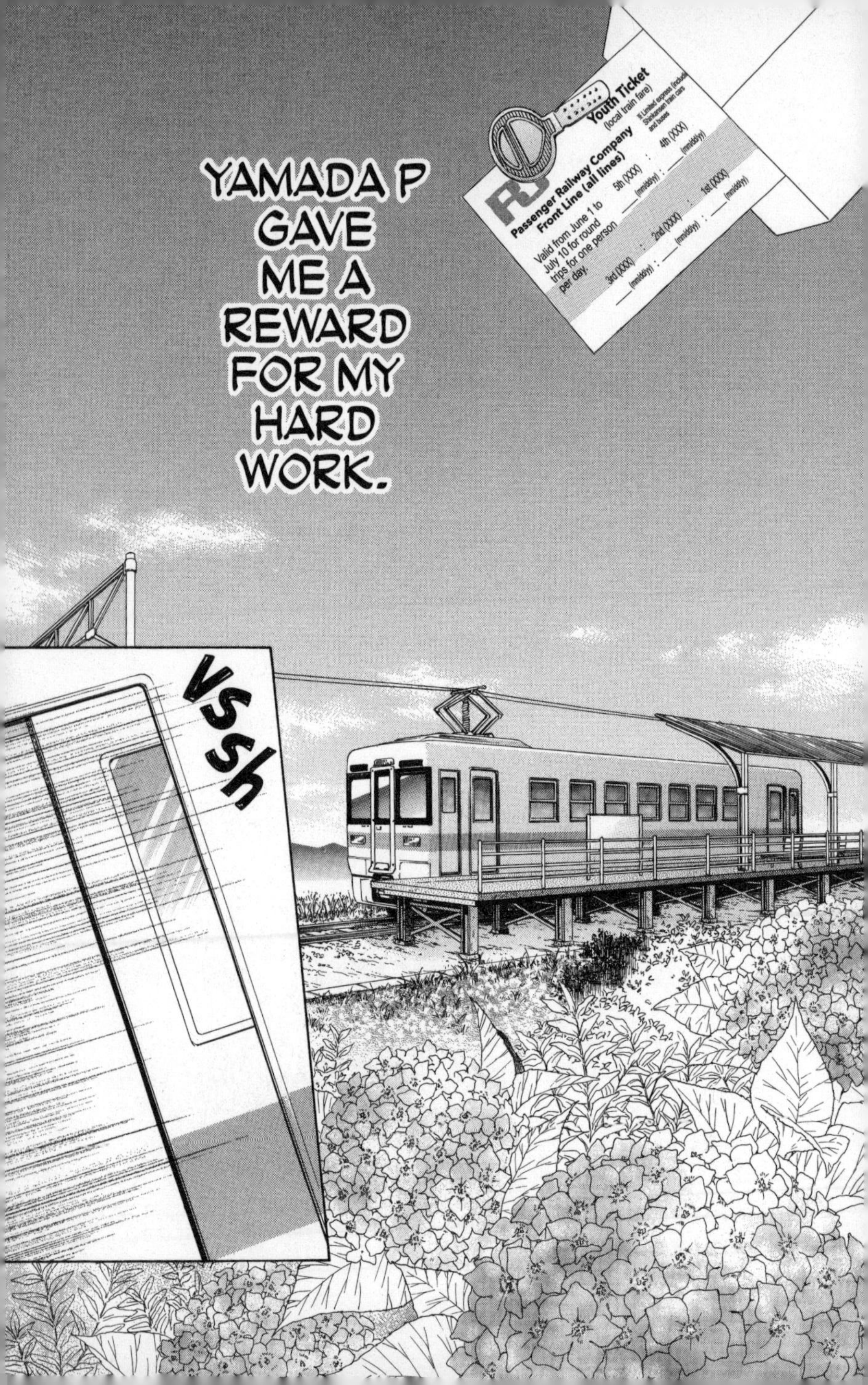
Youth Ticket
(local train fare)
Passenger Railway Company
Front Line (all lines)
Valid from June 1 to July 10 for round trips for one person per day.
YAMADA P GAVE ME A REWARD FOR MY HARD WORK.
VSSh

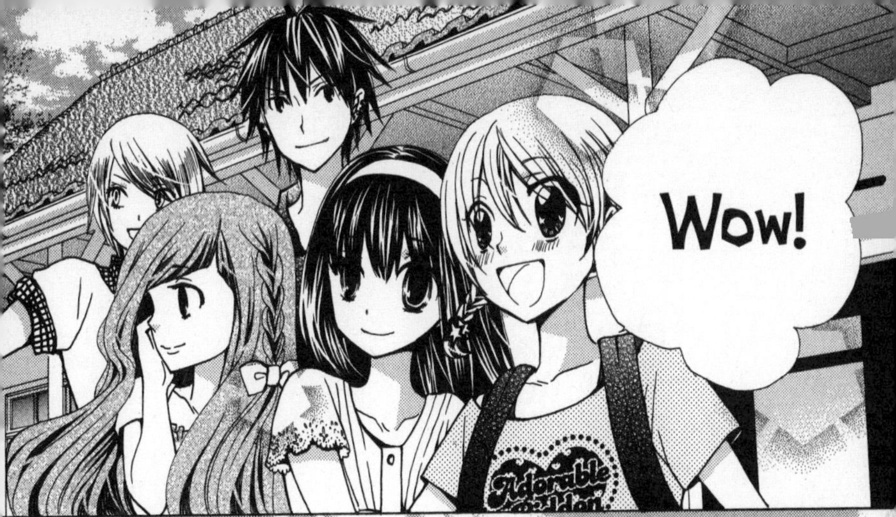
Wow!
Adorable
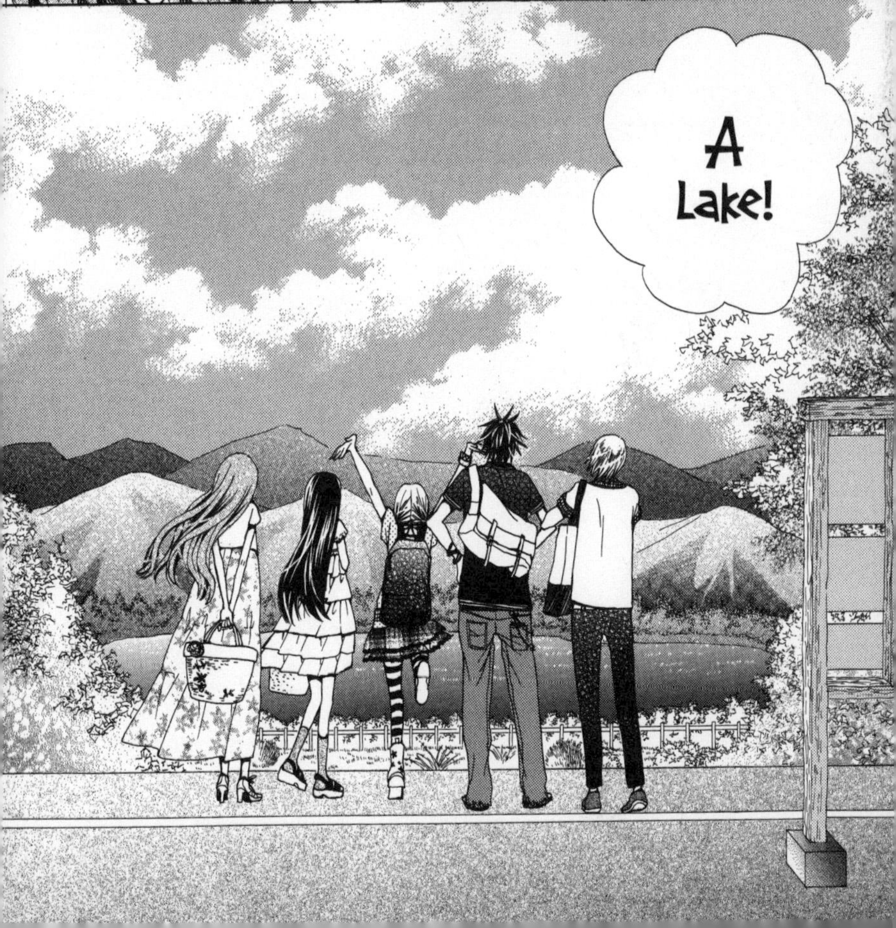
A Lake!

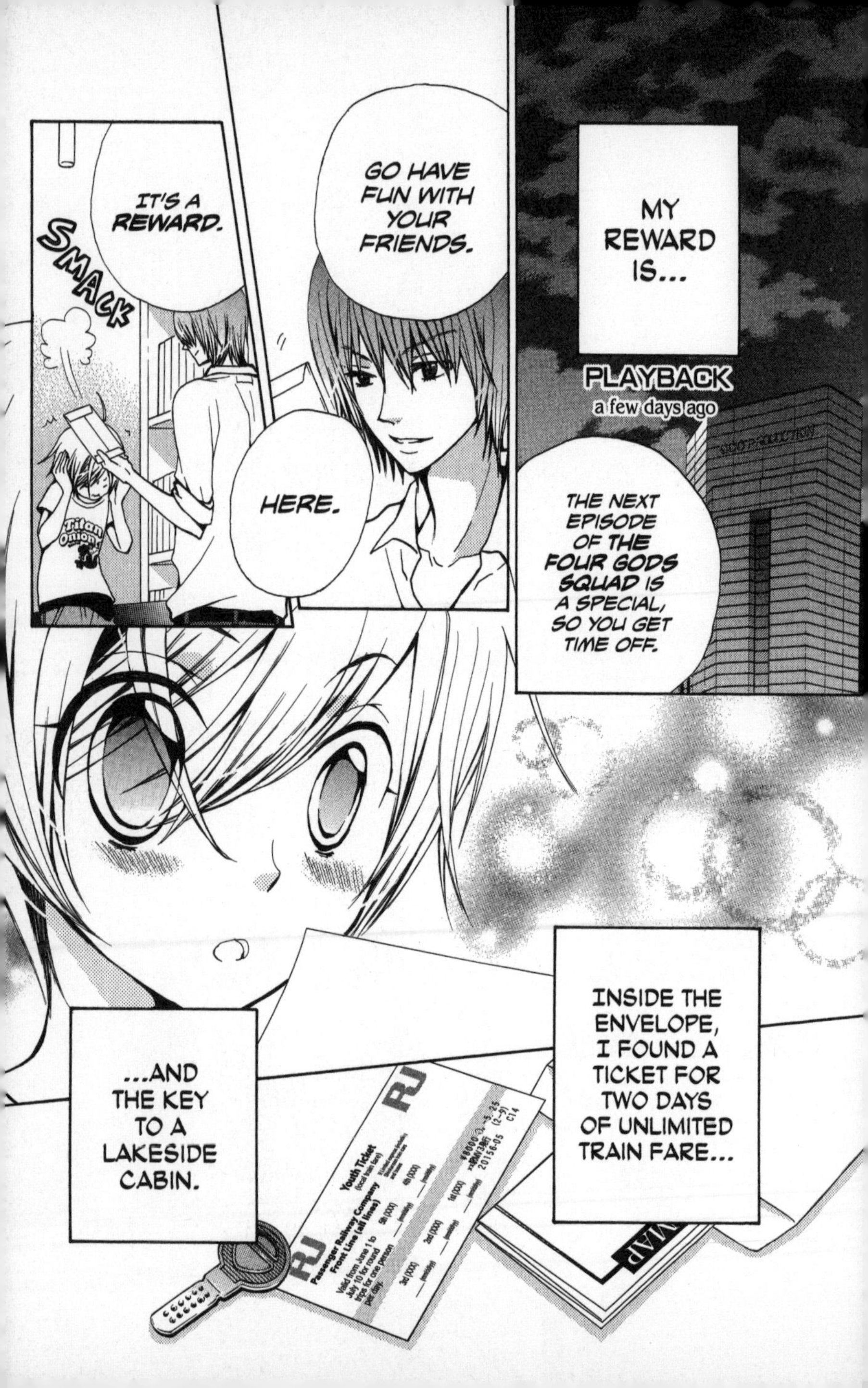

MY REWARD IS...
PLAYBACK
a few days ago
THE NEXT EPISODE OF THE FOUR GODS SQUAD IS A SPECIAL, SO YOU GET TIME OFF.
GO HAVE FUN WITH YOUR FRIENDS.
HERE.
IT'S A REWARD.
SMACK
INSIDE THE ENVELOPE, I FOUND A TICKET FOR TWO DAYS OF UNLIMITED TRAIN FARE...
...AND THE KEY TO A LAKESIDE CABIN.

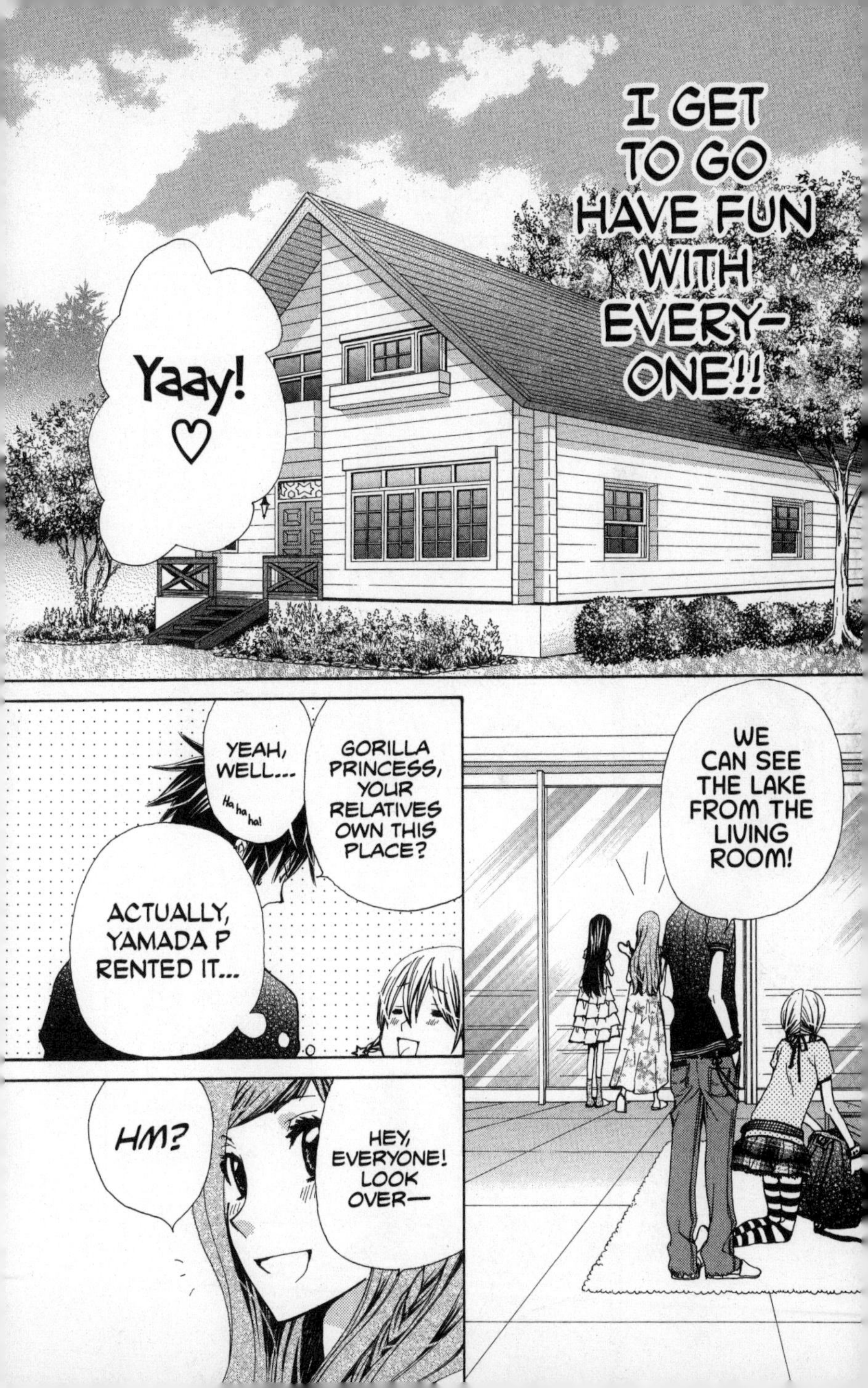
I GET TO GO HAVE FUN WITH EVERY-ONE!!
Yaay! ♡
WE CAN SEE THE LAKE FROM THE LIVING ROOM!
GORILLA PRINCESS, YOUR RELATIVES OWN THIS PLACE?
YEAH, WELL...
Ha ha ha!
ACTUALLY, YAMADA P RENTED IT...
HEY, EVERYONE! LOOK OVER—
HM?

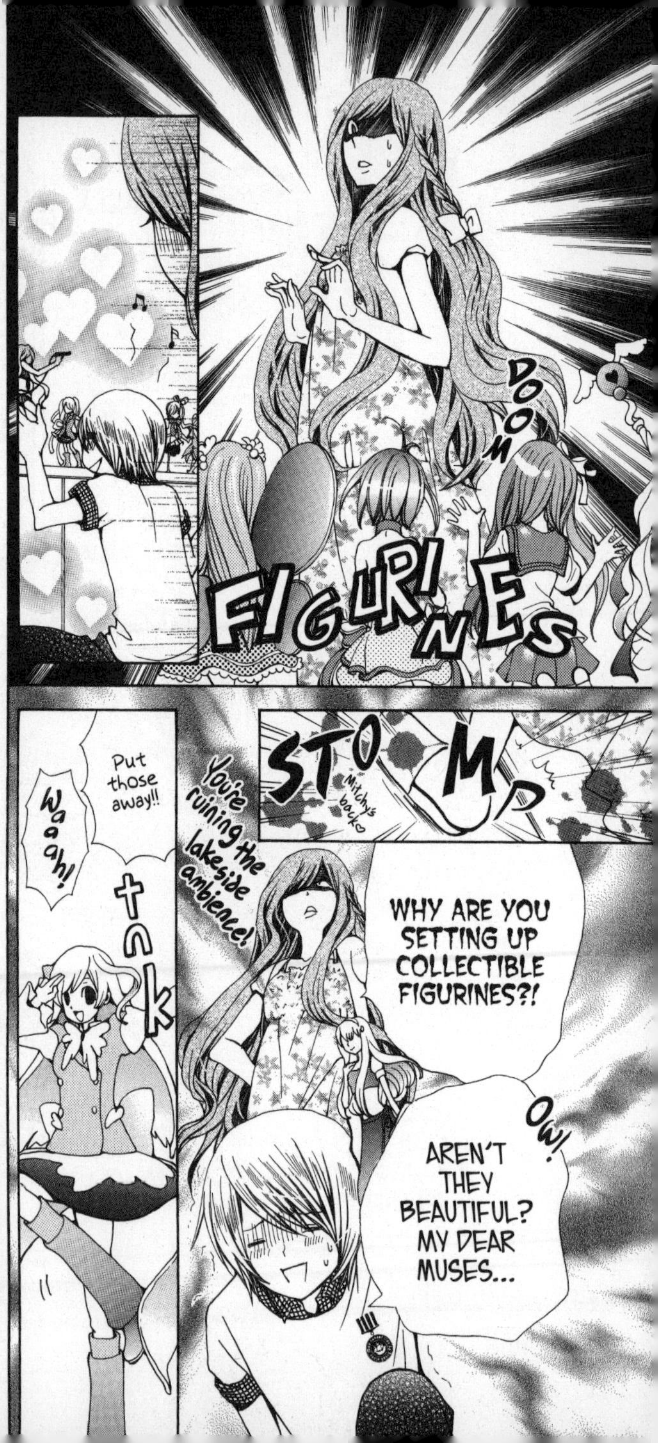
DOOM
FIGURINES
STOMP
Mitchy's back♡
WHY ARE YOU SETTING UP COLLECTIBLE FIGURINES?!
You're ruining the lakeside ambience!
OW!
AREN'T THEY BEAUTIFUL? MY DEAR MUSES...
Put those away!!
Waaah!
tuck

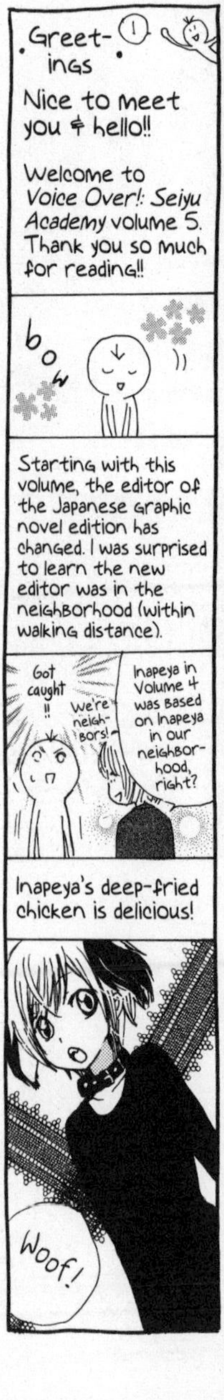
Greet-ings
!
Nice to meet you & hello!!
Welcome to *Voice Over!: Seiyu Academy* volume 5. Thank you so much for reading!!
bow
Starting with this volume, the editor of the Japanese graphic novel edition has changed. I was surprised to learn the new editor was in the neighborhood (within walking distance).
Inapeya in Volume 4 was based on Inapeya in our neighbor-hood, right?
We're neigh-bors!
Got caught !!
Inapeya's deep-fried chicken is delicious!
Woof!

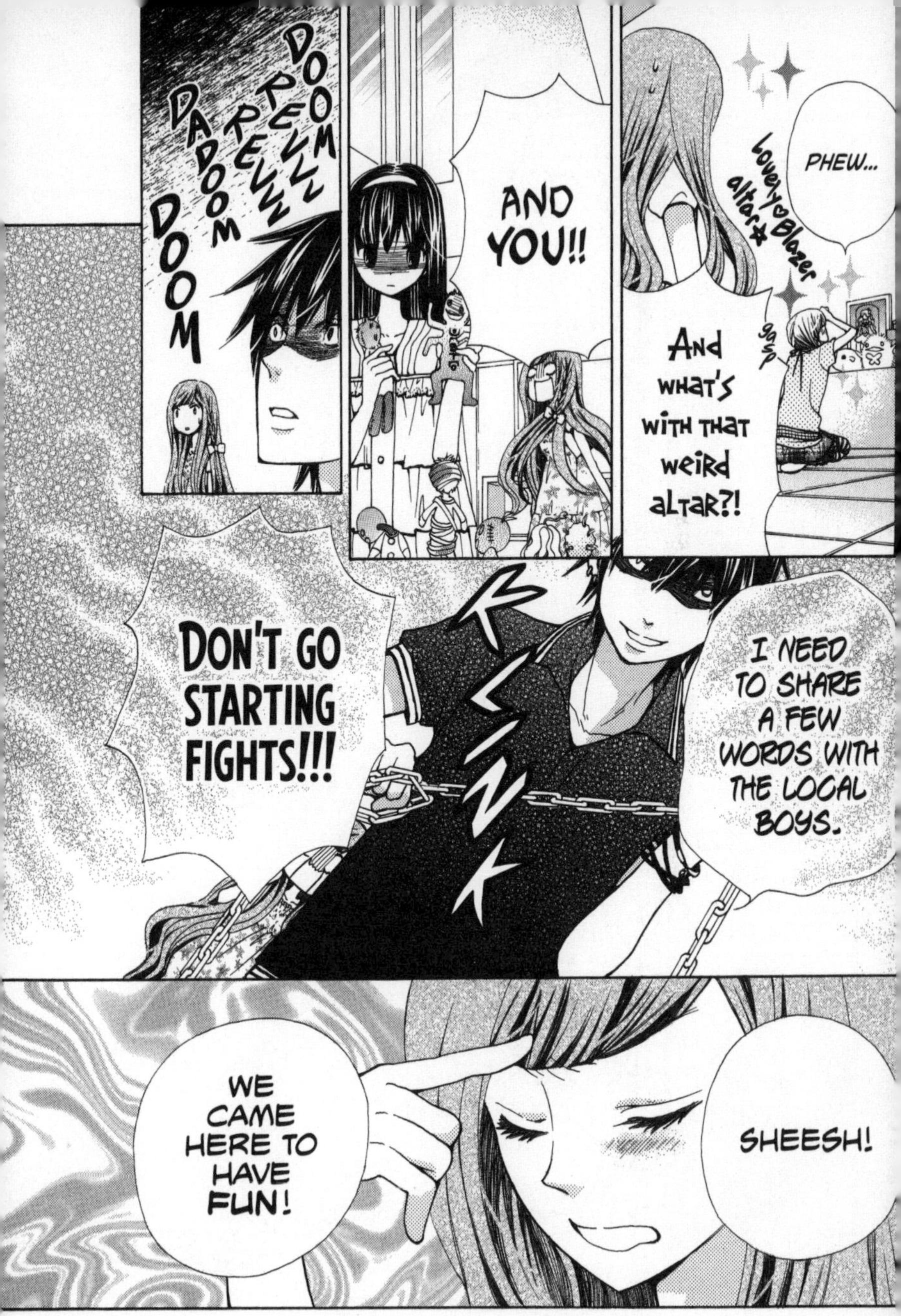
PHEW...
Lovely♡Blazer altar★
gasp
And what's with that weird altar?!
AND YOU!!
DOOM REVVV REVVV DADOOM DOOM
I NEED TO SHARE A FEW WORDS WITH THE LOCAL BOYS.
KLINK
DON'T GO STARTING FIGHTS!!!
SHEESH!
WE CAME HERE TO HAVE FUN!

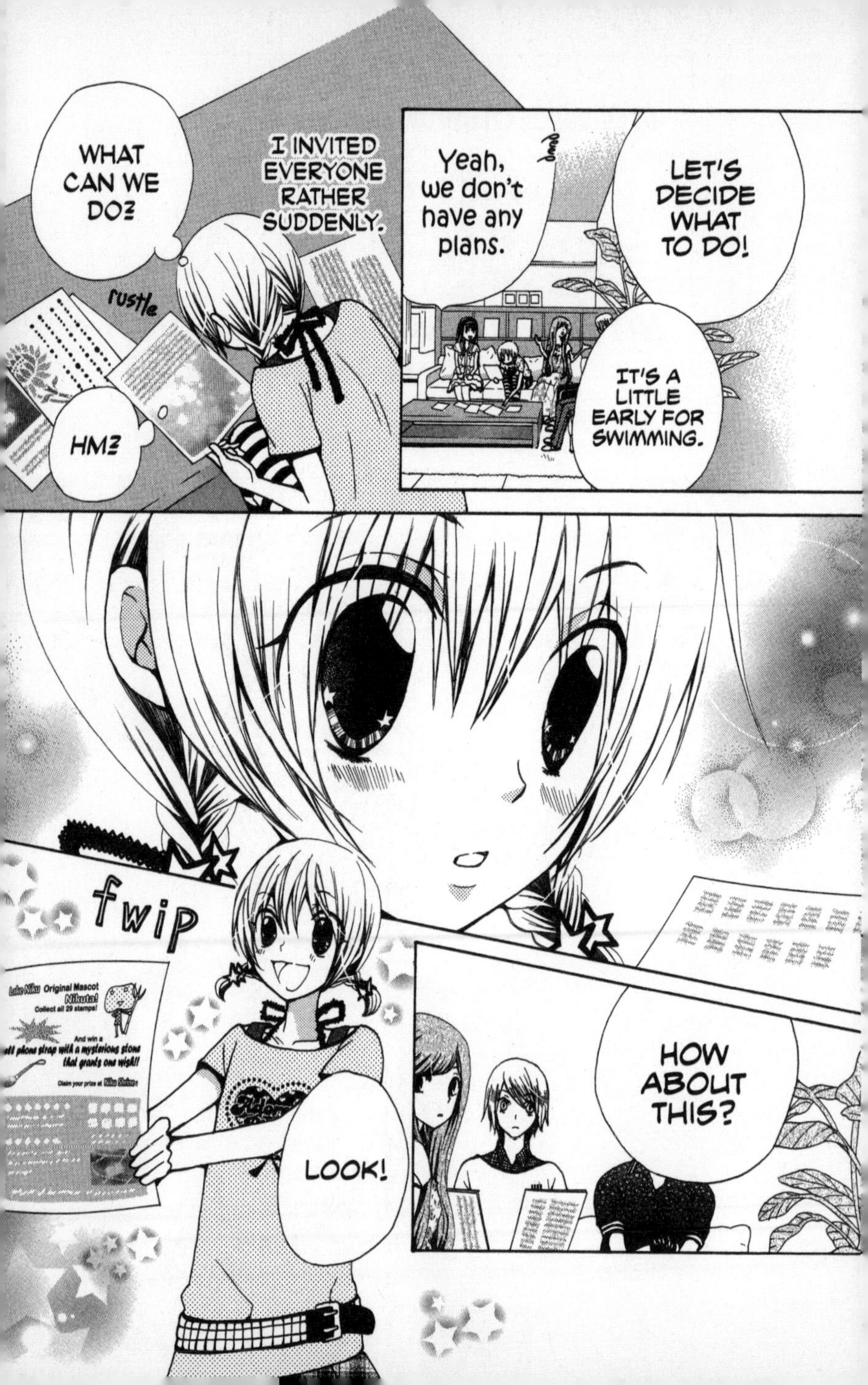
LET'S DECIDE WHAT TO DO!
Yeah, we don't have any plans.
IT'S A LITTLE EARLY FOR SWIMMING.
I INVITED EVERYONE RATHER SUDDENLY.
WHAT CAN WE DO?
rustle
HM?
HOW ABOUT THIS?
fwip
LOOK!
Lake Niku Original Mascot
Nikuta!
Collect all 29 stamps!
And win a
ell phone strap with a mysterious stone
that grants one wish!!
Claim your prize at Niku Shrine!

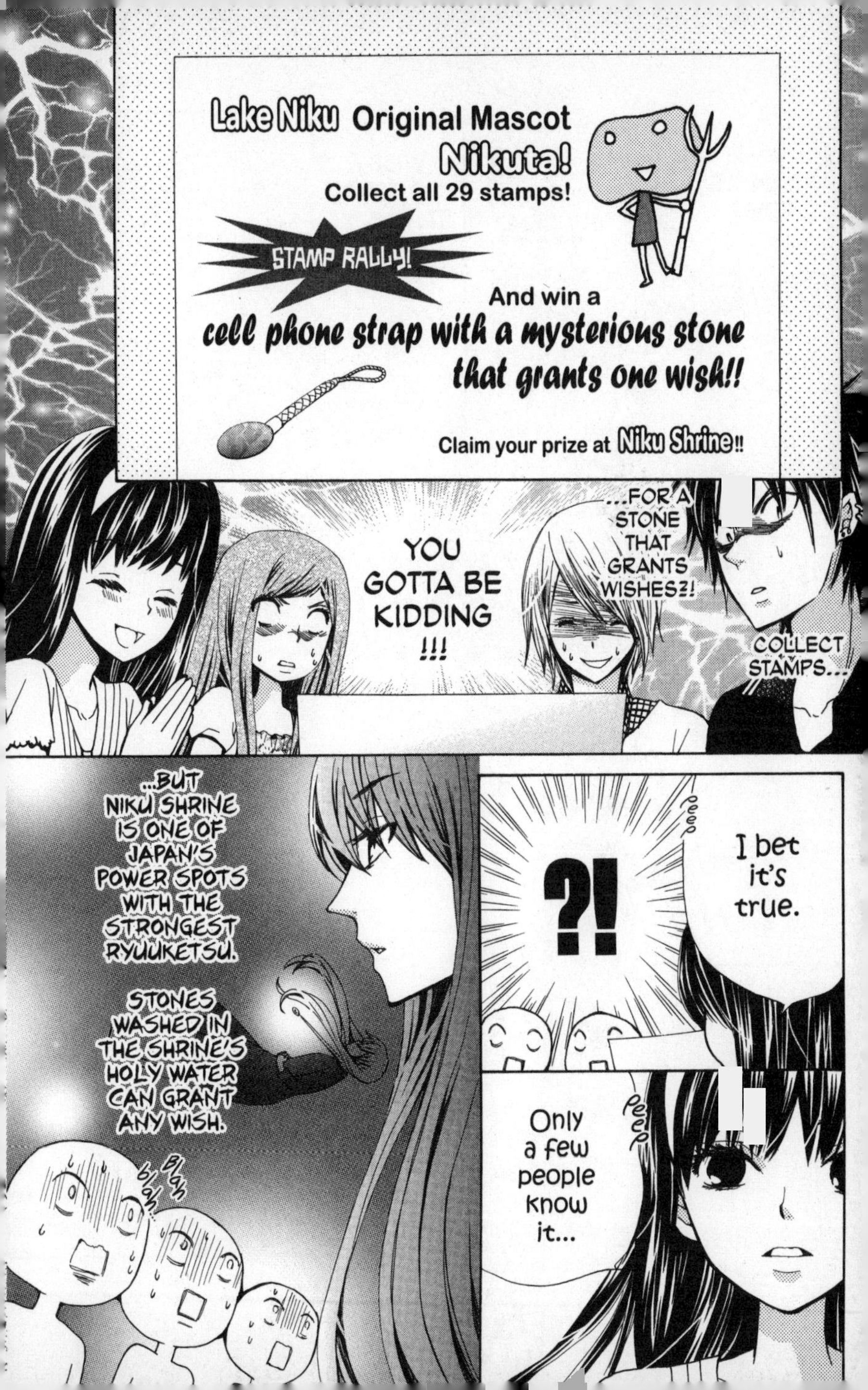
Lake Niku Original Mascot
Nikuta!
Collect all 29 stamps!
STAMP RALLY!
And win a
cell phone strap with a mysterious stone that grants one wish!!
Claim your prize at Niku Shrine!!
COLLECT STAMPS...
...FOR A STONE THAT GRANTS WISHES?!
YOU GOTTA BE KIDDING!!!
peep
I bet it's true.
?!
peep
Only a few people know it...
...BUT NIKU SHRINE IS ONE OF JAPAN'S POWER SPOTS WITH THE STRONGEST RYUUKETSU.
STONES WASHED IN THE SHRINE'S HOLY WATER CAN GRANT ANY WISH.
Blah blah

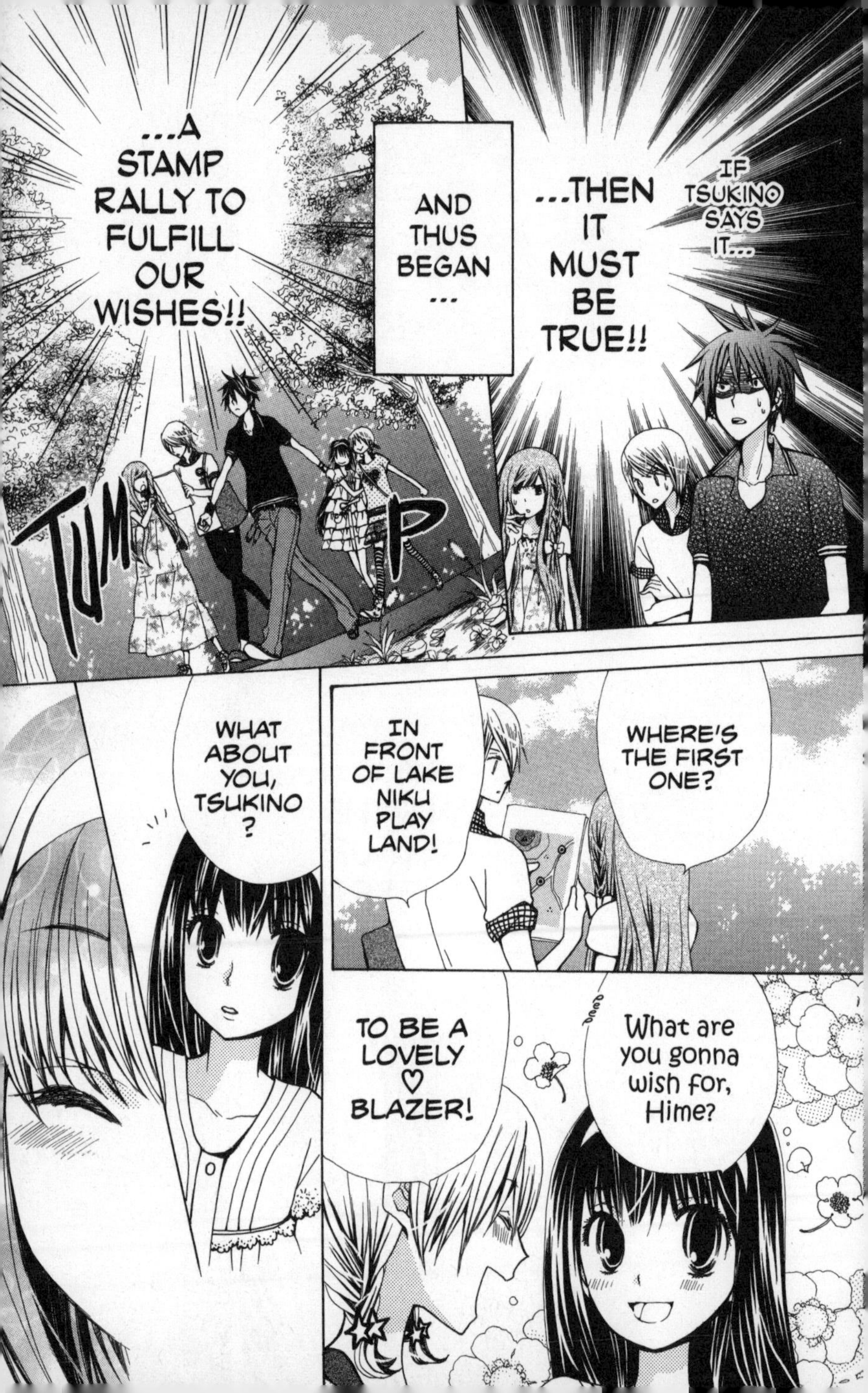
IF TSUKINO SAYS IT...
...THEN IT MUST BE TRUE!!
AND THUS BEGAN ...
...A STAMP RALLY TO FULFILL OUR WISHES!!
TUMP
WHERE'S THE FIRST ONE?
IN FRONT OF LAKE NIKU PLAY LAND!
What are you gonna wish for, Hime?
TO BE A LOVELY ♡ BLAZER!
WHAT ABOUT YOU, TSUKINO?

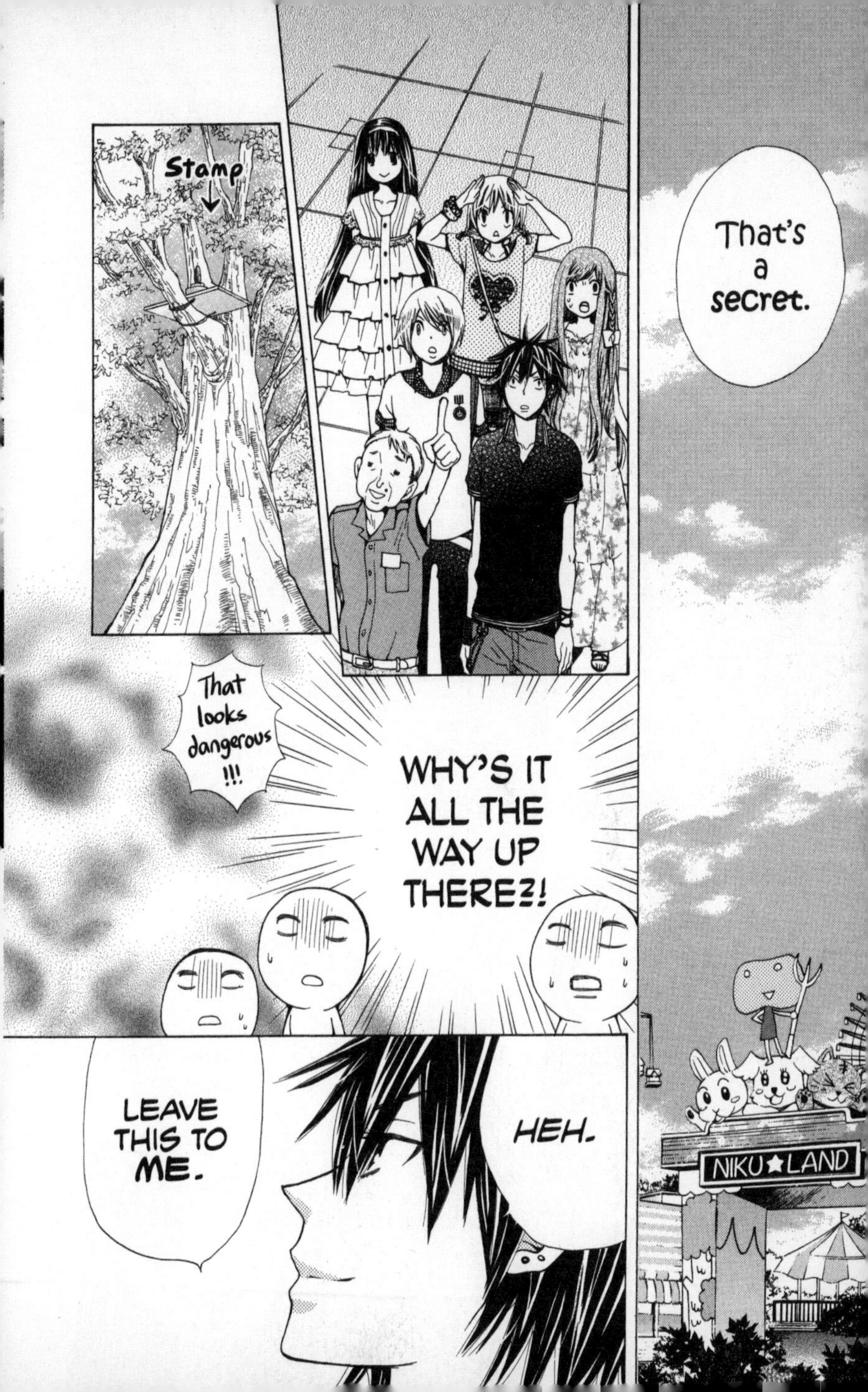
That's a secret.
NIKU★LAND
Stamp
WHY'S IT ALL THE WAY UP THERE?!
That looks dangerous!!!
HEH.
LEAVE THIS TO ME.

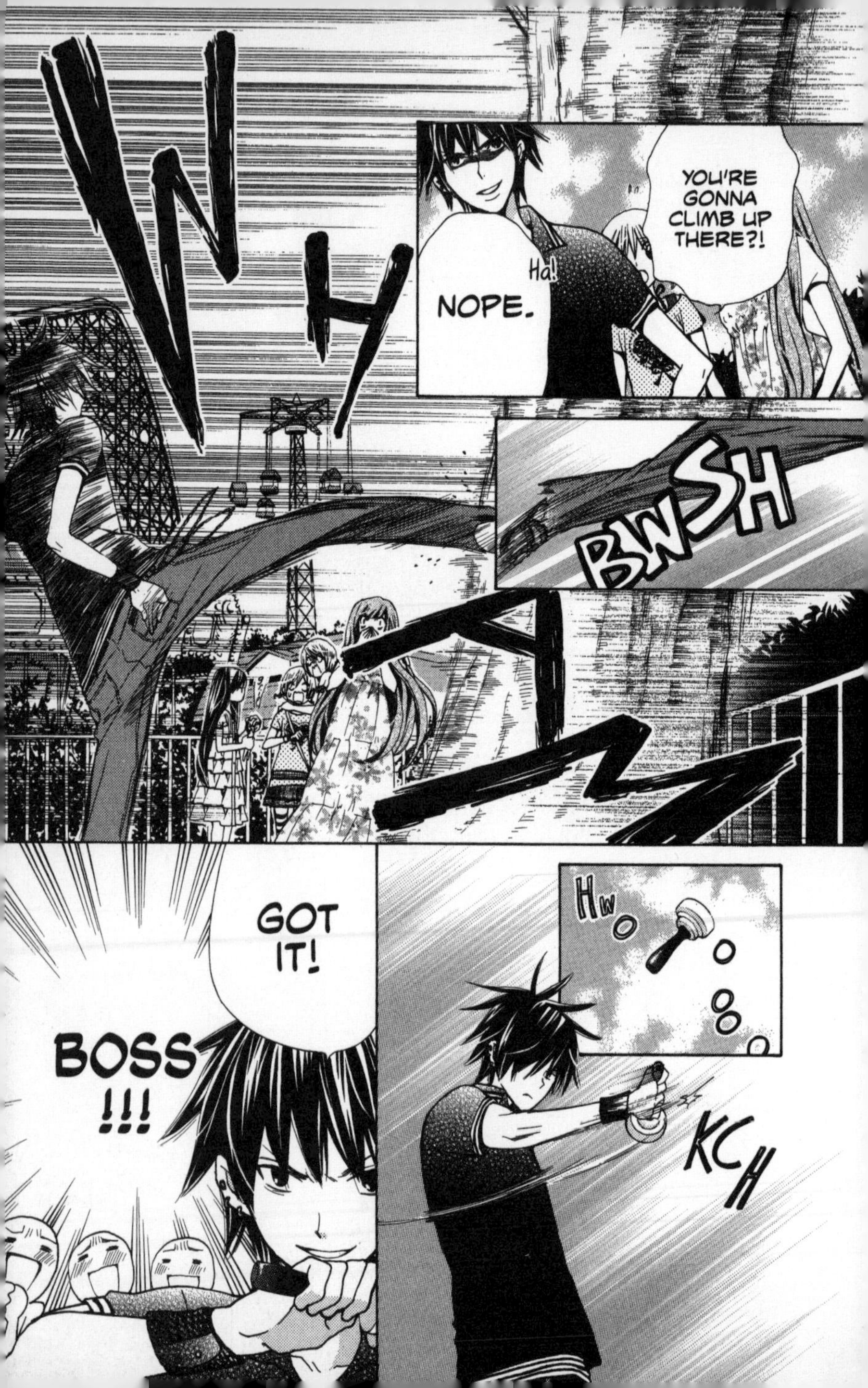
YOU'RE GONNA CLIMB UP THERE?!
Ha!
NOPE.
BWSH
HWOOOOO
KCH
GOT IT!
BOSS !!!

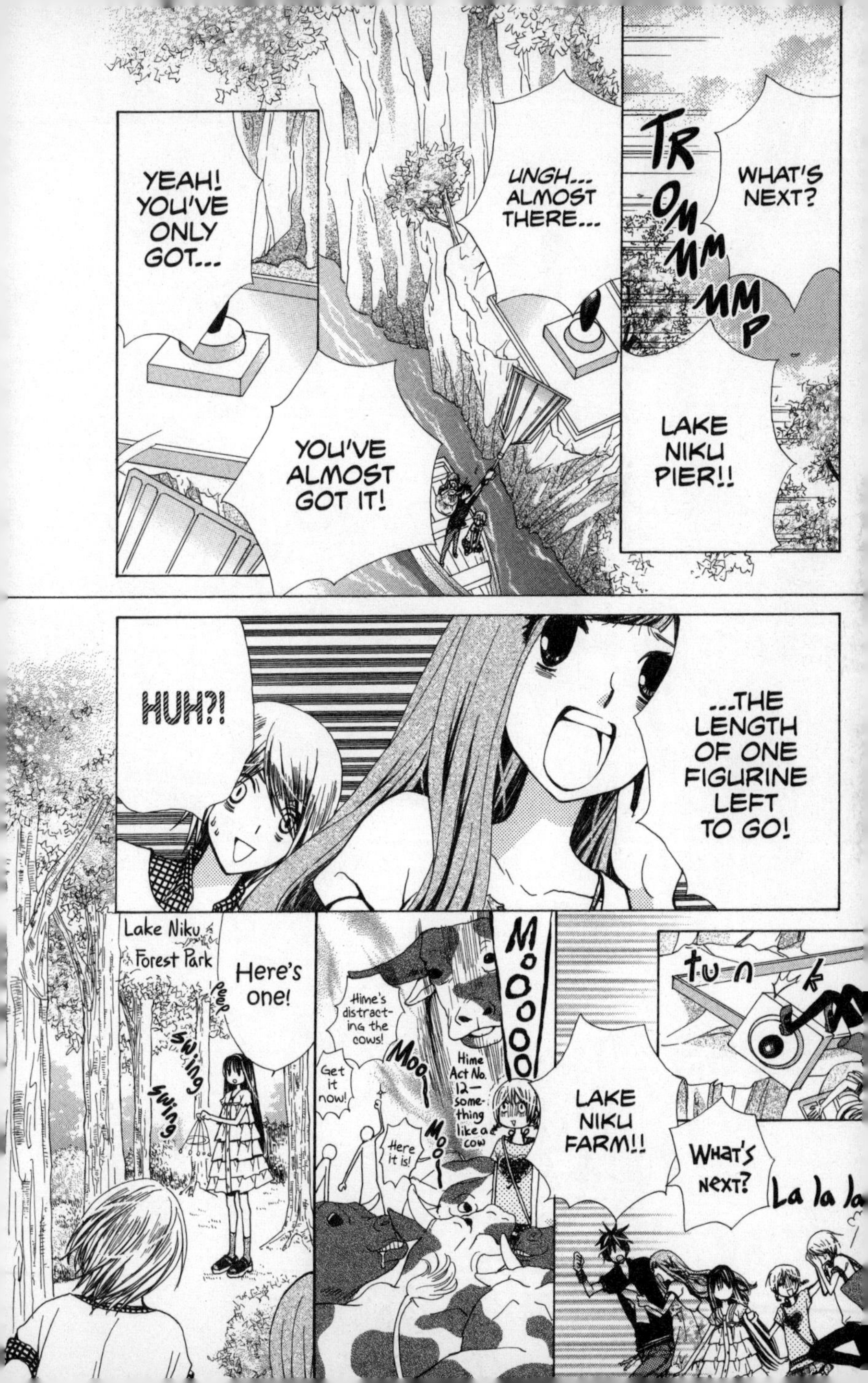
WHAT'S NEXT?
TROMMMMMP
LAKE NIKU PIER!!
UNGH... ALMOST THERE...
YOU'VE ALMOST GOT IT!
YEAH! YOU'VE ONLY GOT...
...THE LENGTH OF ONE FIGURINE LEFT TO GO!
HUH?!
tunk
WHAT'S NEXT?
La la la
LAKE NIKU FARM!!
MOOOOOO
Hime Act No. 12—something like a cow
Moo
Moo
Hime's distracting the cows!
Get it now!
Here it is!
Lake Niku Forest Park
Here's one!
peep
swing
swing

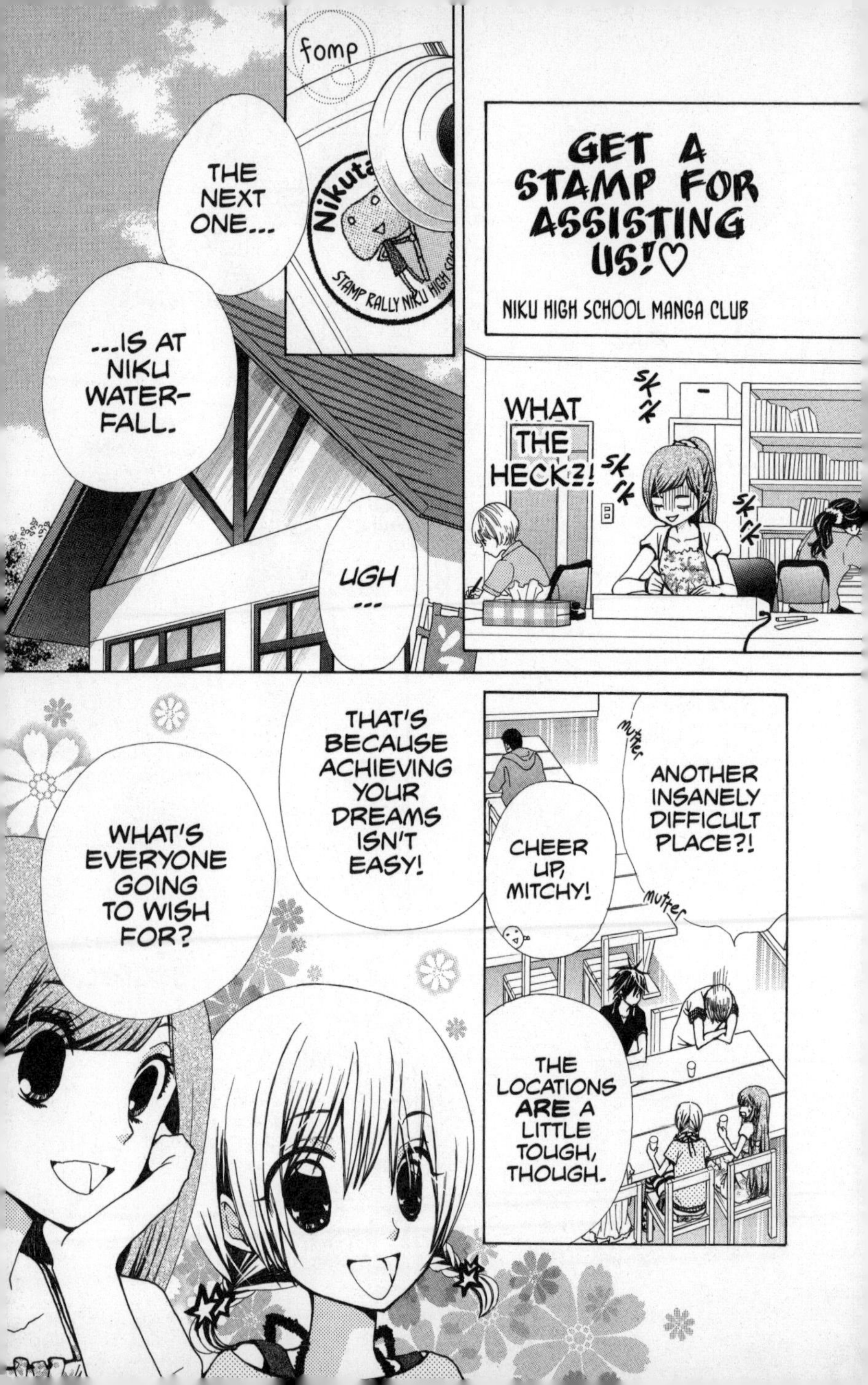
GET A STAMP FOR ASSISTING US!♡
NIKU HIGH SCHOOL MANGA CLUB
WHAT THE HECK?!
skrik
skrik
skrik
fomp
Nikuta
STAMP RALLY NIKU HIGH
THE NEXT ONE...
...IS AT NIKU WATERFALL.
UGH...
mutter
ANOTHER INSANELY DIFFICULT PLACE?!
mutter
CHEER UP, MITCHY!
THE LOCATIONS ARE A LITTLE TOUGH, THOUGH.
THAT'S BECAUSE ACHIEVING YOUR DREAMS ISN'T EASY!
WHAT'S EVERYONE GOING TO WISH FOR?

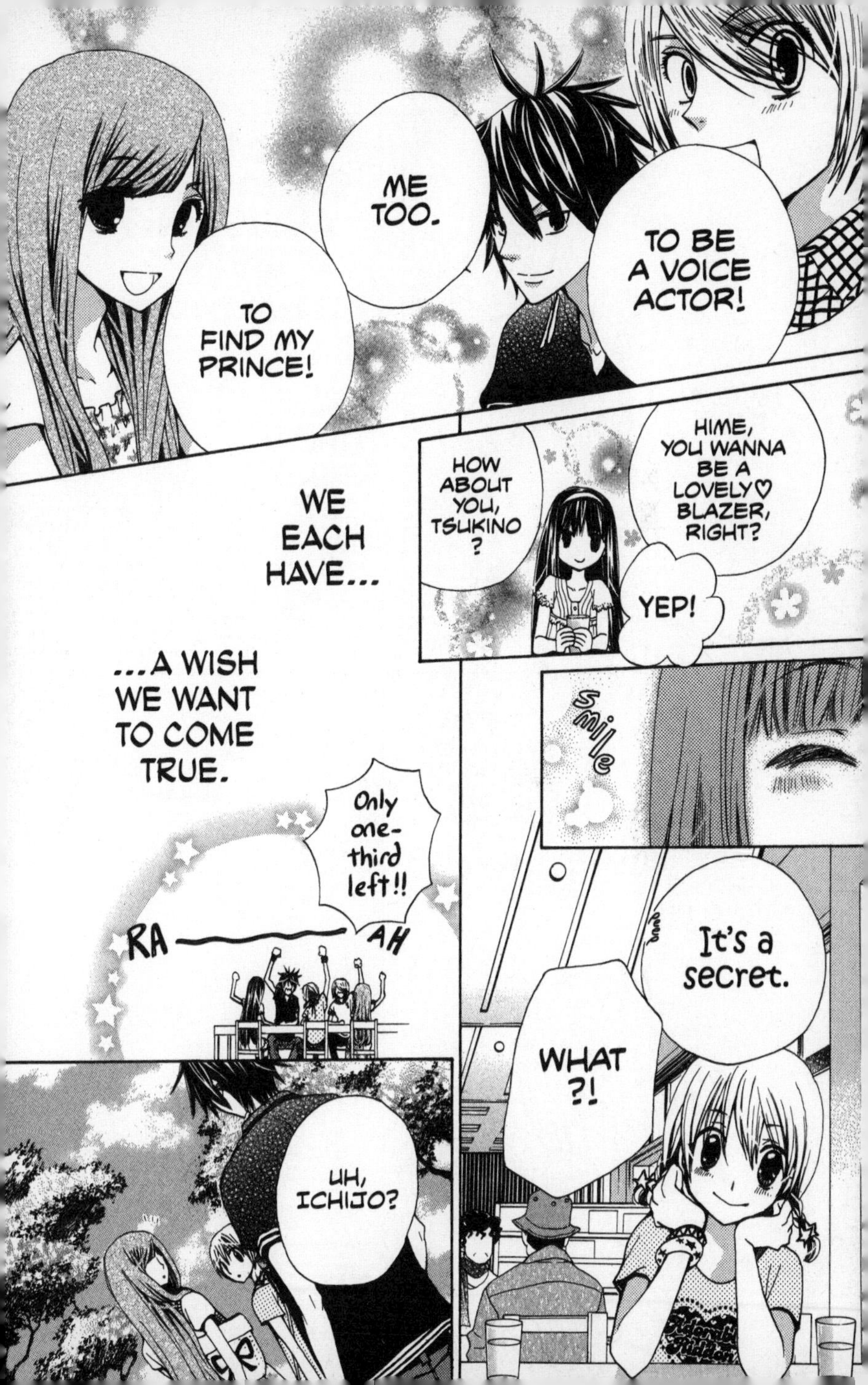
TO BE A VOICE ACTOR!
ME TOO.
TO FIND MY PRINCE!
HIME, YOU WANNA BE A LOVELY♡ BLAZER, RIGHT?
YEP!
HOW ABOUT YOU, TSUKINO?
smile
It's a secret.
WHAT?!
WE EACH HAVE...
...A WISH WE WANT TO COME TRUE.
Only one-third left!!
RA——AH
UH, ICHIJO?

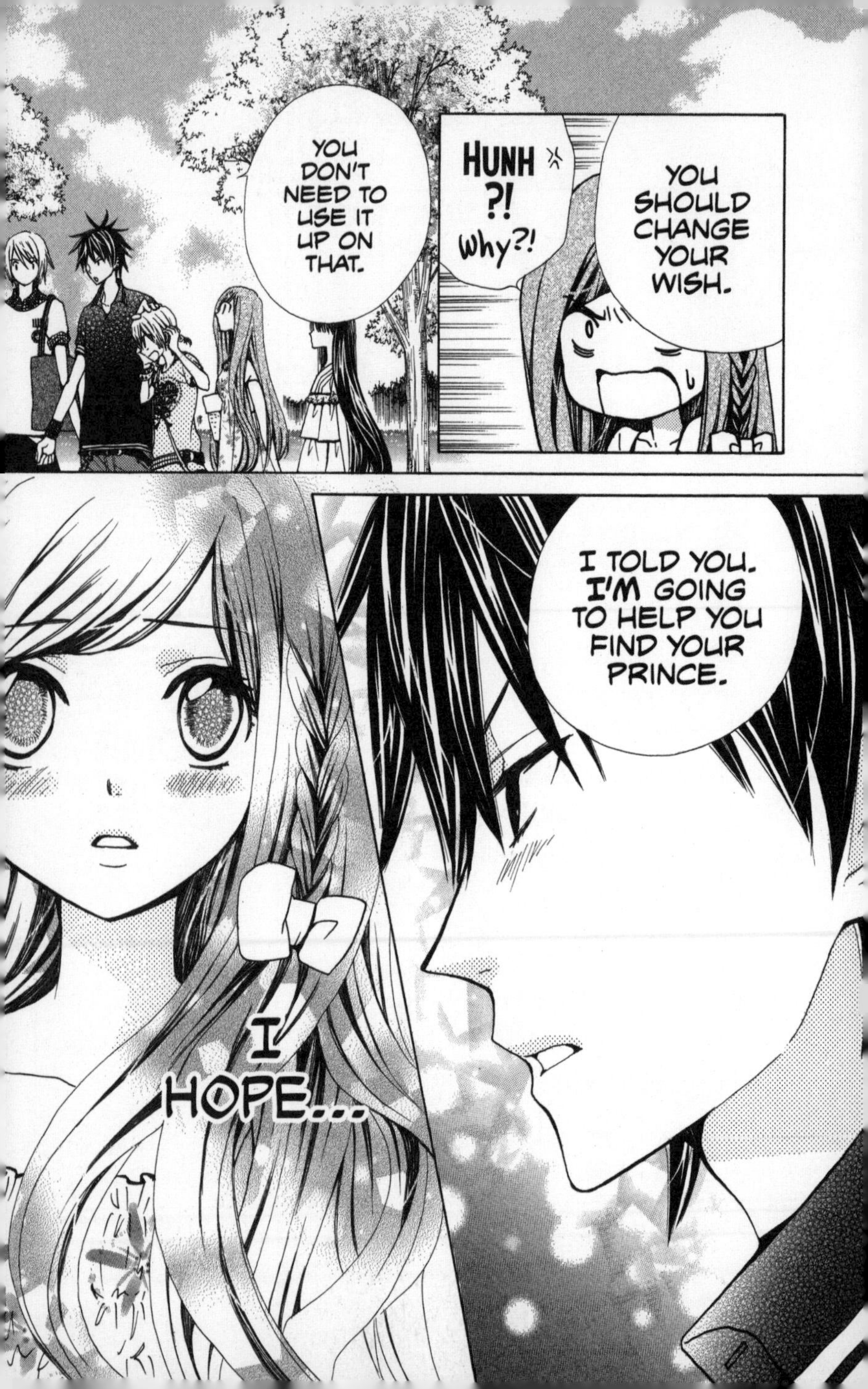
YOU SHOULD CHANGE YOUR WISH.
HUNH?! Why?!
YOU DON'T NEED TO USE IT UP ON THAT.
I TOLD YOU. I'M GOING TO HELP YOU FIND YOUR PRINCE.
I HOPE...

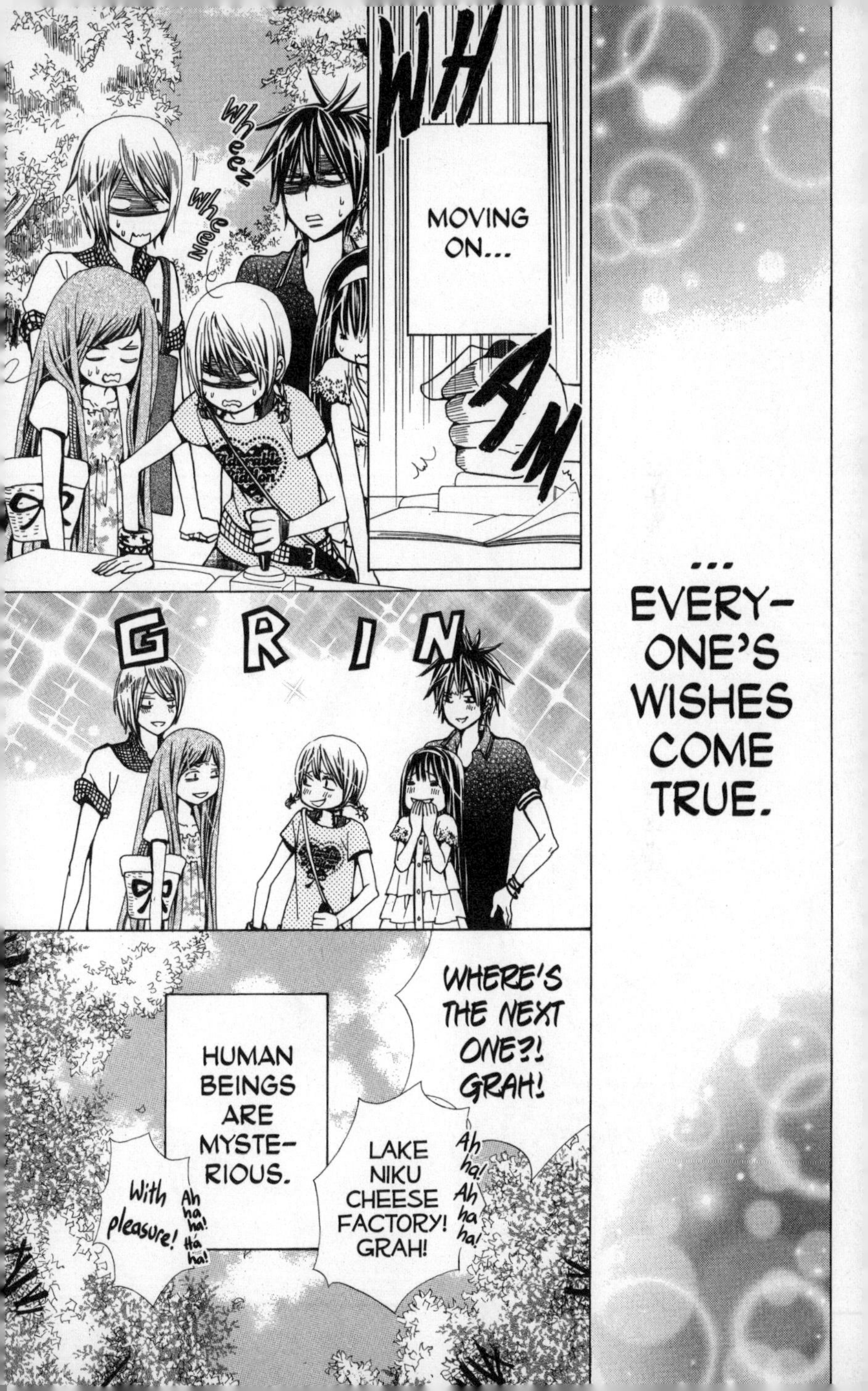

... EVERY-ONE'S WISHES COME TRUE.
WH
MOVING ON...
AM
wheez
wheen
GRIN
WHERE'S THE NEXT ONE?! GRAH!
HUMAN BEINGS ARE MYSTE-RIOUS.
Ah ha! Ah ha ha!
LAKE NIKU CHEESE FACTORY! GRAH!
Ah ha ha! Ha ha!
With pleasure!

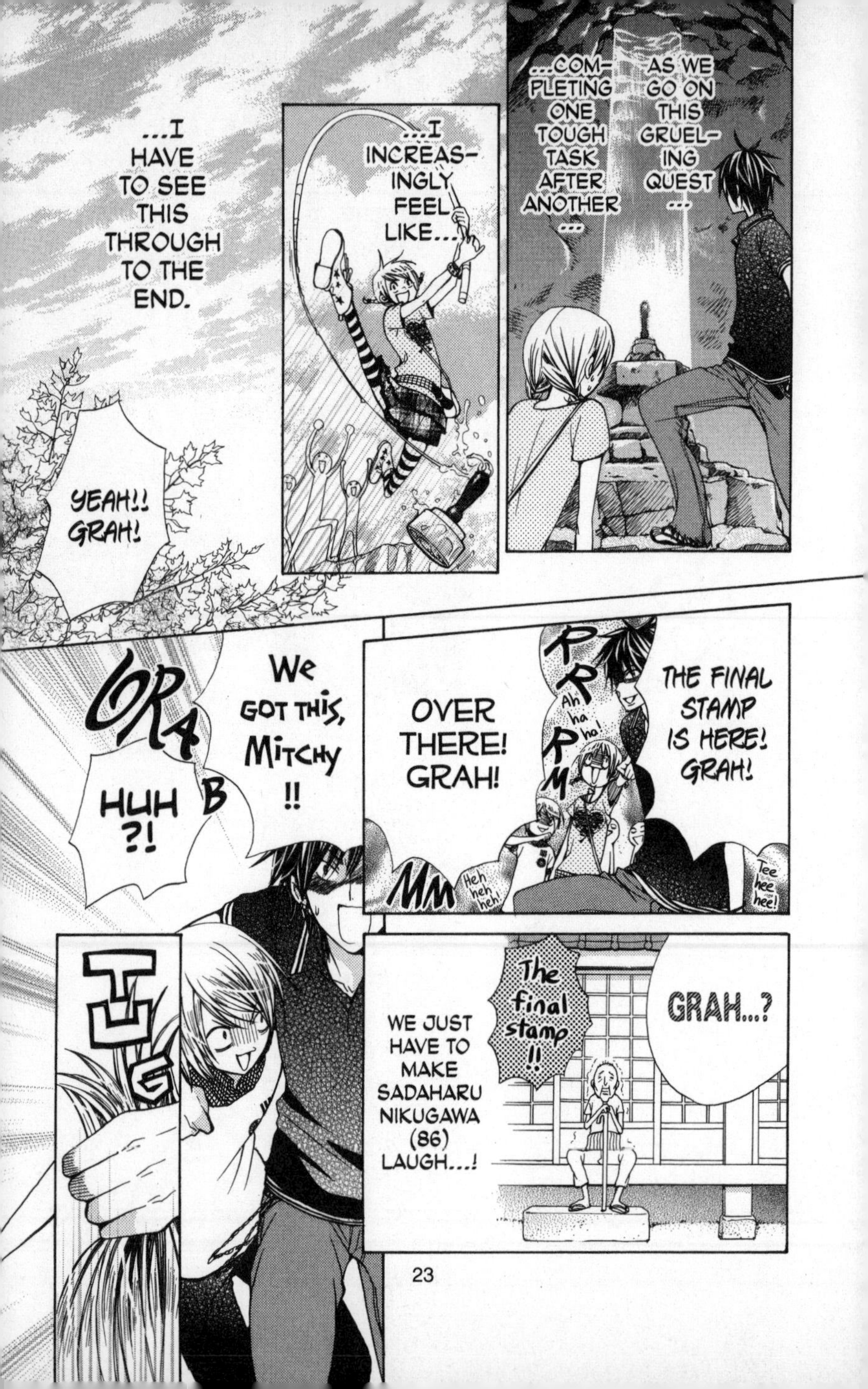
AS WE GO ON THIS GRUEL-ING QUEST...
...COM-PLETING ONE TOUGH TASK AFTER ANOTHER...
...I INCREAS-INGLY FEEL LIKE...
...I HAVE TO SEE THIS THROUGH TO THE END.
YEAH!! GRAH!
THE FINAL STAMP IS HERE! GRAH!
RRRMMM
Ah ha ha!
OVER THERE! GRAH!
Heh heh heh!
Tee hee hee!
We GOT THIS, MITCHY!!
GRAB
HUH?!
GRAH...?
The final stamp!!
WE JUST HAVE TO MAKE SADAHARU NIKUGAWA (86) LAUGH...!
TUG

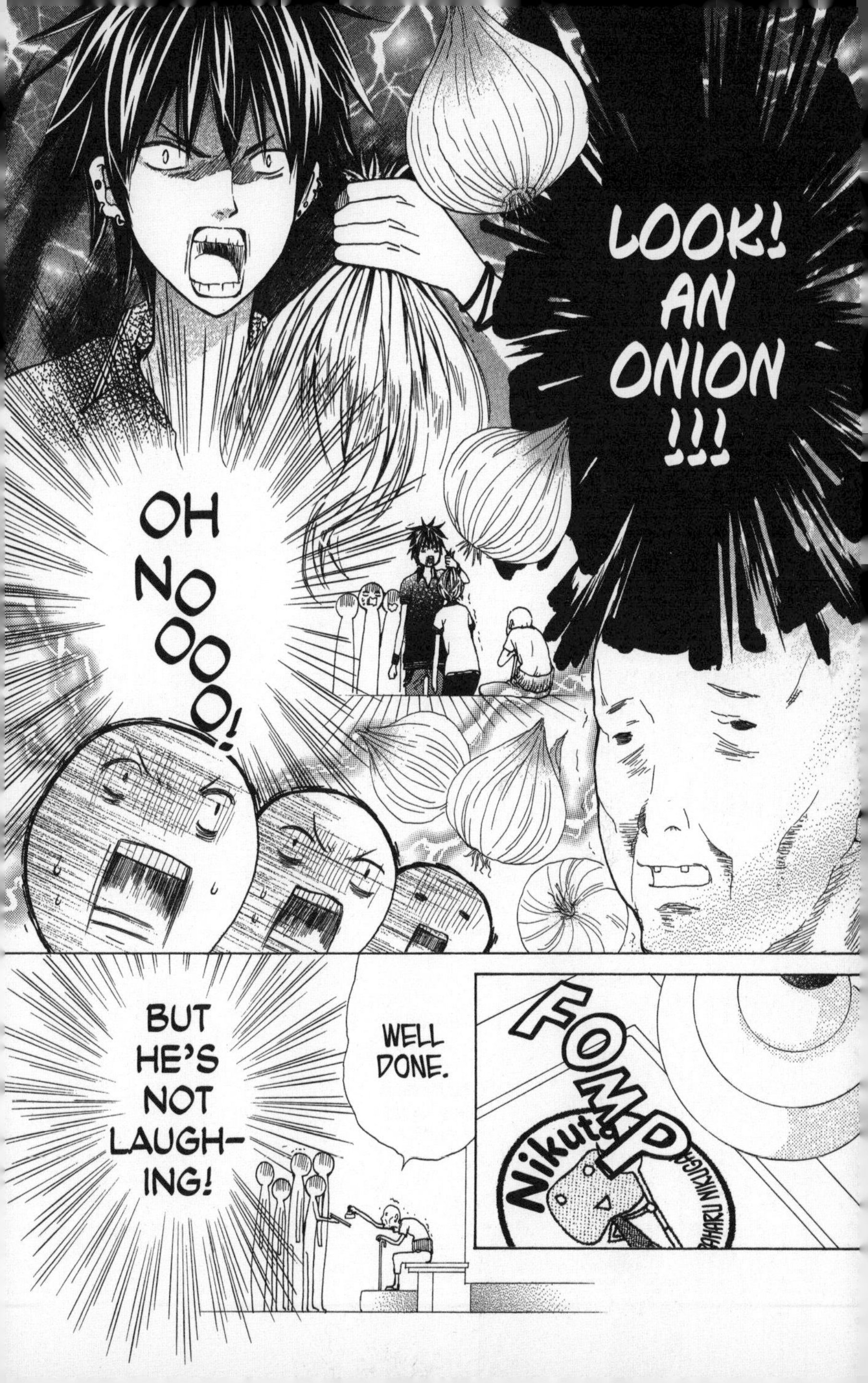
LOOK! AN ONION!!!
OH NOOOO!
FOMP!
WELL DONE.
BUT HE'S NOT LAUGHING!

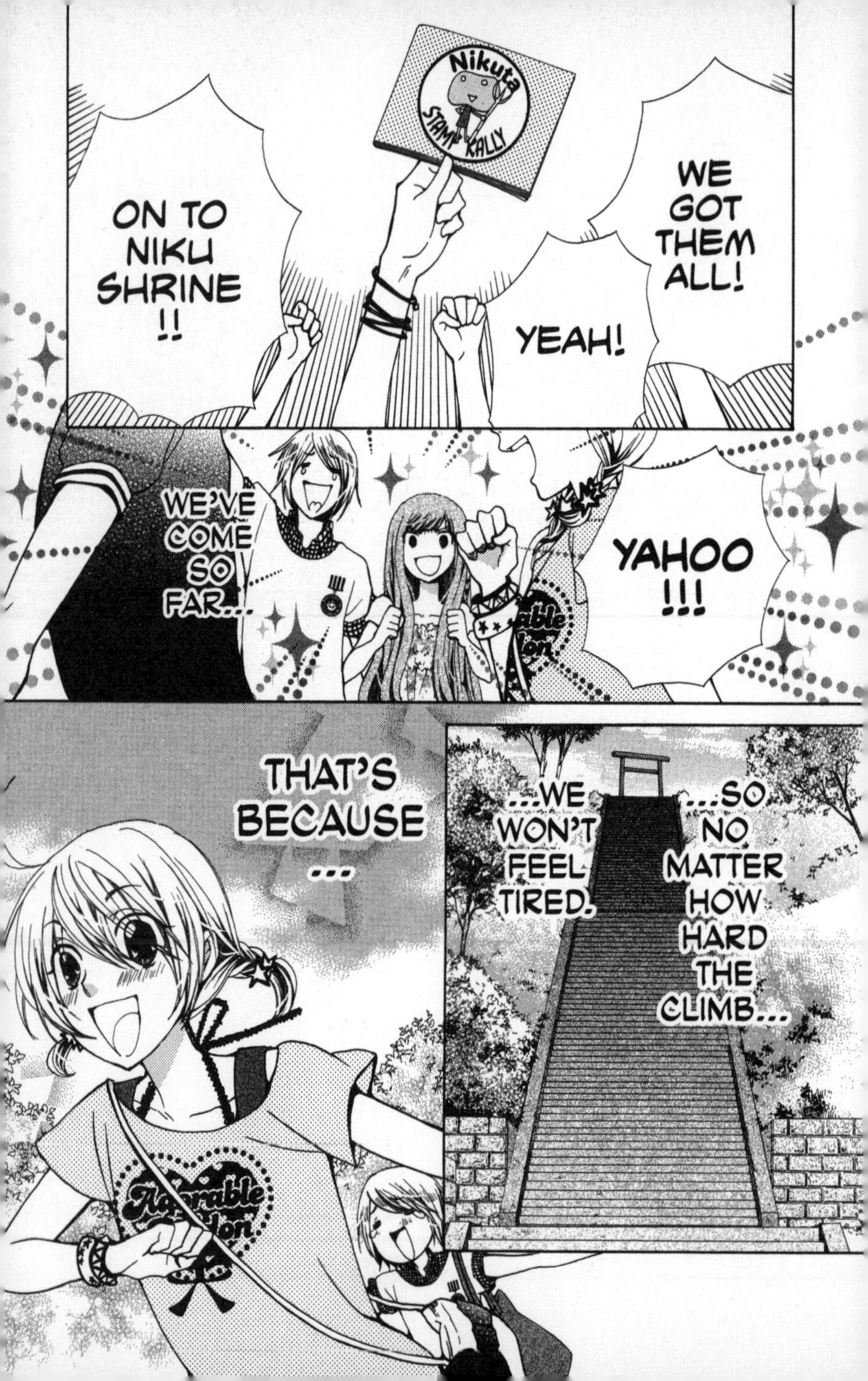
WE GOT THEM ALL!
YEAH!
Nikuta STAMP RALLY
ON TO NIKU SHRINE !!
YAHOO !!!
WE'VE COME SO FAR...
...SO NO MATTER HOW HARD THE CLIMB...
...WE WON'T FEEL TIRED.
THAT'S BECAUSE ...

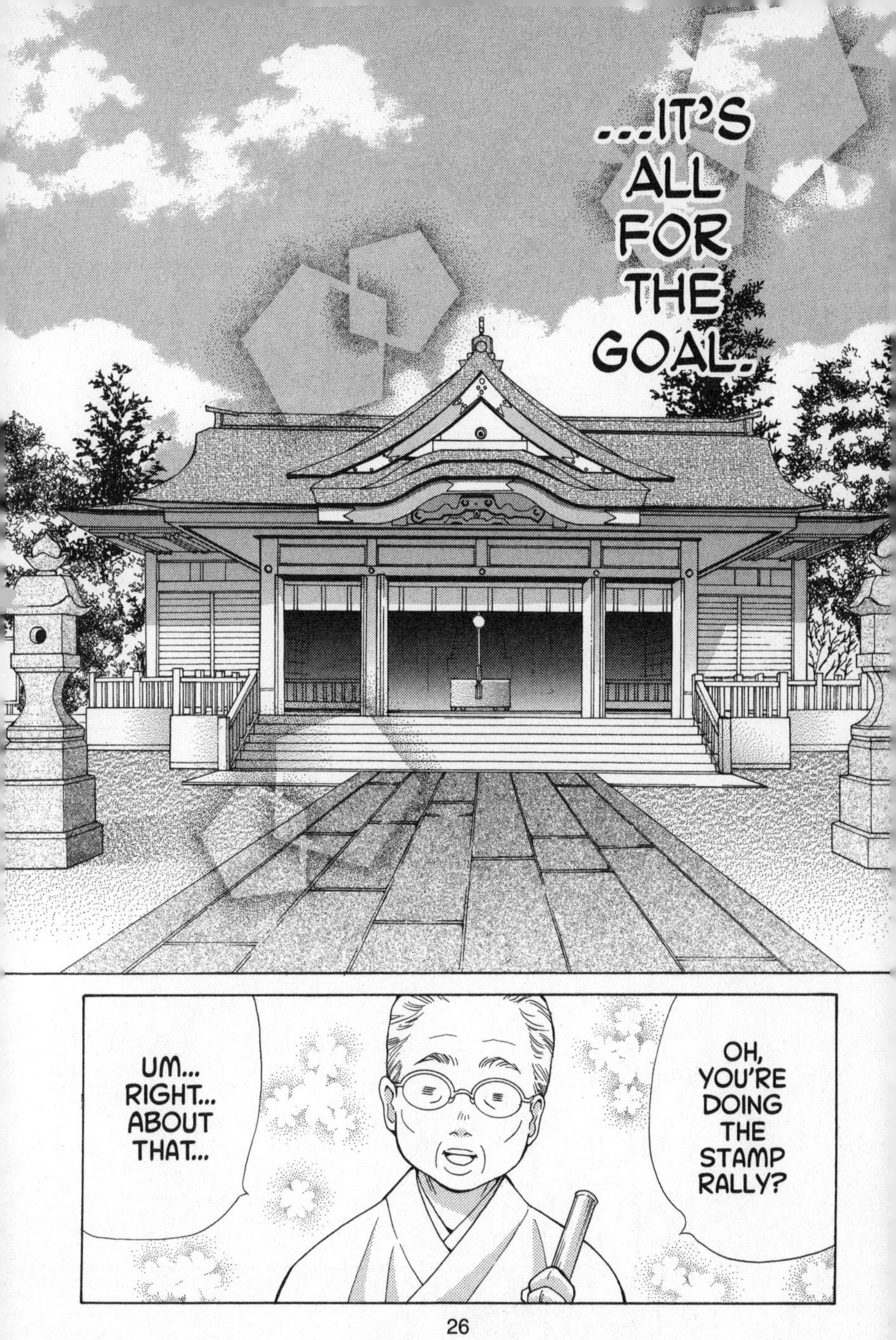
...IT'S ALL FOR THE GOAL.
OH, YOU'RE DOING THE STAMP RALLY?
UM... RIGHT... ABOUT THAT...

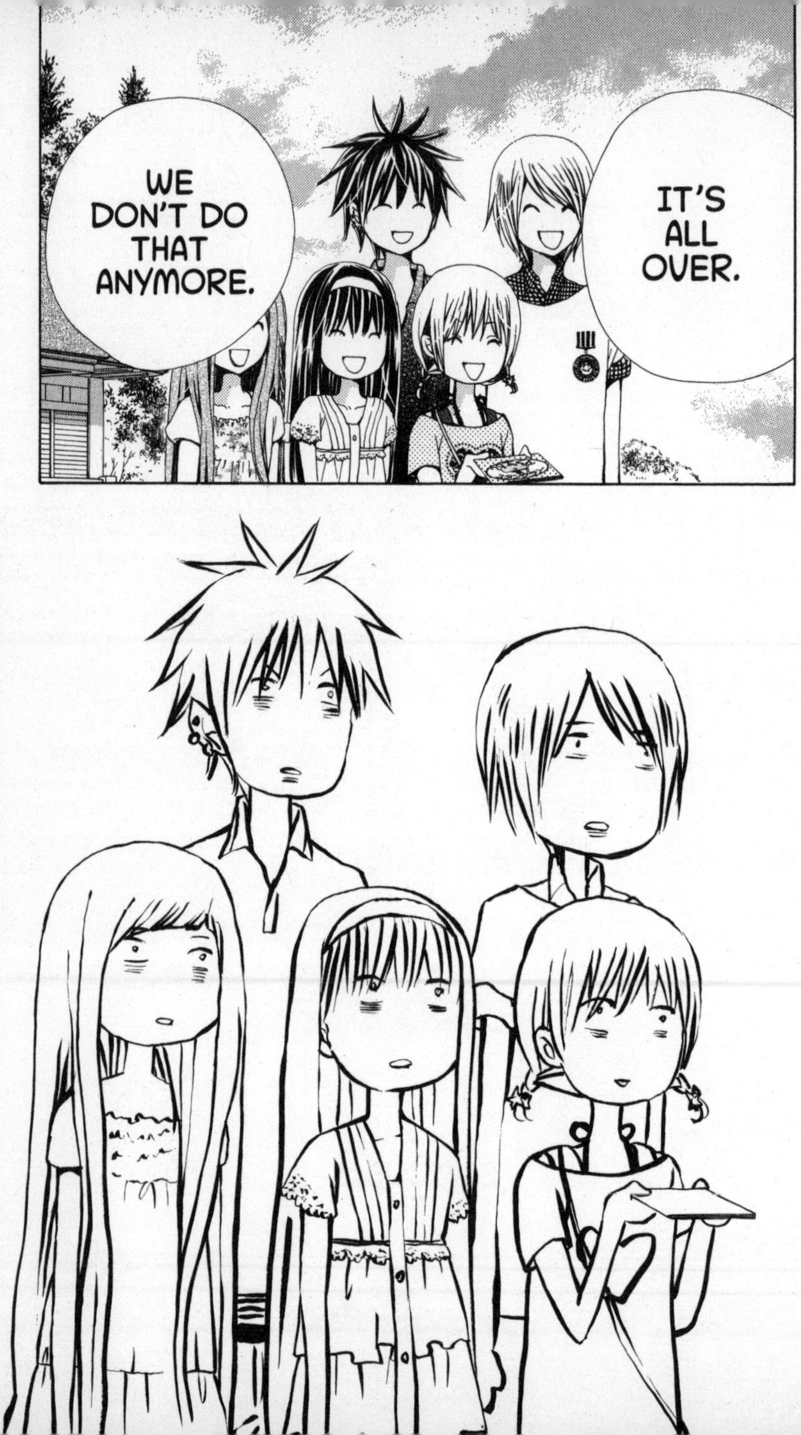
IT'S ALL OVER.
WE DON'T DO THAT ANYMORE.

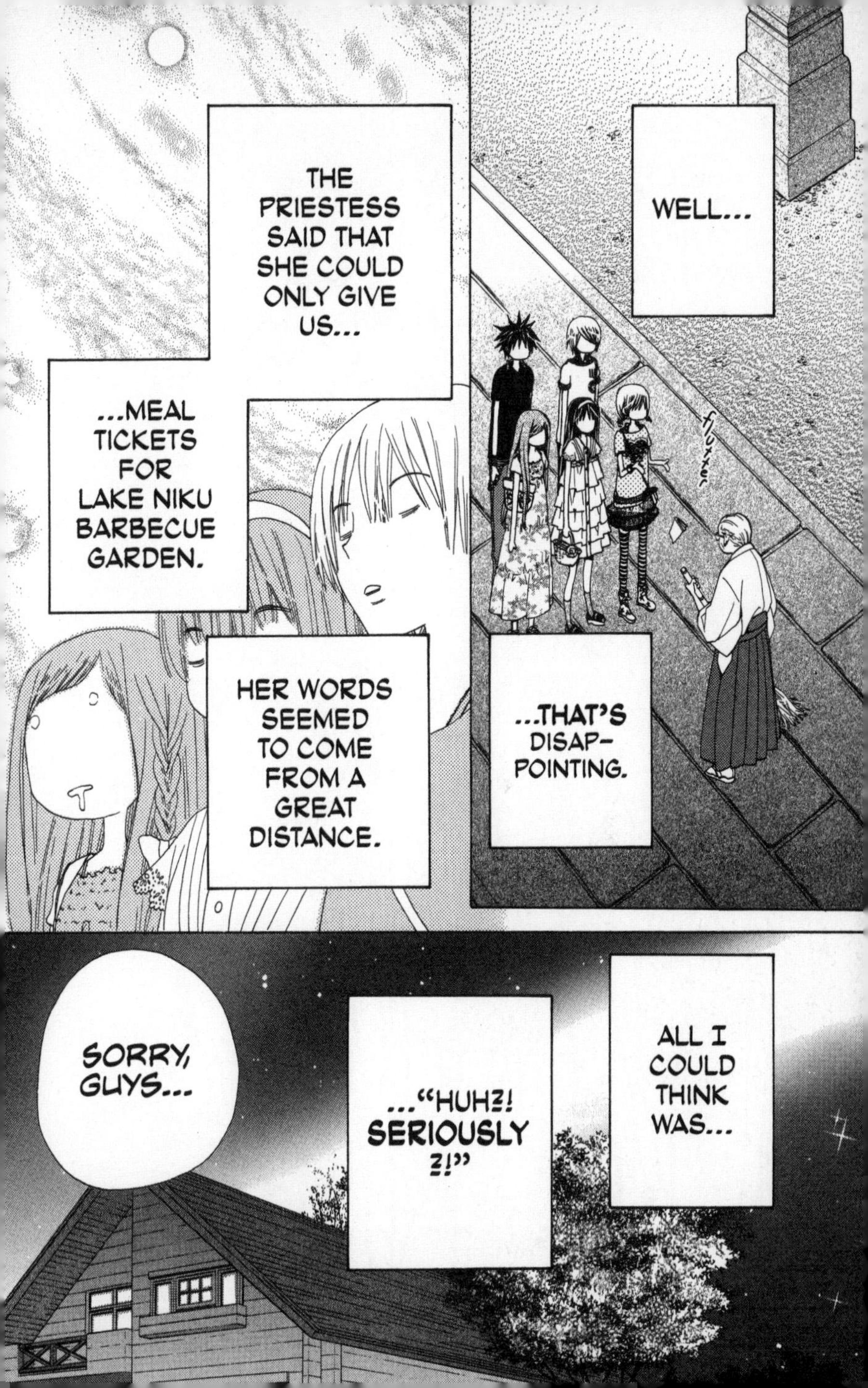
WELL...
flutter
...THAT'S DISAP-POINTING.
THE PRIESTESS SAID THAT SHE COULD ONLY GIVE US...
...MEAL TICKETS FOR LAKE NIKU BARBECUE GARDEN.
HER WORDS SEEMED TO COME FROM A GREAT DISTANCE.
ALL I COULD THINK WAS...
..."HUH?! SERIOUSLY?!"
SORRY, GUYS...

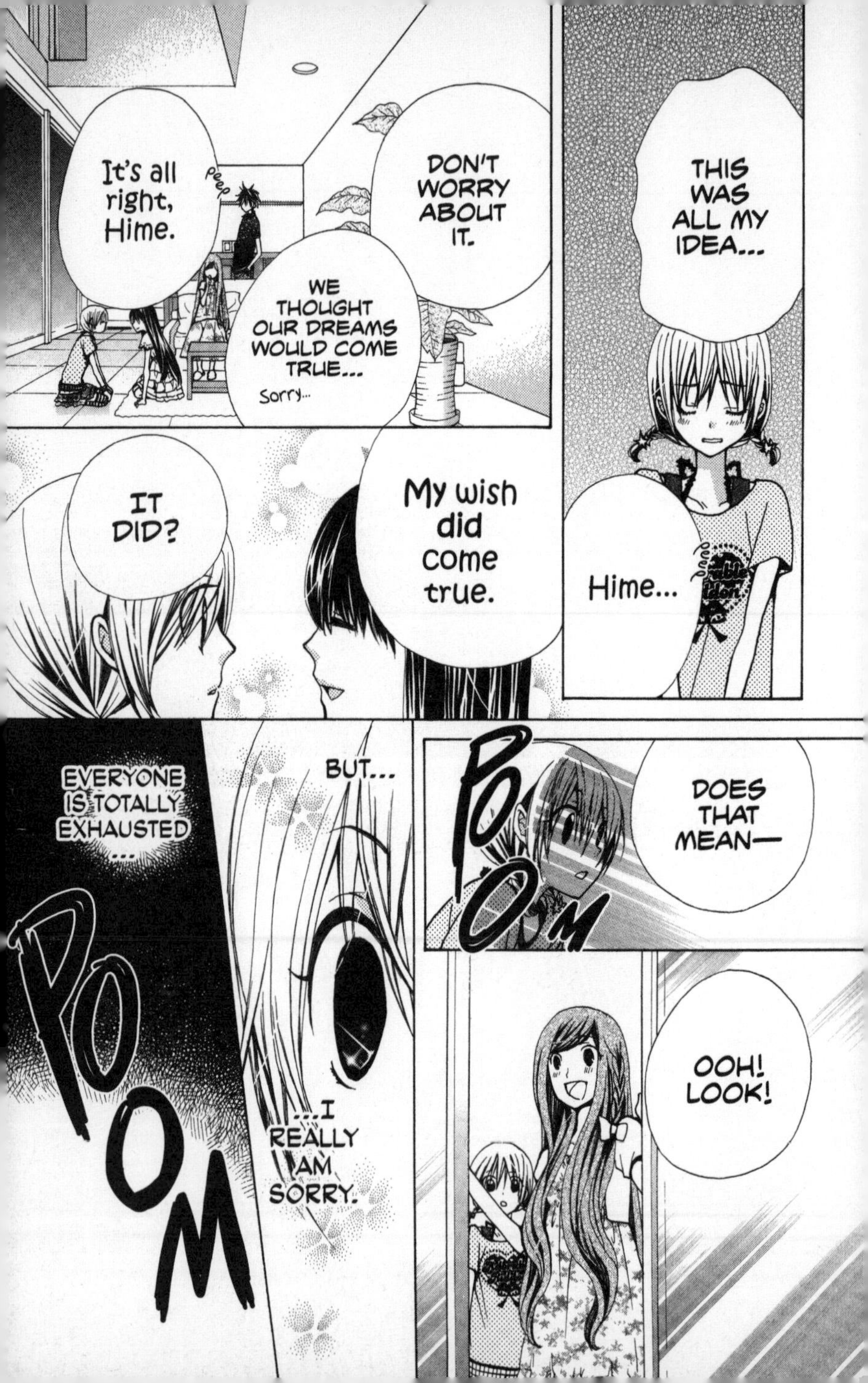
THIS WAS ALL MY IDEA...
peep
Hime...
DON'T WORRY ABOUT IT.
WE THOUGHT OUR DREAMS WOULD COME TRUE...
Sorry...
peep
It's all right, Hime.
My wish did come true.
IT DID?
DOES THAT MEAN—
POOM
OOH! LOOK!
BUT...
...I REALLY AM SORRY.
EVERYONE IS TOTALLY EXHAUSTED...
POOM

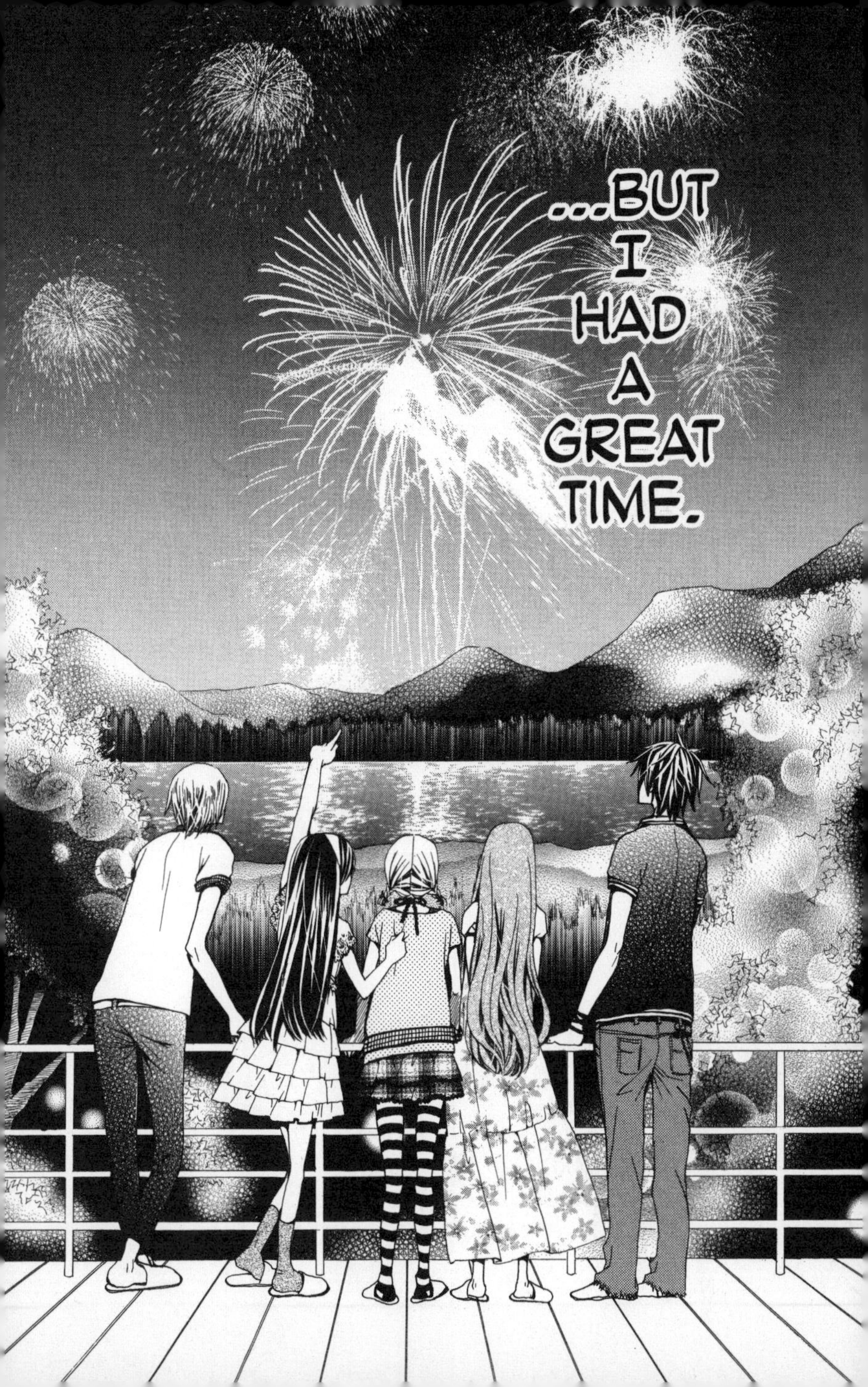
...BUT I HAD A GREAT TIME.

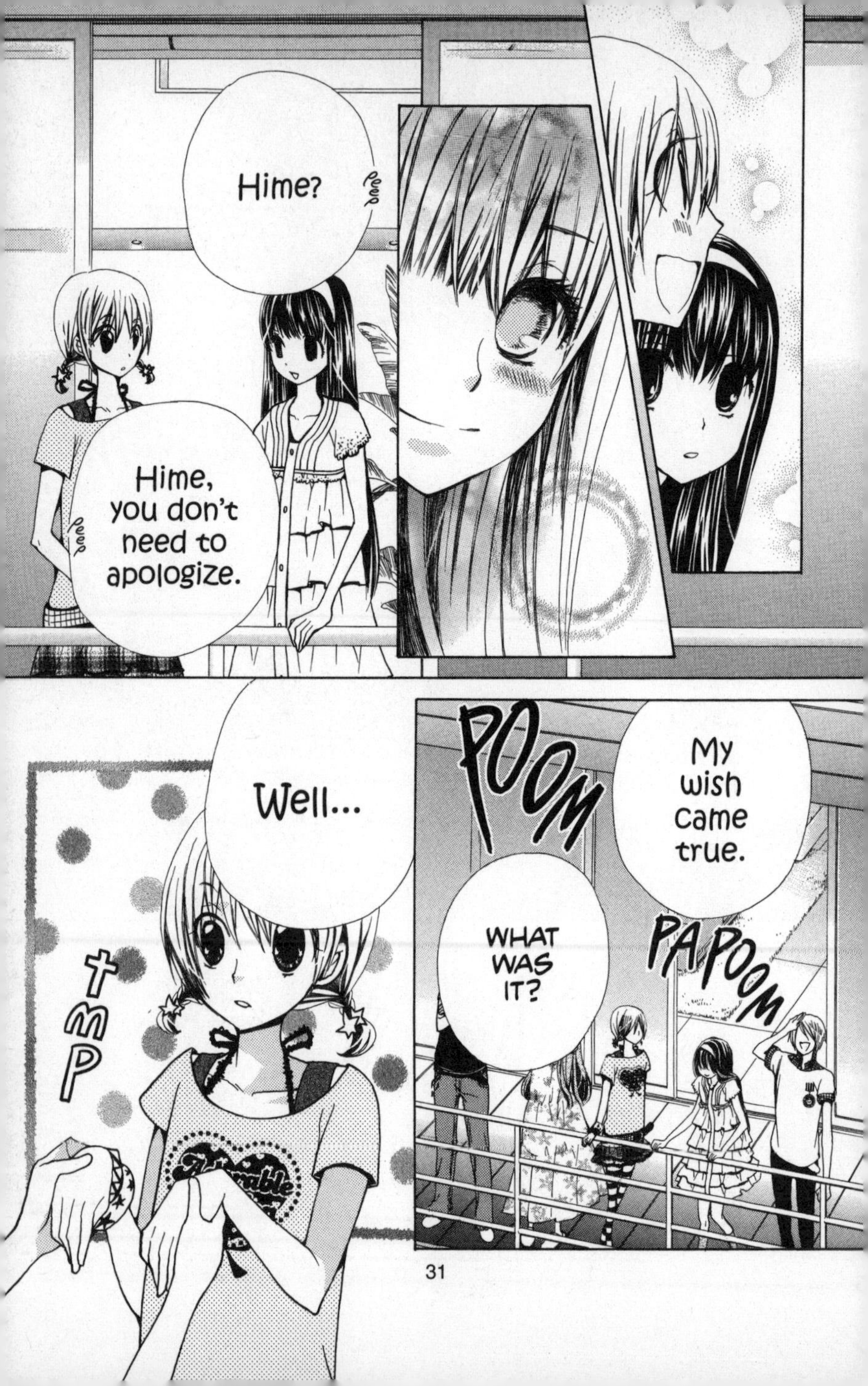
Hime?
peer
Hime, you don't need to apologize.
peer
POOM
My wish came true.
PAPOOM
WHAT WAS IT?
Well...
TMP

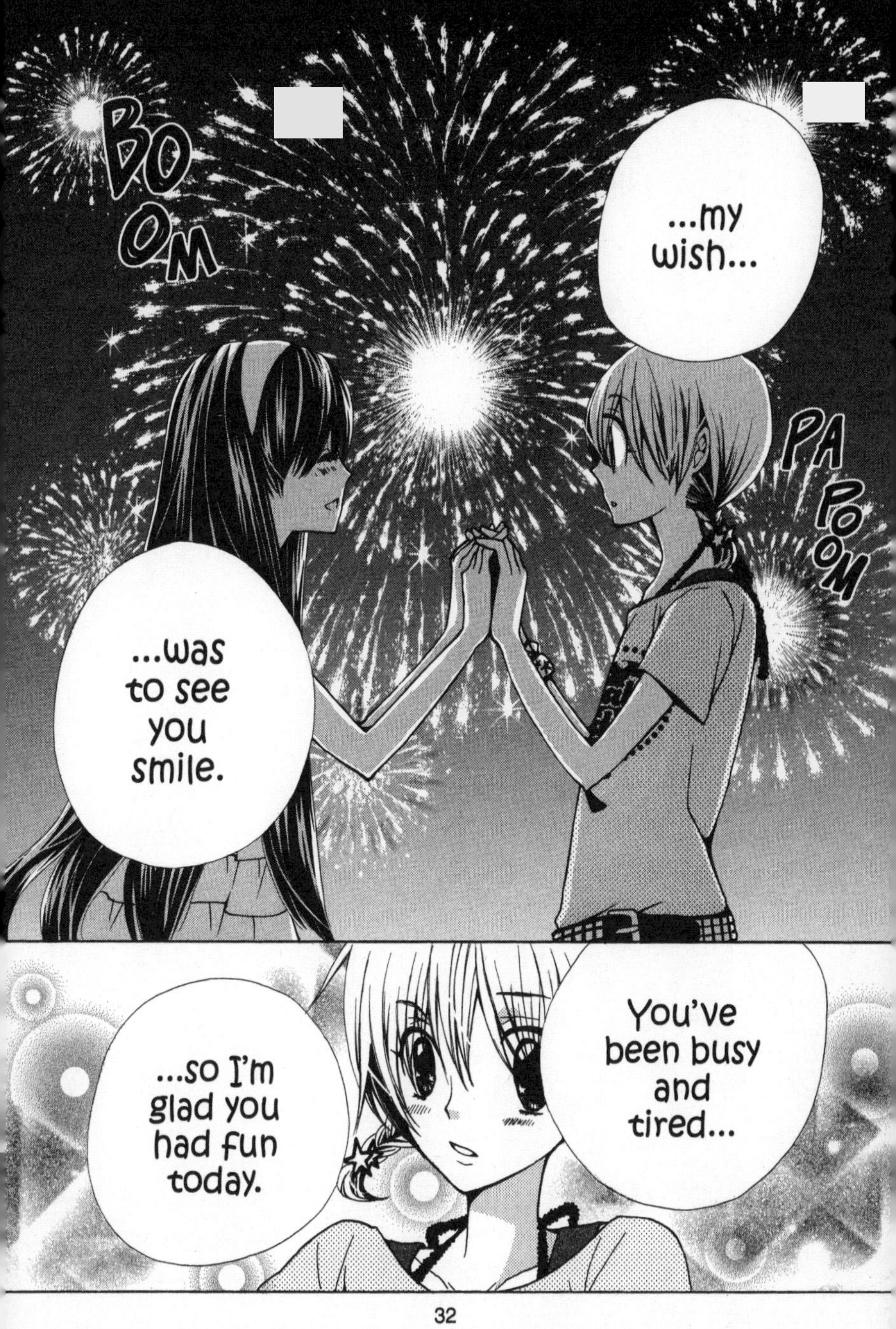
...my wish...
PAPOOM
BOOM
...was to see you smile.
You've been busy and tired...
...so I'm glad you had fun today.

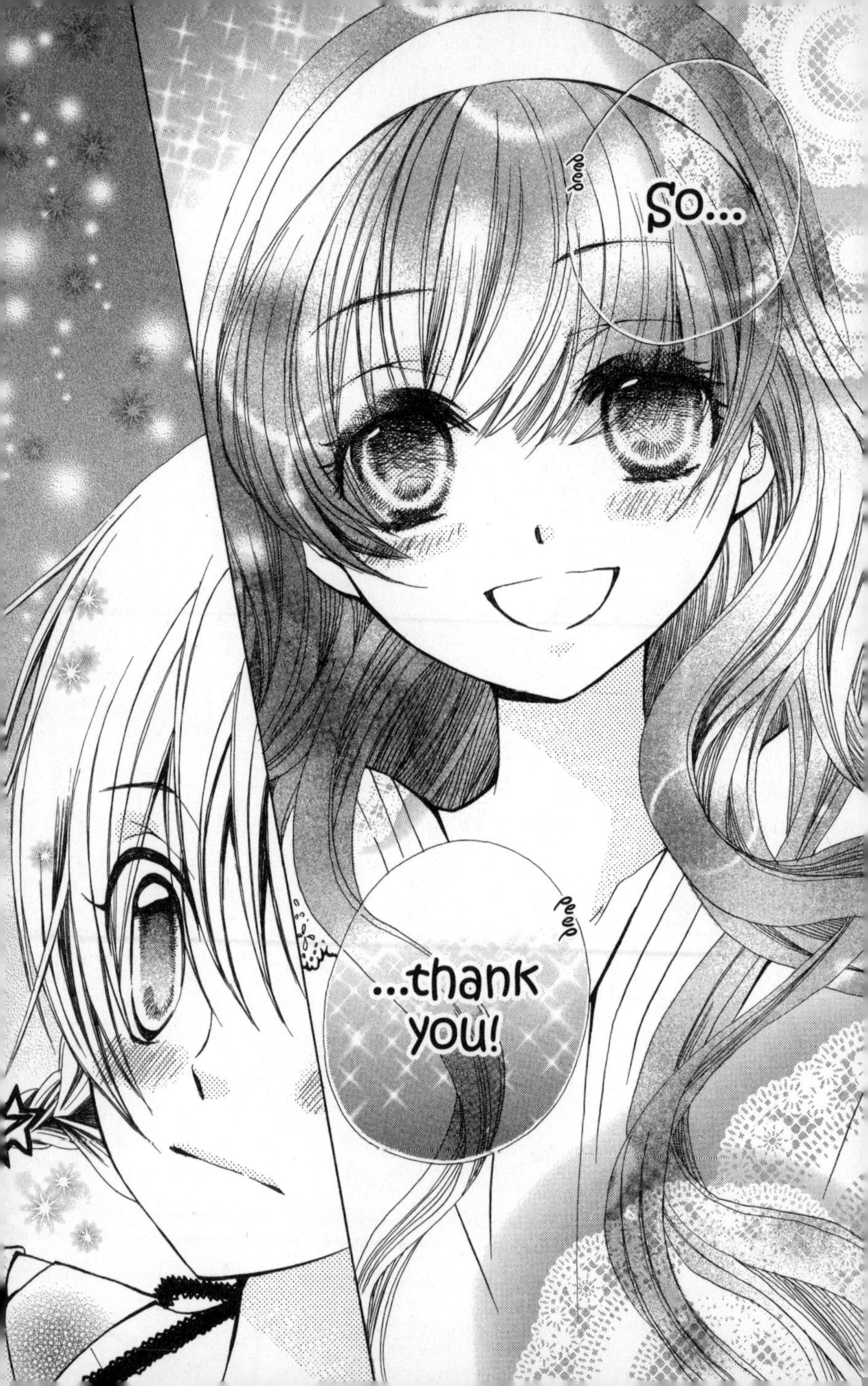
So...
...thank you!

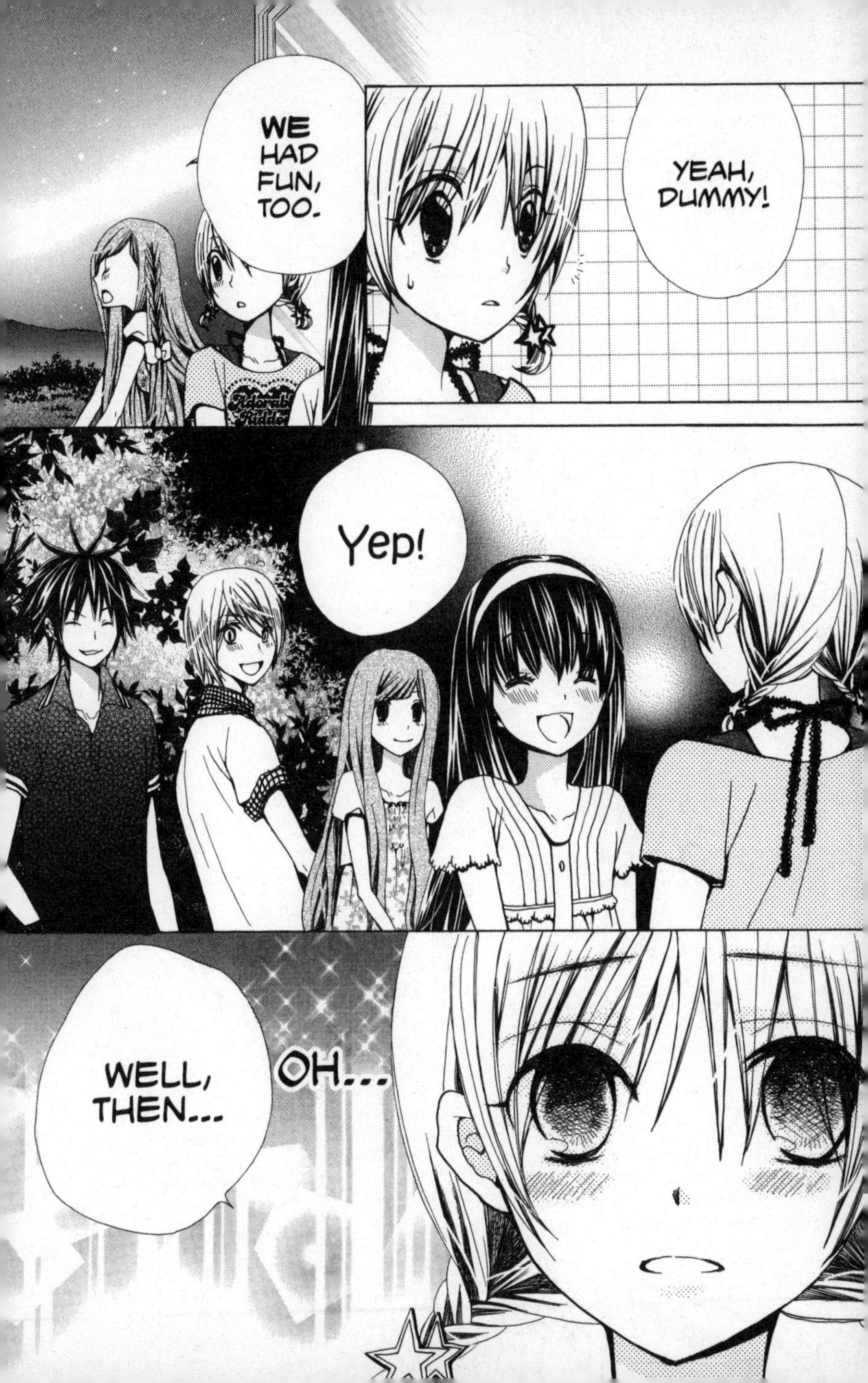
YEAH, DUMMY!
WE HAD FUN, TOO.
Yep!
OH...
WELL, THEN...

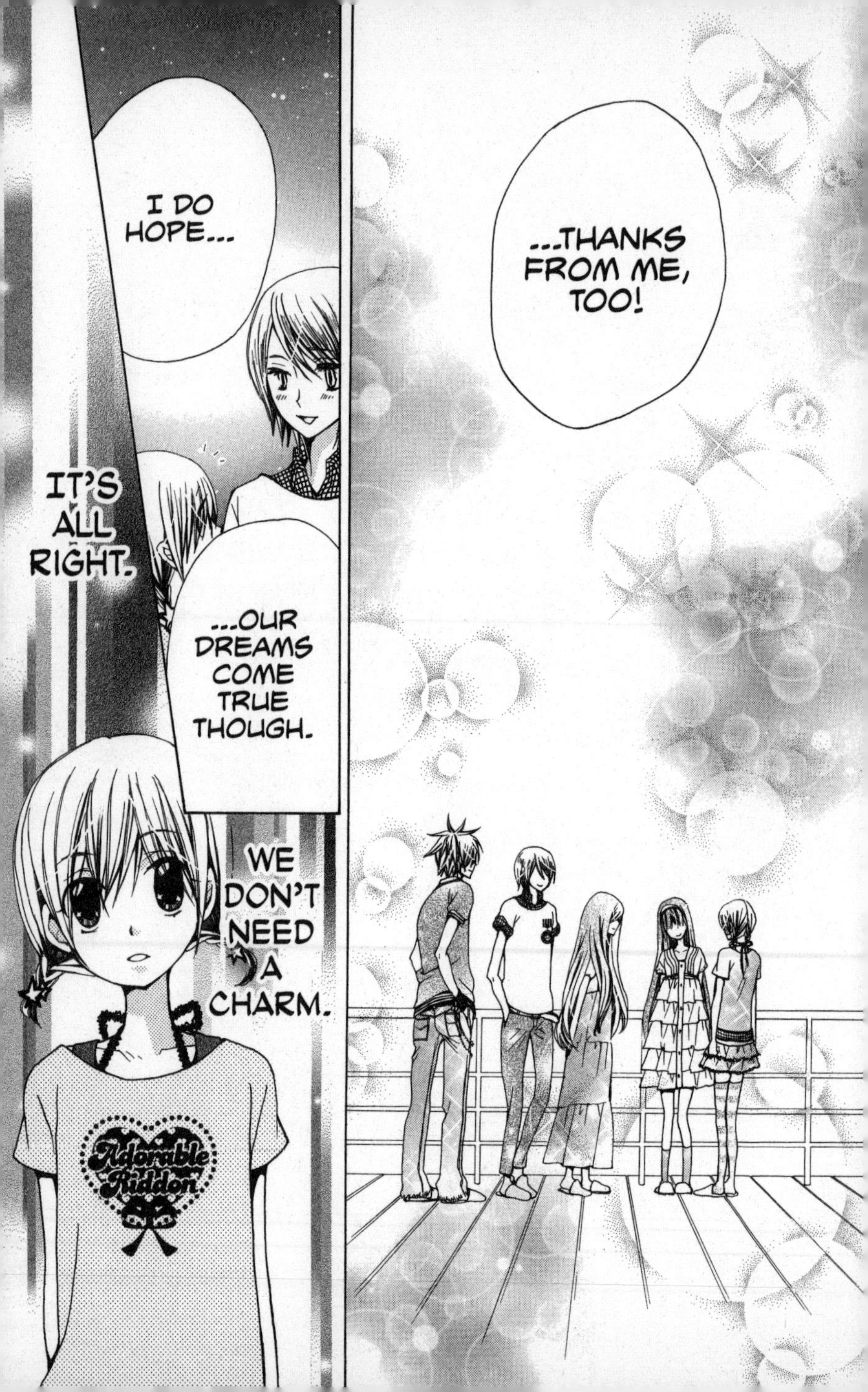
...THANKS FROM ME, TOO!
I DO HOPE...
...OUR DREAMS COME TRUE THOUGH.
IT'S ALL RIGHT.
WE DON'T NEED A CHARM.
Adorable Riddon

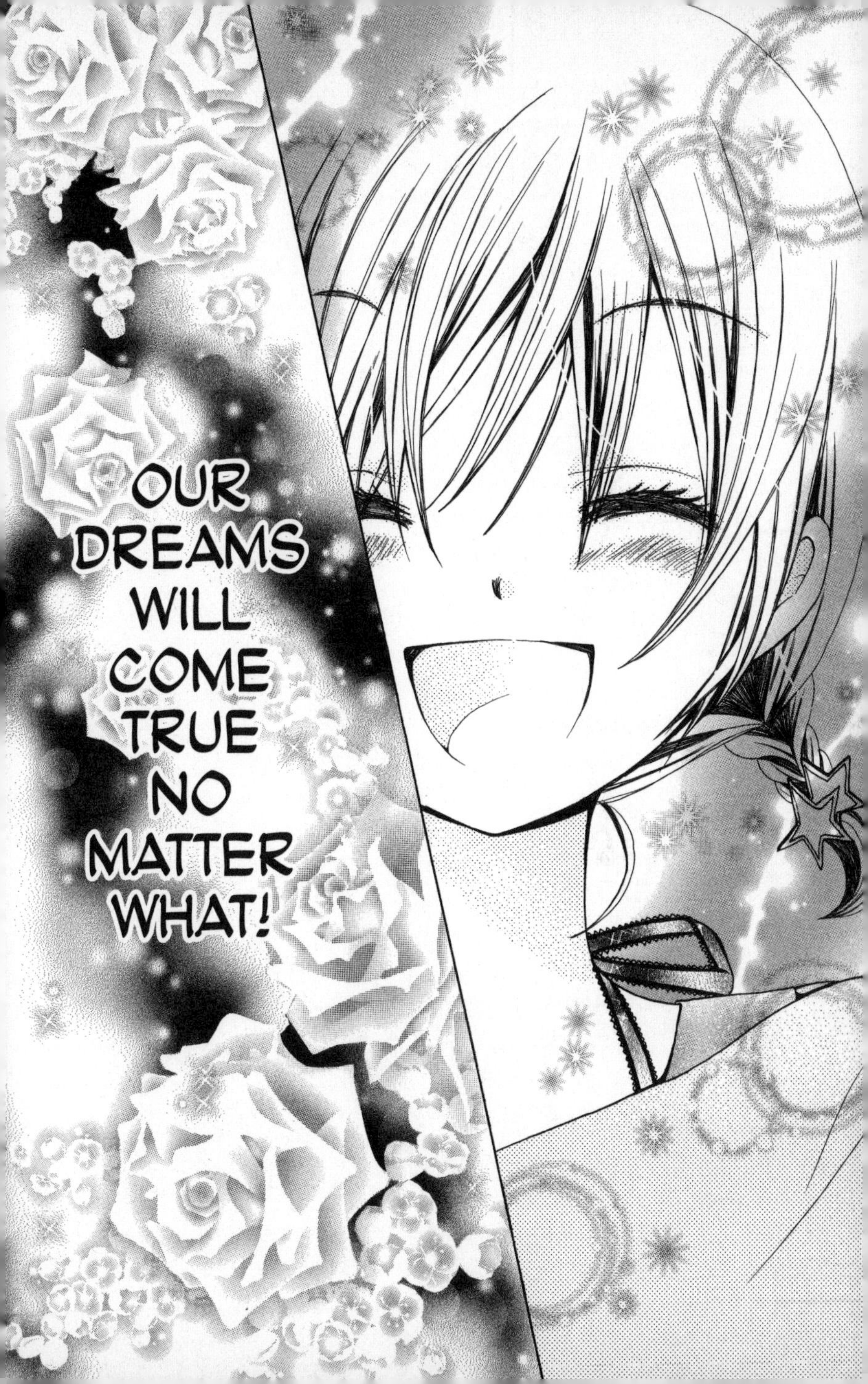
OUR DREAMS WILL COME TRUE NO MATTER WHAT!

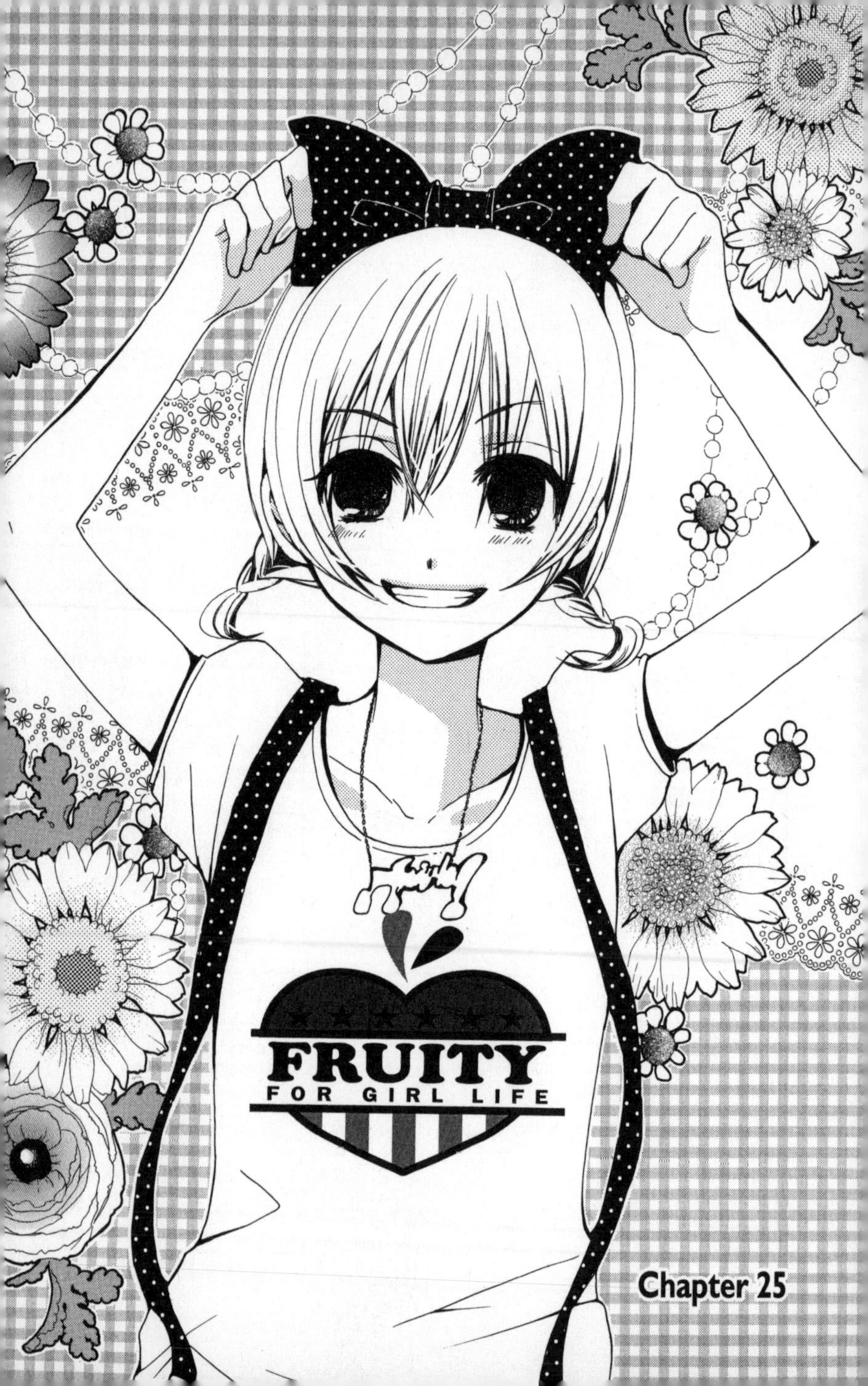
FRUITY
FOR GIRL LIFE

Chapter 25

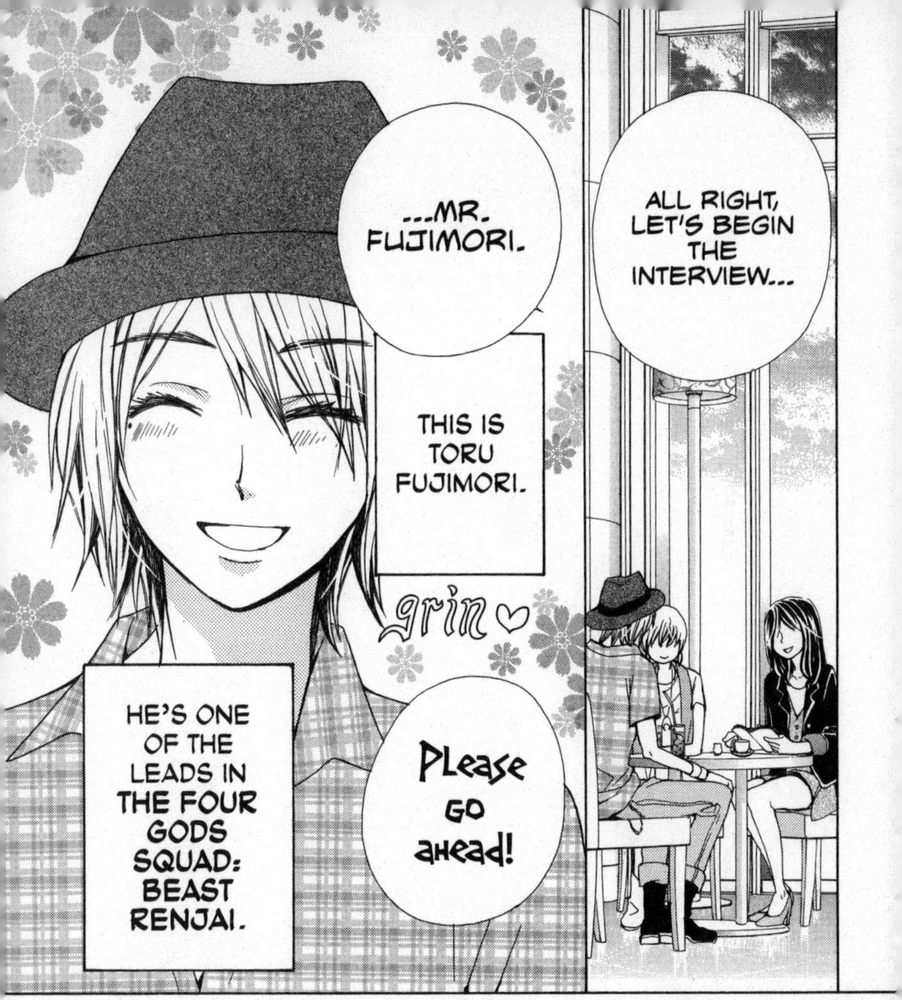
ALL RIGHT, LET'S BEGIN THE INTERVIEW...
...MR. FUJIMORI.
THIS IS TORU FUJIMORI.
grin
Please go ahead!
HE'S ONE OF THE LEADS IN THE FOUR GODS SQUAD: BEAST RENJAI.

• Cover & Various •

Yamada P is on the cover this time. Compared to when he first showed up, his hair is a lot smoother and isn't as wavy. Why does this happen? When I drew a man with wavy hair before, it gradually straightened out too.

Maybe I should just stop drawing guys with wavy hair!

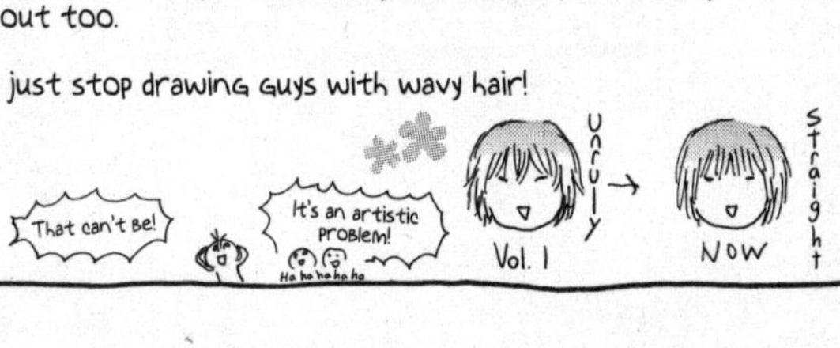
That can't be!
It's an artistic problem!
Ho ho ho ho ho
Unruly
Vol. 1
Straight
NOW

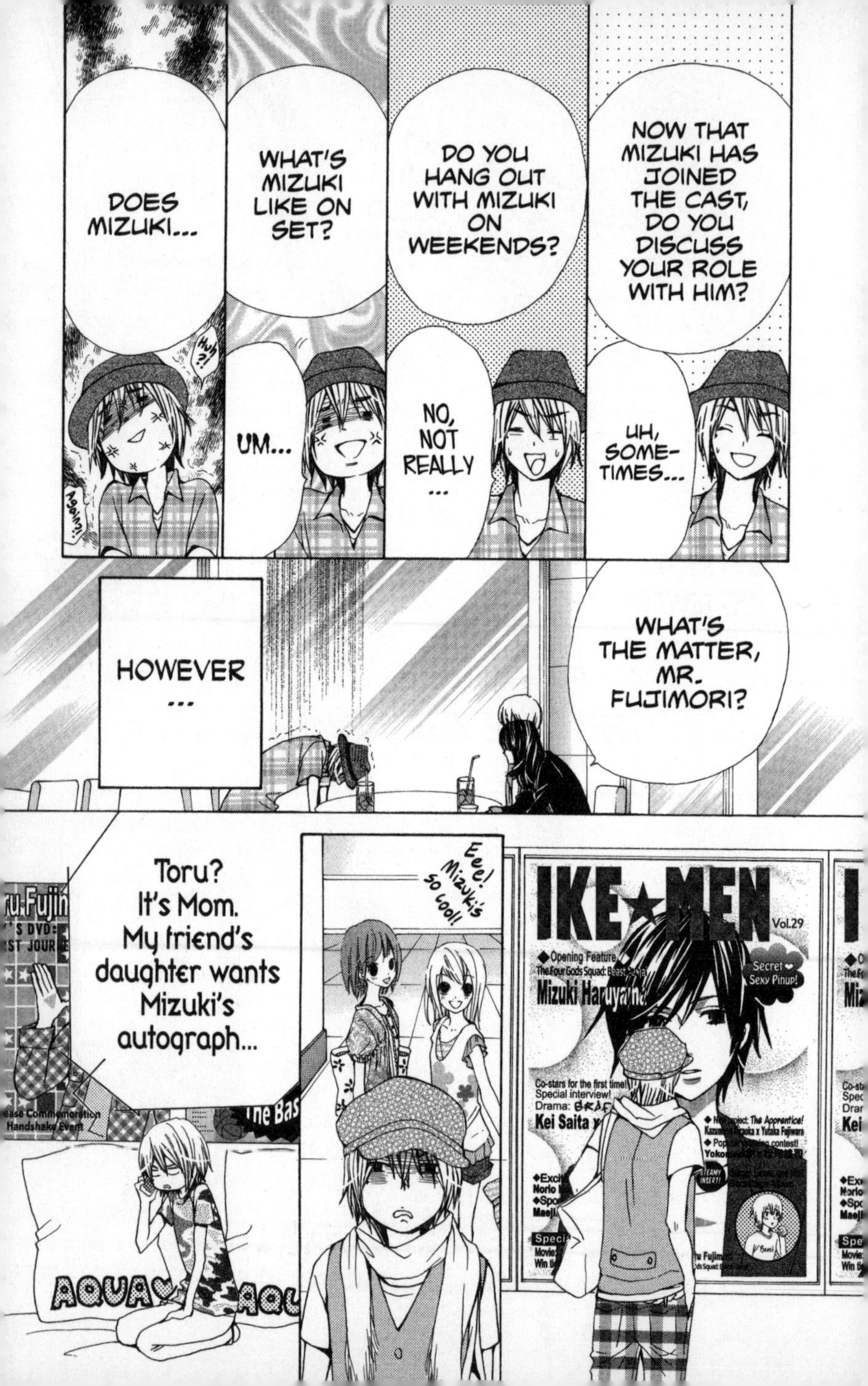
NOW THAT MIZUKI HAS JOINED THE CAST, DO YOU DISCUSS YOUR ROLE WITH HIM?
UH, SOME-TIMES...
DO YOU HANG OUT WITH MIZUKI ON WEEKENDS?
NO, NOT REALLY ...
WHAT'S MIZUKI LIKE ON SET?
UM...
DOES MIZUKI...
Huh?!
Again?!
WHAT'S THE MATTER, MR. FUJIMORI?
HOWEVER ...
Eee! Mizuki's so cool!
IKE★MEN
Vol.29
Opening Feature
Secret Sexy Pinup!
Co-stars for the first time!
Special interview!
Toru? It's Mom. My friend's daughter wants Mizuki's autograph...

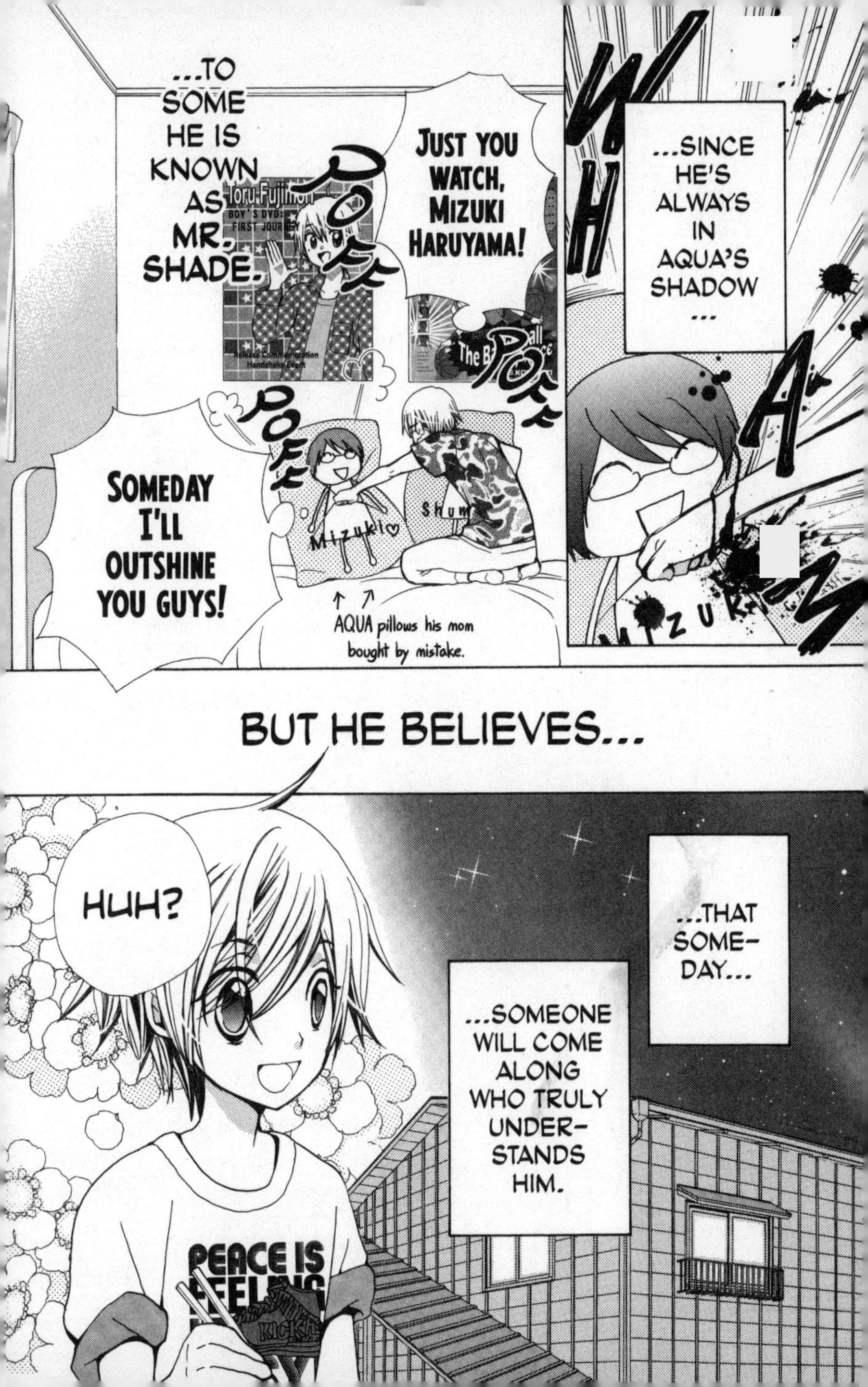
...TO SOME HE IS KNOWN AS MR. SHADE.
JUST YOU WATCH, MIZUKI HARUYAMA!
POKE
POKE
POKE
SOMEDAY I'LL OUTSHINE YOU GUYS!
AQUA pillows his mom bought by mistake.
WHAM
...SINCE HE'S ALWAYS IN AQUA'S SHADOW...
BUT HE BELIEVES...
...THAT SOME-DAY...
...SOMEONE WILL COME ALONG WHO TRULY UNDER-STANDS HIM.
HUH?

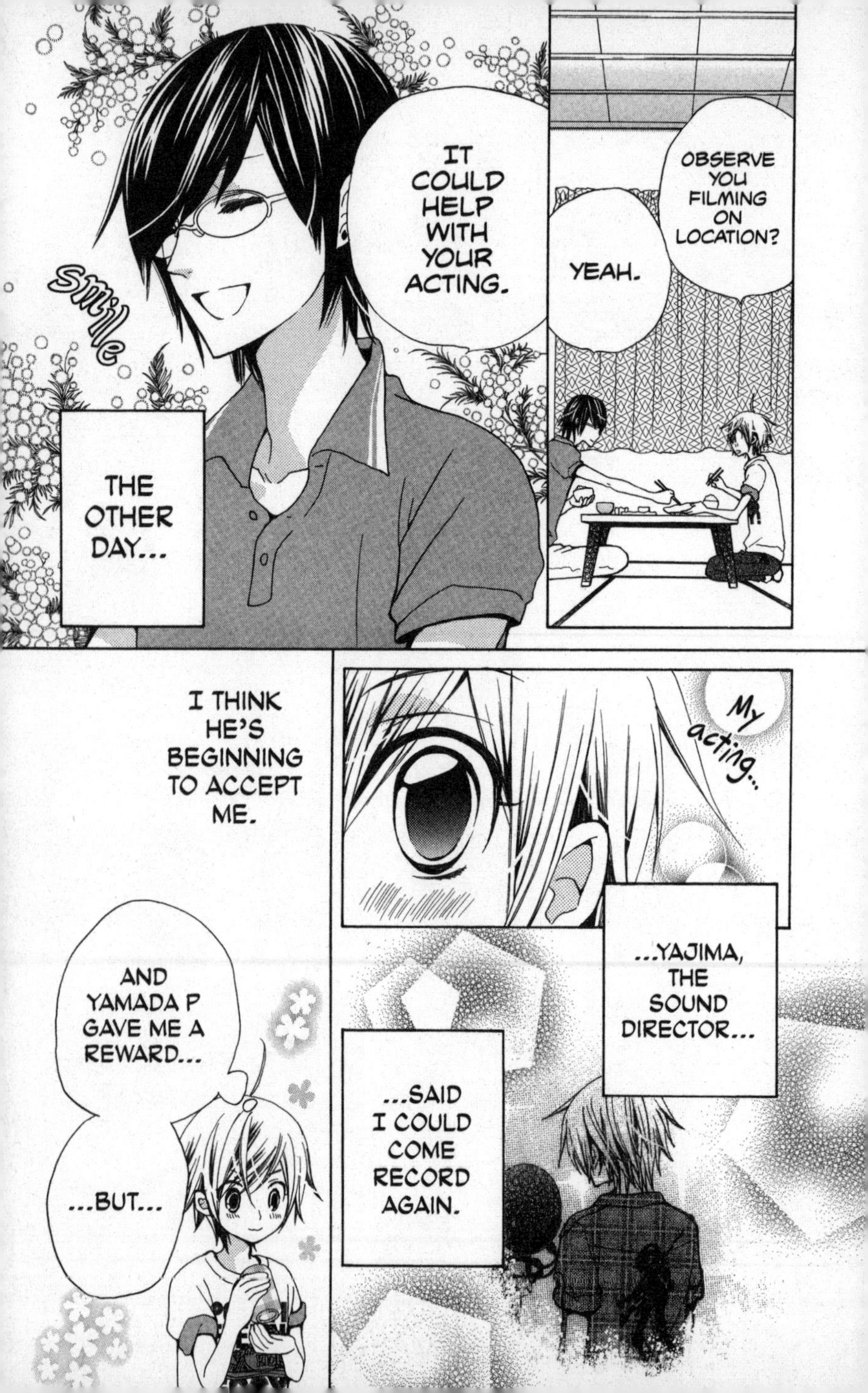
OBSERVE YOU FILMING ON LOCATION?
YEAH.
IT COULD HELP WITH YOUR ACTING.
Smile
THE OTHER DAY...
My acting...
...YAJIMA, THE SOUND DIRECTOR...
...SAID I COULD COME RECORD AGAIN.
I THINK HE'S BEGINNING TO ACCEPT ME.
AND YAMADA P GAVE ME A REWARD...
...BUT...

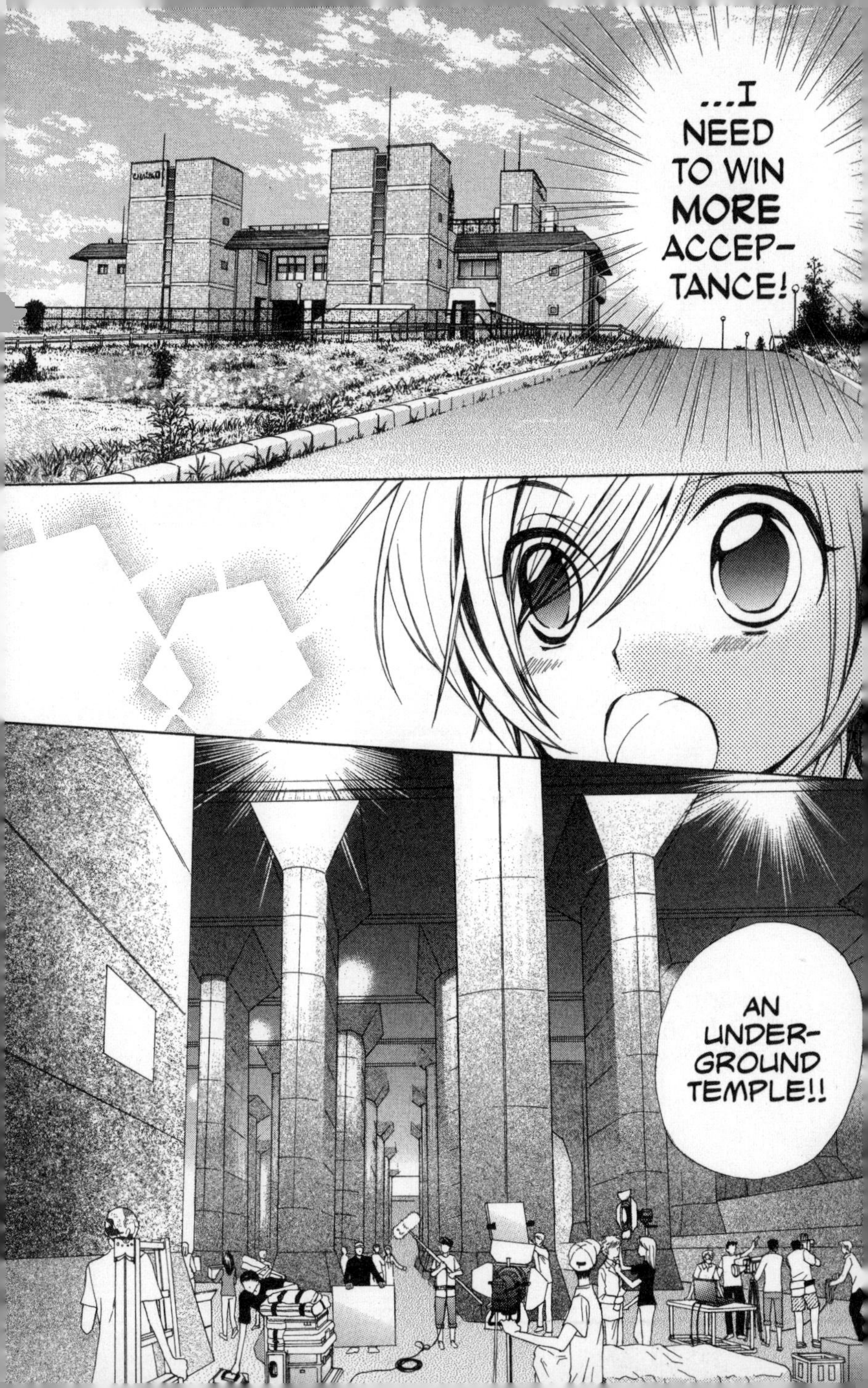
...I NEED TO WIN MORE ACCEPTANCE!
AN UNDERGROUND TEMPLE!!

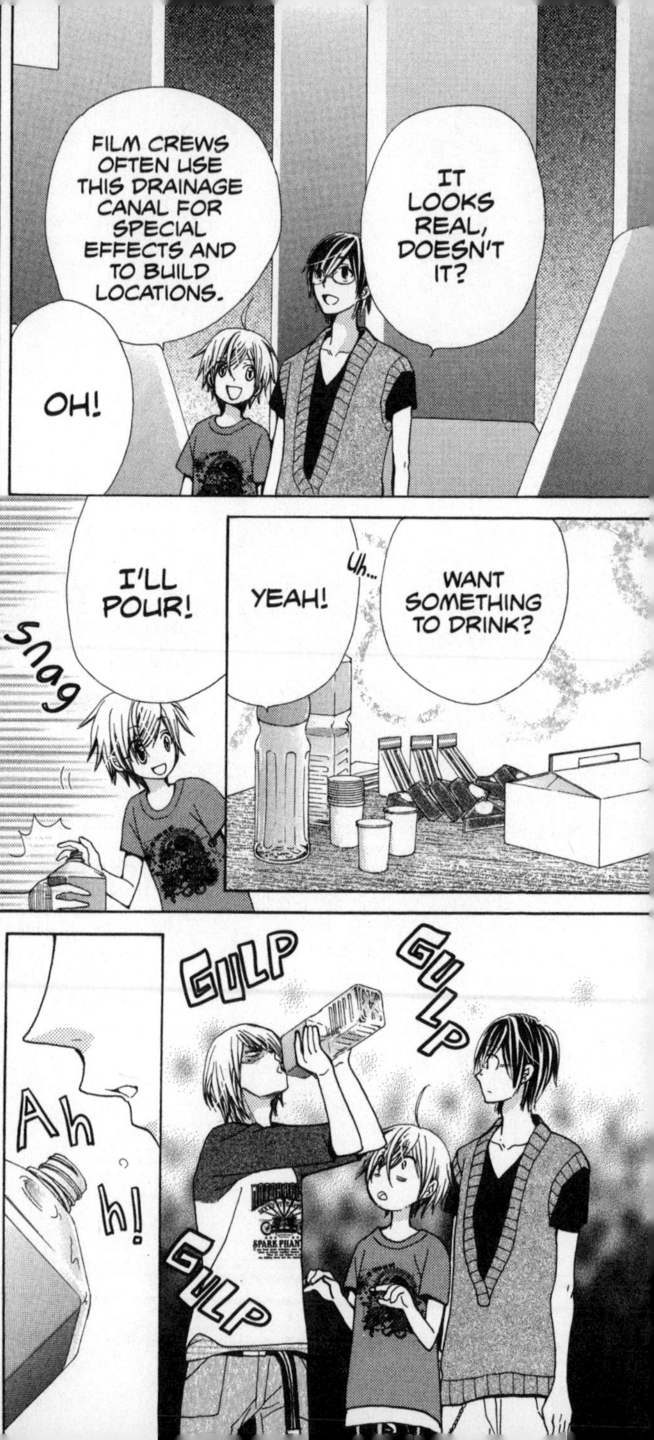
IT LOOKS REAL, DOESN'T IT?
FILM CREWS OFTEN USE THIS DRAINAGE CANAL FOR SPECIAL EFFECTS AND TO BUILD LOCATIONS.
OH!
WANT SOMETHING TO DRINK?
Uh...
YEAH!
I'LL POUR!
Snag
GULP
GULP
GULP
Ah h!

• Hirame ① •

I don't know what I was thinking, but when I was in elementary school, I suddenly said to my friends...

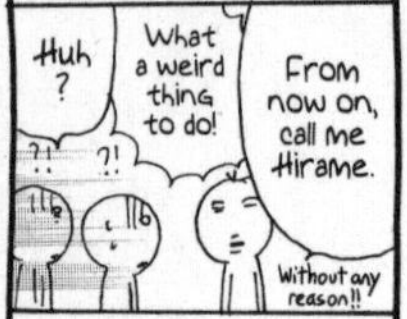
From now on, call me Hirame.
What a weird thing to do!
Huh?
?! ?!
Without any reason!!

In line with my request, my friends called me Hirame. This continued through junior high, but in high school...

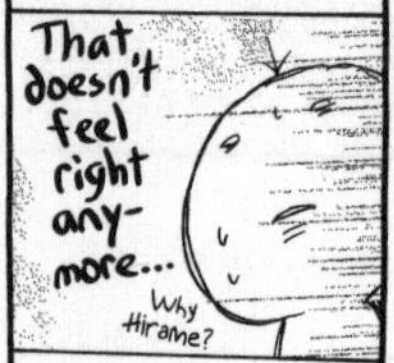
That doesn't feel right any-more...
Why Hirame?

So I had my friends use my normal name. I got used to that, and then after a long time, I had to go to a reunion for a junior high school club.

→ Continued in ②

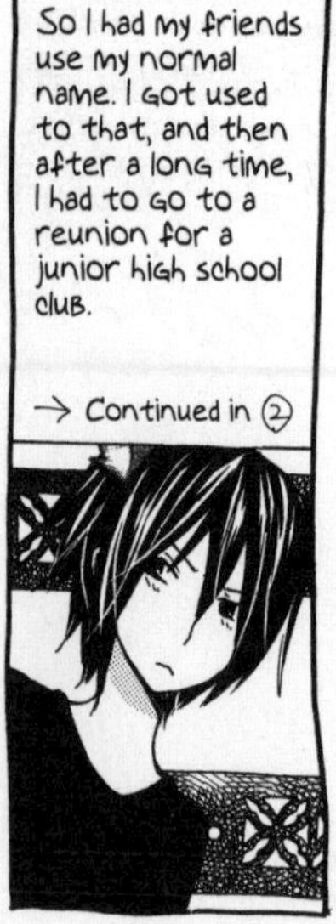

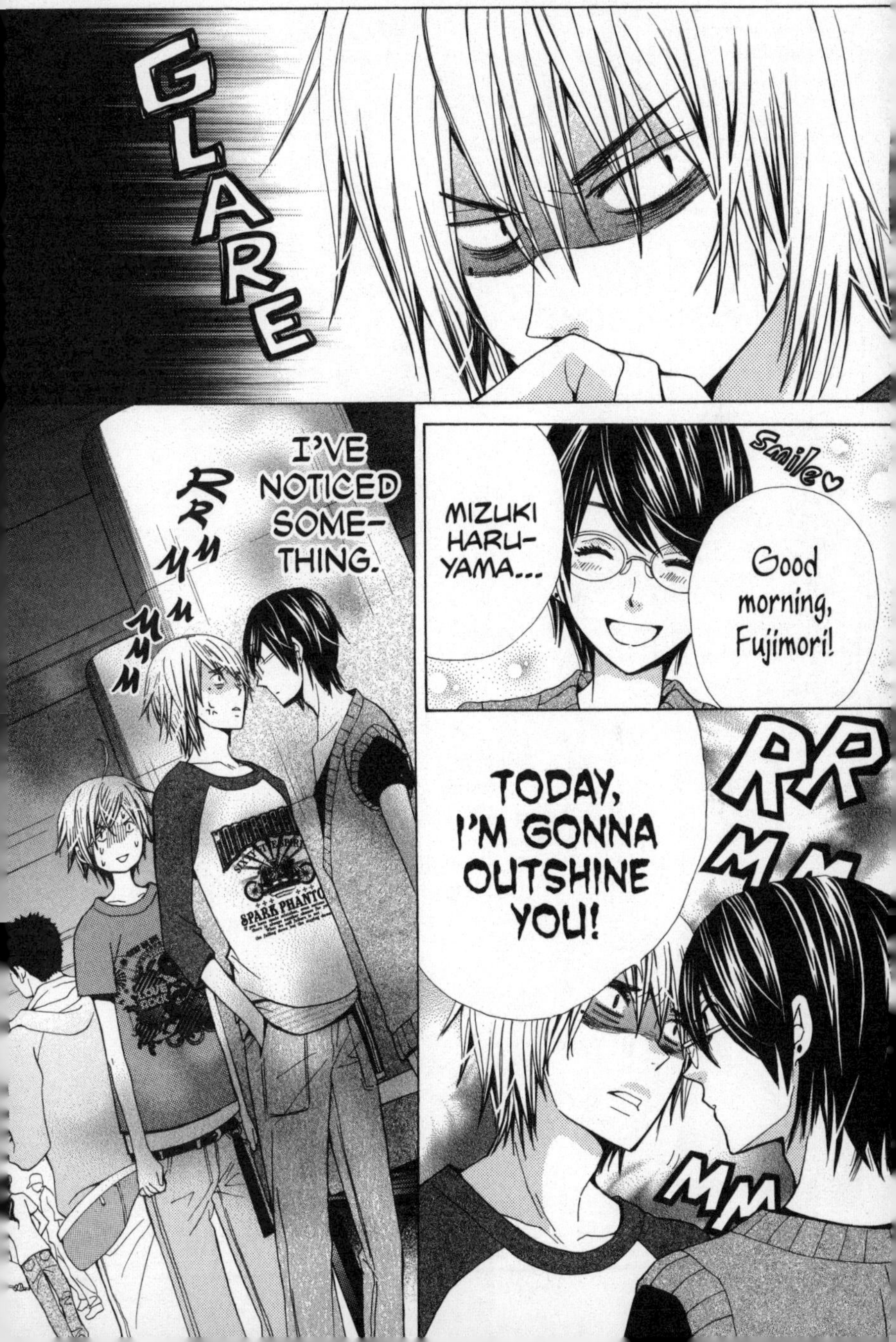
GLARE
Smile♡
Good morning, Fujimori!
MIZUKI HARU-YAMA...
RR
MM MM
TODAY, I'M GONNA OUTSHINE YOU!
MM
I'VE NOTICED SOME-THING.

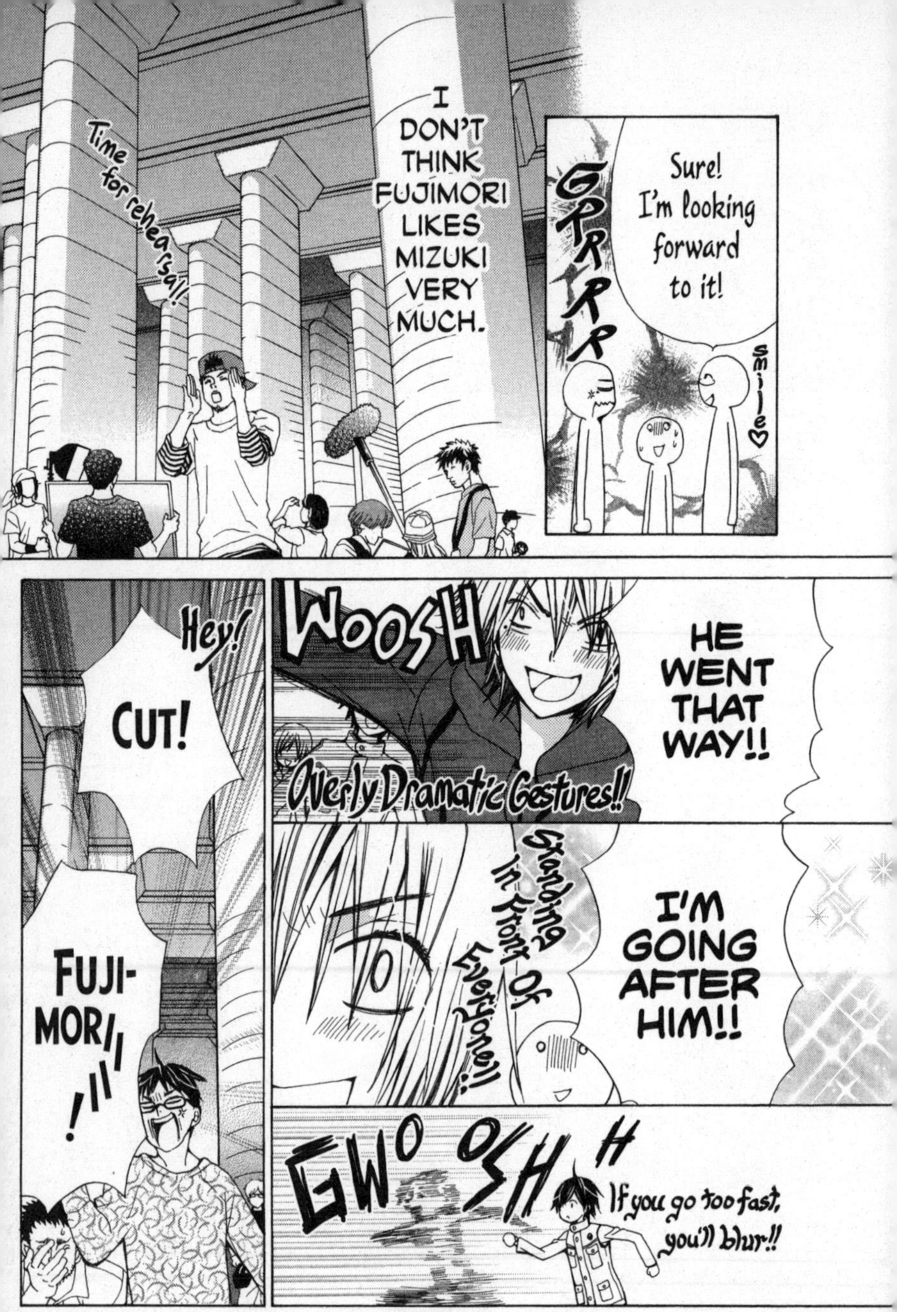
Sure! I'm looking forward to it!
GRRRR
smile♡
I DON'T THINK FUJIMORI LIKES MIZUKI VERY MUCH.
Time for rehearsal!!
WOOSH
HE WENT THAT WAY!!
Overly Dramatic Gestures!!
I'M GOING AFTER HIM!!
Standing In Front Of Everyone!!
GWOOSHH
If you go too fast, you'll blur!!
Hey!
CUT!
FUJIMORI!!!

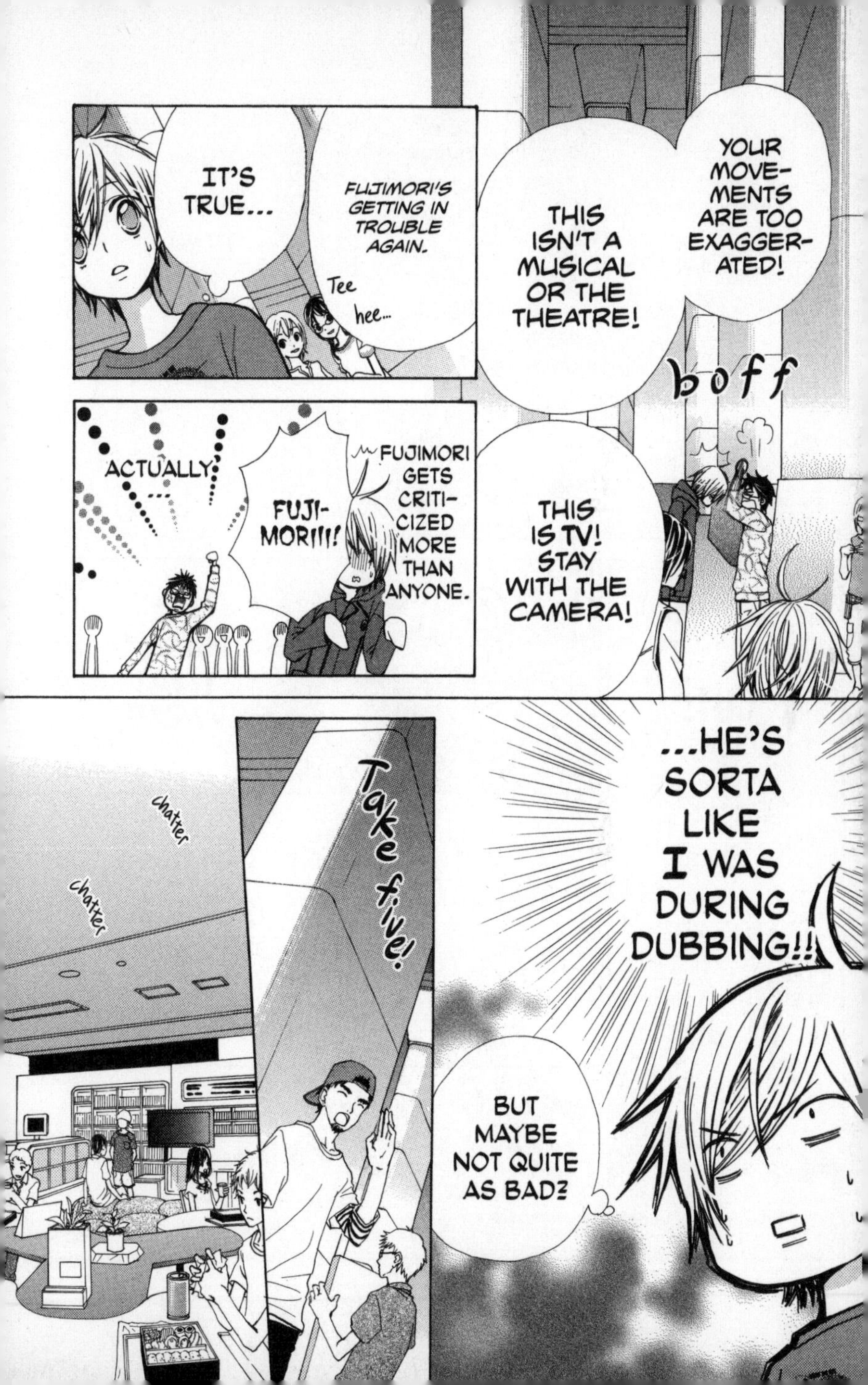
YOUR MOVEMENTS ARE TOO EXAGGERATED!
THIS ISN'T A MUSICAL OR THE THEATRE!
boff
THIS IS TV! STAY WITH THE CAMERA!
FUJIMORI'S GETTING IN TROUBLE AGAIN.
Tee hee...
IT'S TRUE...
FUJIMORI GETS CRITICIZED MORE THAN ANYONE.
FUJI-MORI!!!
ACTUALLY...
...HE'S SORTA LIKE I WAS DURING DUBBING!!
BUT MAYBE NOT QUITE AS BAD?
Take five!
chatter
chatter

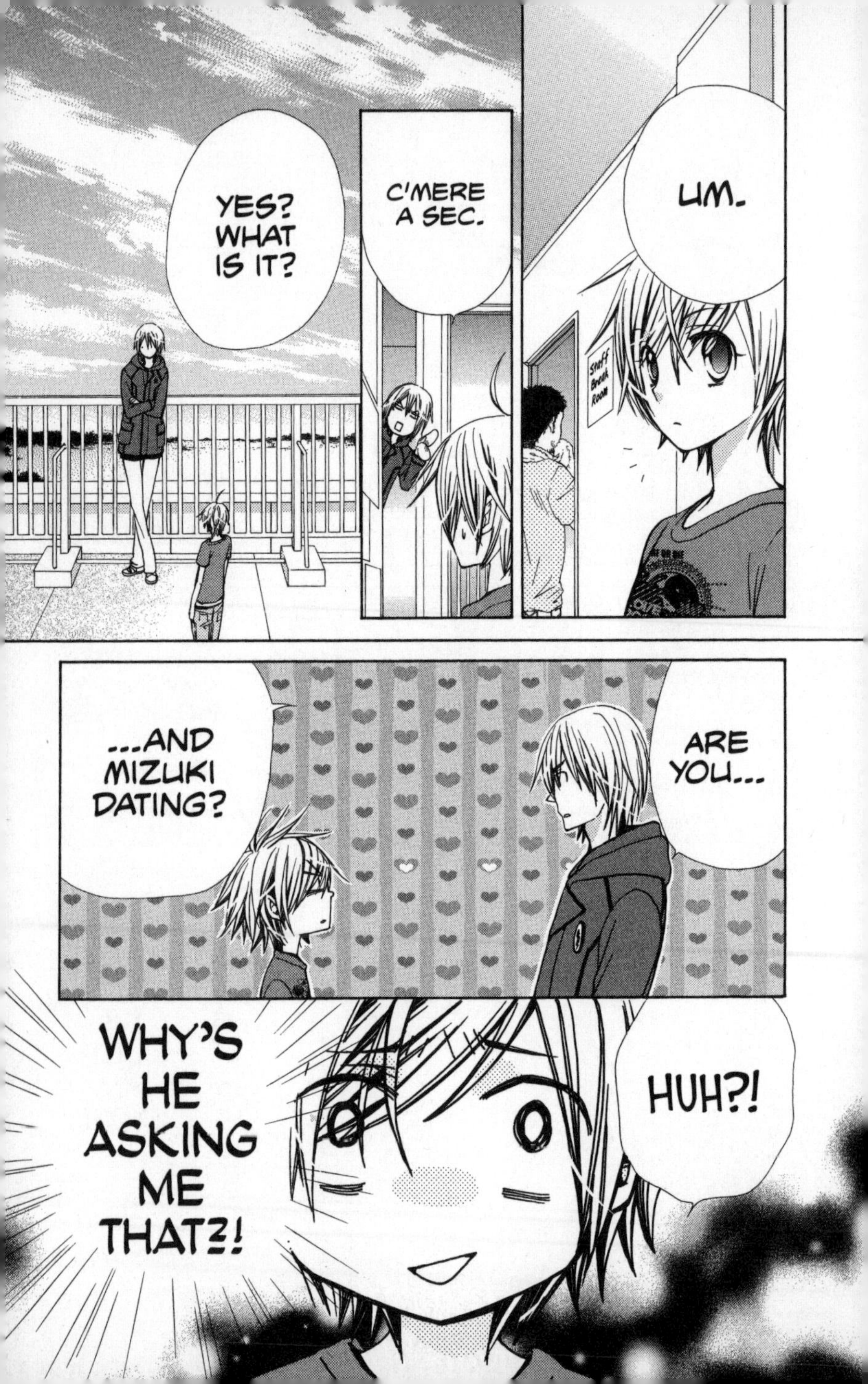
UM.
Staff Break Room
C'MERE A SEC.
YES? WHAT IS IT?
ARE YOU...
...AND MIZUKI DATING?
HUH?!
WHY'S HE ASKING ME THAT?!

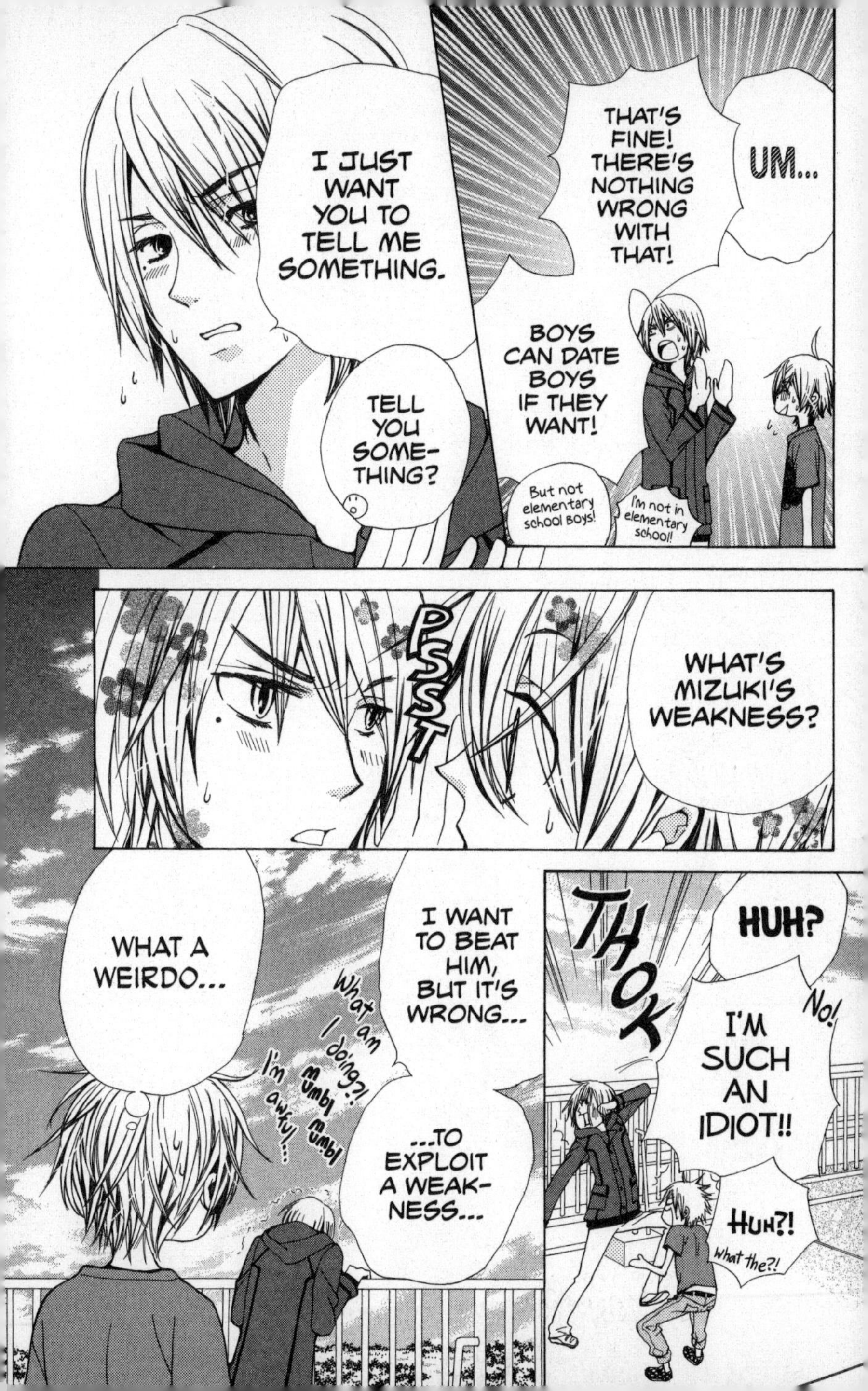
UM...
THAT'S FINE! THERE'S NOTHING WRONG WITH THAT!
BOYS CAN DATE BOYS IF THEY WANT!
I'm not in elementary school!
But not elementary school boys!
I JUST WANT YOU TO TELL ME SOMETHING.
TELL YOU SOMETHING?
PSST
WHAT'S MIZUKI'S WEAKNESS?
THOK
HUH?
No!
I'M SUCH AN IDIOT!!
HUH?!
What the?!
I WANT TO BEAT HIM, BUT IT'S WRONG...
...TO EXPLOIT A WEAKNESS...
What am I doing?!
mumbl mumbl
I'm awful...
WHAT A WEIRDO...

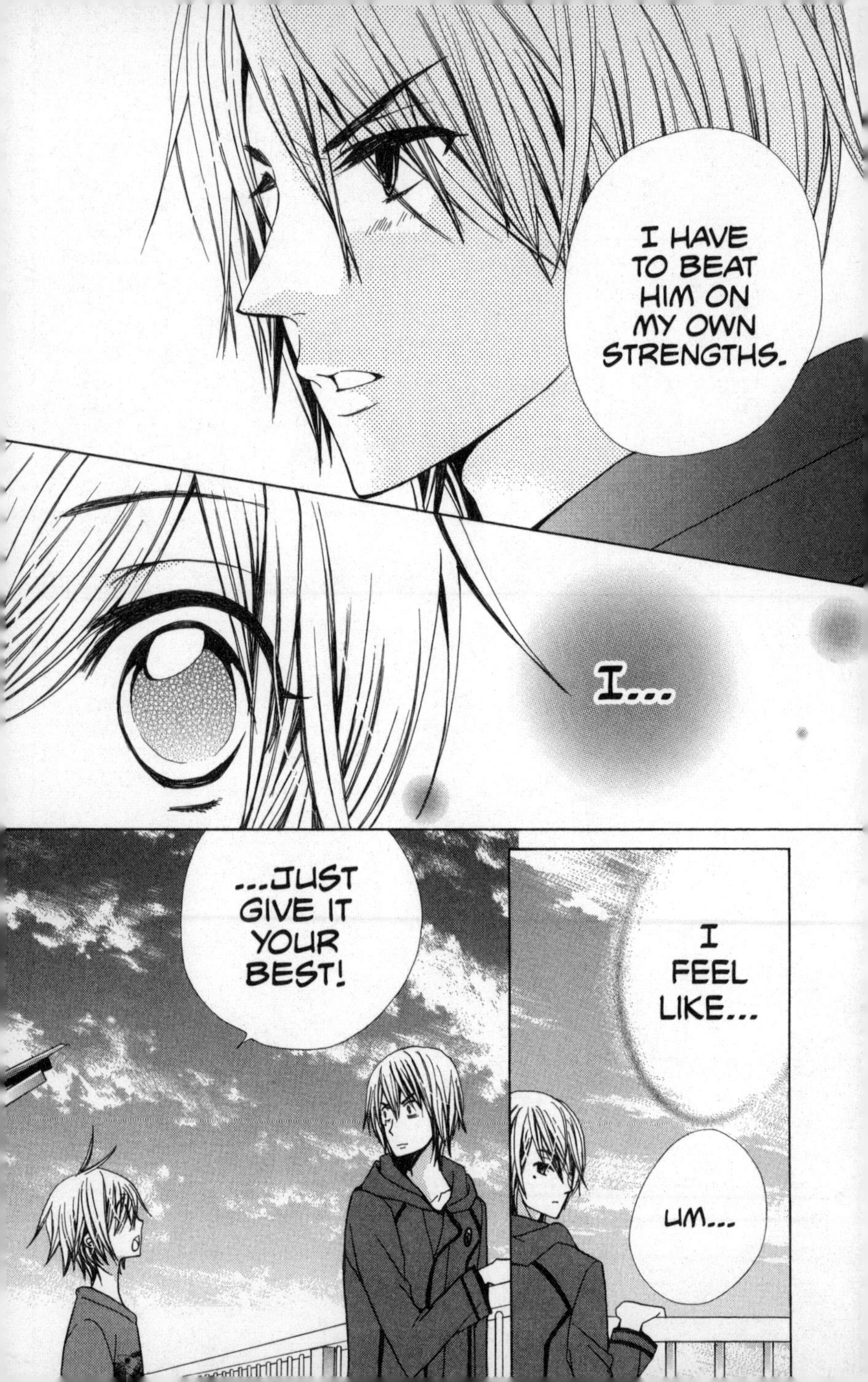
I HAVE TO BEAT HIM ON MY OWN STRENGTHS.
I...
I FEEL LIKE...
UM...
...JUST GIVE IT YOUR BEST!

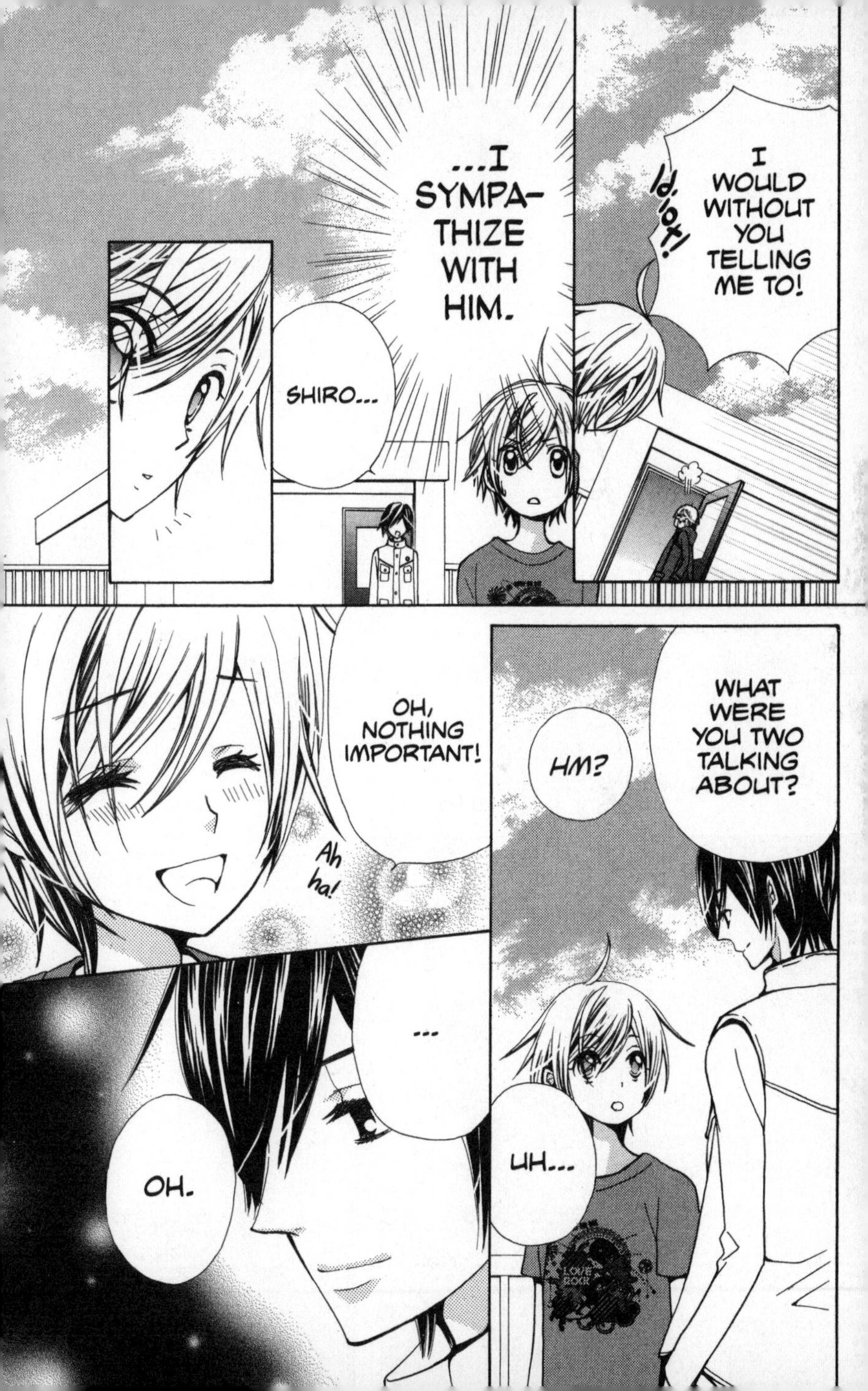
Idiot!
I WOULD WITHOUT YOU TELLING ME TO!
...I SYMPATHIZE WITH HIM.
SHIRO...
WHAT WERE YOU TWO TALKING ABOUT?
HM?
UH...
OH, NOTHING IMPORTANT!
Ah ha!
...
OH.

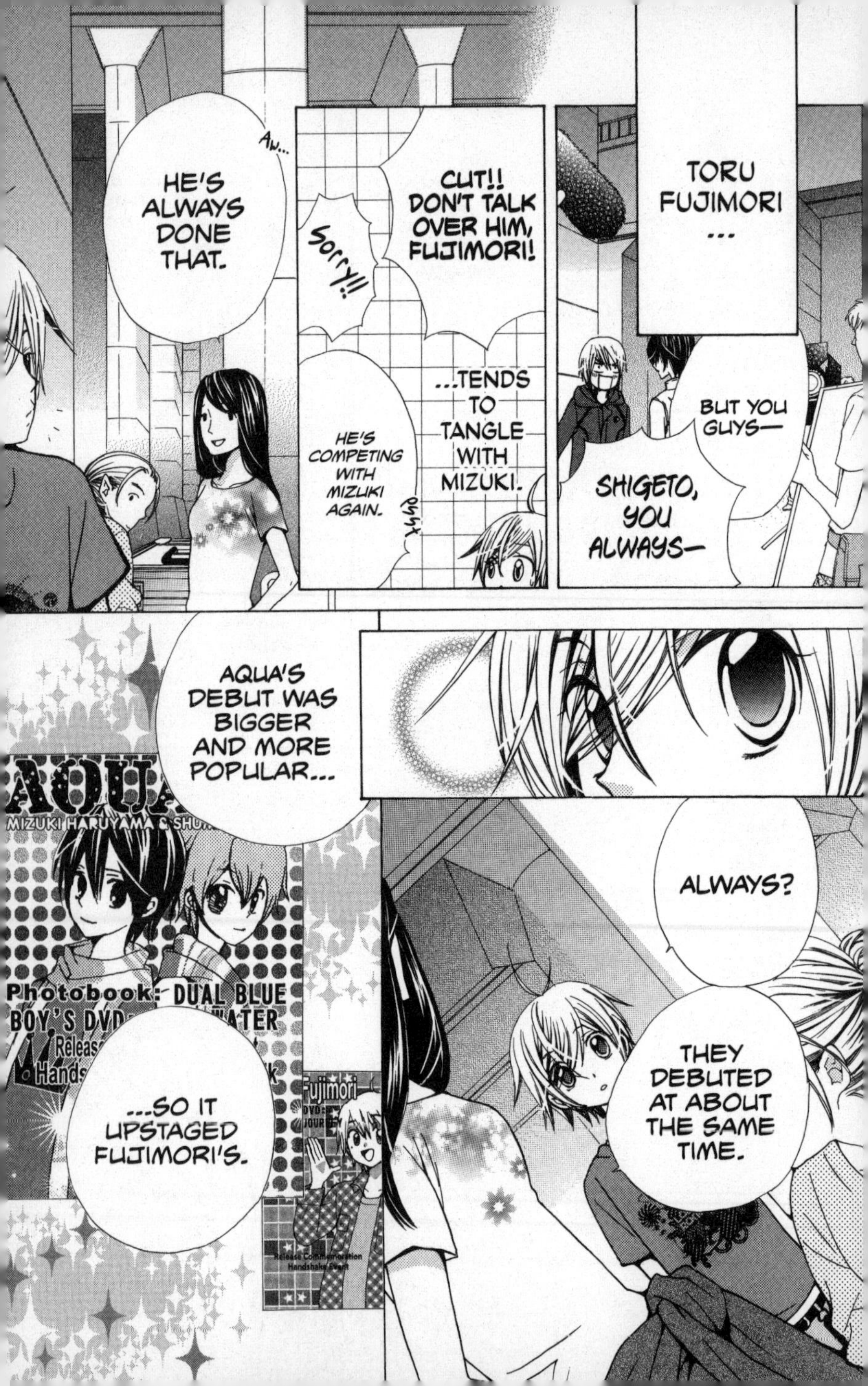
TORU FUJIMORI ...
BUT YOU GUYS—
SHIGETO, YOU ALWAYS—
CUT!! DON'T TALK OVER HIM, FUJIMORI!
Sorry!!
...TENDS TO TANGLE WITH MIZUKI.
HE'S COMPETING WITH MIZUKI AGAIN.
Aw...
HE'S ALWAYS DONE THAT.
ALWAYS?
THEY DEBUTED AT ABOUT THE SAME TIME.
AQUA'S DEBUT WAS BIGGER AND MORE POPULAR...
Photobook: DUAL BLUE
...SO IT UPSTAGED FUJIMORI'S.
Fujimori
Release Commemoration Handshake Event

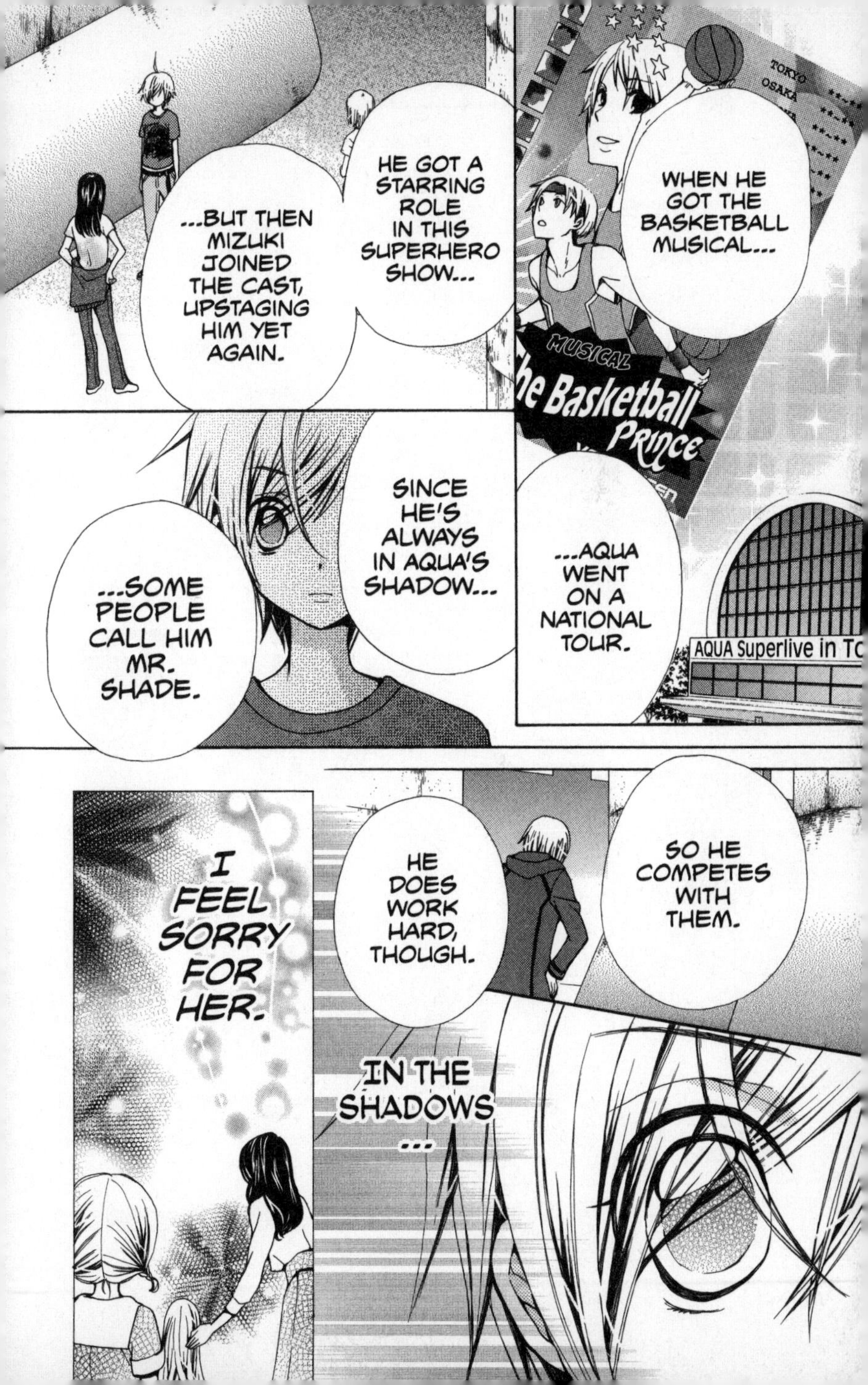
WHEN HE GOT THE BASKETBALL MUSICAL...
TOKYO
OSAKA
MUSICAL
he Basketball PRINCE
HE GOT A STARRING ROLE IN THIS SUPERHERO SHOW...
...BUT THEN MIZUKI JOINED THE CAST, UPSTAGING HIM YET AGAIN.
...AQUA WENT ON A NATIONAL TOUR.
AQUA Superlive in To
SINCE HE'S ALWAYS IN AQUA'S SHADOW...
...SOME PEOPLE CALL HIM MR. SHADE.
SO HE COMPETES WITH THEM.
HE DOES WORK HARD, THOUGH.
IN THE SHADOWS...
I FEEL SORRY FOR HER.

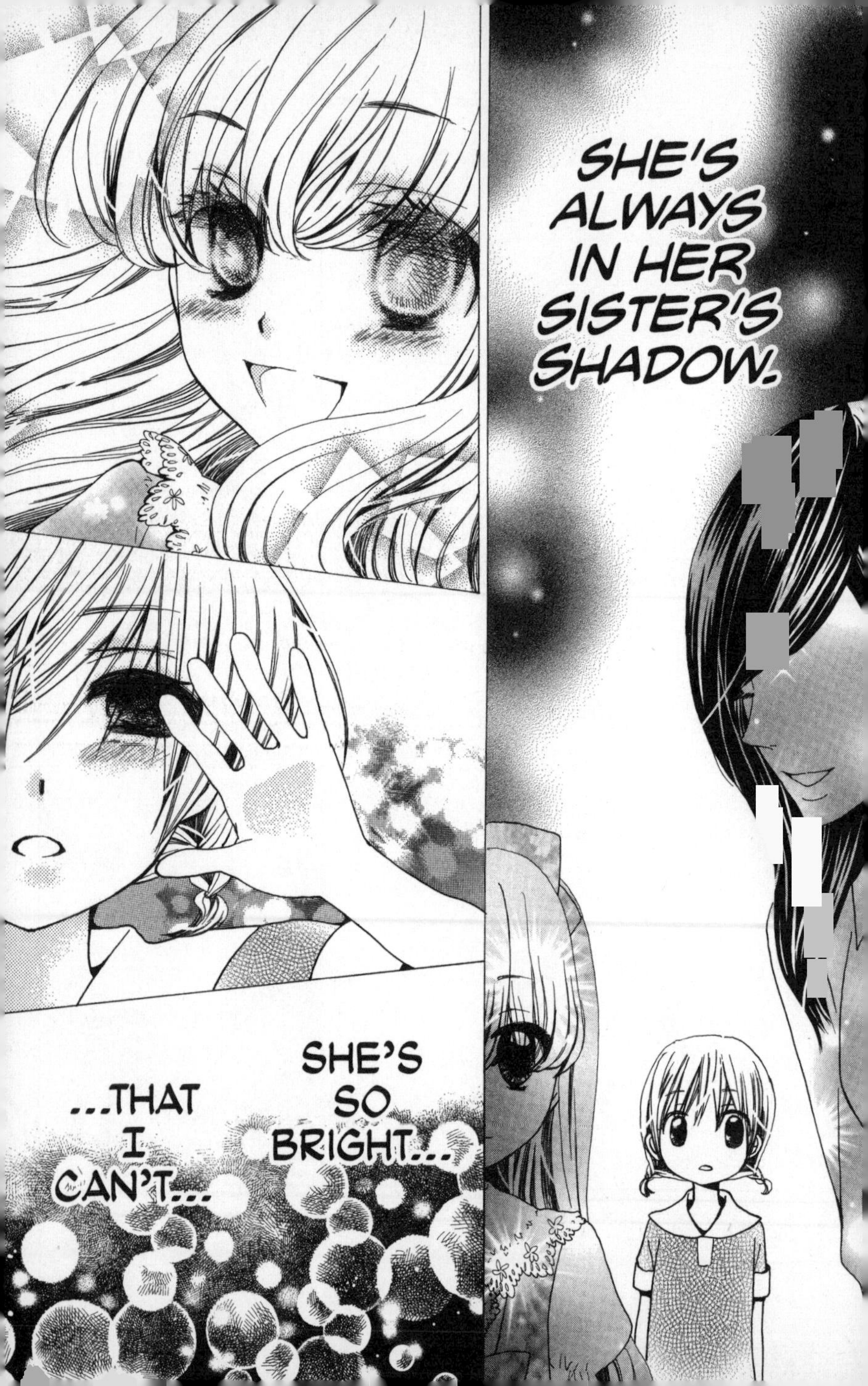
SHE'S ALWAYS IN HER SISTER'S SHADOW.
SHE'S SO BRIGHT...
...THAT I CAN'T...

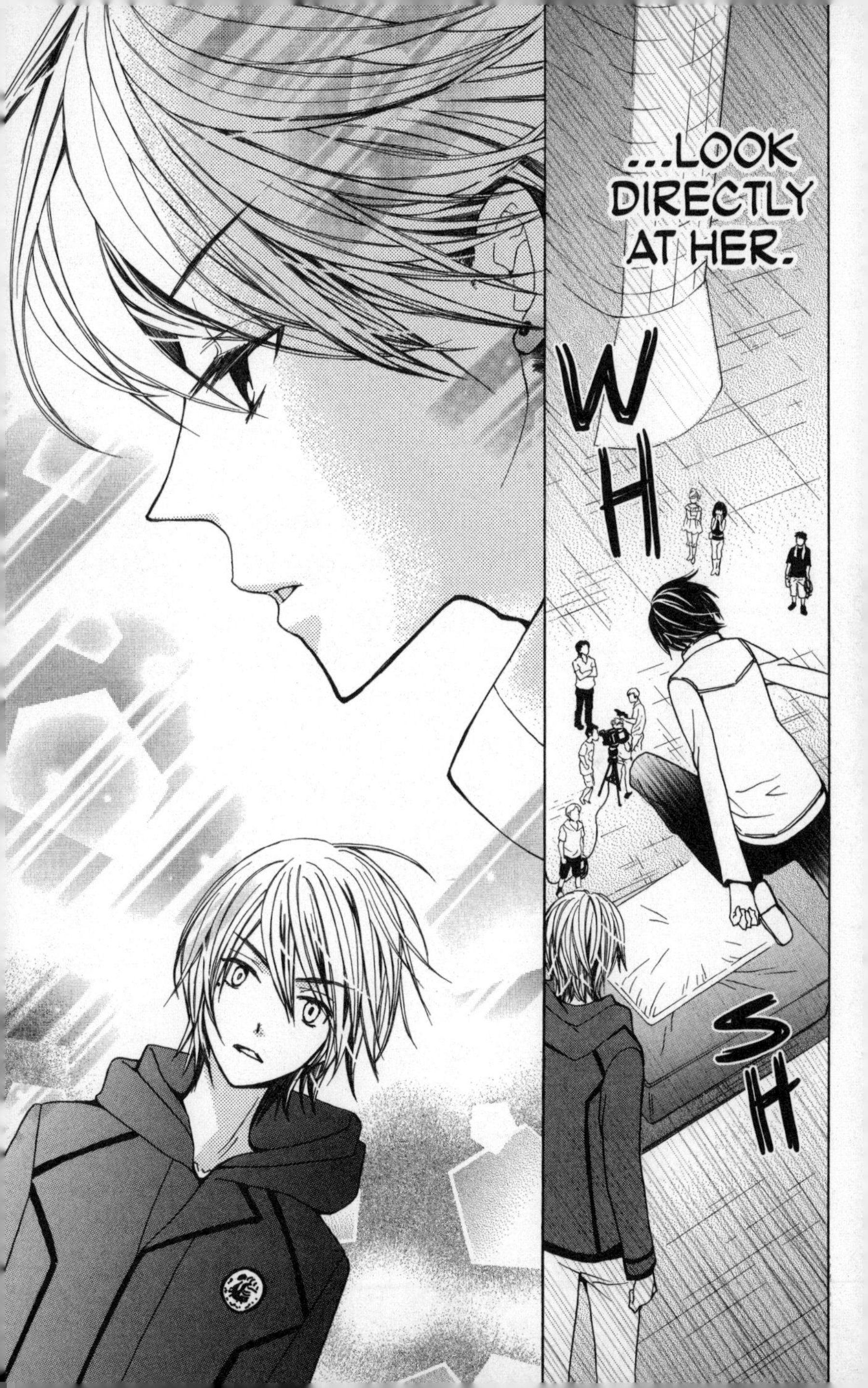
...LOOK DIRECTLY AT HER.
WHSH

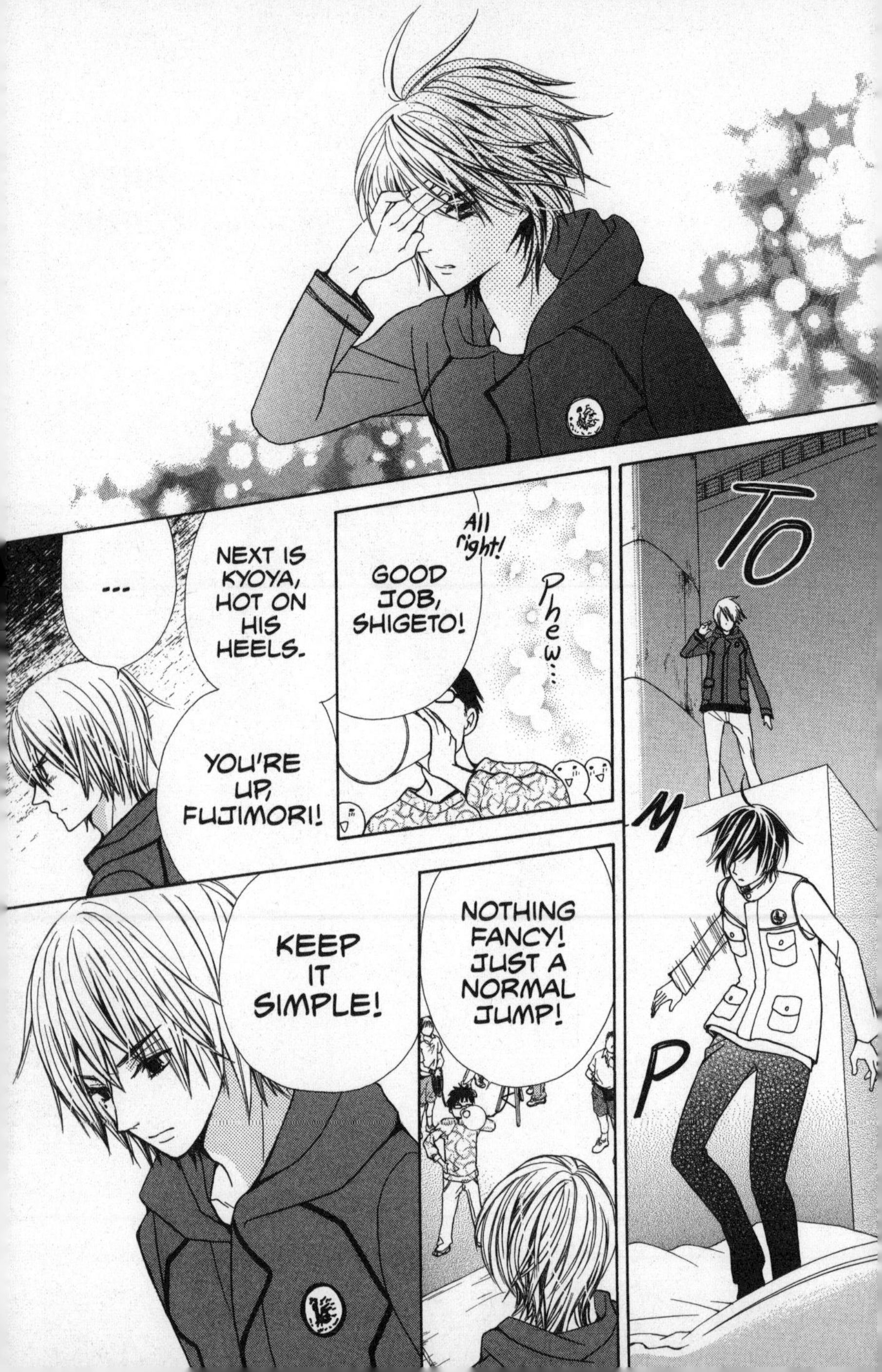
TOMP
All right!
GOOD JOB, SHIGETO!
Phew...
NEXT IS KYOYA, HOT ON HIS HEELS.
...
YOU'RE UP, FUJIMORI!
NOTHING FANCY! JUST A NORMAL JUMP!
KEEP IT SIMPLE!

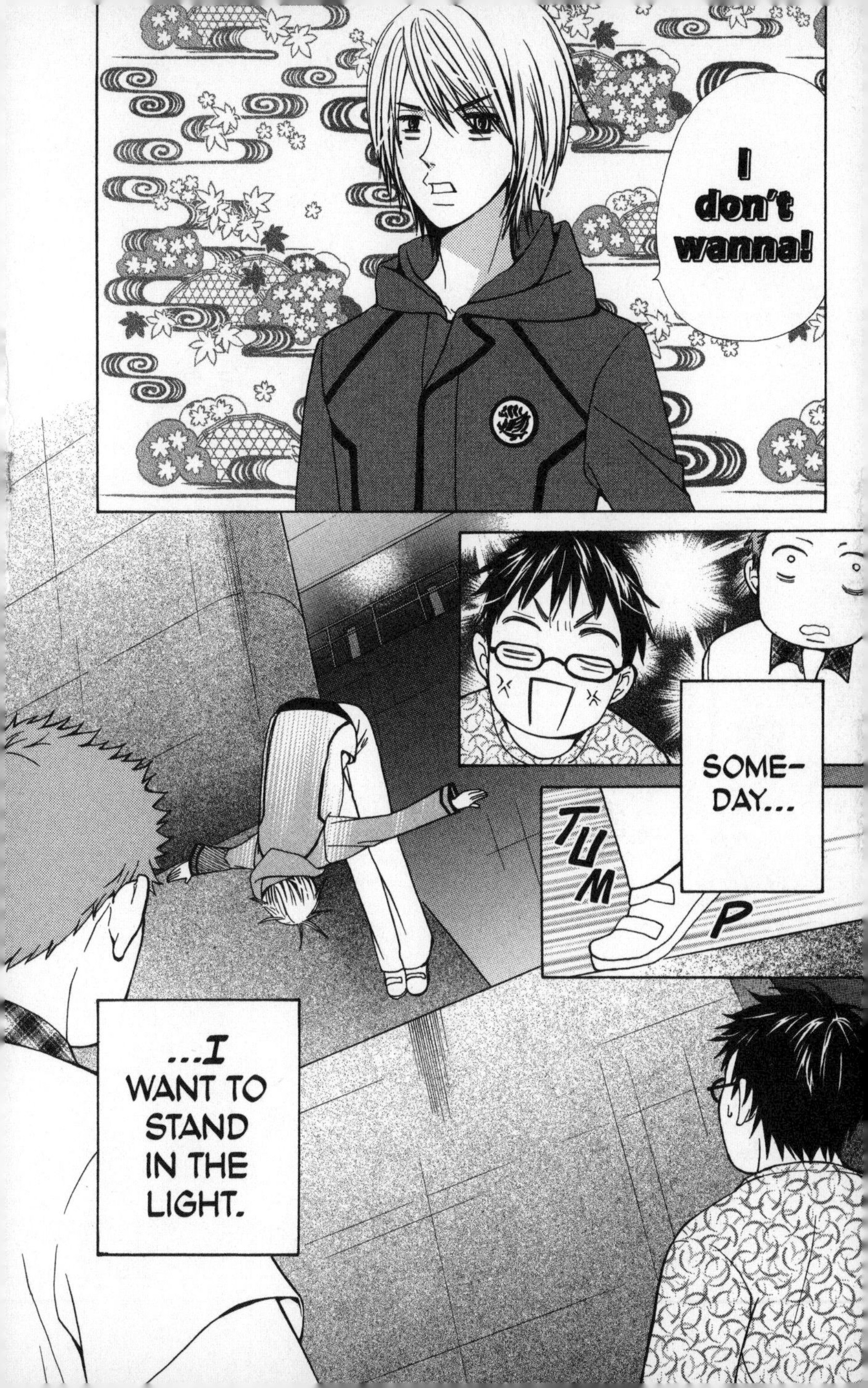
I don't wanna!
SOME-DAY...
TUMP
...I WANT TO STAND IN THE LIGHT.

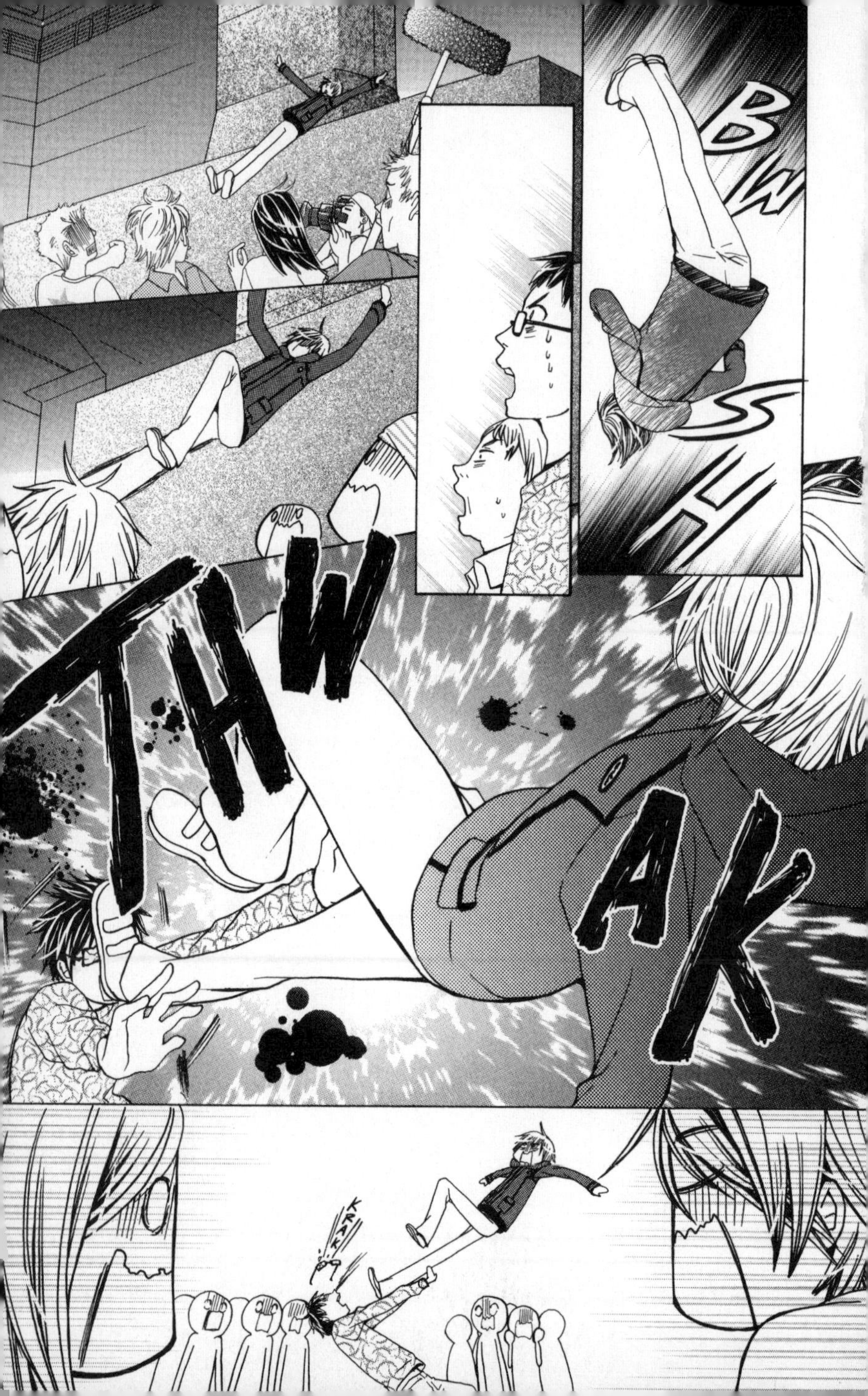
BWSH
THWAK
KRAK

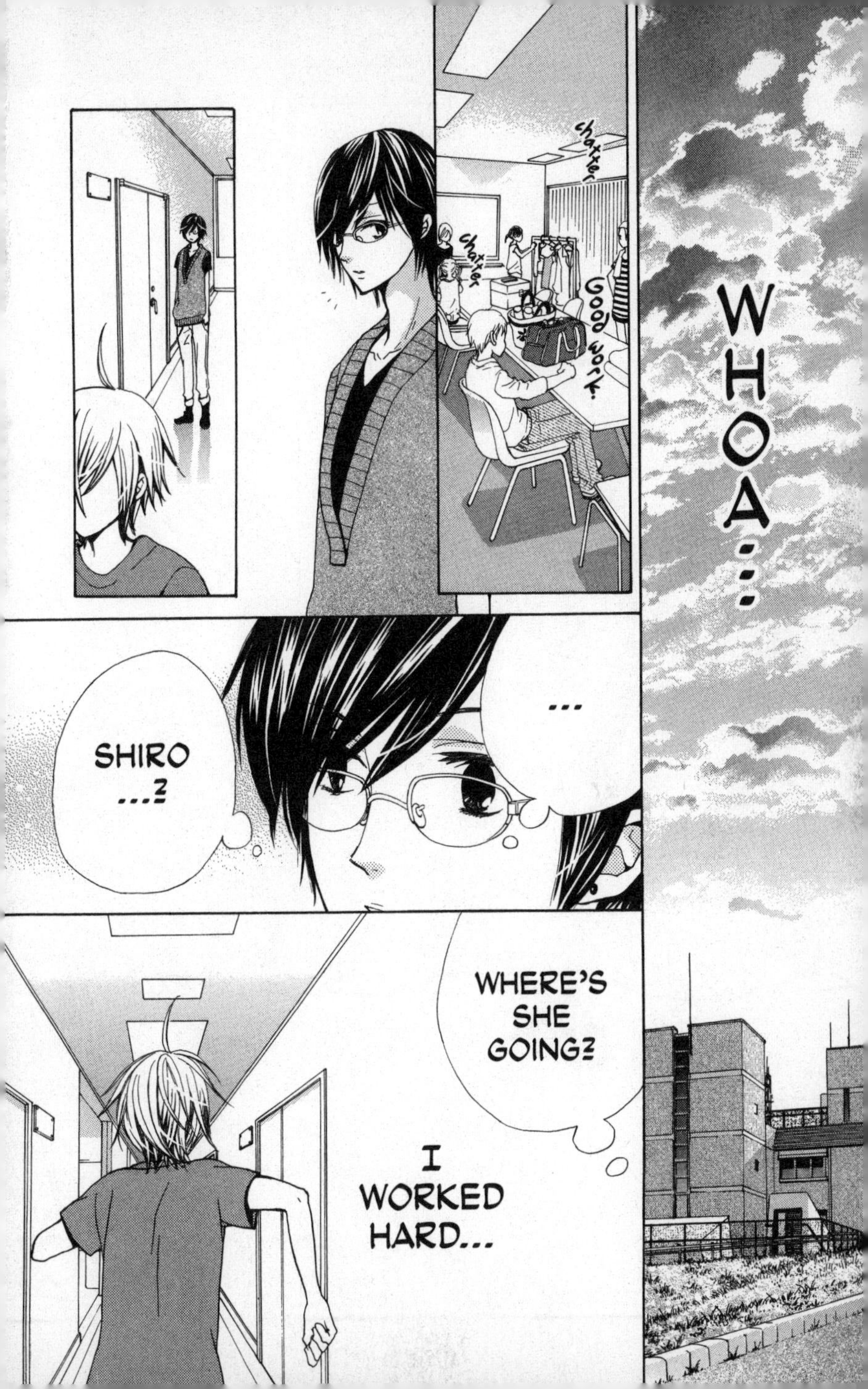

WHOA...
chatter
Good work.
chatter
...
SHIRO...?
WHERE'S SHE GOING?
I WORKED HARD...

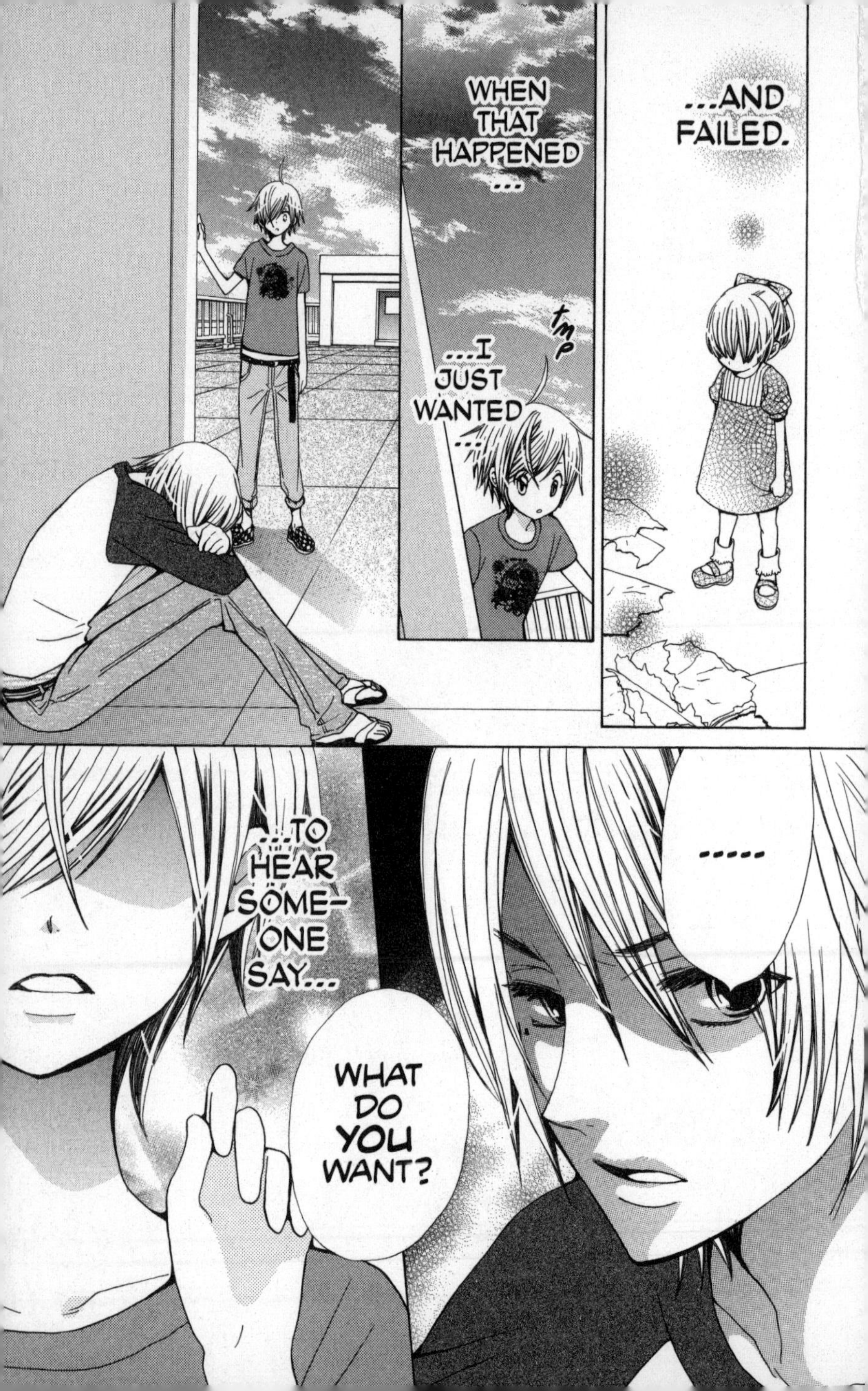
...AND FAILED.
WHEN THAT HAPPENED ...
tmp
...I JUST WANTED ...
.....
...TO HEAR SOME-ONE SAY...
WHAT DO YOU WANT?

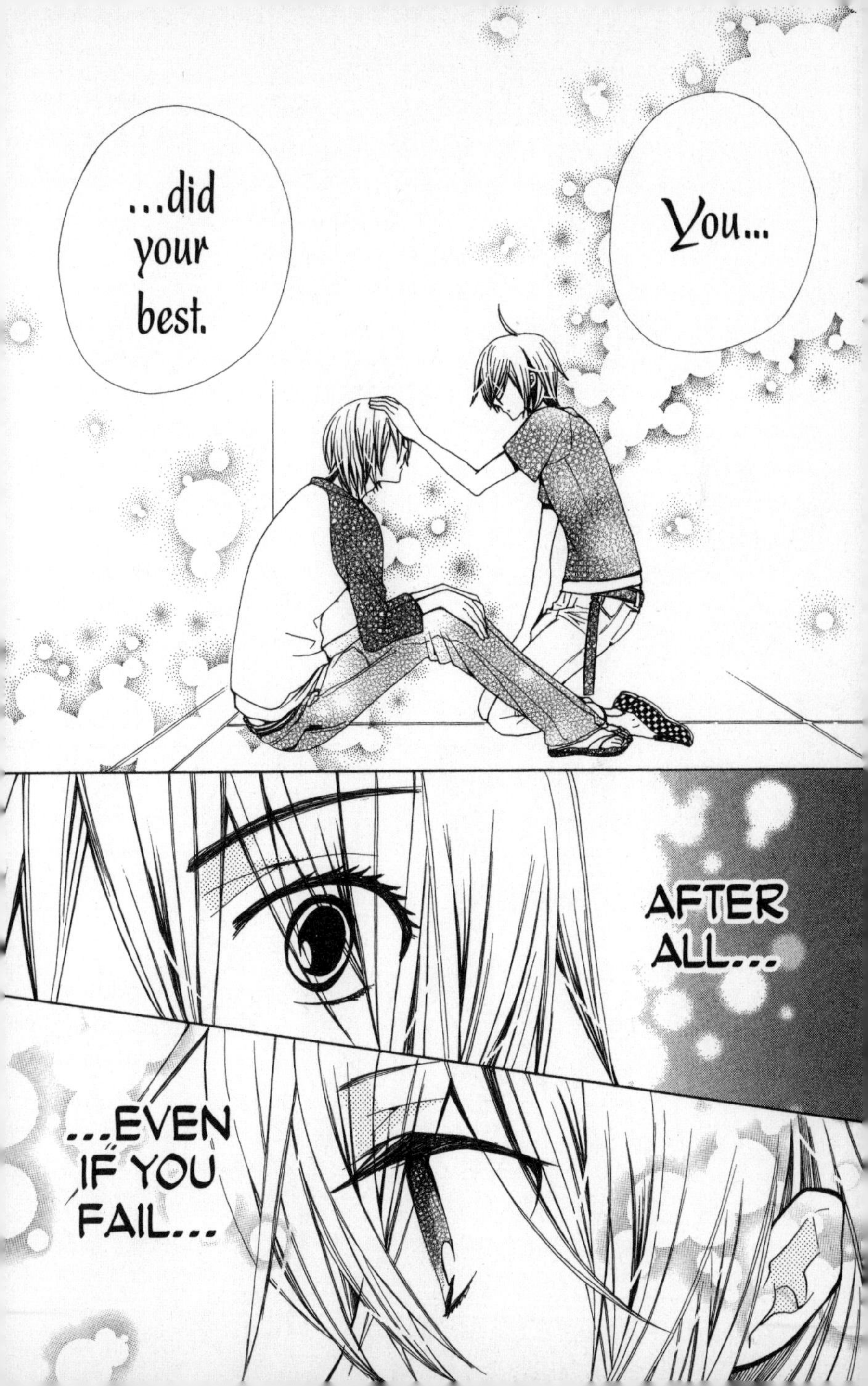
You...
...did your best.
AFTER ALL...
...EVEN IF YOU FAIL...

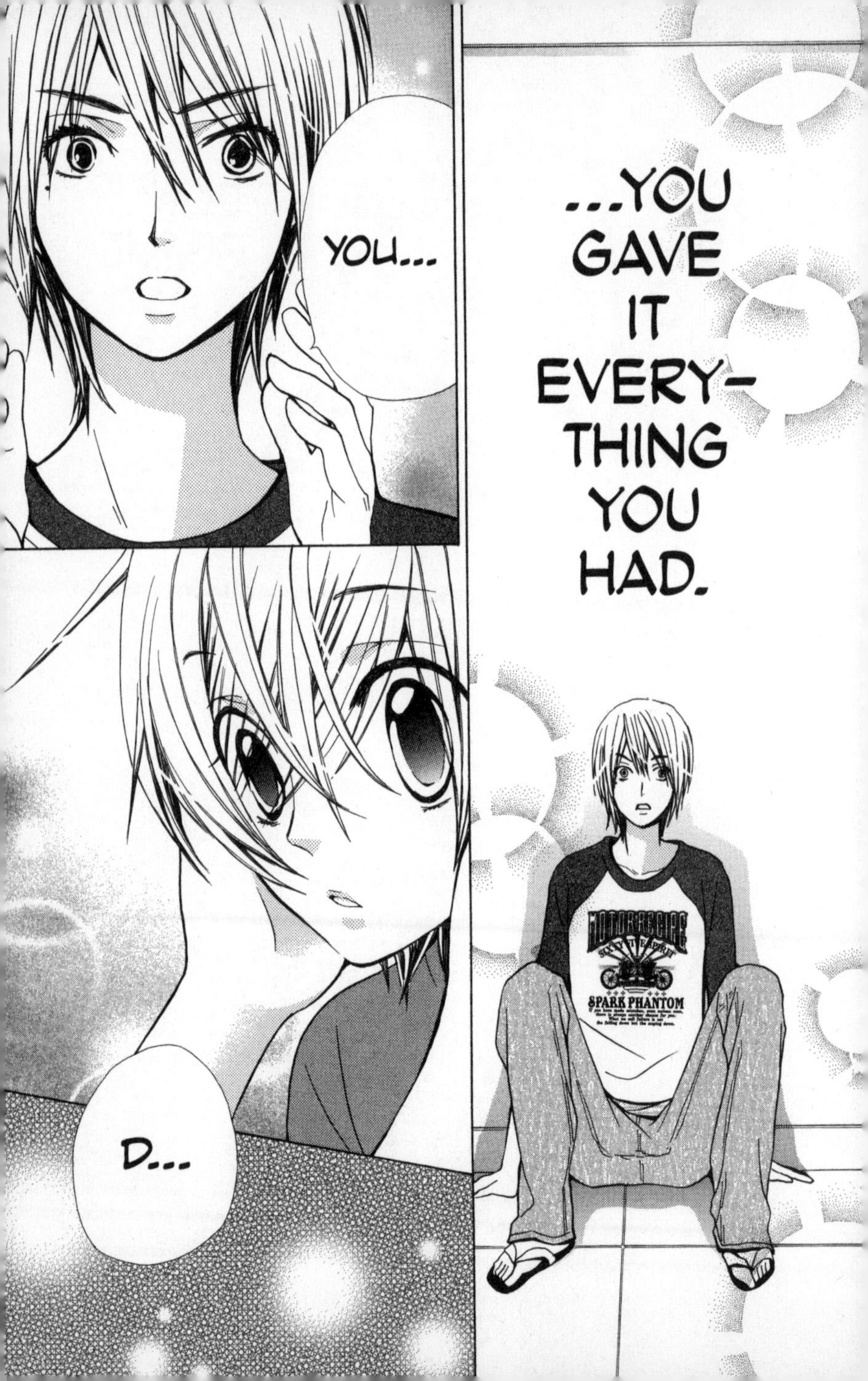
...YOU GAVE IT EVERYTHING YOU HAD.
SPARK PHANTOM
YOU...
D...

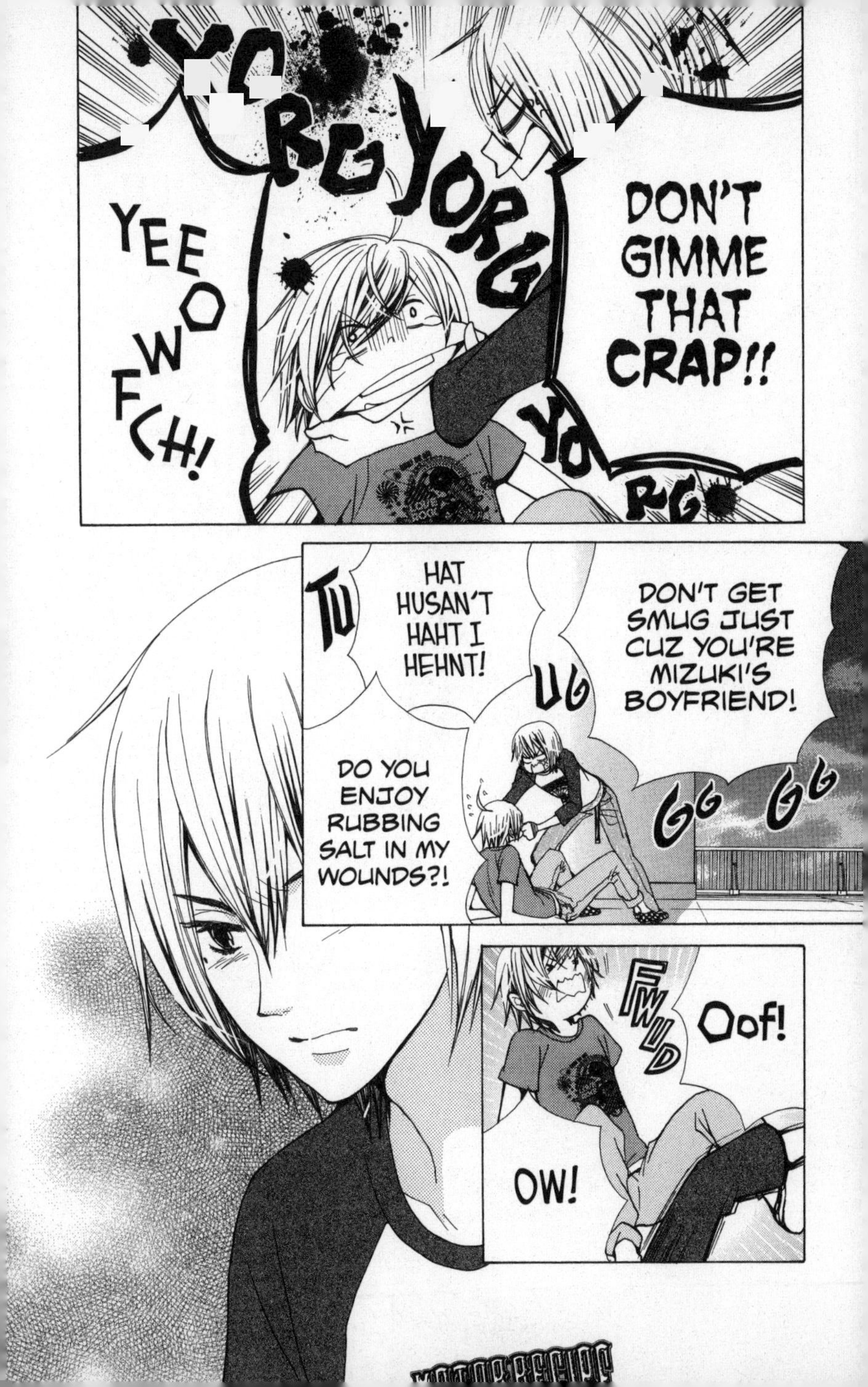
DON'T GIMME THAT CRAP!!
YORG YORG YORG YORG
YEEOWFCH!
DON'T GET SMUG JUST CUZ YOU'RE MIZUKI'S BOYFRIEND!
GG GG
UG
TU
HAT HUSAN'T HAHT I HEHNT!
DO YOU ENJOY RUBBING SALT IN MY WOUNDS?!
Oof!
FWUD
OW!

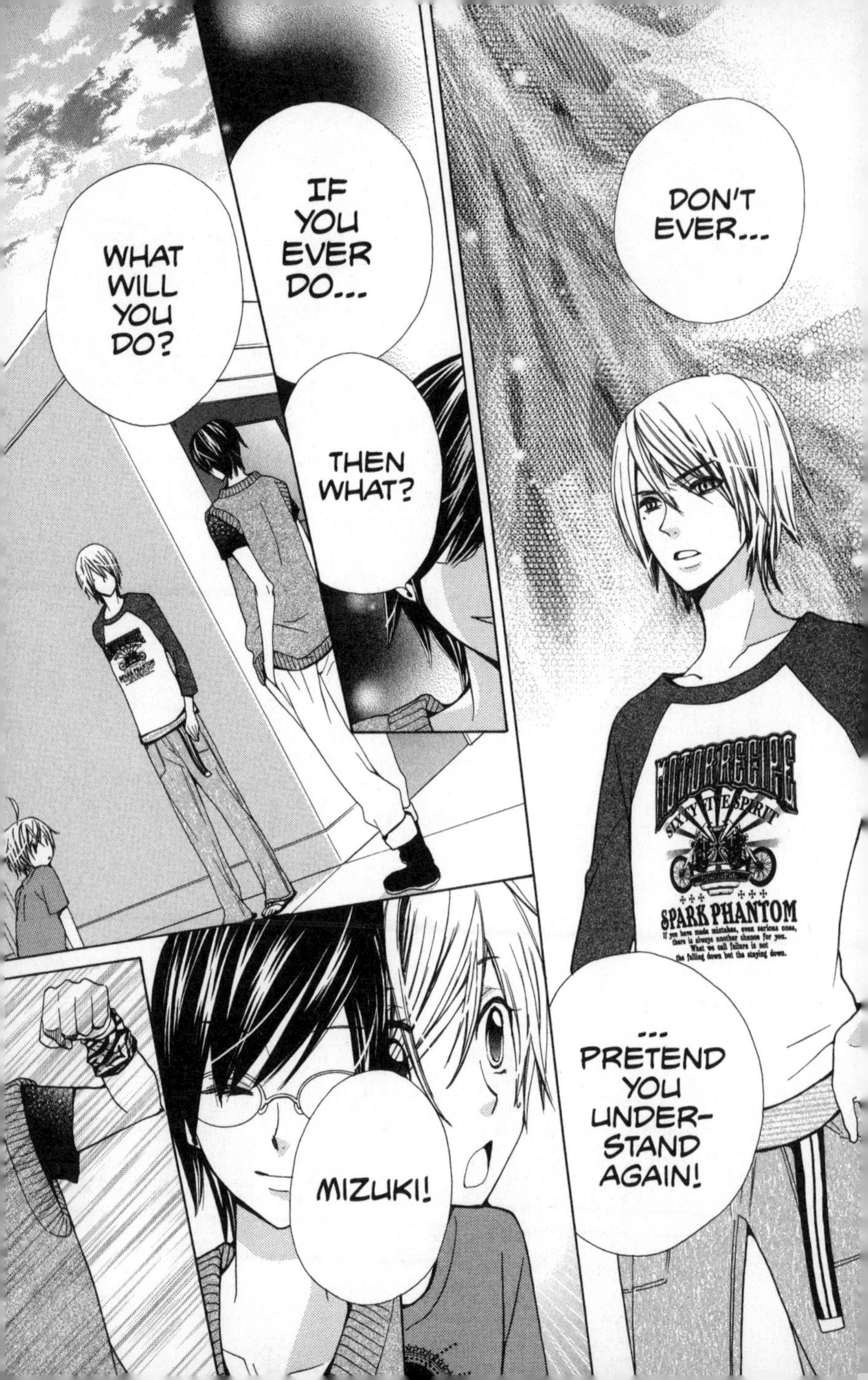
DON'T EVER...
MOTOR RECIPE
SIXTY FIVE SPIRIT
SPARK PHANTOM
If you have made mistakes, even serious ones, there is always another chance for you. What we call failure is not the falling down but the staying down.
...PRETEND YOU UNDER-STAND AGAIN!
IF YOU EVER DO...
THEN WHAT?
WHAT WILL YOU DO?
MIZUKI!

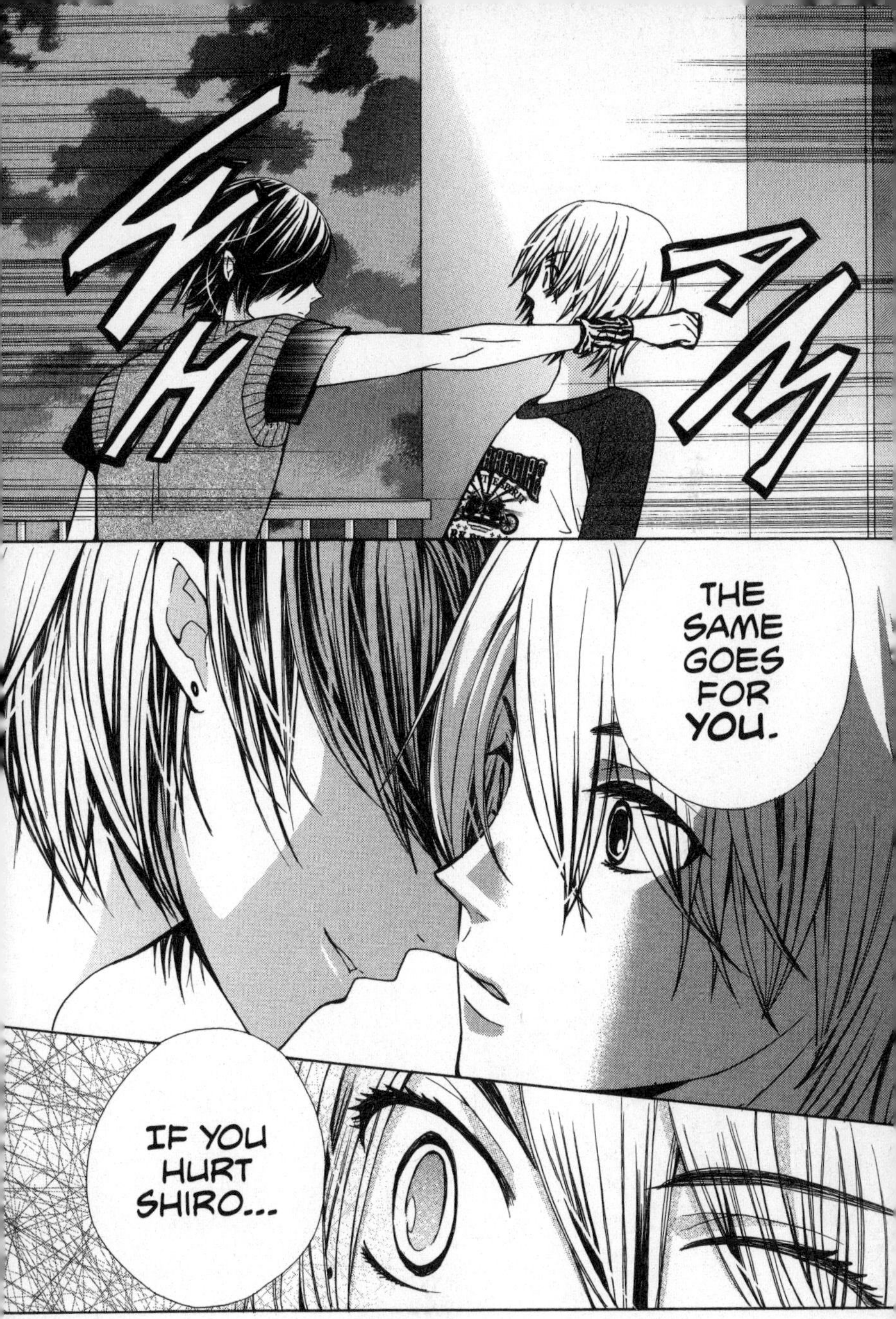
WHAM
THE SAME GOES FOR YOU.
IF YOU HURT SHIRO...

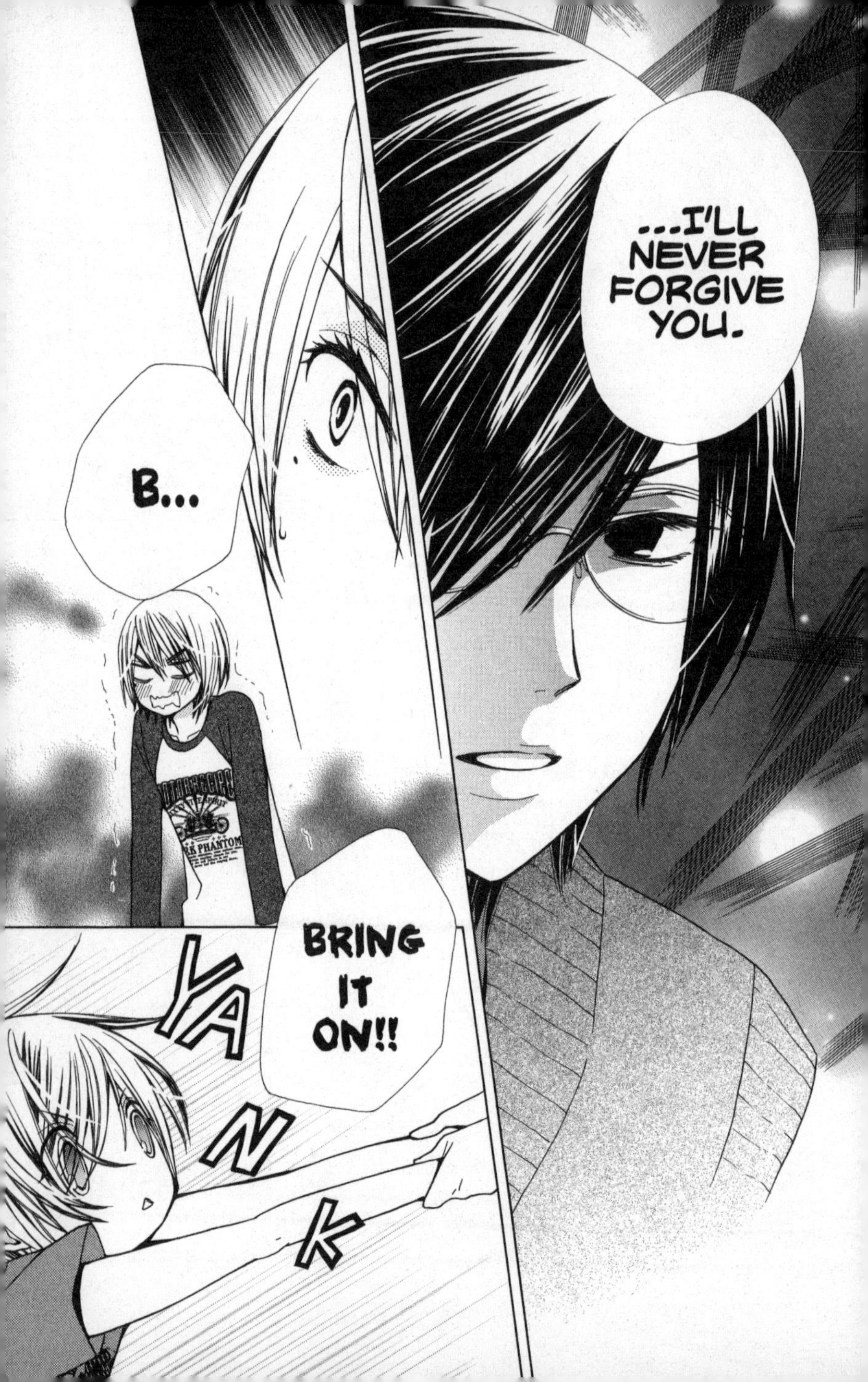
...I'LL NEVER FORGIVE YOU.
B...
BRING IT ON!!
YANK

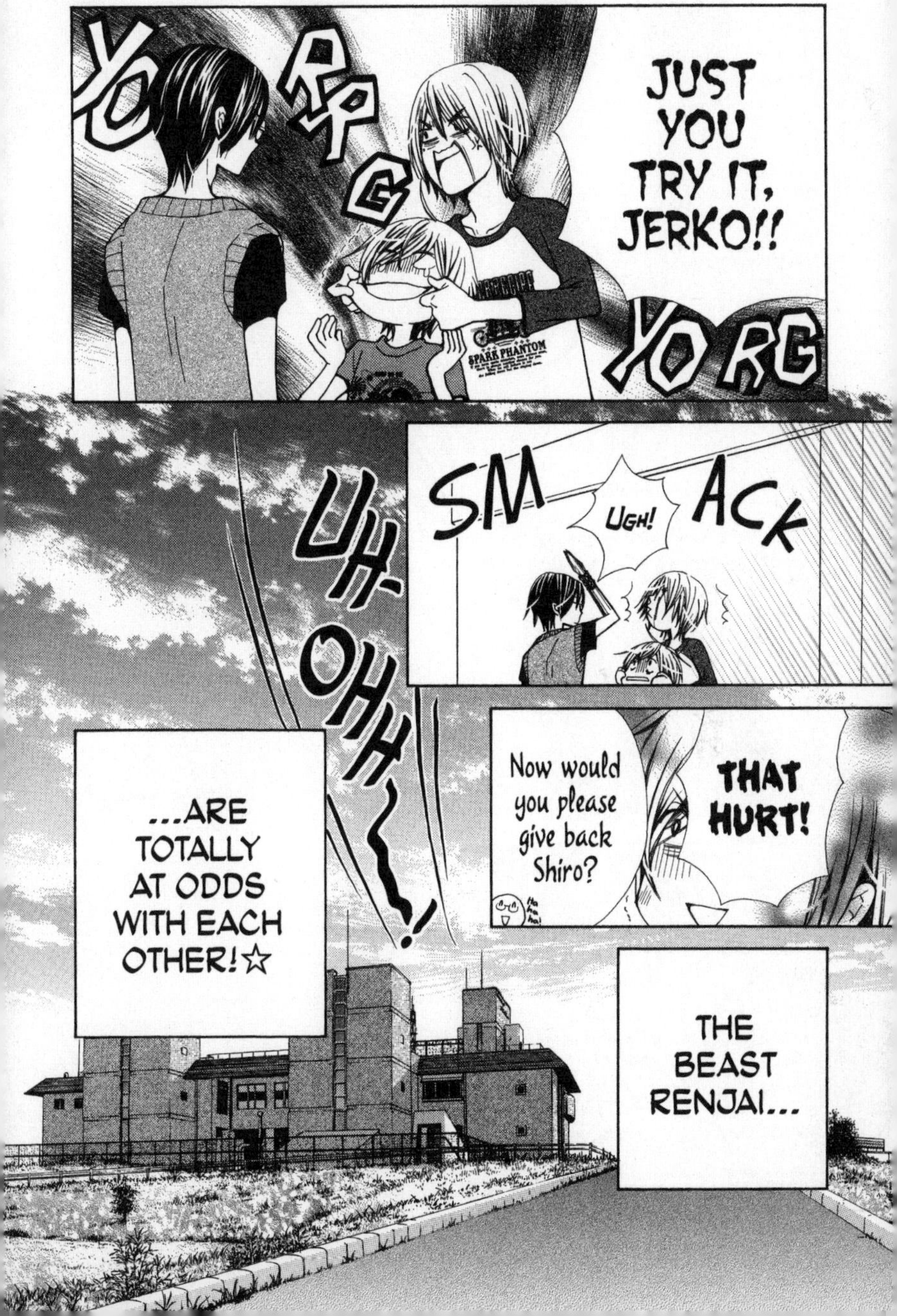
JUST YOU TRY IT, JERKO!!
YORG
YORRG
SMACK
UGH!
UH-OHHH~!
THAT HURT!
Now would you please give back Shiro?
Ha ha ha!
THE BEAST RENJAI...
...ARE TOTALLY AT ODDS WITH EACH OTHER!☆

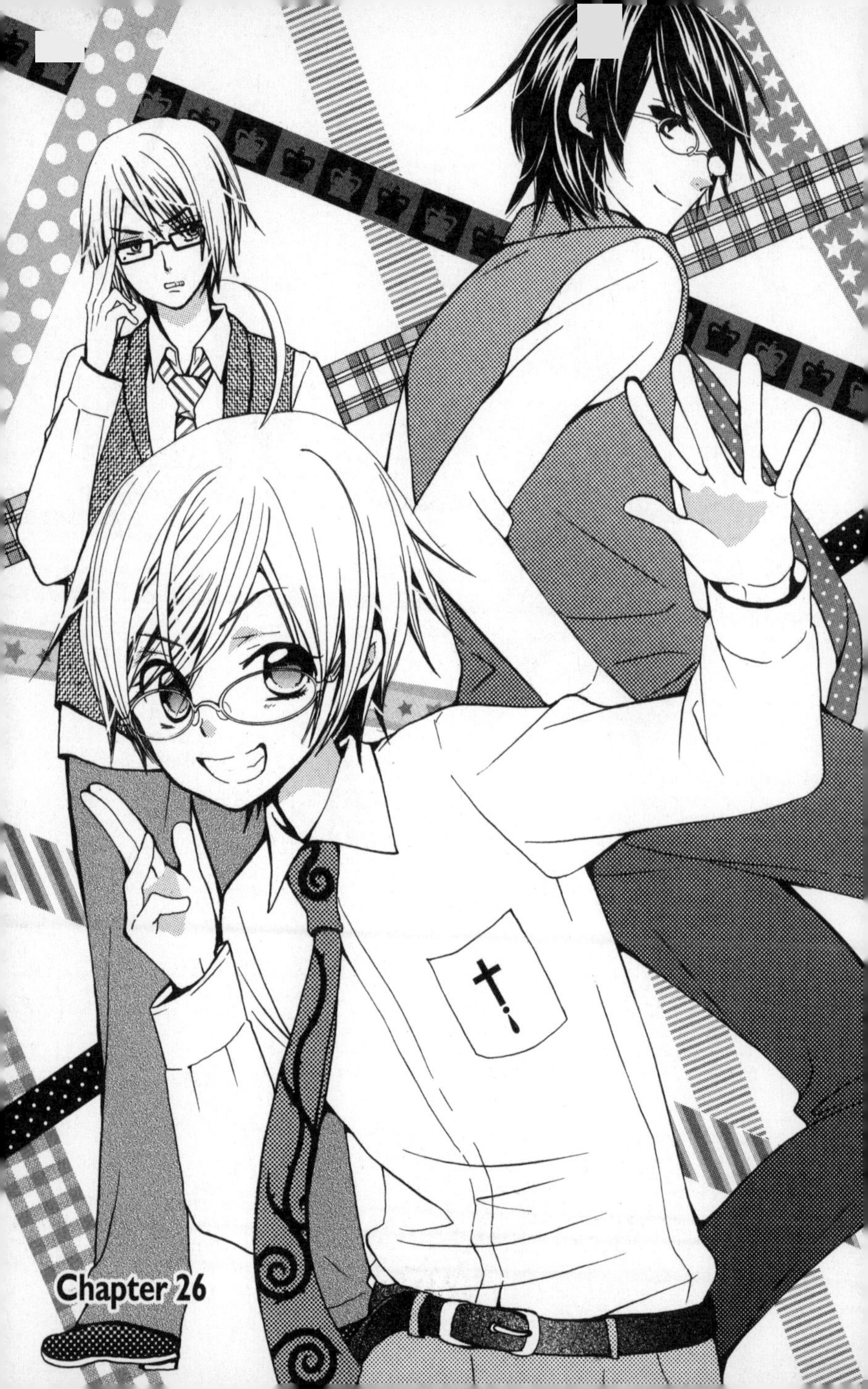
Chapter 26

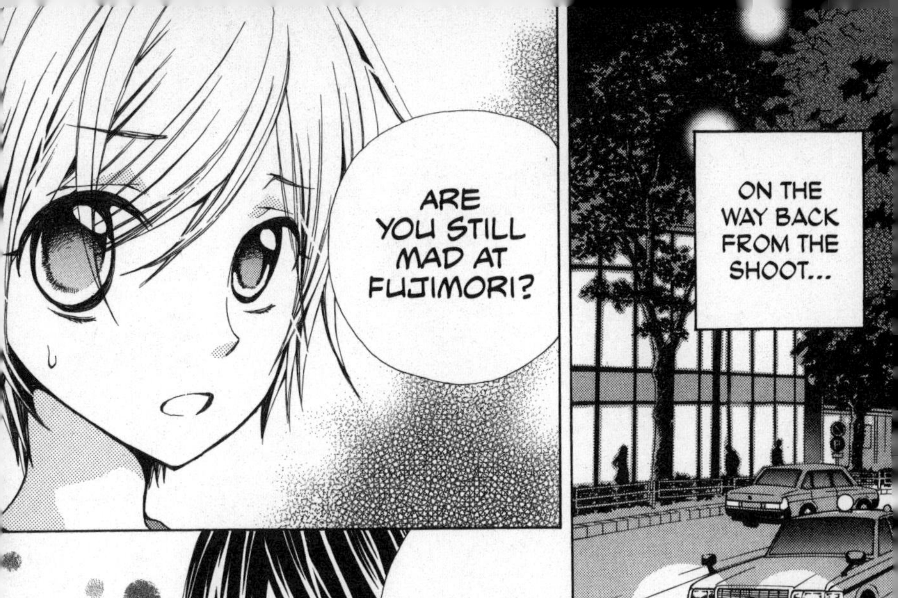
ON THE WAY BACK FROM THE SHOOT...
...I ASKED MIZUKI SOMETHING I'D BEEN WONDERING.
ARE YOU STILL MAD AT FUJIMORI?
MAD AT FUJIMORI?
ME?

• Bonus Pages •

Senri didn't show up in the main manga at all this time, so I drew him in the bonus pages. It's a veritable Senri festival! (A mystery festival!)

His personality's different and the craziest stuff is happening, but it's a festival, so overlook that, please! (Forgive what?!)

And *The Hana to Yume* website let me draw a bonus manga about Takayanagi and Ume. Check it out!

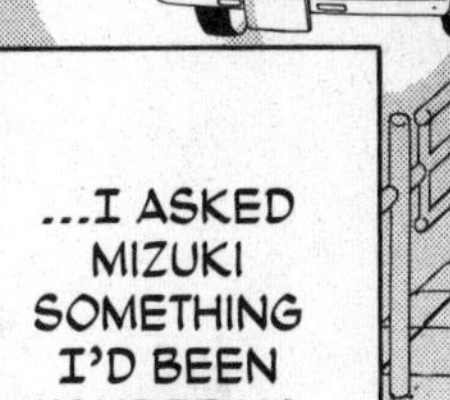
B
All 13 pages are for me!!

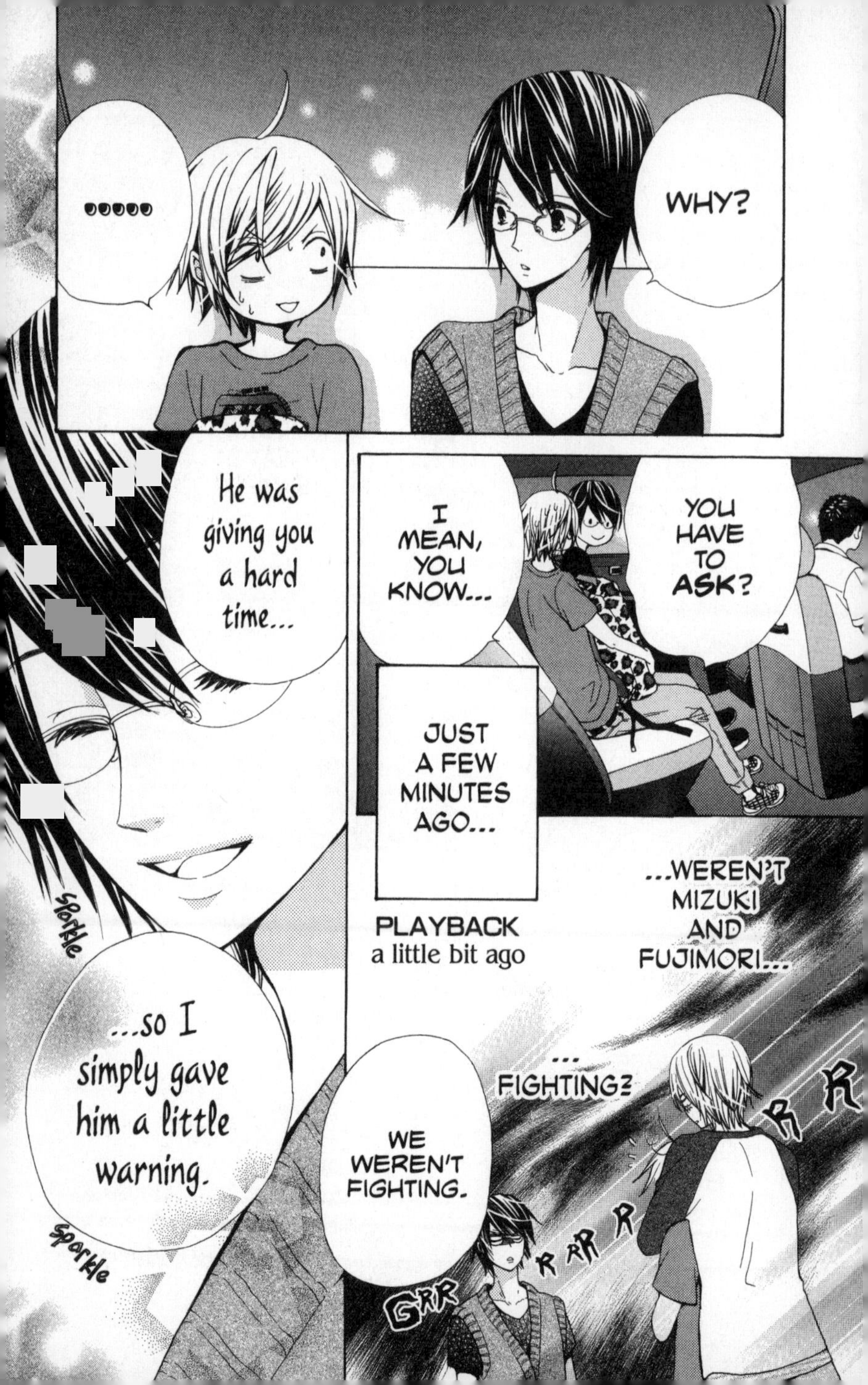
WHY?
.....
YOU HAVE TO ASK?
I MEAN, YOU KNOW...
JUST A FEW MINUTES AGO...
PLAYBACK
a little bit ago
...WEREN'T MIZUKI AND FUJIMORI...
...FIGHTING?
WE WEREN'T FIGHTING.
R R
R R R R
GRR
He was giving you a hard time...
...so I simply gave him a little warning.
sparkle
sparkle

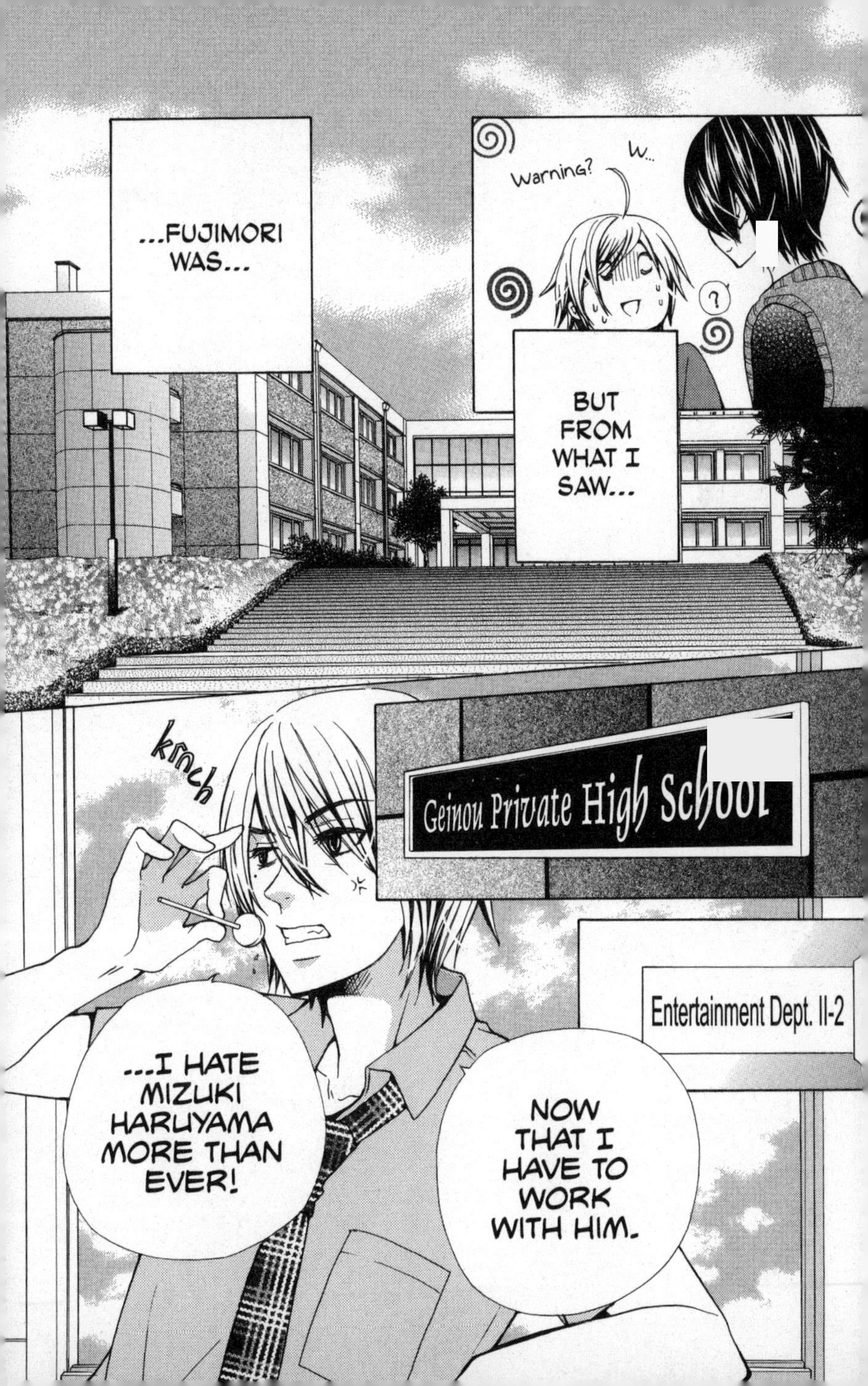
W...
Warning?
BUT FROM WHAT I SAW...
...FUJIMORI WAS...
Geinou Private High School
krnch
Entertainment Dept. II-2
NOW THAT I HAVE TO WORK WITH HIM.
...I HATE MIZUKI HARUYAMA MORE THAN EVER!

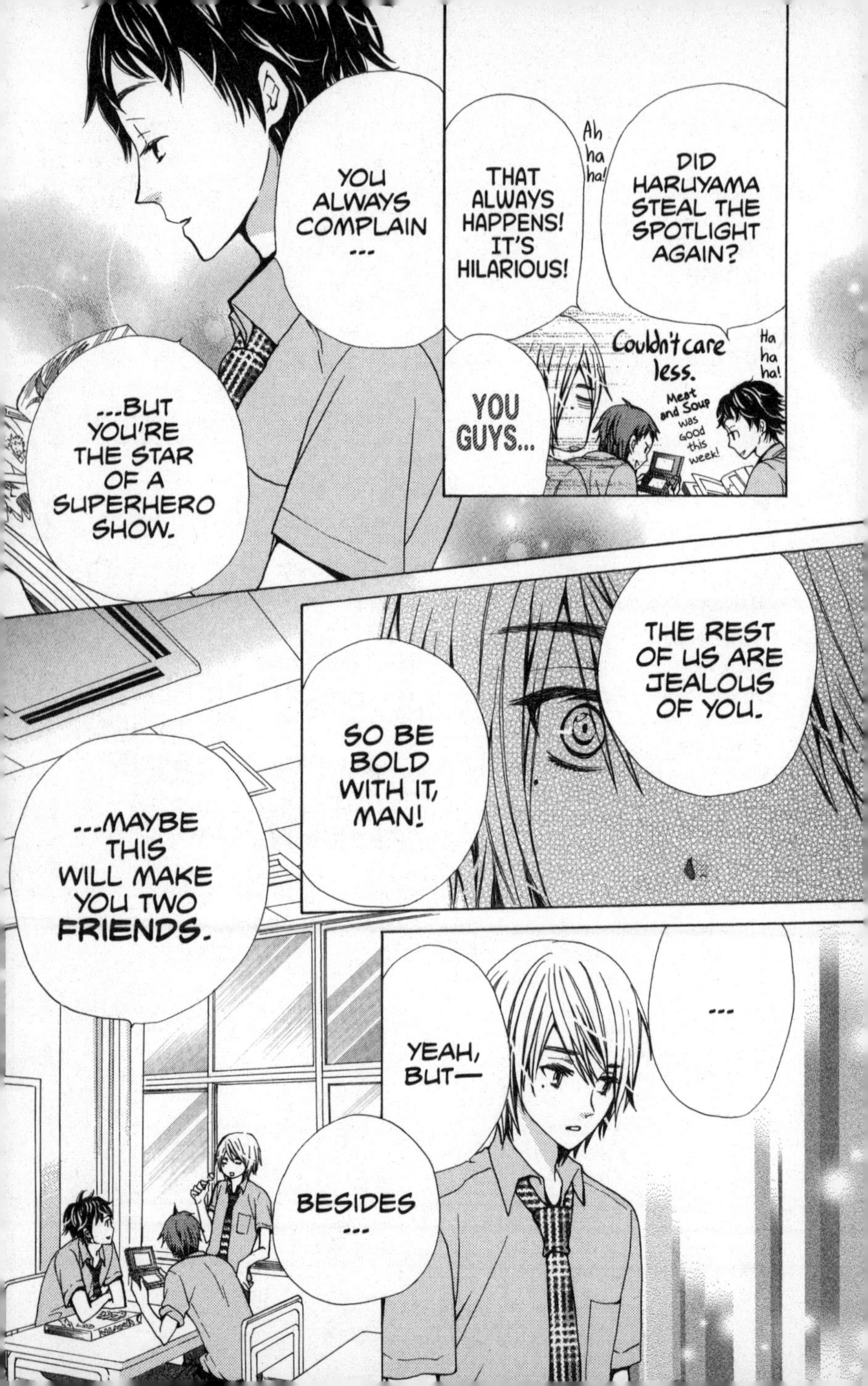
DID HARUYAMA STEAL THE SPOTLIGHT AGAIN?
Ah ha ha!
THAT ALWAYS HAPPENS! IT'S HILARIOUS!
Ha ha ha!
Couldn't care less.
Meat and Soup was good this week!
YOU GUYS...
YOU ALWAYS COMPLAIN ...
...BUT YOU'RE THE STAR OF A SUPERHERO SHOW.
THE REST OF US ARE JEALOUS OF YOU.
SO BE BOLD WITH IT, MAN!
...
YEAH, BUT—
BESIDES ...
...MAYBE THIS WILL MAKE YOU TWO FRIENDS.

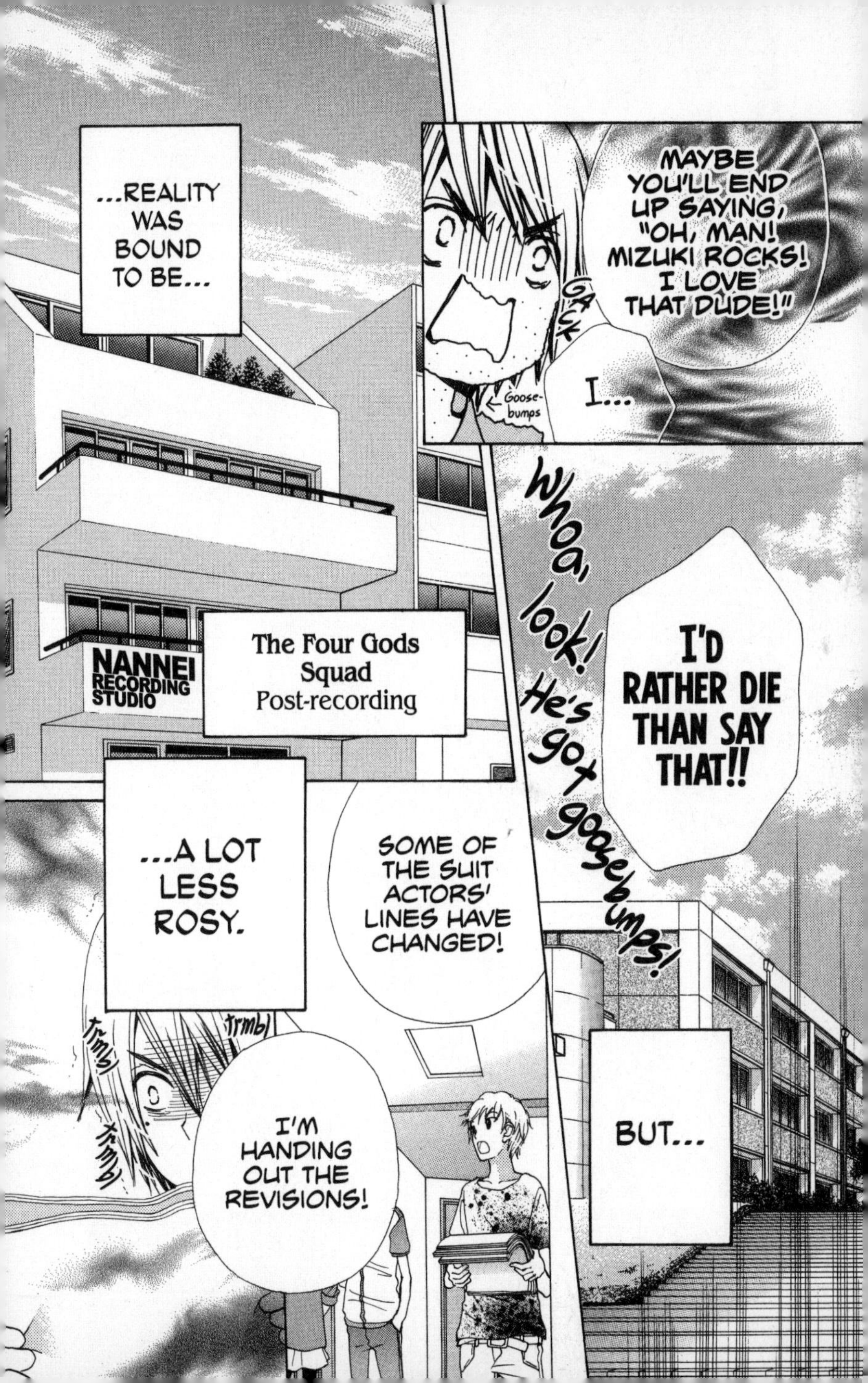
MAYBE YOU'LL END UP SAYING, "OH, MAN! MIZUKI ROCKS! I LOVE THAT DUDE!"
GACK
Goose-bumps
I...
I'D RATHER DIE THAN SAY THAT!!
Whoa, look! He's got goosebumps!
BUT...
...REALITY WAS BOUND TO BE...
NANNEI RECORDING STUDIO
The Four Gods Squad Post-recording
...A LOT LESS ROSY.
SOME OF THE SUIT ACTORS' LINES HAVE CHANGED!
I'M HANDING OUT THE REVISIONS!
trmbl
trmbl
trmbl

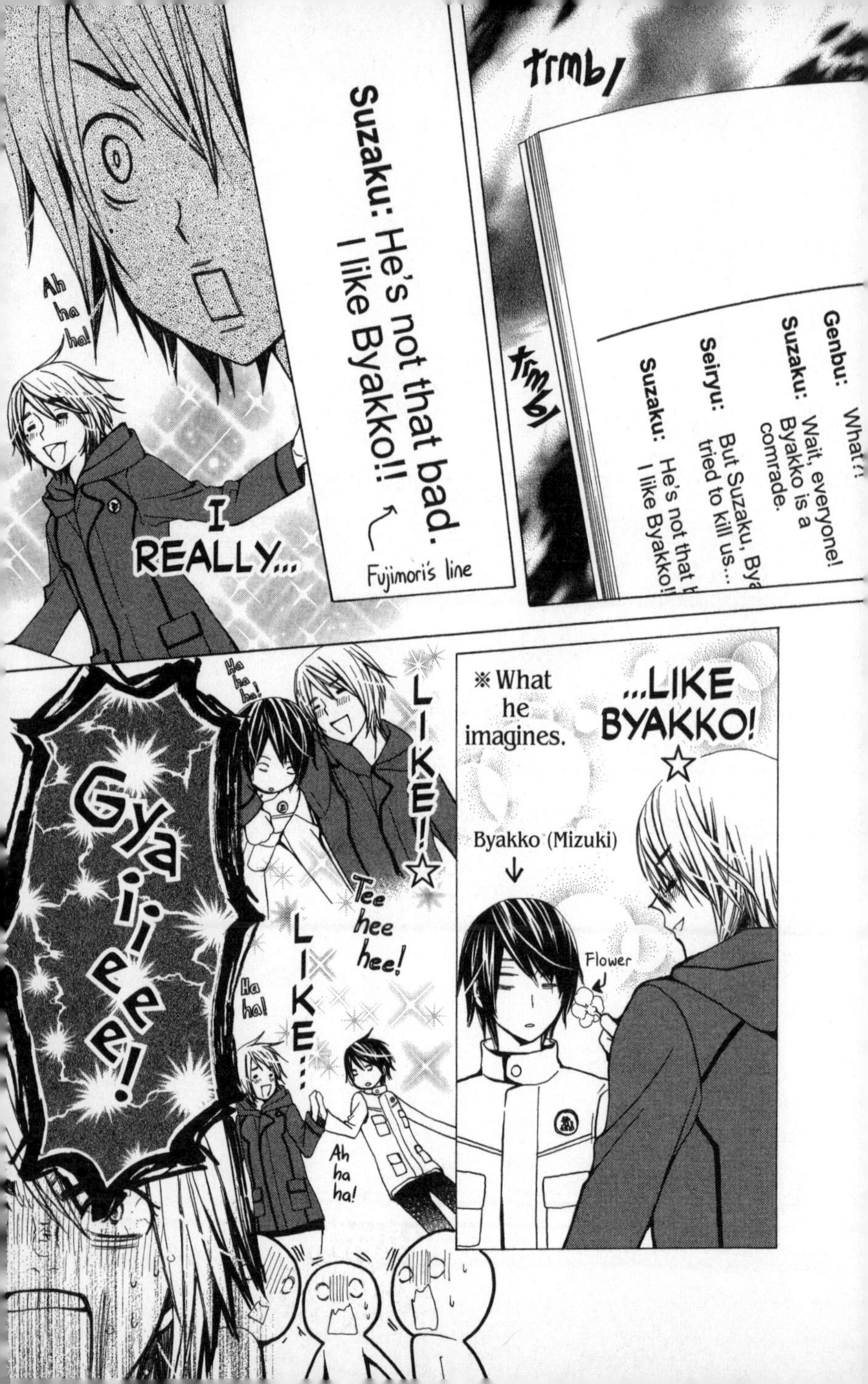

trmbl
Genbu: What?!
Suzaku: Wait, everyone! Byakko is a comrade.
Seiryu: But Suzaku, Bya
tried to kill us...
Suzaku: He's not that b
I like Byakko!
trmbl
Suzaku: He's not that bad.
I like Byakko!!
Fujimori's line
Ah ha ha!
I REALLY...
...LIKE BYAKKO! ☆
※ What he imagines.
Byakko (Mizuki)
Flower
LIKE! ☆
Ha ha ha!
Tee hee hee!
LIKE...
Ha ha!
Ah ha ha!
Gyaiiieee!

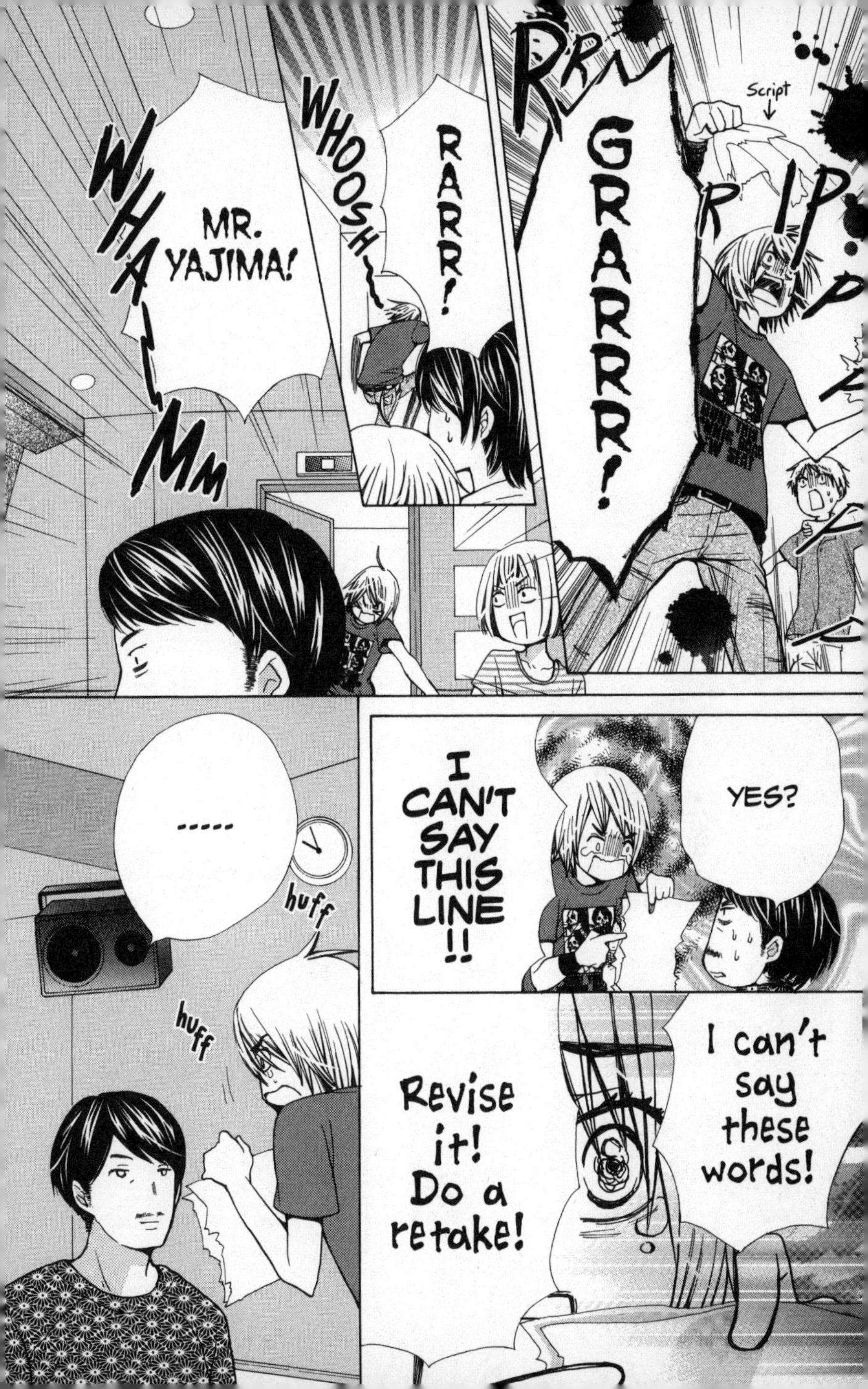
Script
RIP!
GRARRRR!
RARRR!
WHOOSH
MR. YAJIMA!
WHAMM
YES?
I CAN'T SAY THIS LINE!!
.....
huff
huff
I can't say these words!
Revise it! Do a retake!

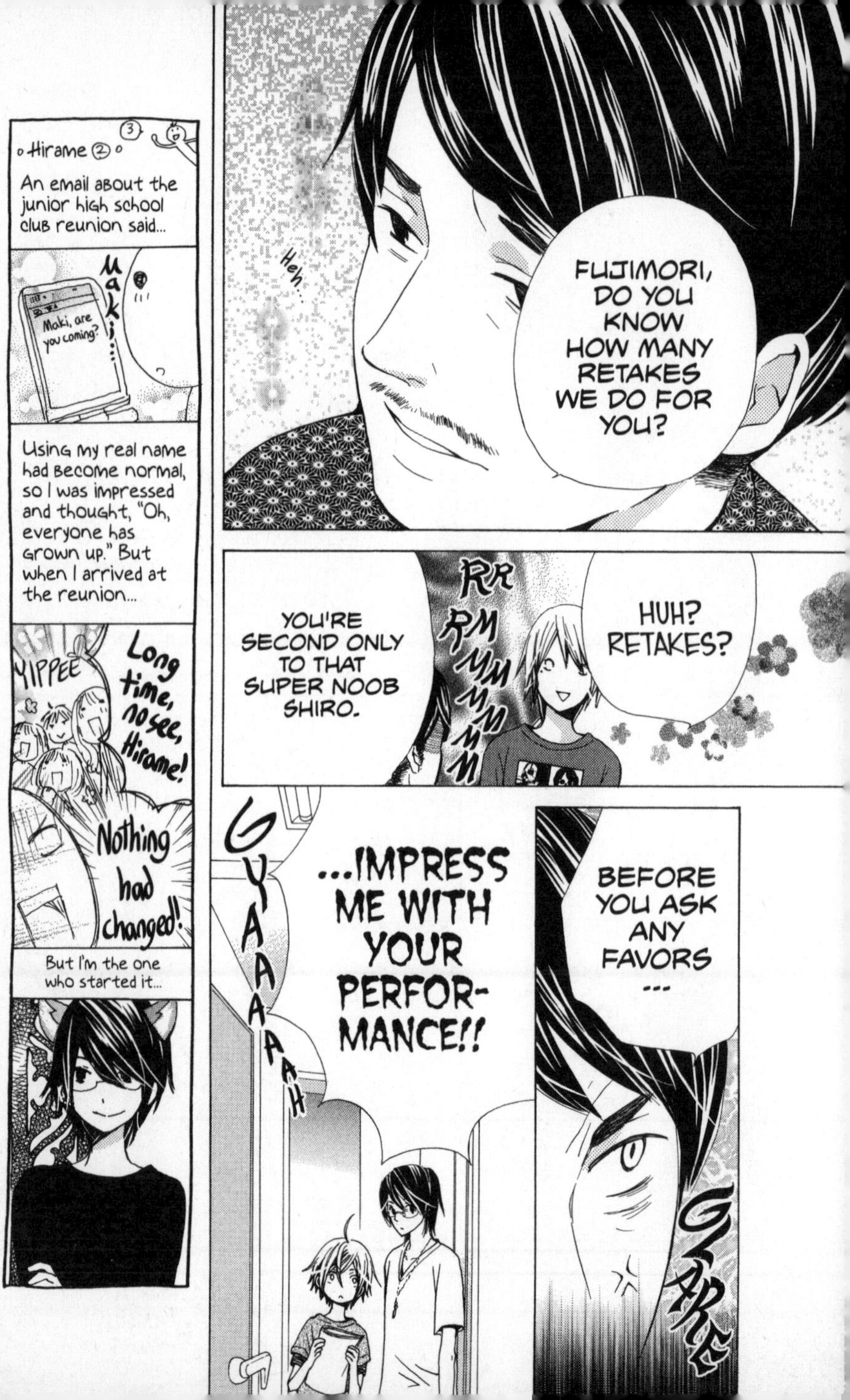
Heh...
FUJIMORI, DO YOU KNOW HOW MANY RETAKES WE DO FOR YOU?
HUH? RETAKES?
RRRMMMMMMM
YOU'RE SECOND ONLY TO THAT SUPER NOOB SHIRO.
BEFORE YOU ASK ANY FAVORS...
GLARE
...IMPRESS ME WITH YOUR PERFORMANCE!!
GYAAAAAAH
Hirame ② ③
An email about the junior high school club reunion said...
Maki, are you coming?
Maki...
Using my real name had become normal, so I was impressed and thought, "Oh, everyone has grown up." But when I arrived at the reunion...
YIPPEE
Long time, no see, Hirame!
Nothing had changed!
But I'm the one who started it...

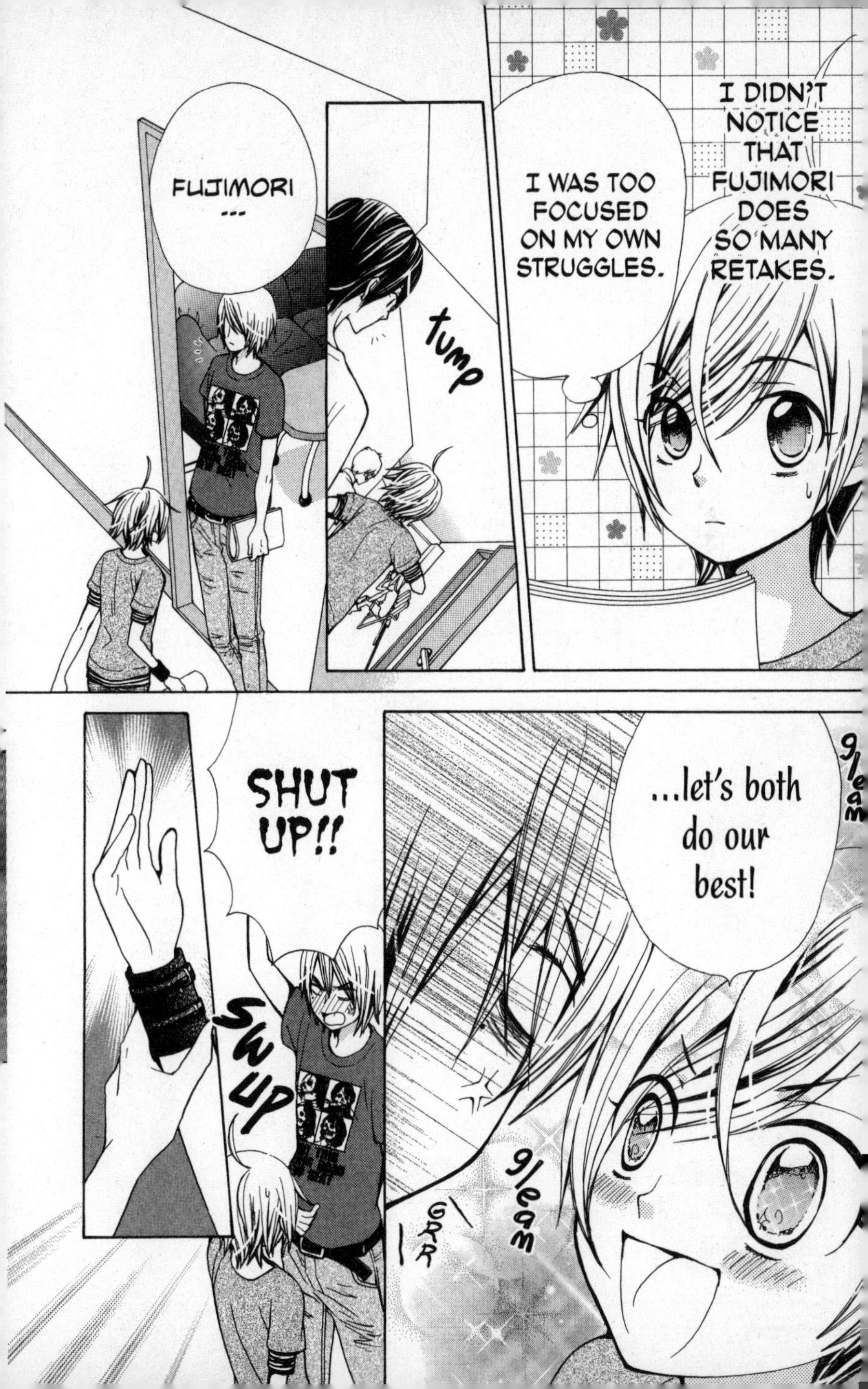
I DIDN'T NOTICE THAT FUJIMORI DOES SO MANY RETAKES.
I WAS TOO FOCUSED ON MY OWN STRUGGLES.
tump
FUJIMORI ...
...let's both do our best!
gleam
gleam
GRR
SHUT UP!!
SWUP

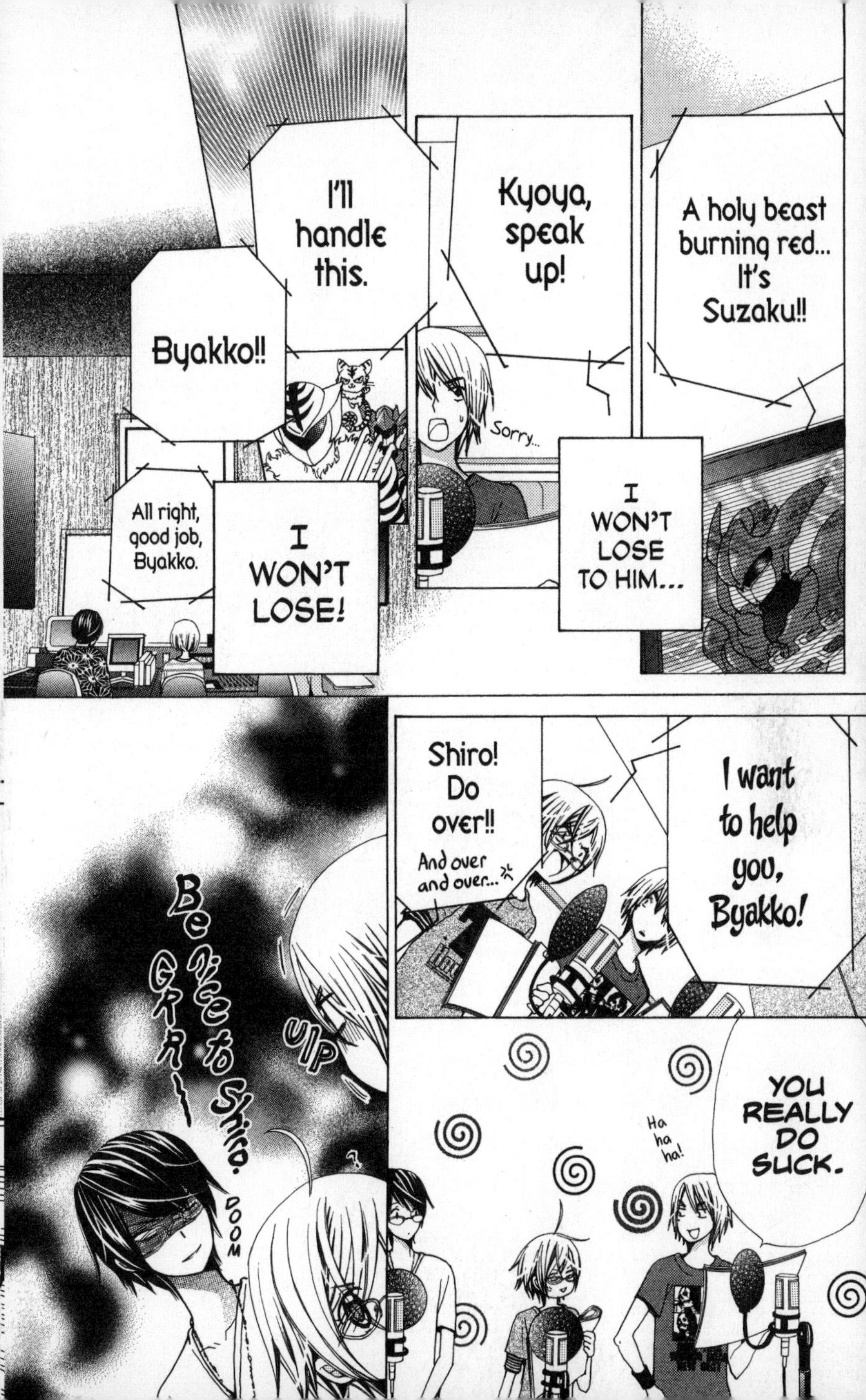
A holy beast burning red... It's Suzaku!!
I WON'T LOSE TO HIM...
Kyoya, speak up!
Sorry...
I'll handle this.
Byakko!!
I WON'T LOSE!
All right, good job, Byakko.
I want to help you, Byakko!
Shiro! Do over!!
And over and over...
YOU REALLY DO SUCK.
Ha ha ha!
Be nice to Shiro.
GRR...
ULP
DOOOM

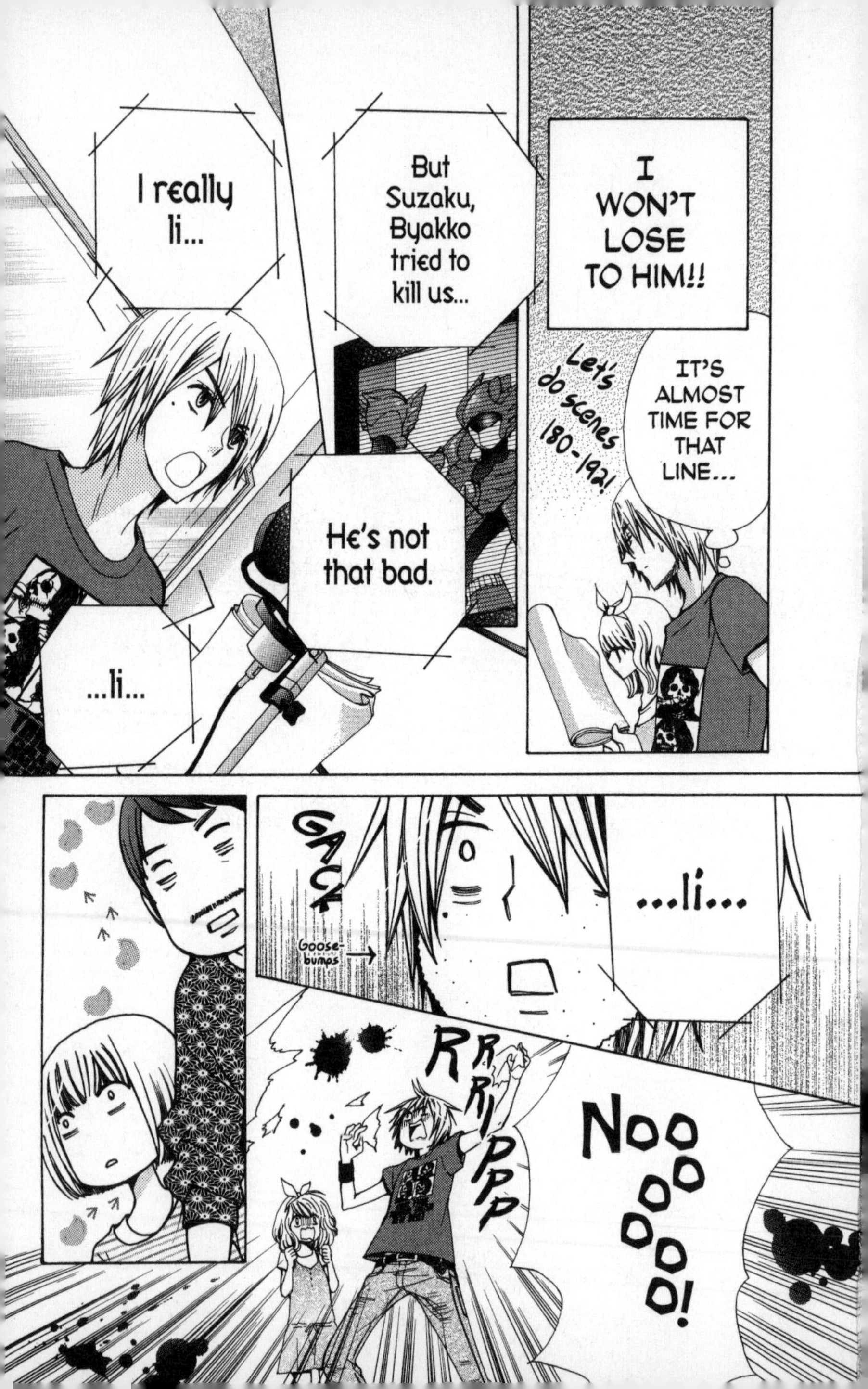
I WON'T LOSE TO HIM!!
IT'S ALMOST TIME FOR THAT LINE...
Let's do scenes 180-192!
But Suzaku, Byakko tried to kill us...
He's not that bad.
I really li...
...li...
GACK
...li...
Goose-bumps
RRRIPPP
NOOOOOOOOO!

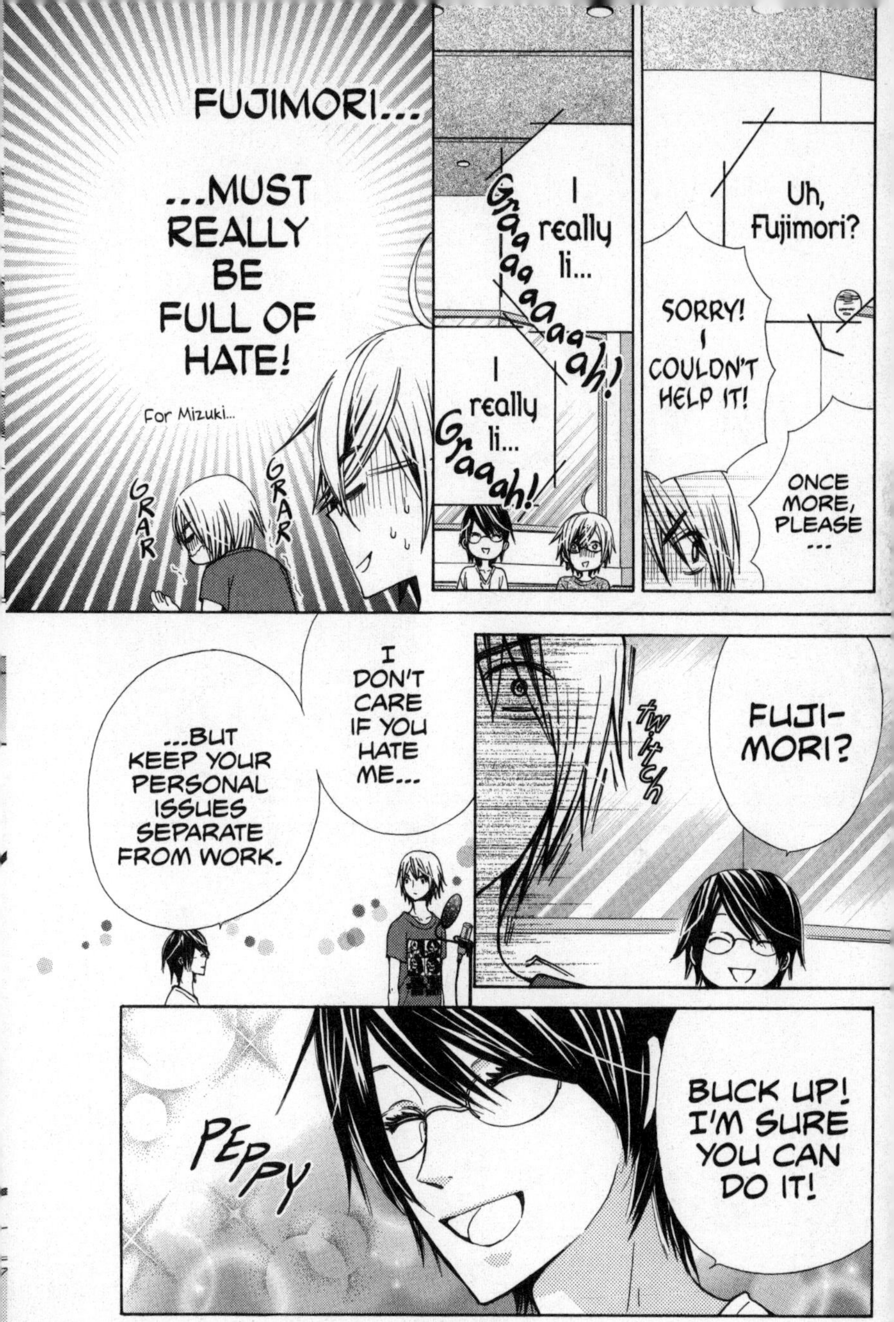
Uh, Fujimori?
SORRY! I COULDN'T HELP IT!
ONCE MORE, PLEASE...
I really li...
Graaaaaaaaah!
I really li...
Graaaah!
FUJIMORI...
...MUST REALLY BE FULL OF HATE!
For Mizuki...
GRAR
GRAR
FUJI-MORI?
twitch
I DON'T CARE IF YOU HATE ME...
...BUT KEEP YOUR PERSONAL ISSUES SEPARATE FROM WORK.
BUCK UP! I'M SURE YOU CAN DO IT!
PEPPY

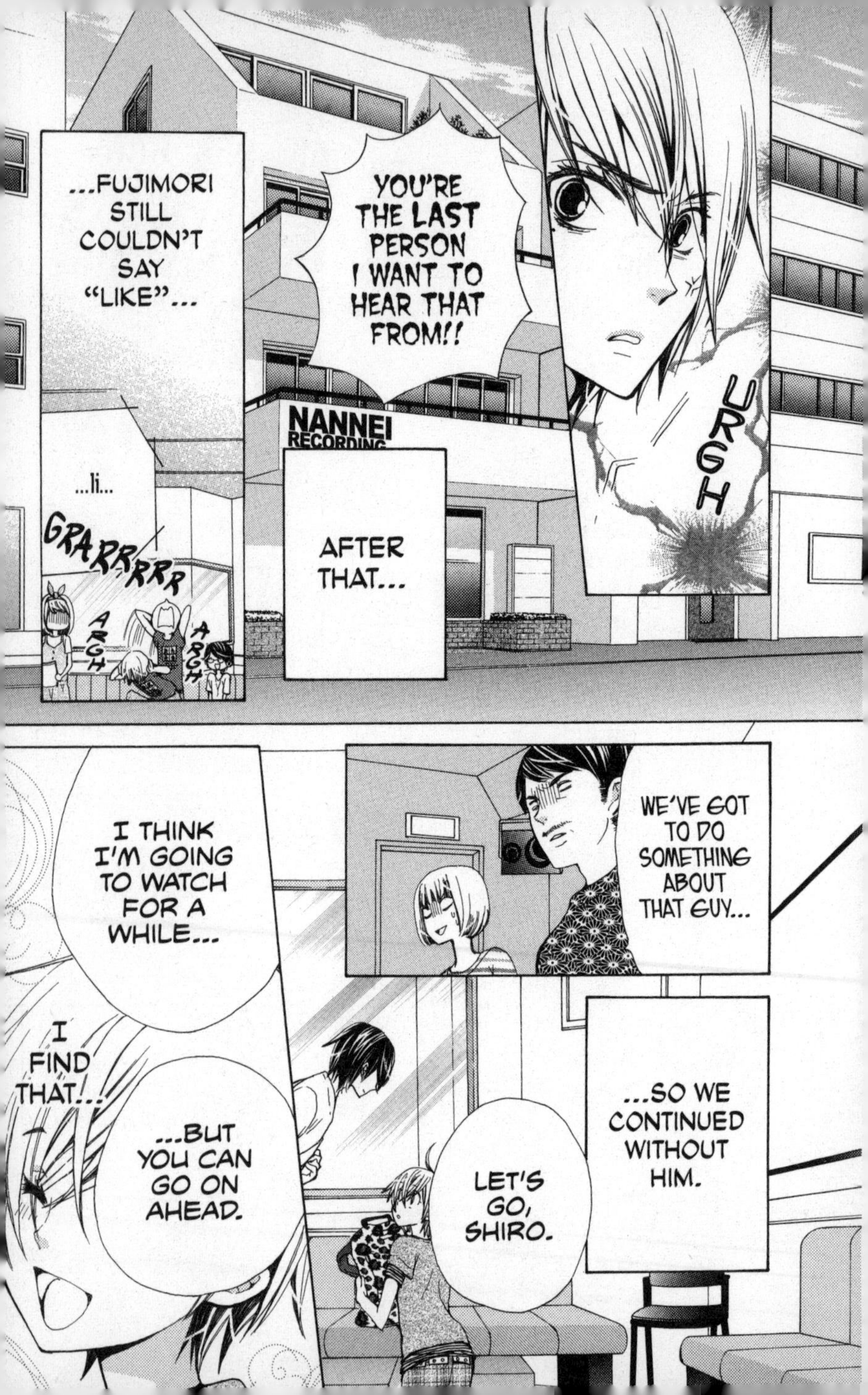
YOU'RE THE LAST PERSON I WANT TO HEAR THAT FROM!!
URGH
NANNEI RECORDING
AFTER THAT...
...FUJIMORI STILL COULDN'T SAY "LIKE"...
...li...
GRARRRRRR
ARGH
ARGH
WE'VE GOT TO DO SOMETHING ABOUT THAT GUY...
...SO WE CONTINUED WITHOUT HIM.
LET'S GO, SHIRO.
I THINK I'M GOING TO WATCH FOR A WHILE...
I FIND THAT...
...BUT YOU CAN GO ON AHEAD.

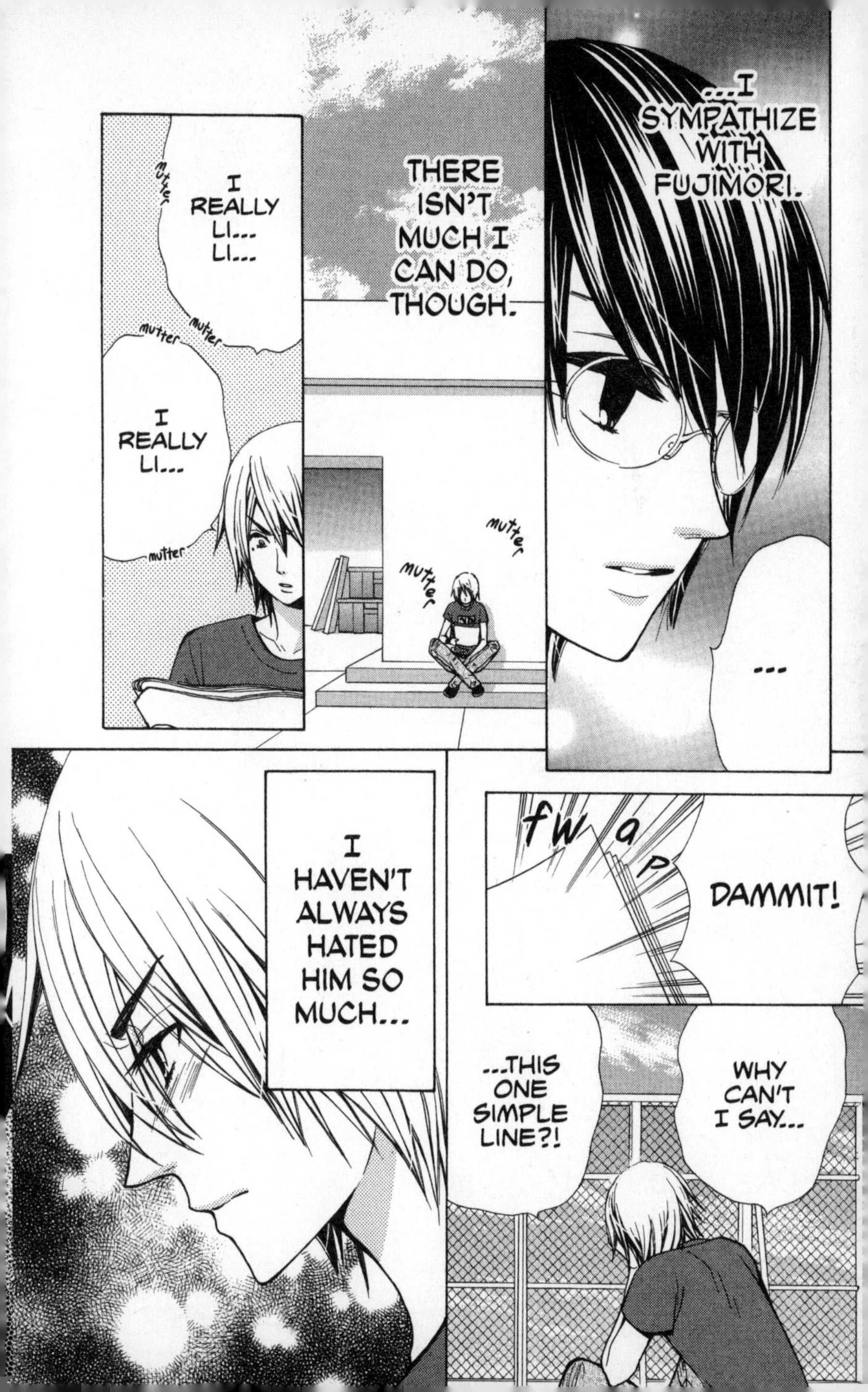
...I SYMPATHIZE WITH FUJIMORI.
...
THERE ISN'T MUCH I CAN DO, THOUGH.
mutter
mutter
I REALLY LI... LI...
mutter
mutter
mutter
I REALLY LI...
mutter
fwap
DAMMIT!
WHY CAN'T I SAY...
...THIS ONE SIMPLE LINE?!
I HAVEN'T ALWAYS HATED HIM SO MUCH...

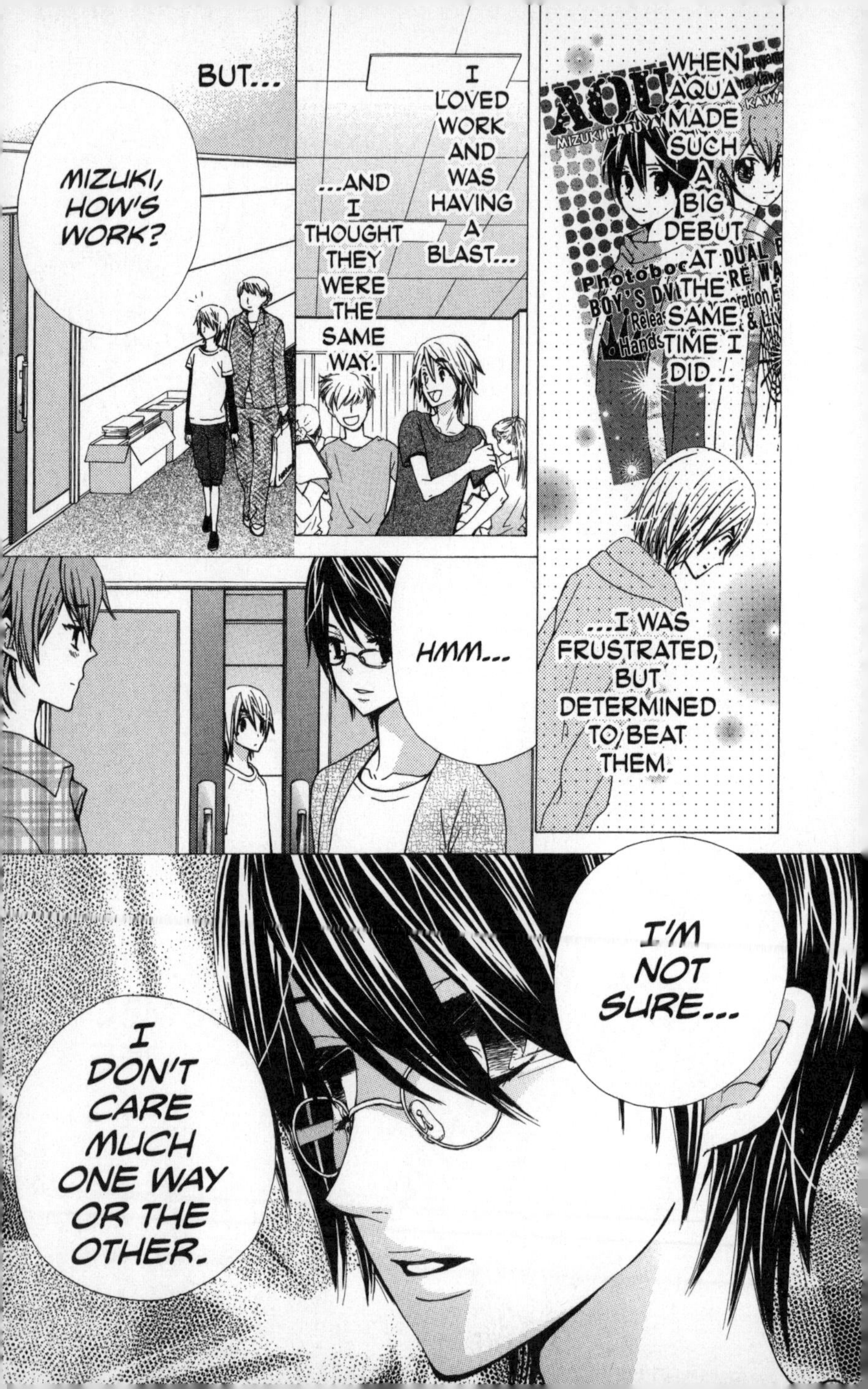
WHEN AQUA MADE SUCH A BIG DEBUT AT THE SAME TIME I DID...
...I WAS FRUSTRATED, BUT DETERMINED TO BEAT THEM.
I LOVED WORK AND WAS HAVING A BLAST...
...AND I THOUGHT THEY WERE THE SAME WAY.
BUT...
MIZUKI, HOW'S WORK?
HMM...
I'M NOT SURE...
I DON'T CARE MUCH ONE WAY OR THE OTHER.

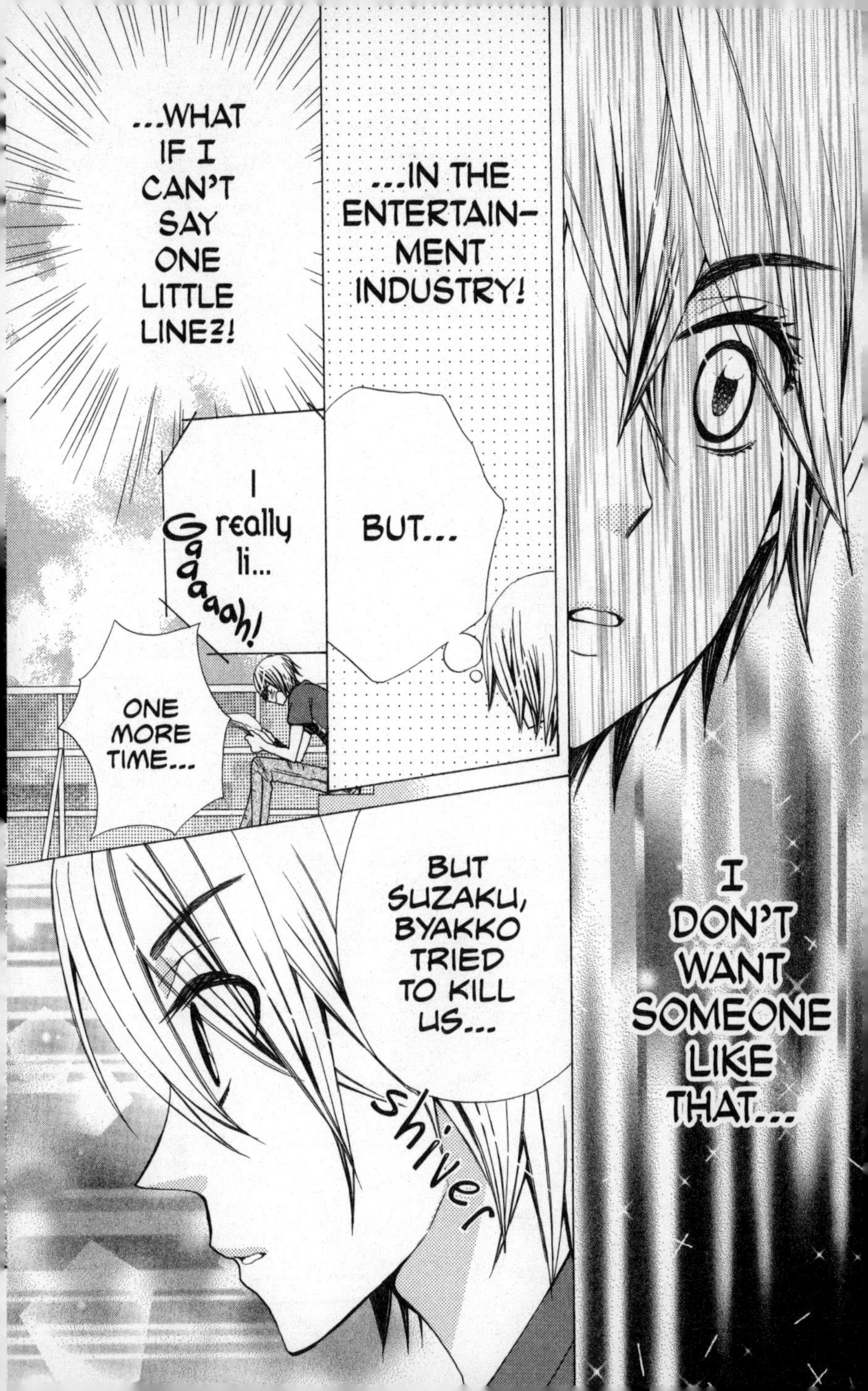
I DON'T WANT SOMEONE LIKE THAT...
...IN THE ENTERTAINMENT INDUSTRY!
BUT...
...WHAT IF I CAN'T SAY ONE LITTLE LINE?!
I really li...
Gaaaaah!
ONE MORE TIME...
BUT SUZAKU, BYAKKO TRIED TO KILL US...
shiver

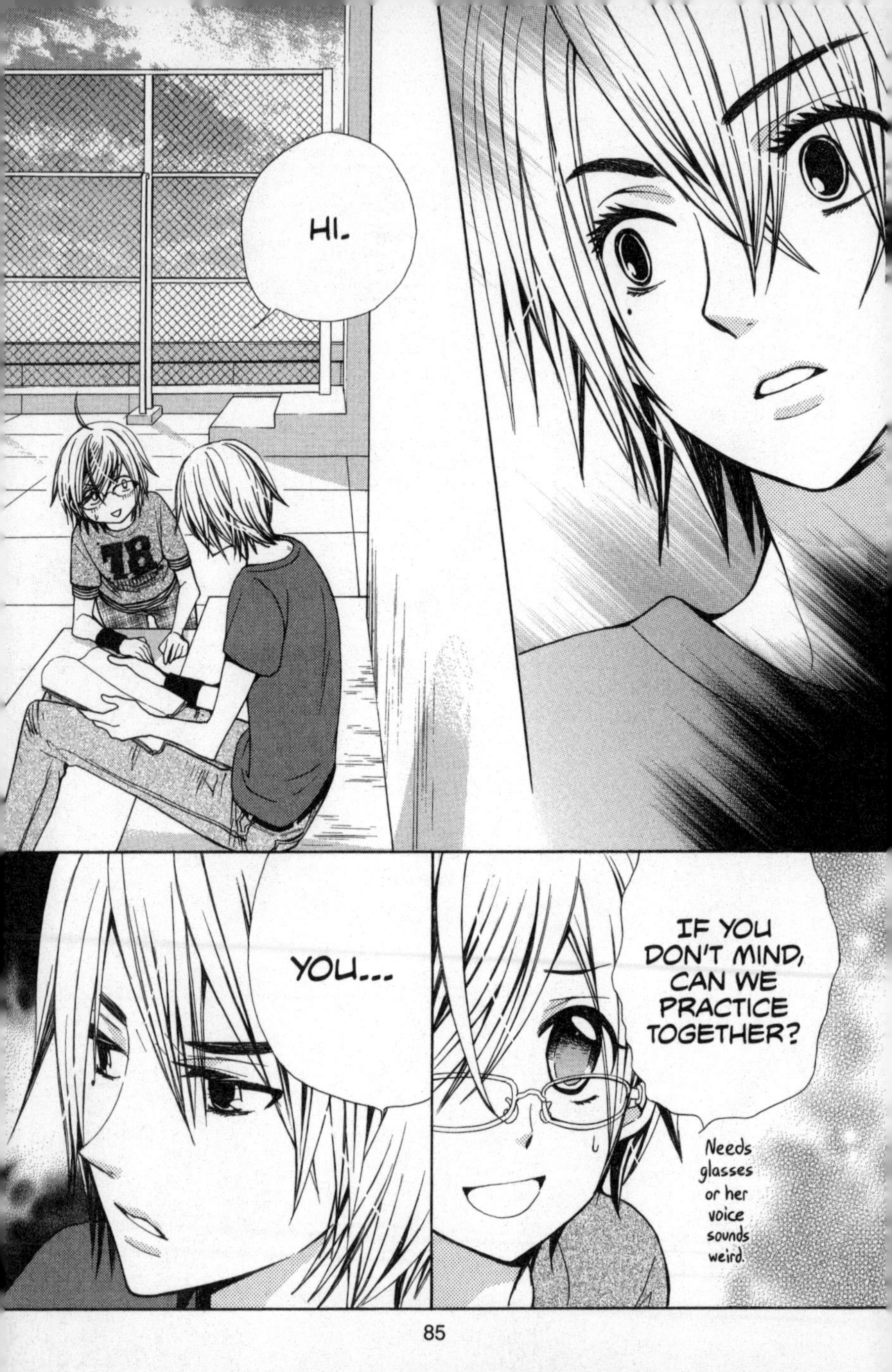
HI.
IF YOU DON'T MIND, CAN WE PRACTICE TOGETHER?
Needs glasses or her voice sounds weird.
YOU...

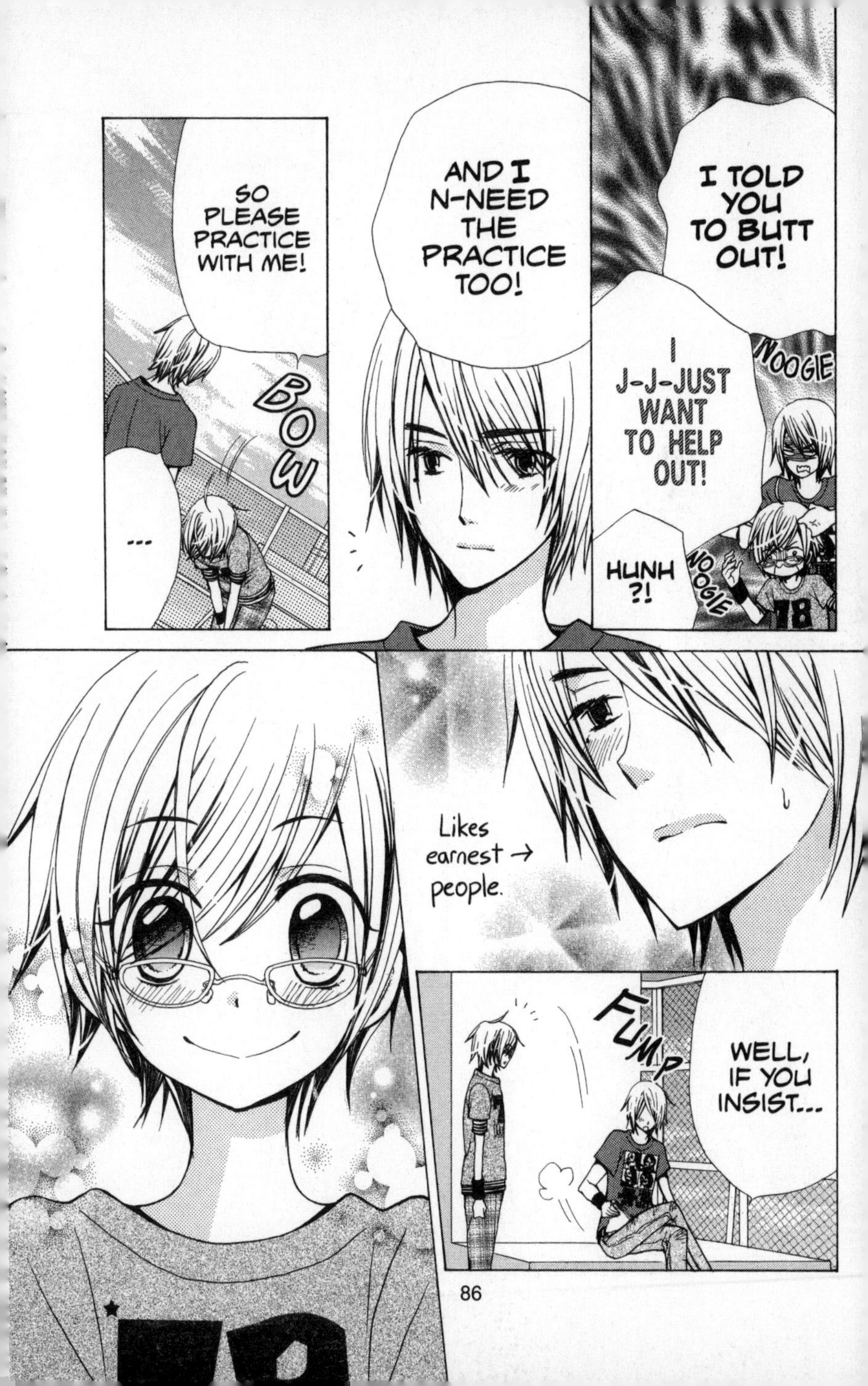
I TOLD YOU TO BUTT OUT!
NOOGIE
I J-J-JUST WANT TO HELP OUT!
HUNH ?!
NOOGIE
AND I N-NEED THE PRACTICE TOO!
SO PLEASE PRACTICE WITH ME!
BOW
...
Likes earnest → people.
WELL, IF YOU INSIST...
FUMP

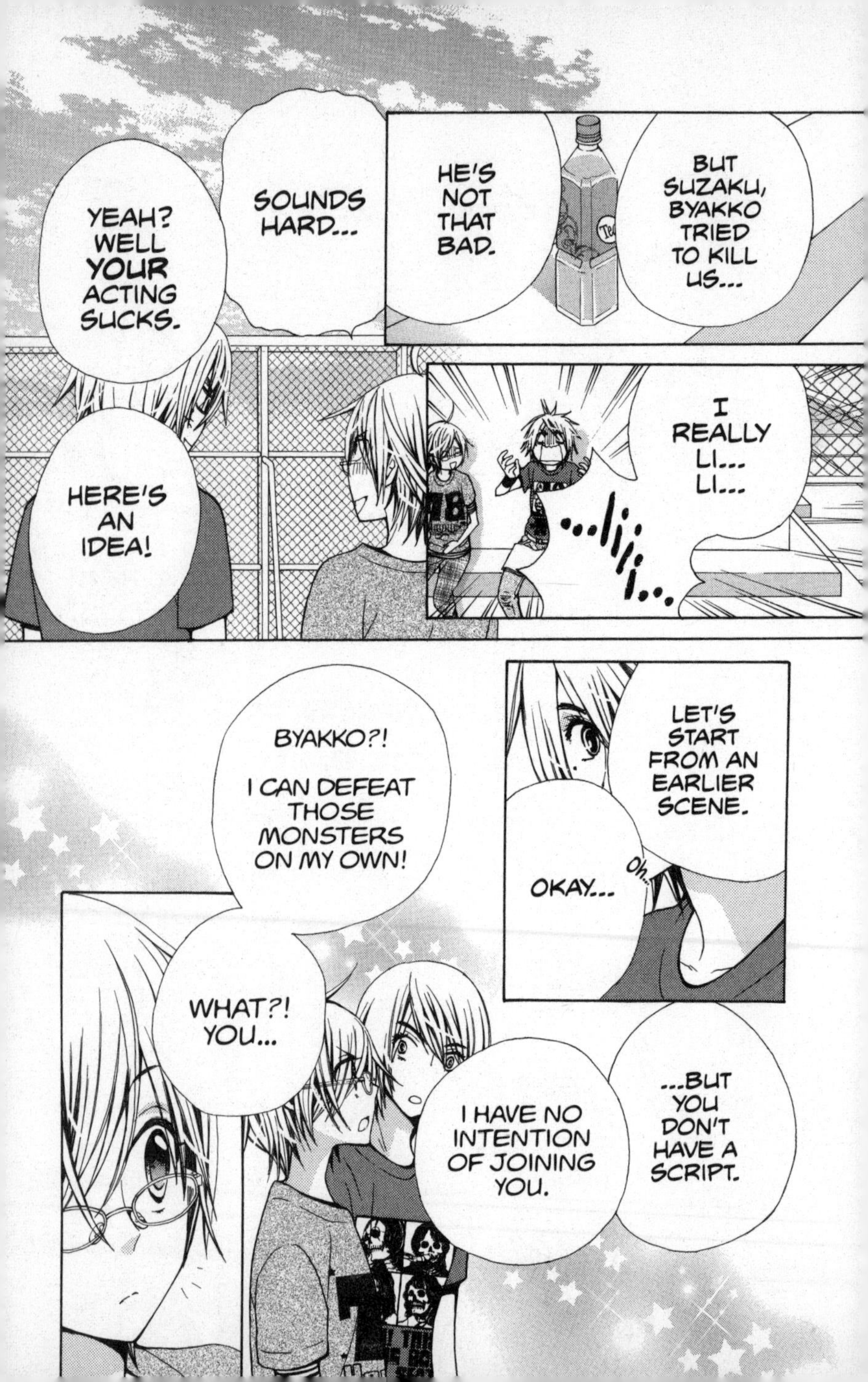
BUT SUZAKU, BYAKKO TRIED TO KILL US...
HE'S NOT THAT BAD.
I REALLY LI... LI...
...lili...
SOUNDS HARD...
YEAH? WELL YOUR ACTING SUCKS.
HERE'S AN IDEA!
LET'S START FROM AN EARLIER SCENE.
Oh...
OKAY...
BYAKKO?! I CAN DEFEAT THOSE MONSTERS ON MY OWN!
WHAT?! YOU...
I HAVE NO INTENTION OF JOINING YOU.
...BUT YOU DON'T HAVE A SCRIPT.

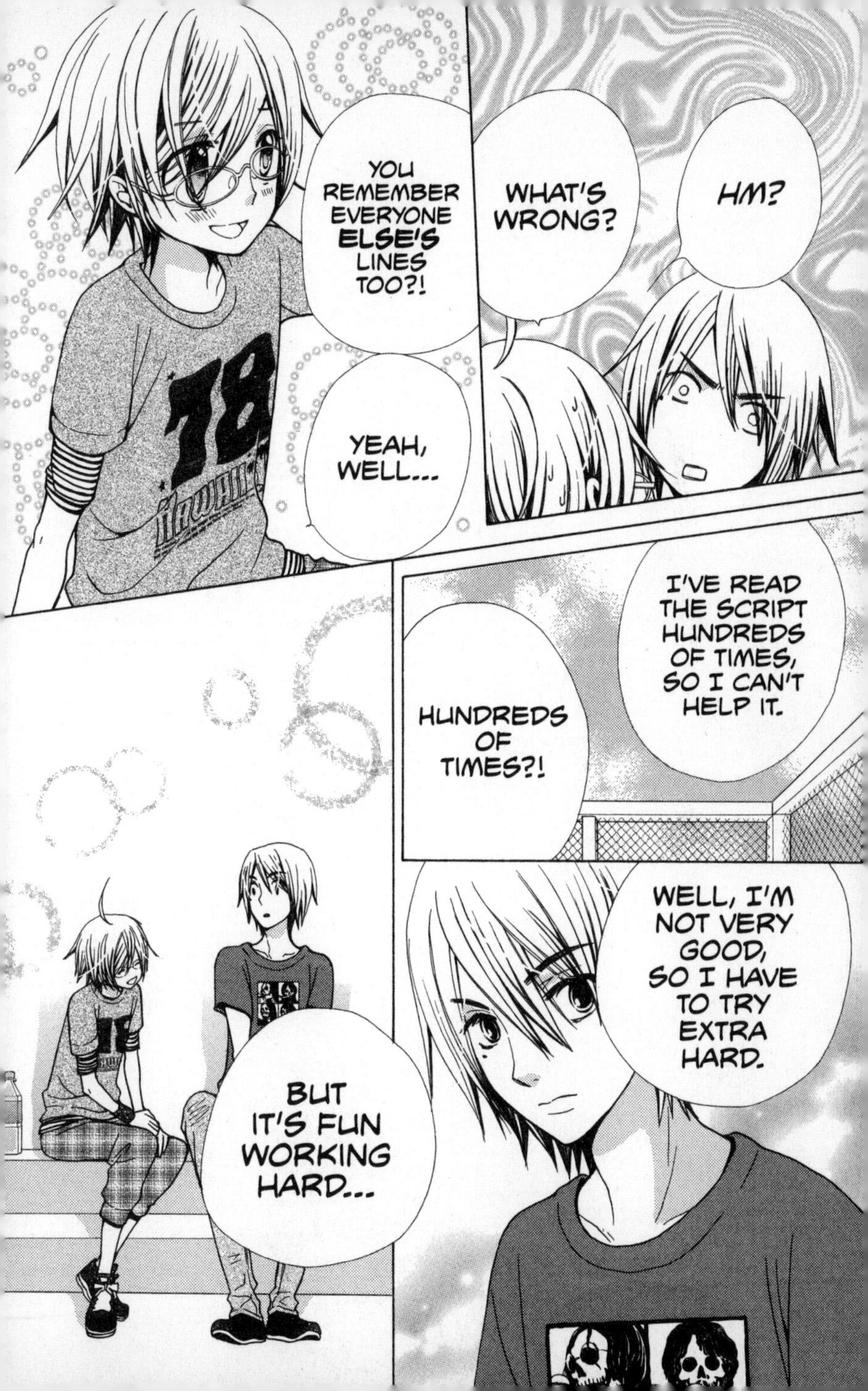
HM?
WHAT'S WRONG?
YOU REMEMBER EVERYONE ELSE'S LINES TOO?!
YEAH, WELL...
I'VE READ THE SCRIPT HUNDREDS OF TIMES, SO I CAN'T HELP IT.
HUNDREDS OF TIMES?!
WELL, I'M NOT VERY GOOD, SO I HAVE TO TRY EXTRA HARD.
BUT IT'S FUN WORKING HARD...

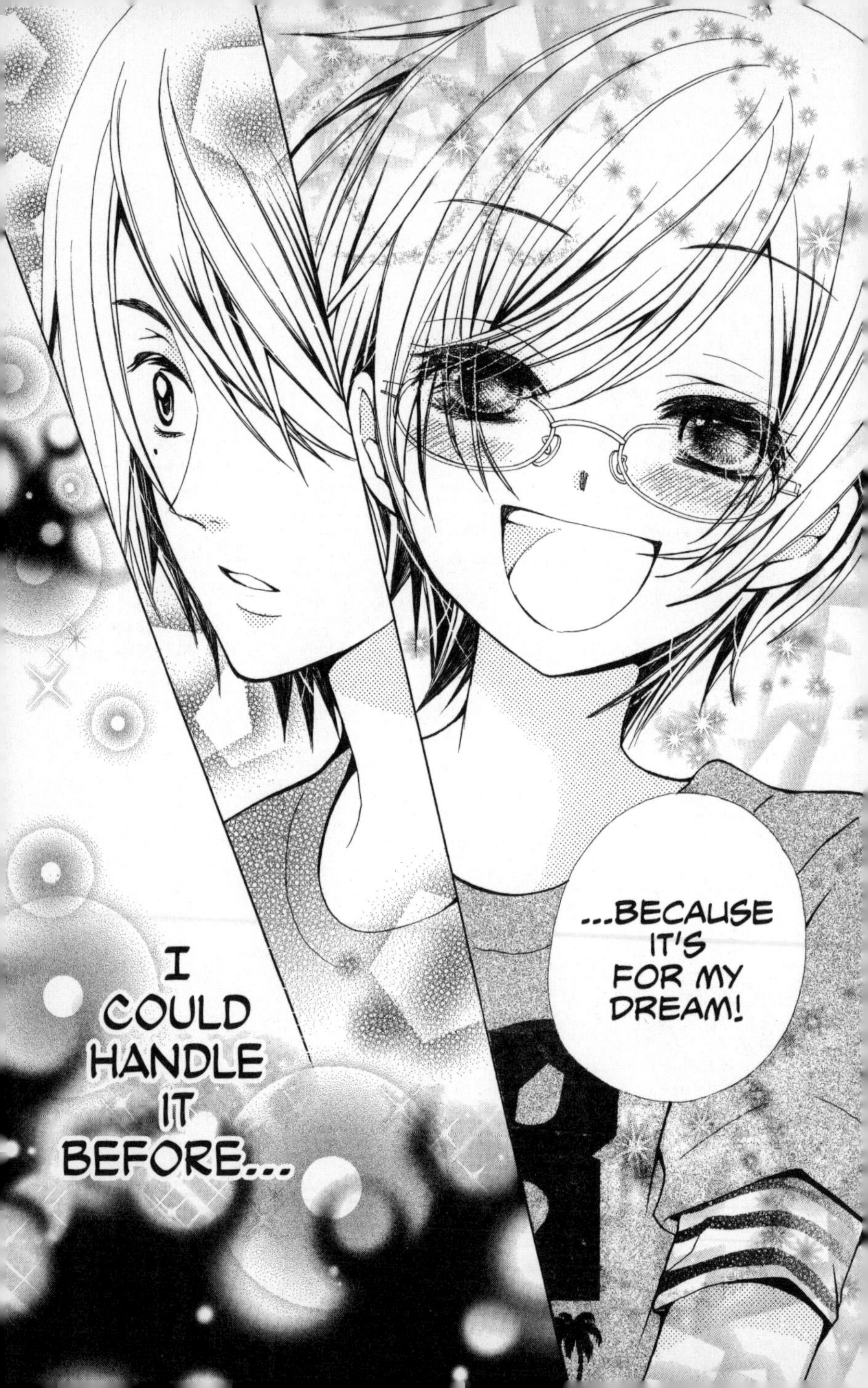
...BECAUSE IT'S FOR MY DREAM!
I COULD HANDLE IT BEFORE...

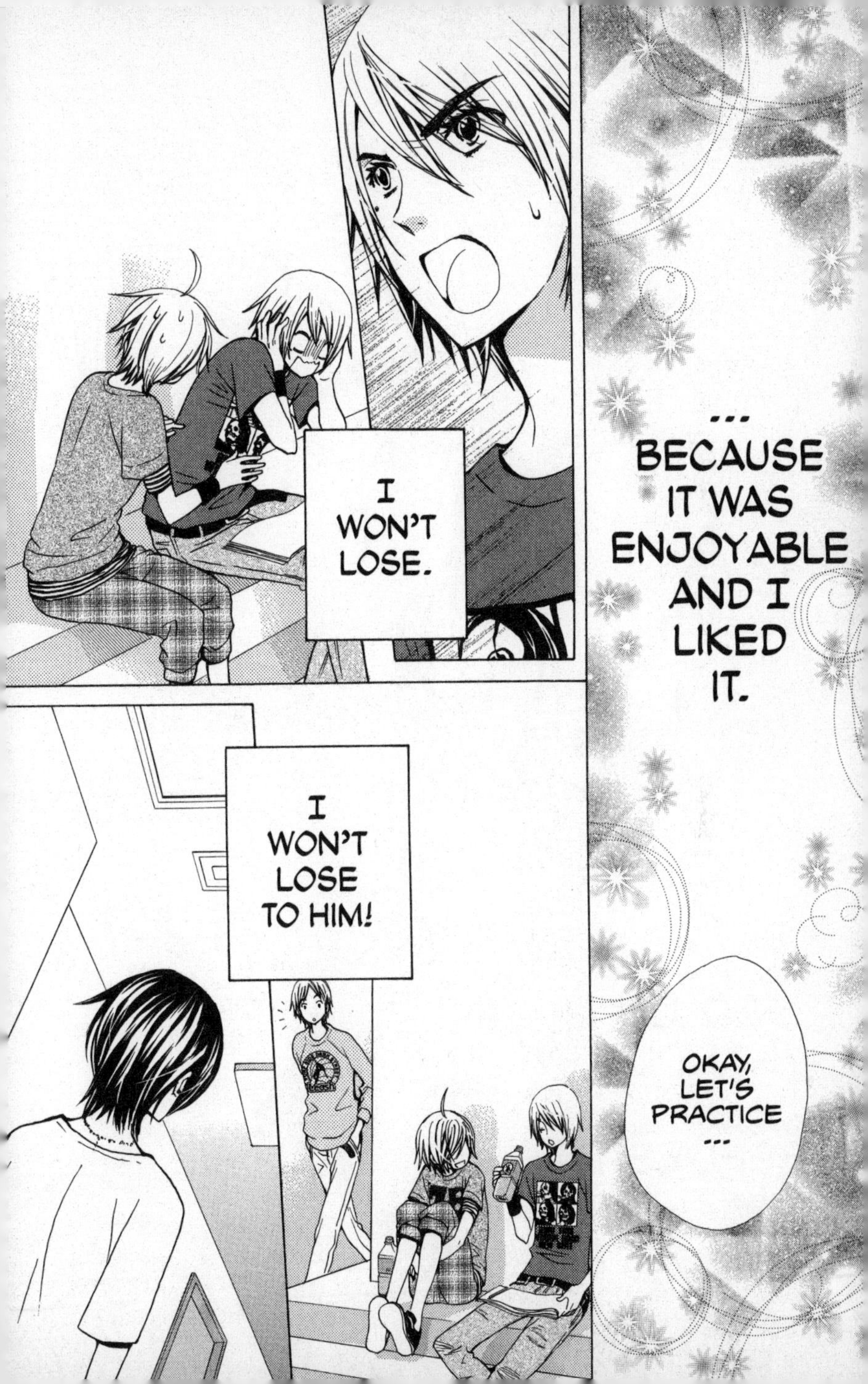

... BECAUSE IT WAS ENJOYABLE AND I LIKED IT.
OKAY, LET'S PRACTICE ...
I WON'T LOSE.
I WON'T LOSE TO HIM!

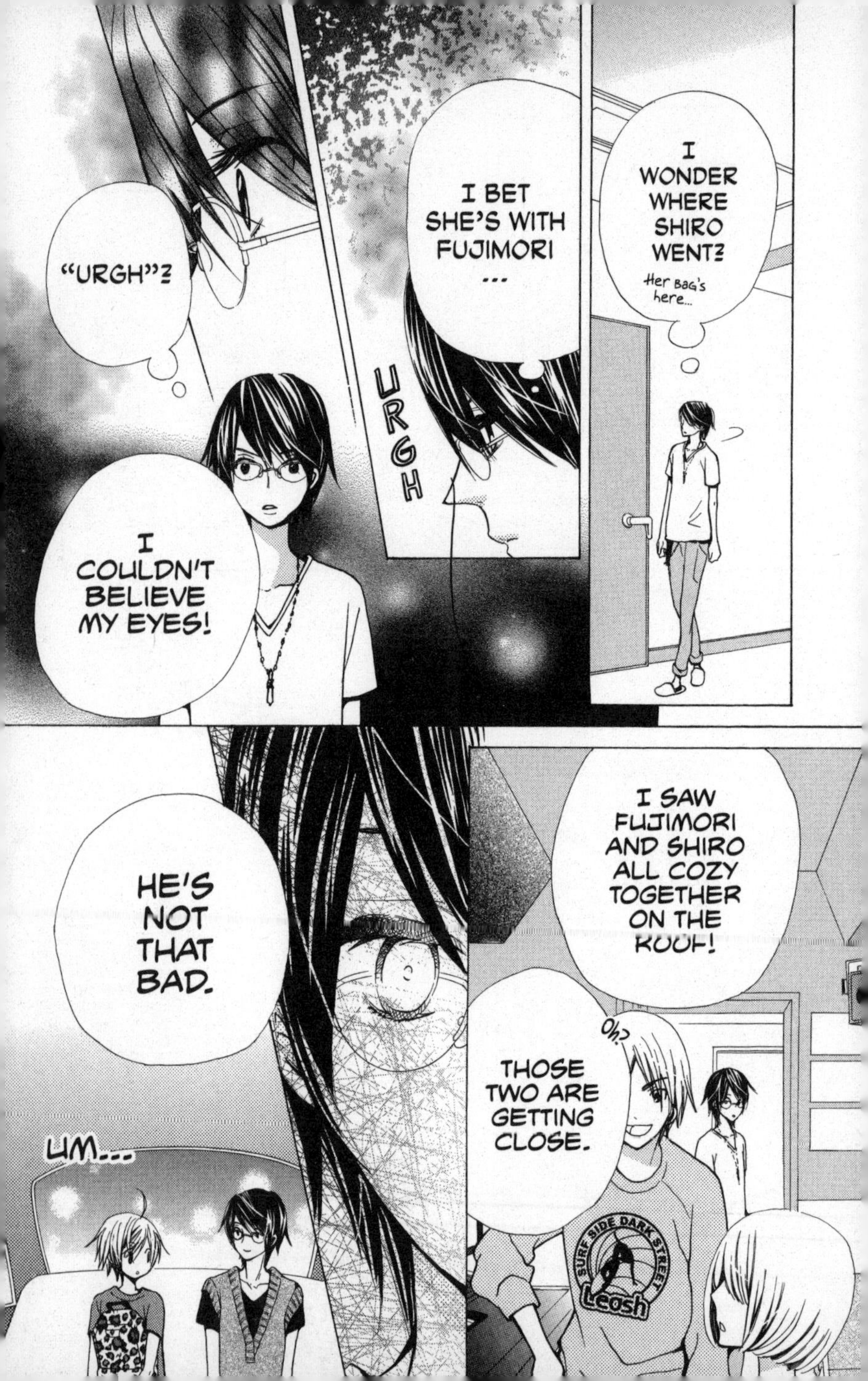
I WONDER WHERE SHIRO WENT?
Her bag's here...
I BET SHE'S WITH FUJIMORI...
URGH
"URGH"?
I COULDN'T BELIEVE MY EYES!
I SAW FUJIMORI AND SHIRO ALL COZY TOGETHER ON THE ROOF!
Oh?
THOSE TWO ARE GETTING CLOSE.
SURF SIDE DARK STREET
Leosh
HE'S NOT THAT BAD.
UM...

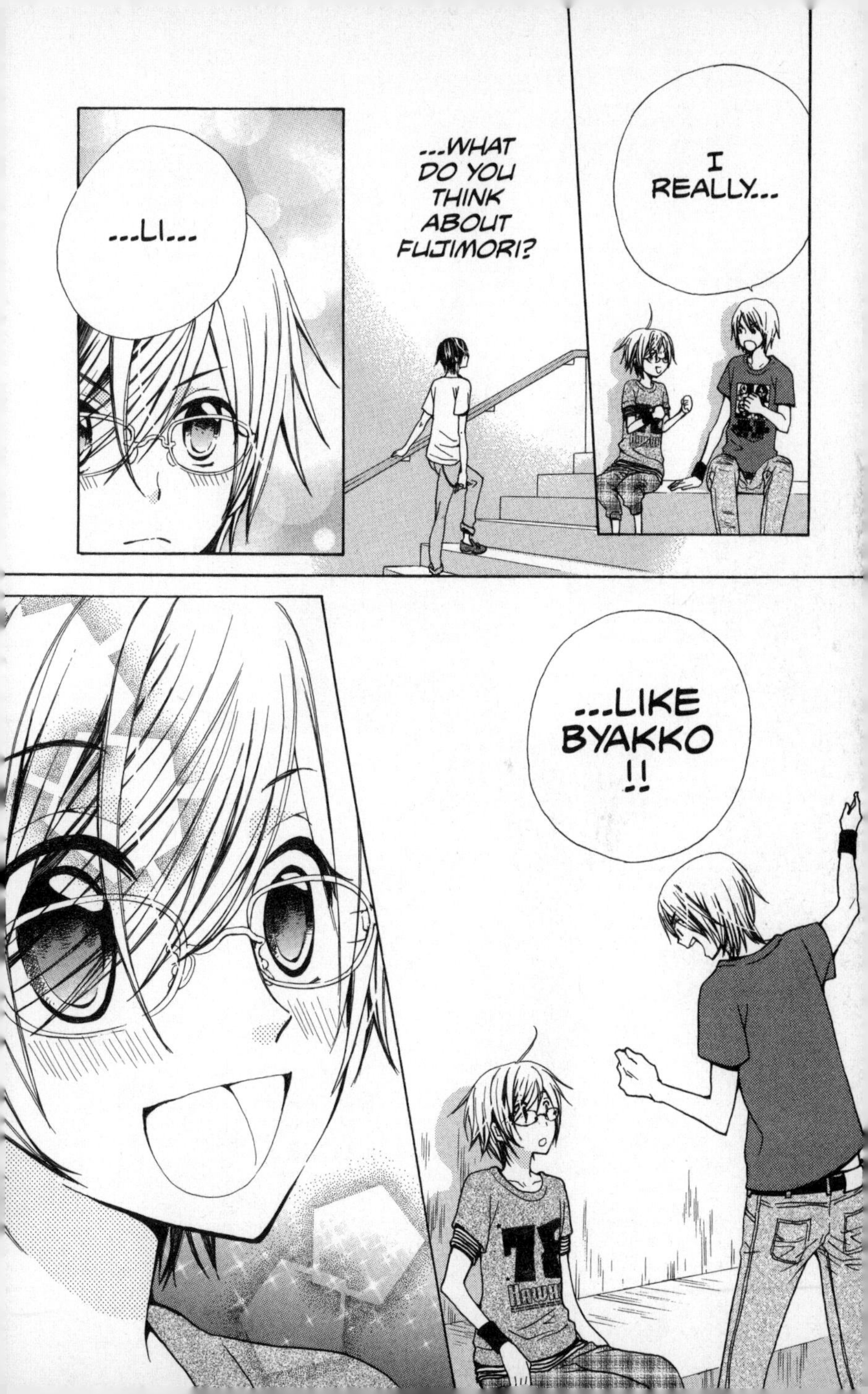
I REALLY...
...WHAT DO YOU THINK ABOUT FUJIMORI?
...LI...
...LIKE BYAKKO !!

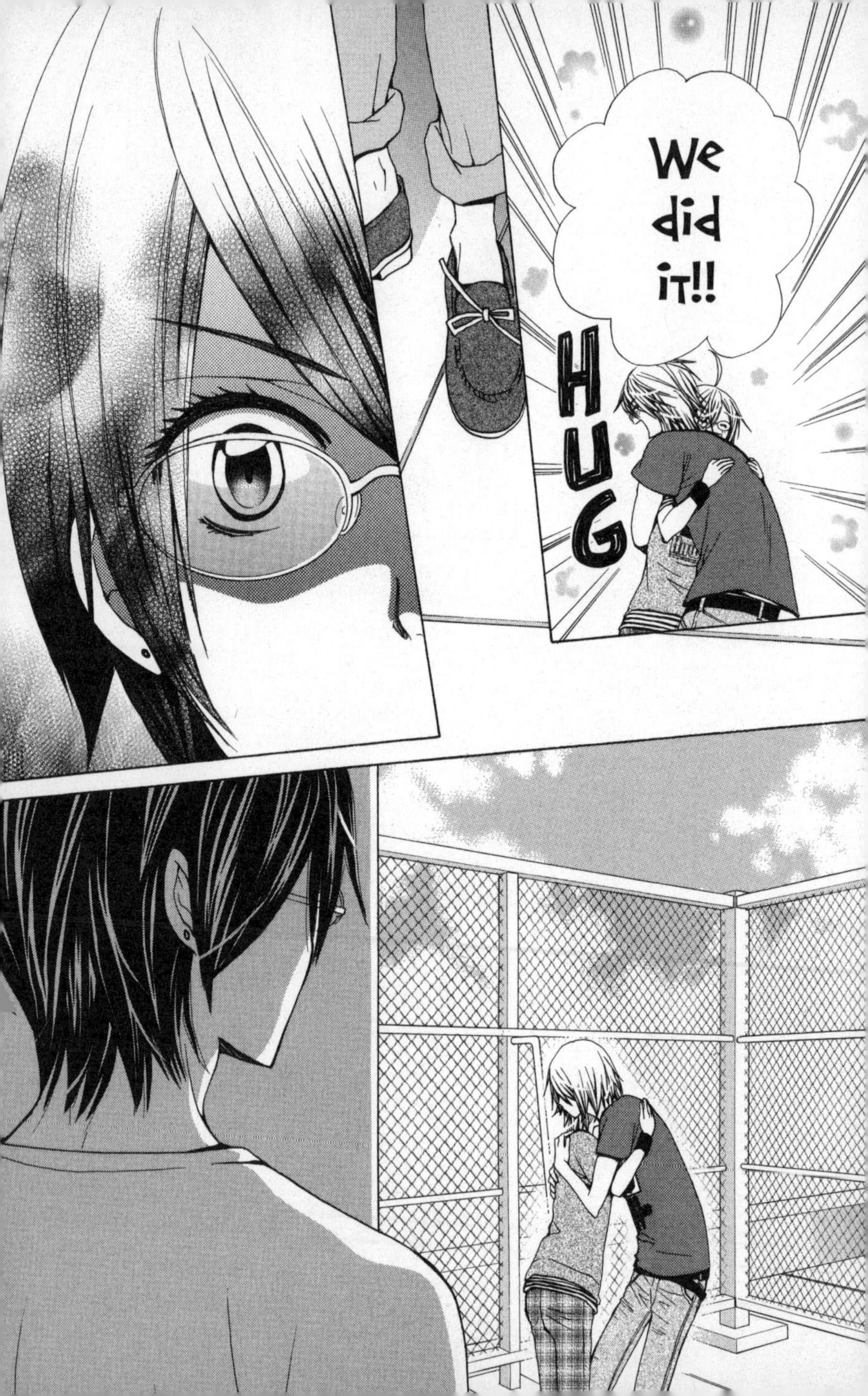
We did it!!
HUG

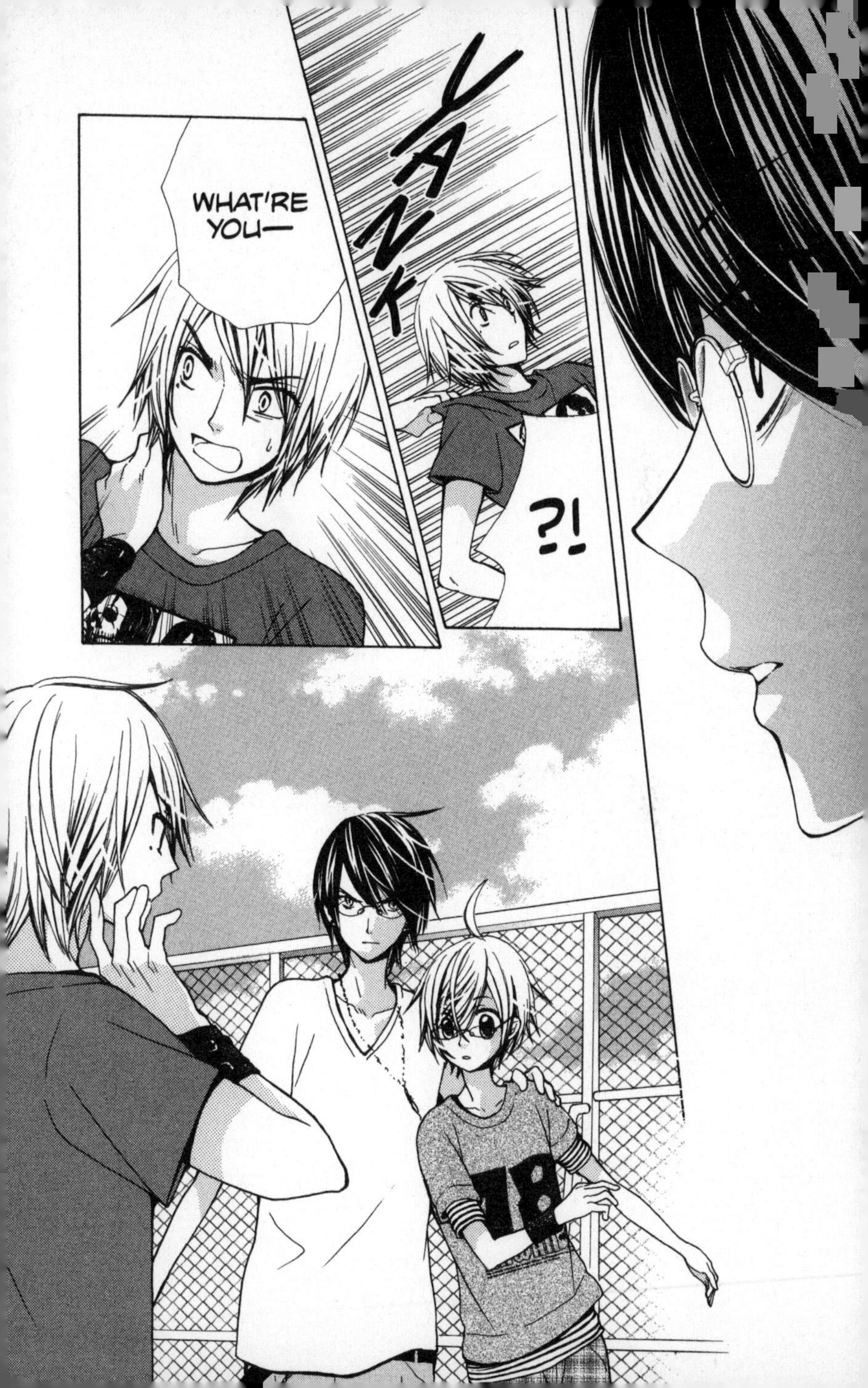
YANK
?!
WHAT'RE YOU—

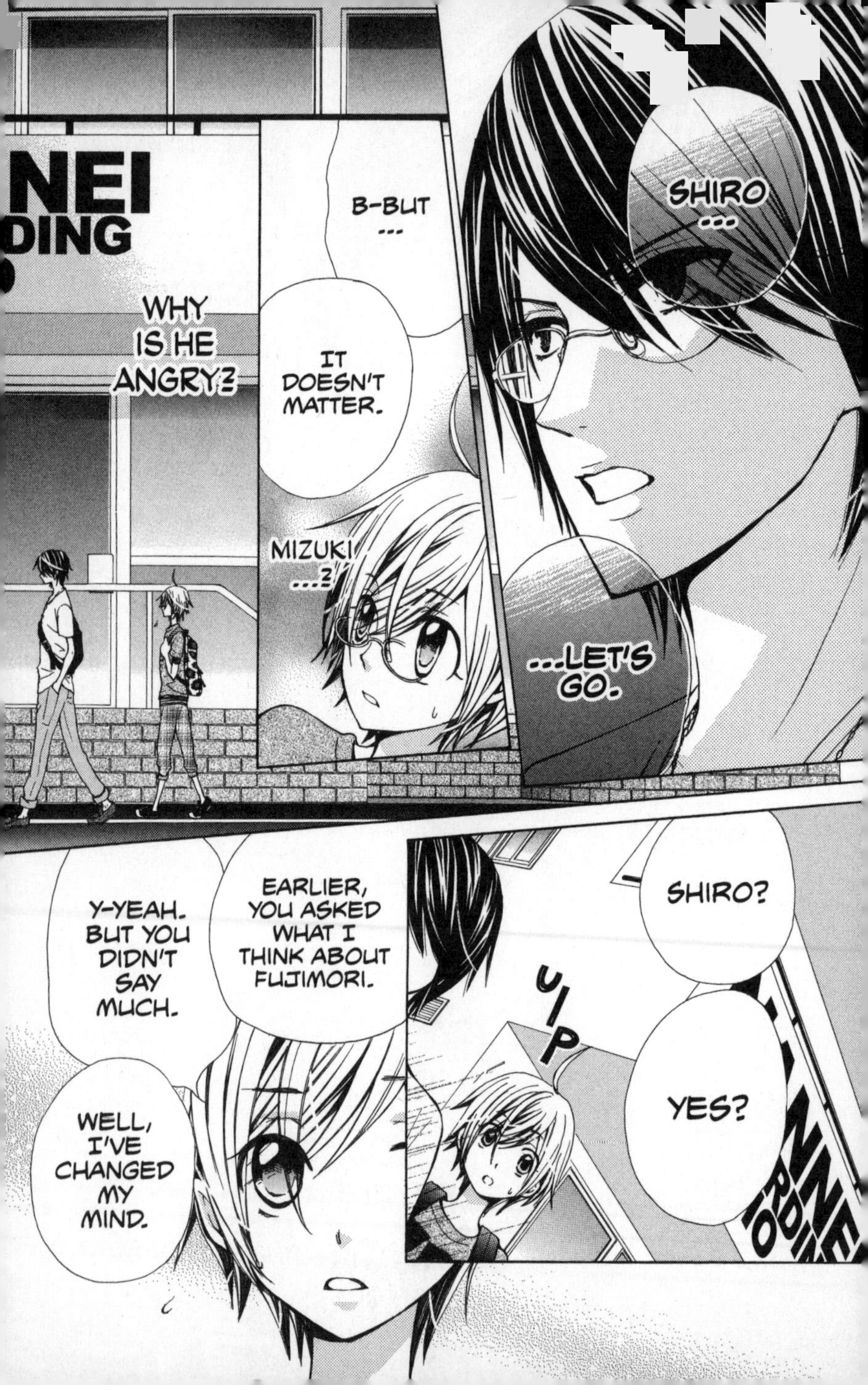
SHIRO ...
...LET'S GO.
B-BUT ...
IT DOESN'T MATTER.
MIZUKI ...?
NEI
DING
WHY IS HE ANGRY?
SHIRO?
U/P
YES?
EARLIER, YOU ASKED WHAT I THINK ABOUT FUJIMORI.
Y-YEAH. BUT YOU DIDN'T SAY MUCH.
WELL, I'VE CHANGED MY MIND.

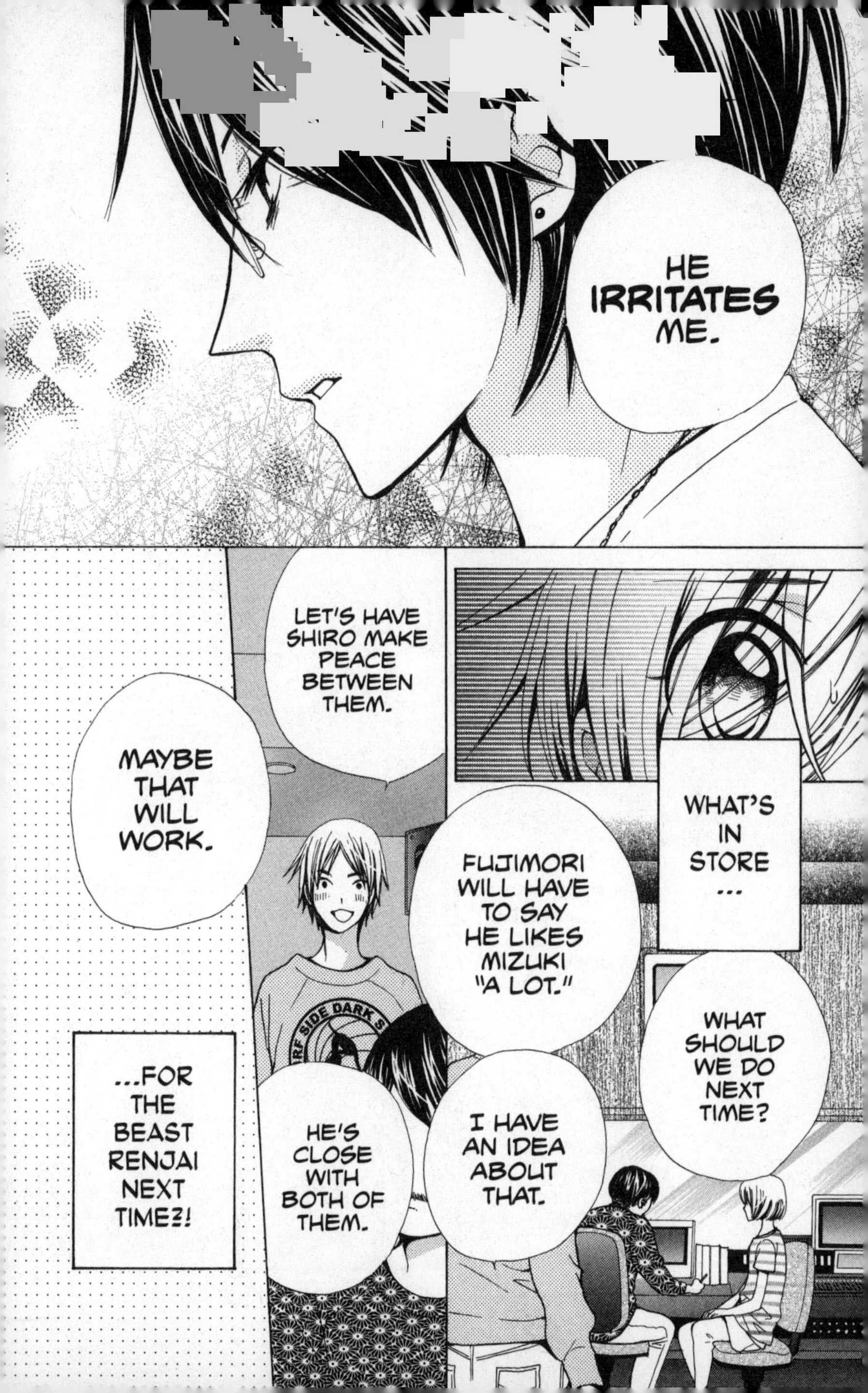
HE IRRITATES ME.
WHAT'S IN STORE ...
WHAT SHOULD WE DO NEXT TIME?
I HAVE AN IDEA ABOUT THAT.
FUJIMORI WILL HAVE TO SAY HE LIKES MIZUKI "A LOT."
LET'S HAVE SHIRO MAKE PEACE BETWEEN THEM.
HE'S CLOSE WITH BOTH OF THEM.
MAYBE THAT WILL WORK.
...FOR THE BEAST RENJAI NEXT TIME?!

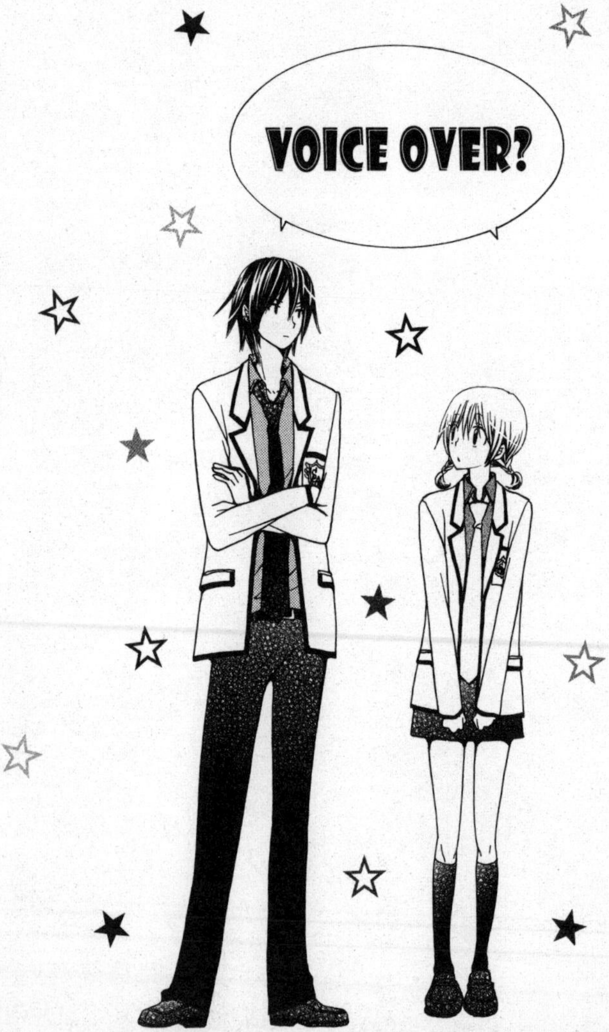
VOICE OVER?

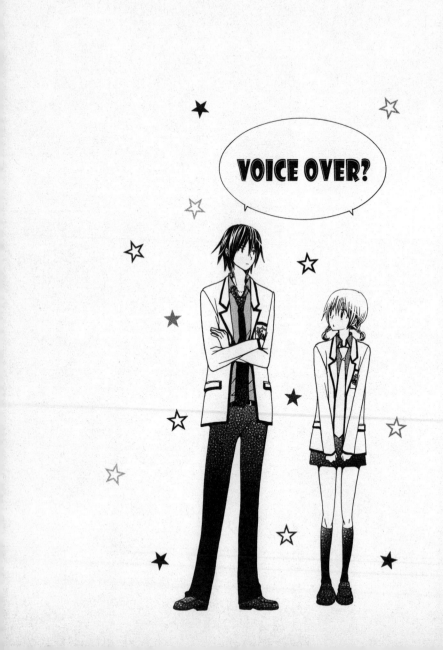

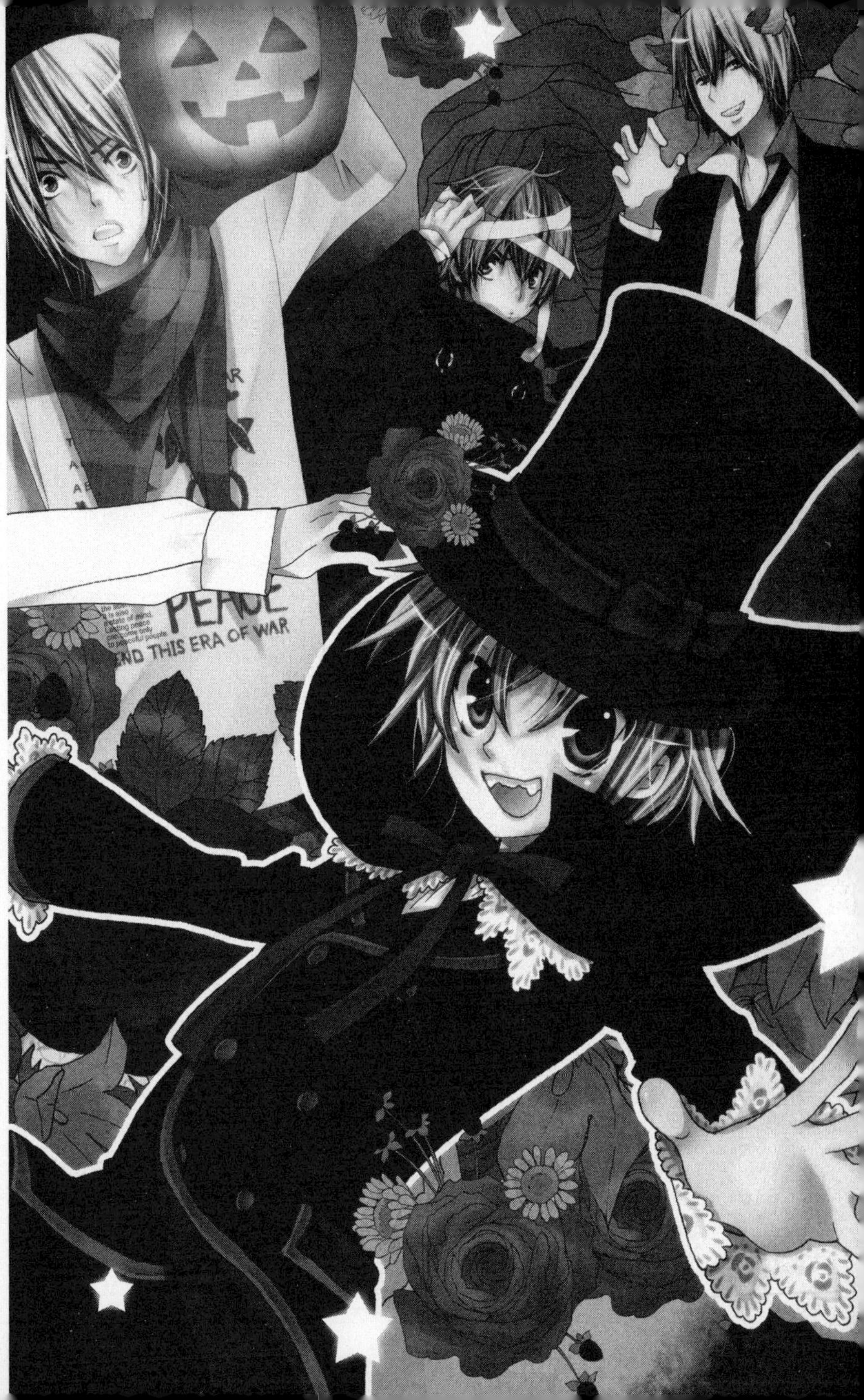

PEACE
END THIS ERA OF WAR

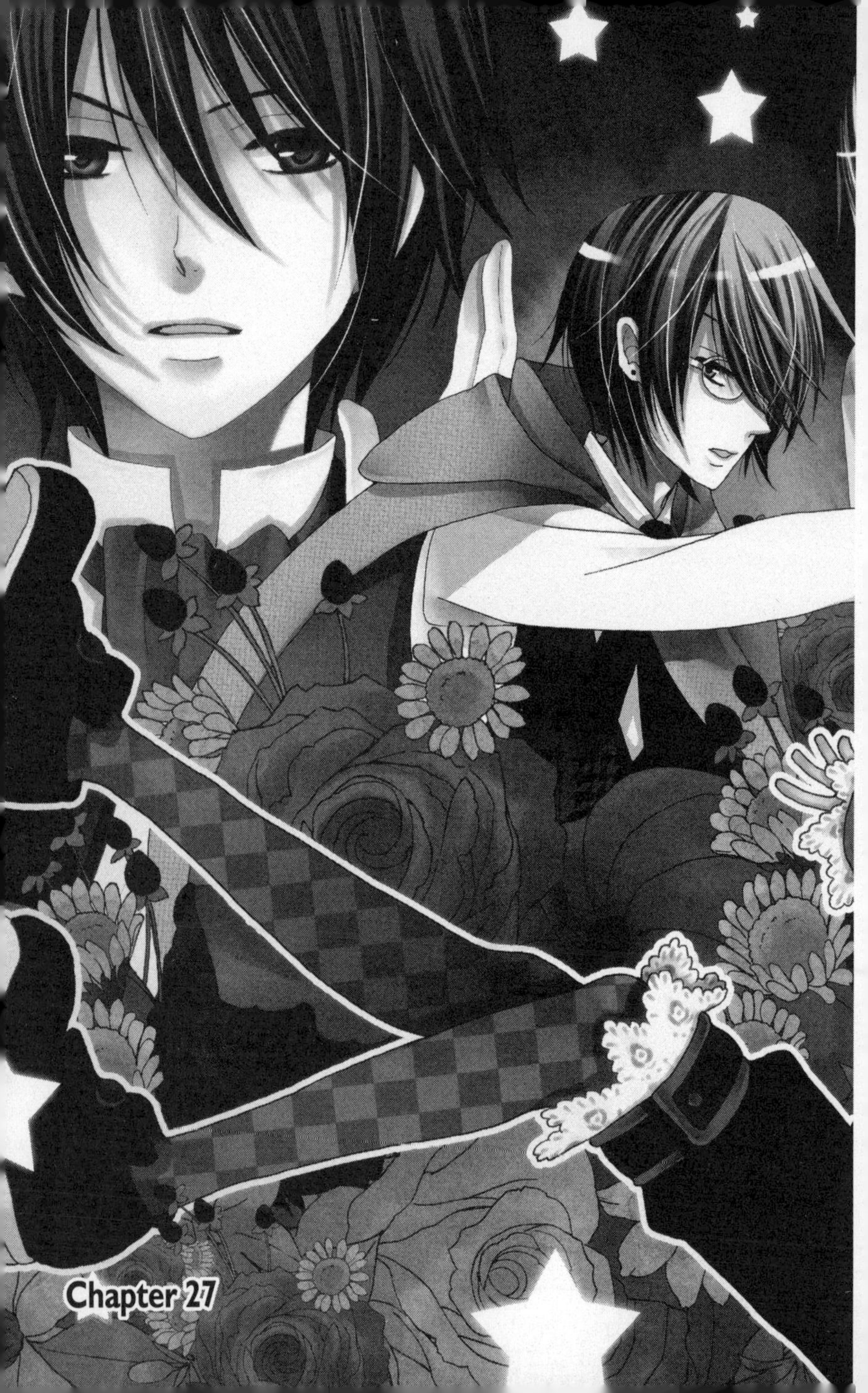
Chapter 27

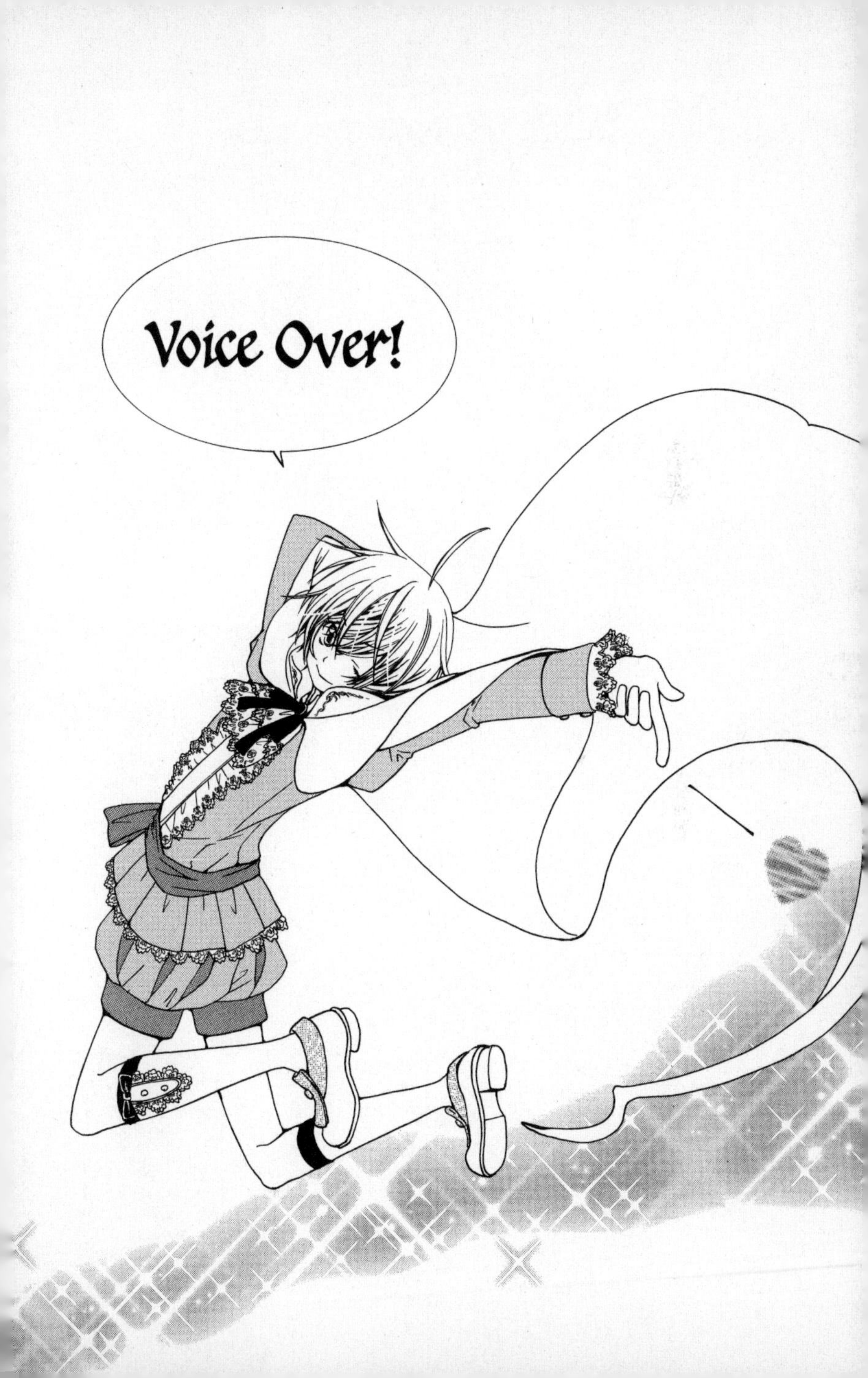
Voice Over!

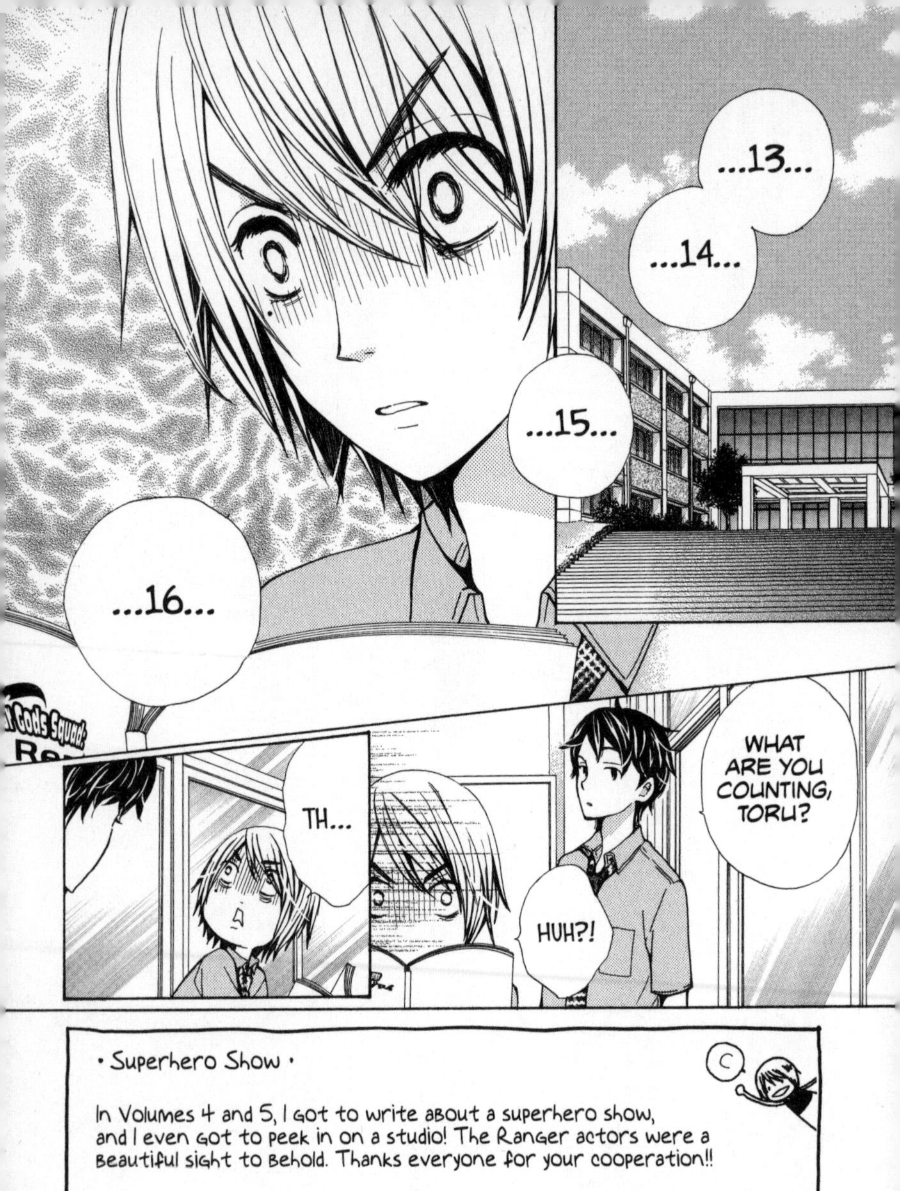
...13...
...14...
...15...
...16...
Gods Squad:
WHAT ARE YOU COUNTING, TORU?
HUH?!
TH...

• Superhero Show •

In Volumes 4 and 5, I got to write about a superhero show, and I even got to peek in on a studio! The Ranger actors were a beautiful sight to behold. Thanks everyone for your cooperation!!

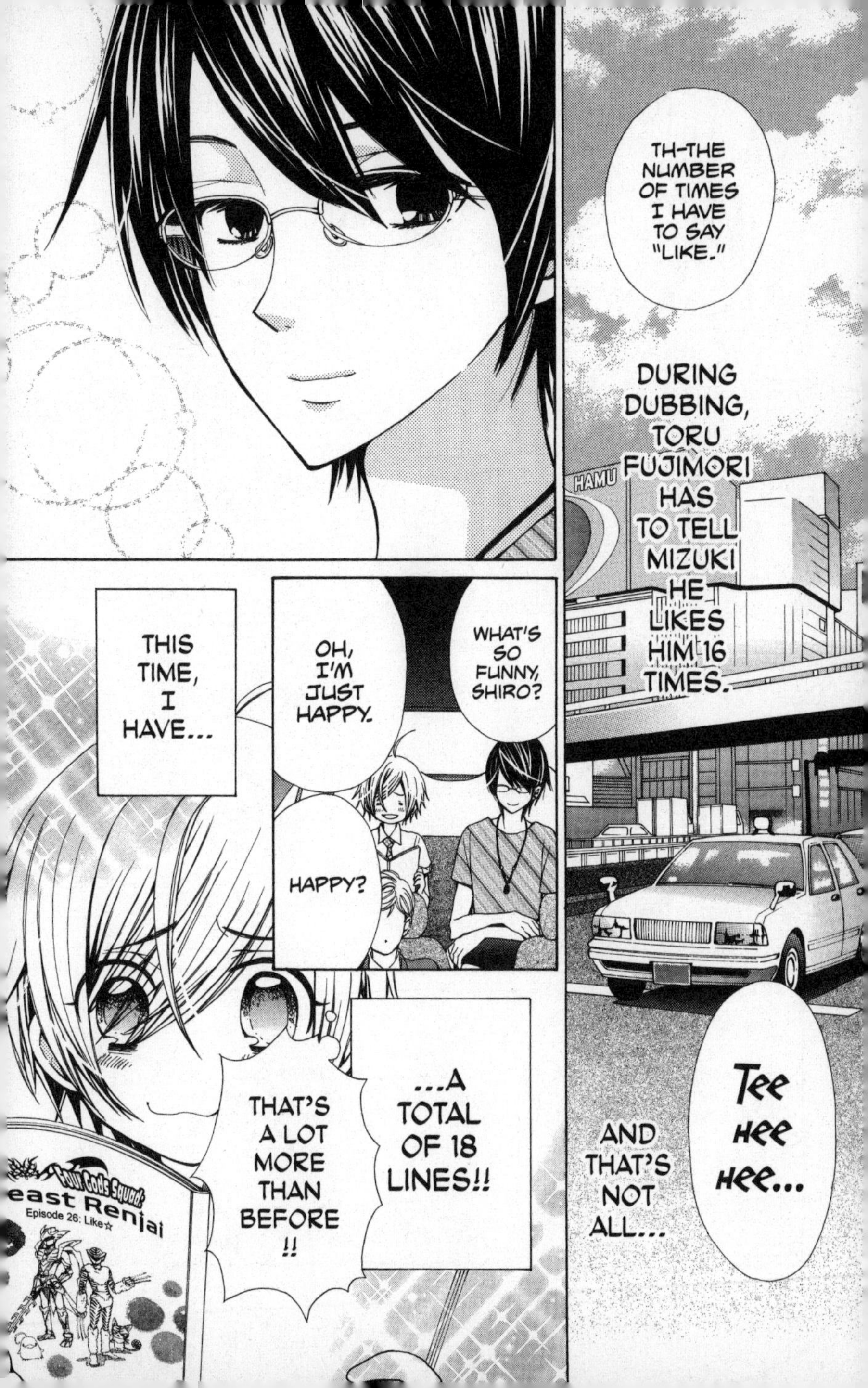

TH-THE NUMBER OF TIMES I HAVE TO SAY "LIKE."
HAMU
DURING DUBBING, TORU FUJIMORI HAS TO TELL MIZUKI HE LIKES HIM 16 TIMES.
TEE HEE HEE...
AND THAT'S NOT ALL...
WHAT'S SO FUNNY, SHIRO?
OH, I'M JUST HAPPY.
HAPPY?
THIS TIME, I HAVE...
...A TOTAL OF 18 LINES!!
THAT'S A LOT MORE THAN BEFORE!!
Four Gods Squad:
east Renjai
Episode 26: Like☆

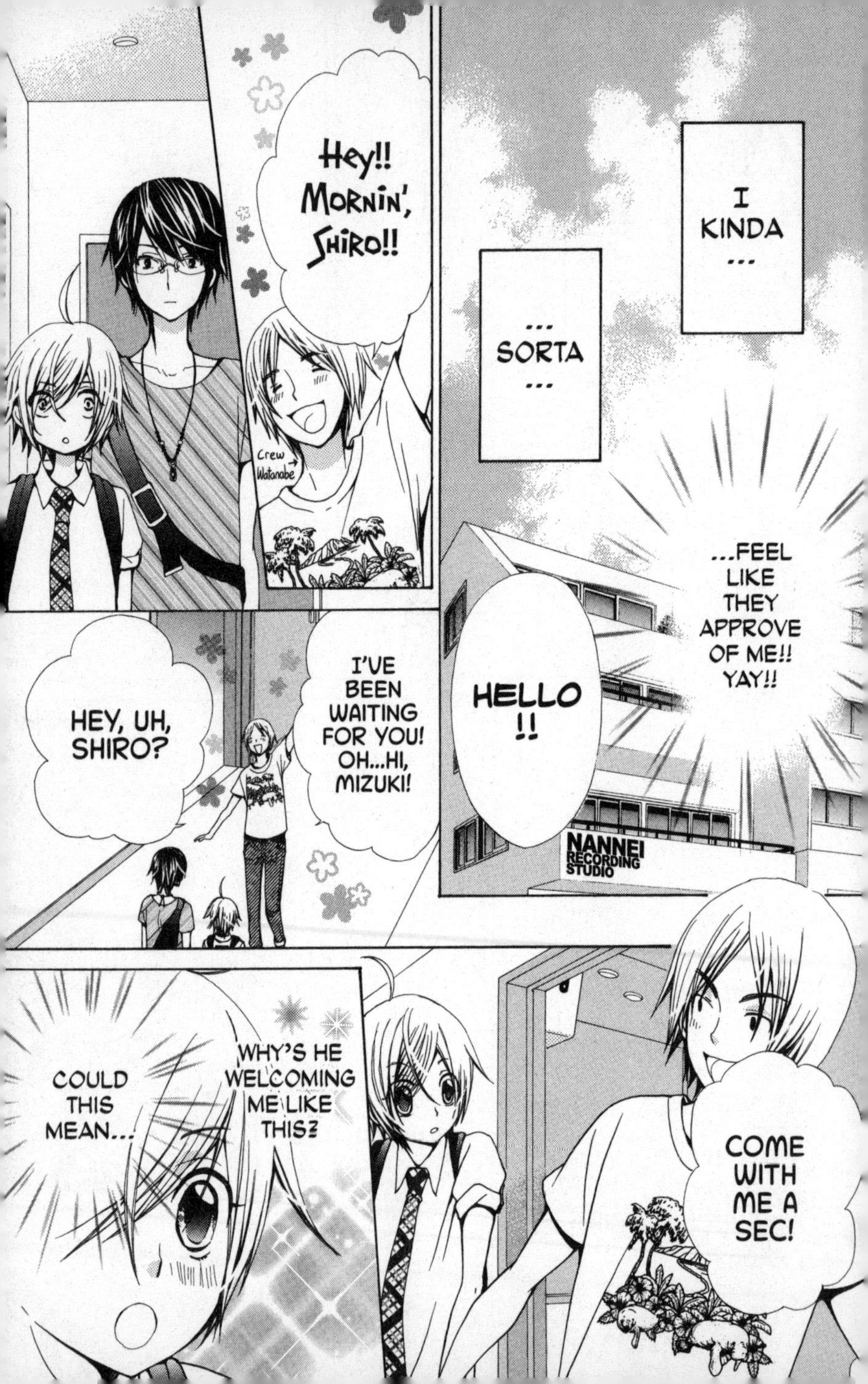
I KINDA...
...SORTA...
...FEEL LIKE THEY APPROVE OF ME!! YAY!!
HELLO!!
NANNEI RECORDING STUDIO
Hey!! Mornin', Shiro!!
Crew Watanabe
I'VE BEEN WAITING FOR YOU! OH...HI, MIZUKI!
HEY, UH, SHIRO?
COME WITH ME A SEC!
WHY'S HE WELCOMING ME LIKE THIS?
COULD THIS MEAN...

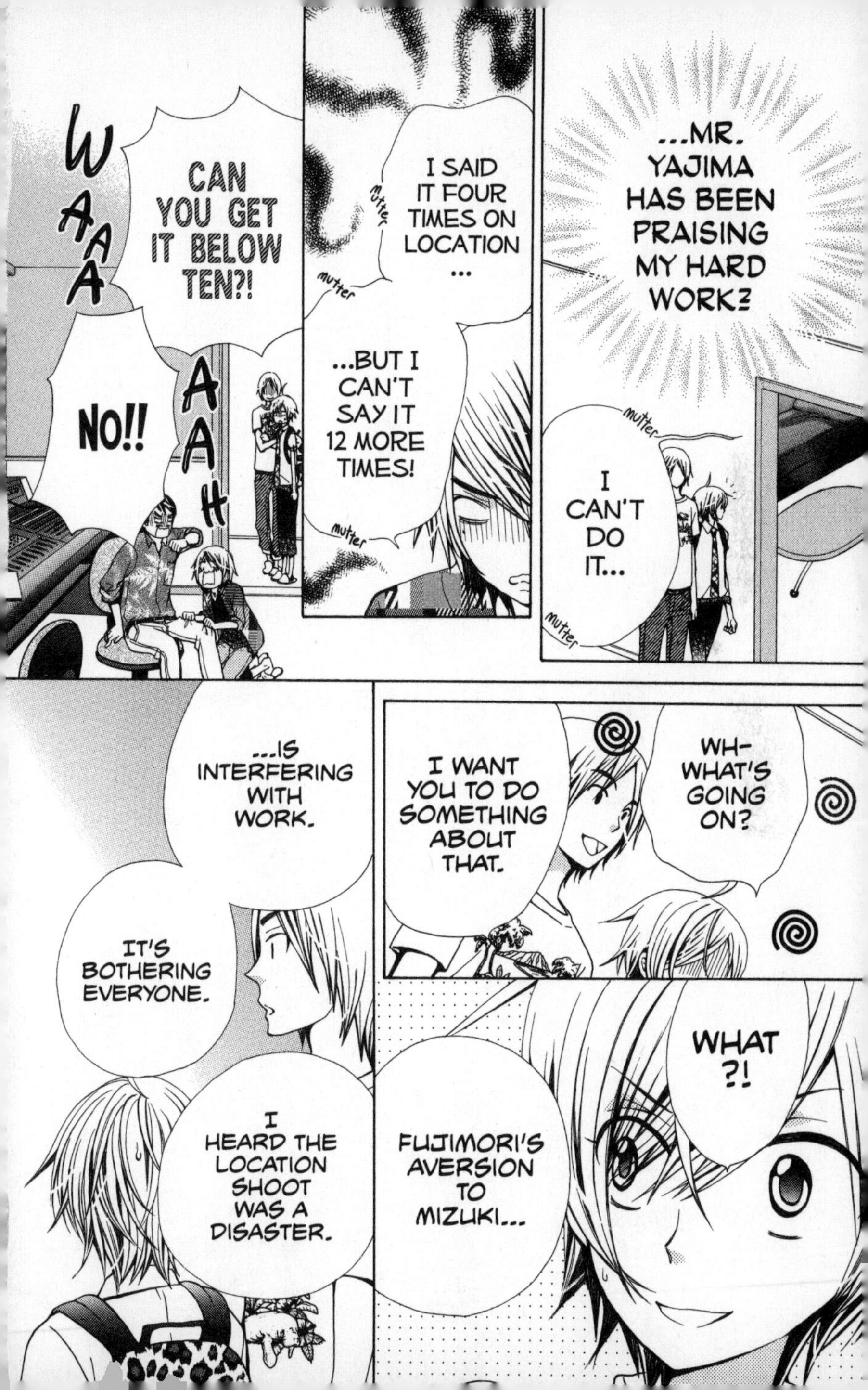
...MR. YAJIMA HAS BEEN PRAISING MY HARD WORK?
mutter
I CAN'T DO IT...
mutter
mutter
I SAID IT FOUR TIMES ON LOCATION ...
mutter
...BUT I CAN'T SAY IT 12 MORE TIMES!
mutter
CAN YOU GET IT BELOW TEN?!
NO!!
WAAAAAAH
WH- WHAT'S GOING ON?
I WANT YOU TO DO SOMETHING ABOUT THAT.
WHAT ?!
FUJIMORI'S AVERSION TO MIZUKI...
...IS INTERFERING WITH WORK.
IT'S BOTHERING EVERYONE.
I HEARD THE LOCATION SHOOT WAS A DISASTER.

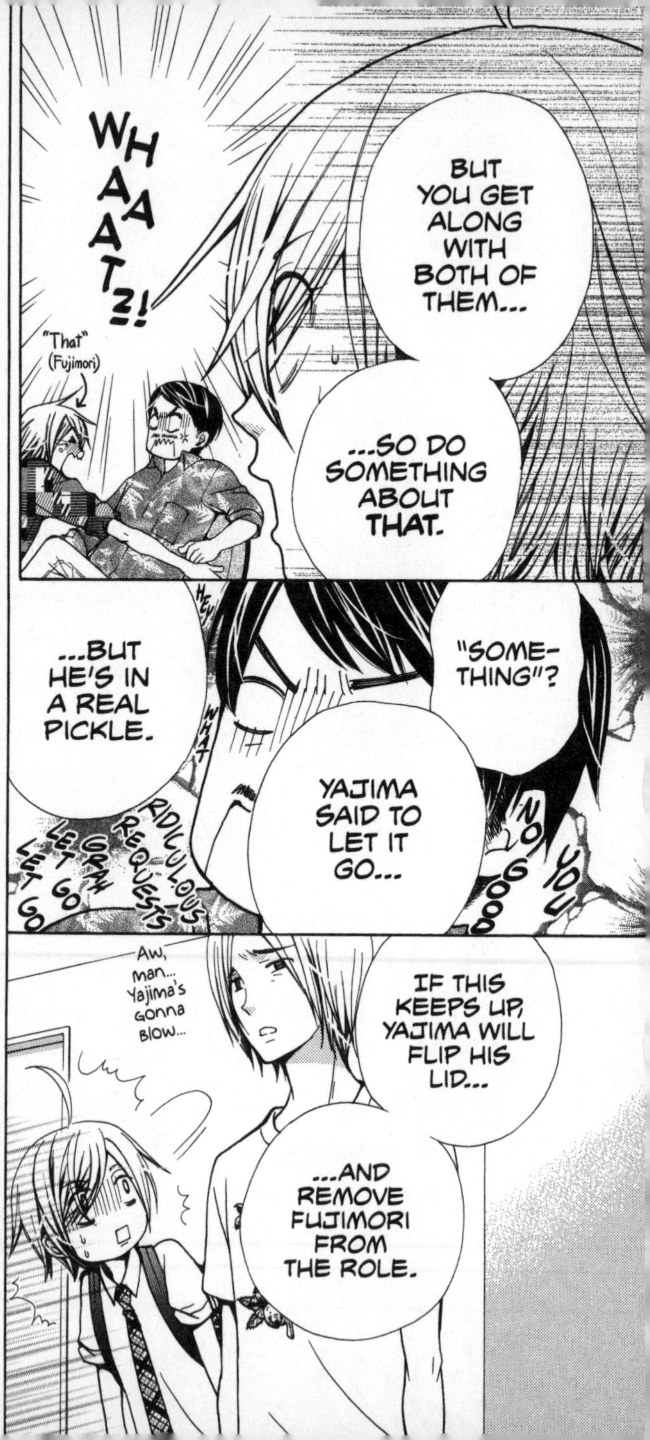
BUT YOU GET ALONG WITH BOTH OF THEM...
...SO DO SOMETHING ABOUT THAT.
WHAAAT?!
"That" (Fujimori)
"SOME-THING"?
YAJIMA SAID TO LET IT GO...
NO GOOD
YOU
...BUT HE'S IN A REAL PICKLE.
HEY
WHAT
RIDICULOUS REQUESTS
GRAH
LET GO LET GO
IF THIS KEEPS UP, YAJIMA WILL FLIP HIS LID...
...AND REMOVE FUJIMORI FROM THE ROLE.
Aw, man... Yajima's gonna blow...

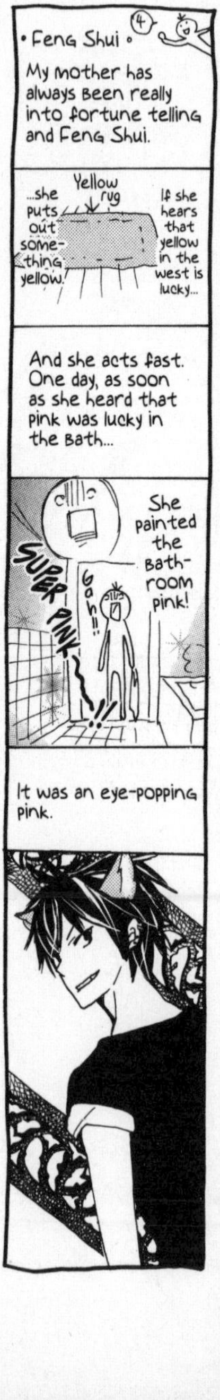
• Feng Shui • ④
My mother has always been really into fortune telling and Feng Shui.
If she hears that yellow in the west is lucky...
...she puts out something yellow.
Yellow rug
And she acts fast. One day, as soon as she heard that pink was lucky in the bath...
She painted the bathroom pink!
SUPER PINK
Gah!!
It was an eye-popping pink.

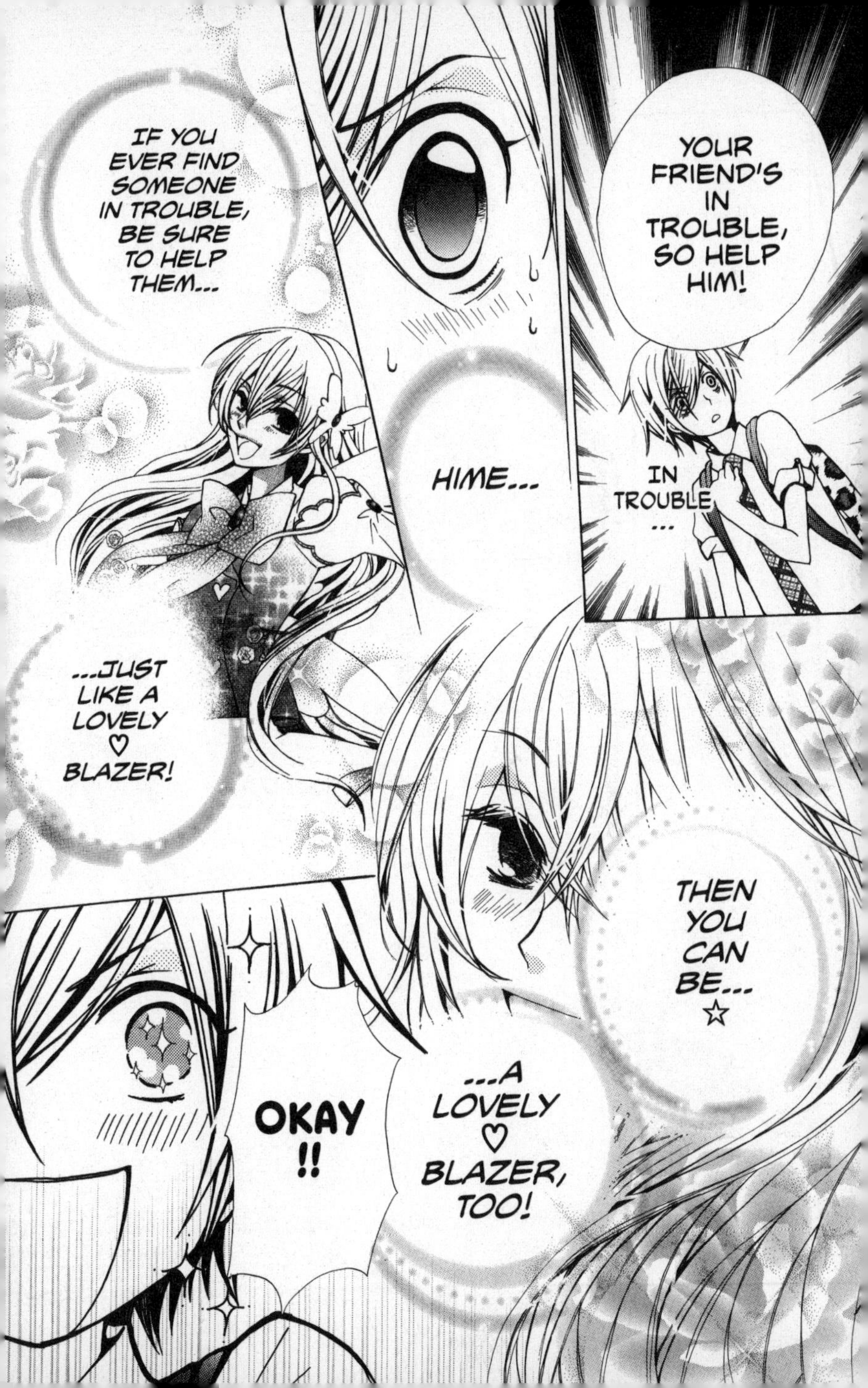
YOUR FRIEND'S IN TROUBLE, SO HELP HIM!
IN TROUBLE...
HIME...
IF YOU EVER FIND SOMEONE IN TROUBLE, BE SURE TO HELP THEM...
...JUST LIKE A LOVELY ♡ BLAZER!
THEN YOU CAN BE... ☆
...A LOVELY ♡ BLAZER, TOO!
OKAY!!

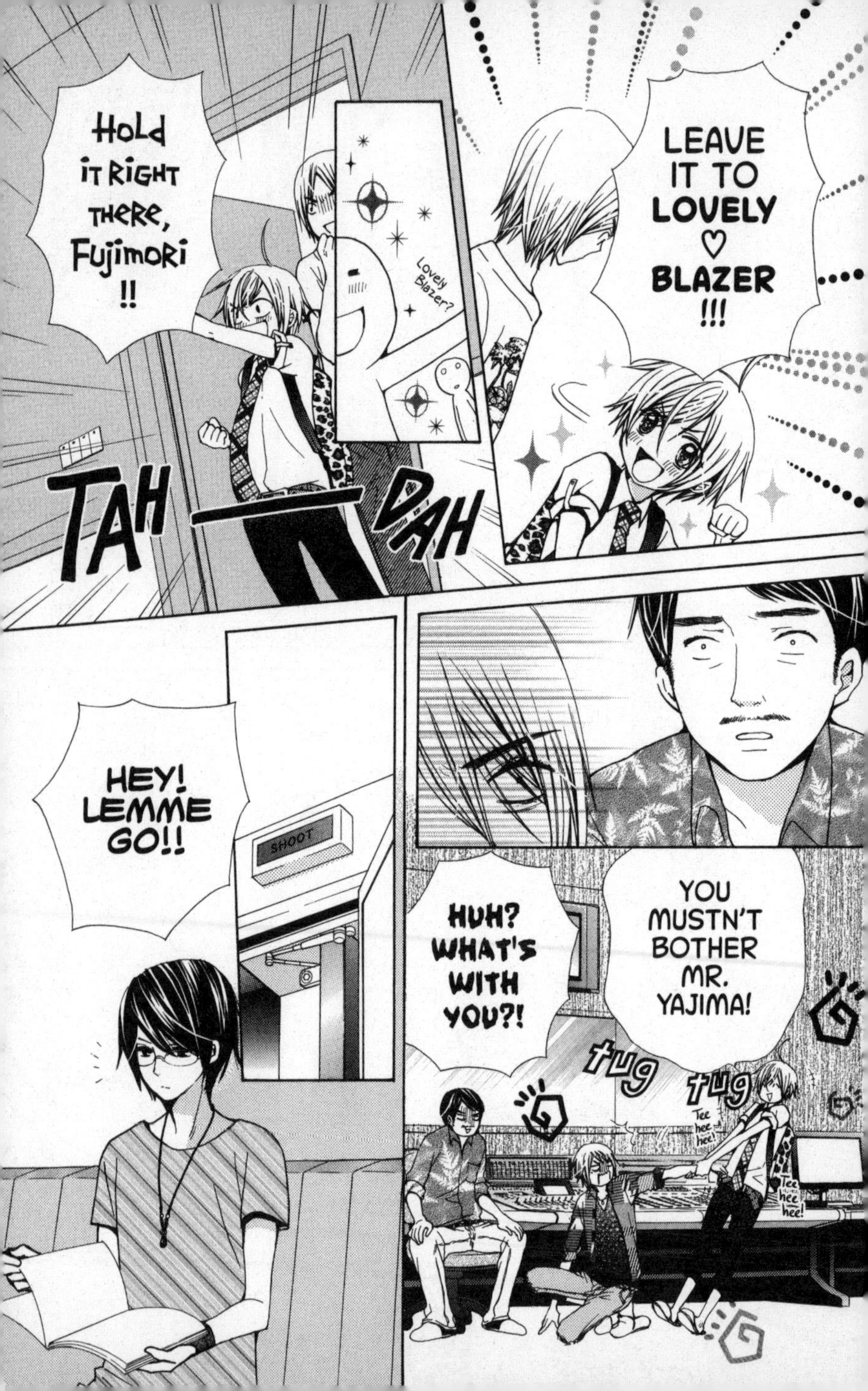
LEAVE IT TO LOVELY ♡ BLAZER!!!
Lovely Blazer?
Hold it RIGHT there, Fujimori!!
TAH—DAH
YOU MUSTN'T BOTHER MR. YAJIMA!
HUH? WHAT'S WITH YOU?!
tug tug
Tee hee hee!
Tee hee hee!
SHOOT
HEY! LEMME GO!!

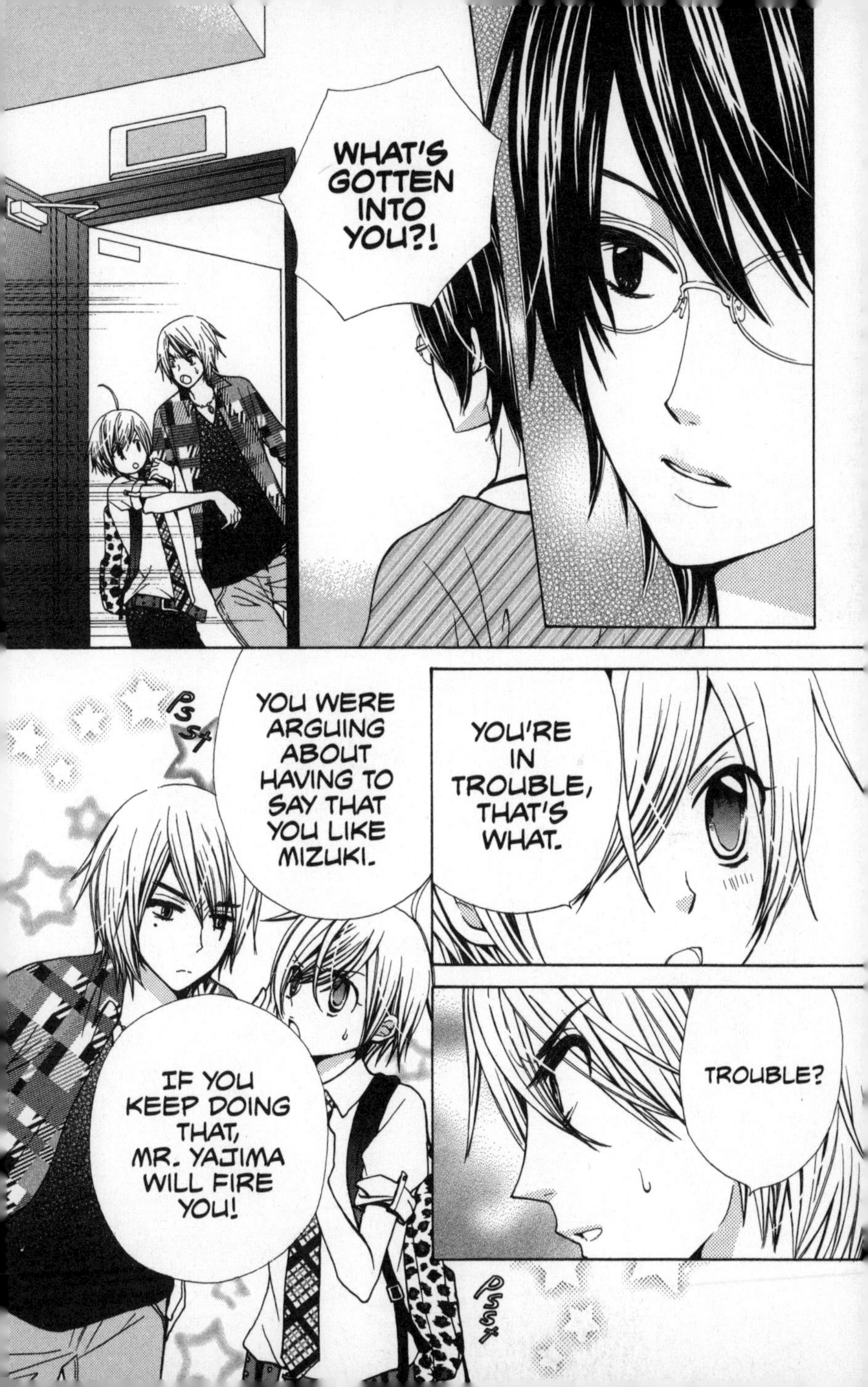
WHAT'S GOTTEN INTO YOU?!
YOU'RE IN TROUBLE, THAT'S WHAT.
TROUBLE?
Psst
YOU WERE ARGUING ABOUT HAVING TO SAY THAT YOU LIKE MIZUKI.
Psst
IF YOU KEEP DOING THAT, MR. YAJIMA WILL FIRE YOU!

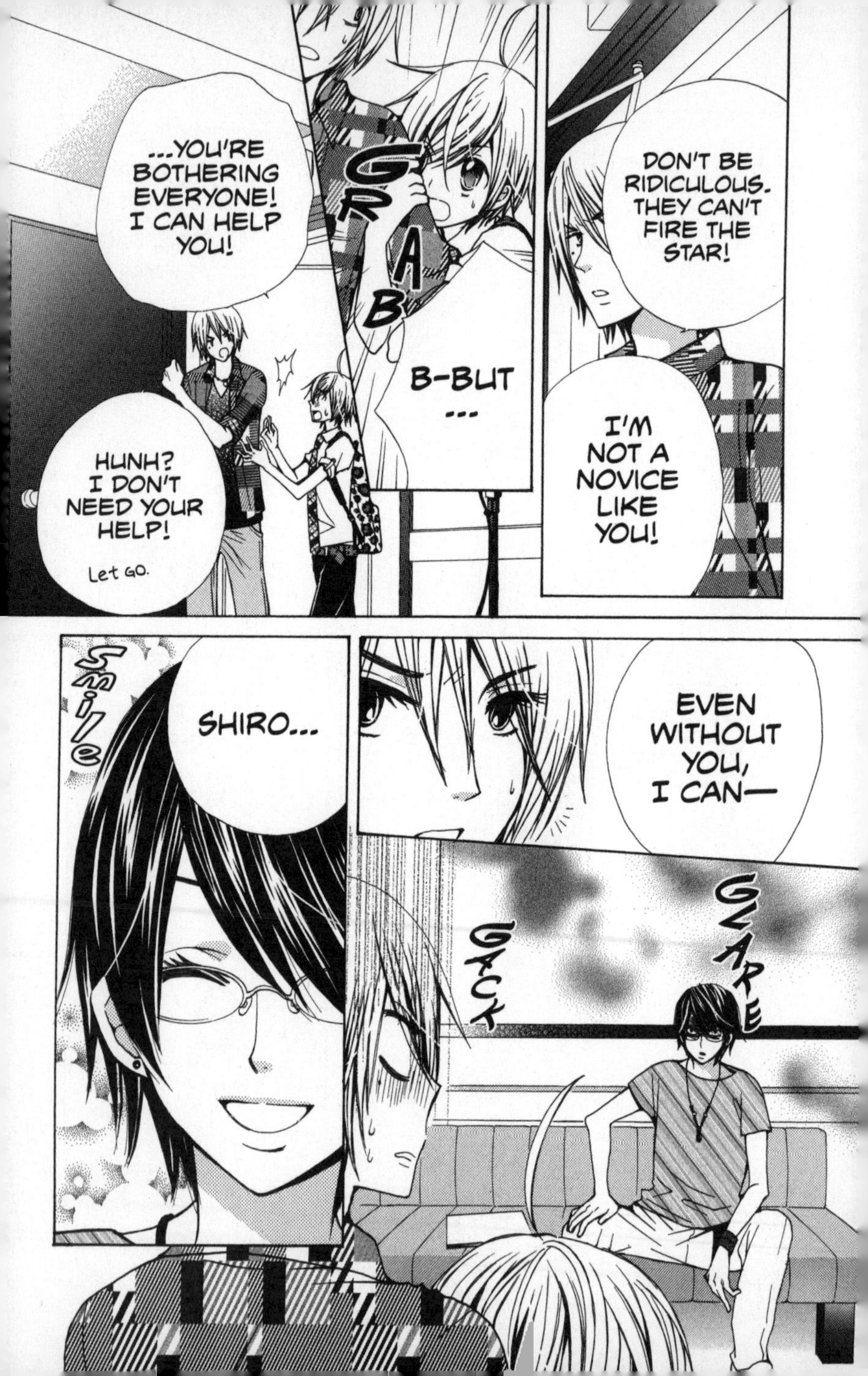
DON'T BE RIDICULOUS. THEY CAN'T FIRE THE STAR!
I'M NOT A NOVICE LIKE YOU!
GRAB
B-BUT ...
...YOU'RE BOTHERING EVERYONE! I CAN HELP YOU!
HUNH? I DON'T NEED YOUR HELP!
Let GO.
EVEN WITHOUT YOU, I CAN—
Smile
SHIRO...
GLARE
GACK

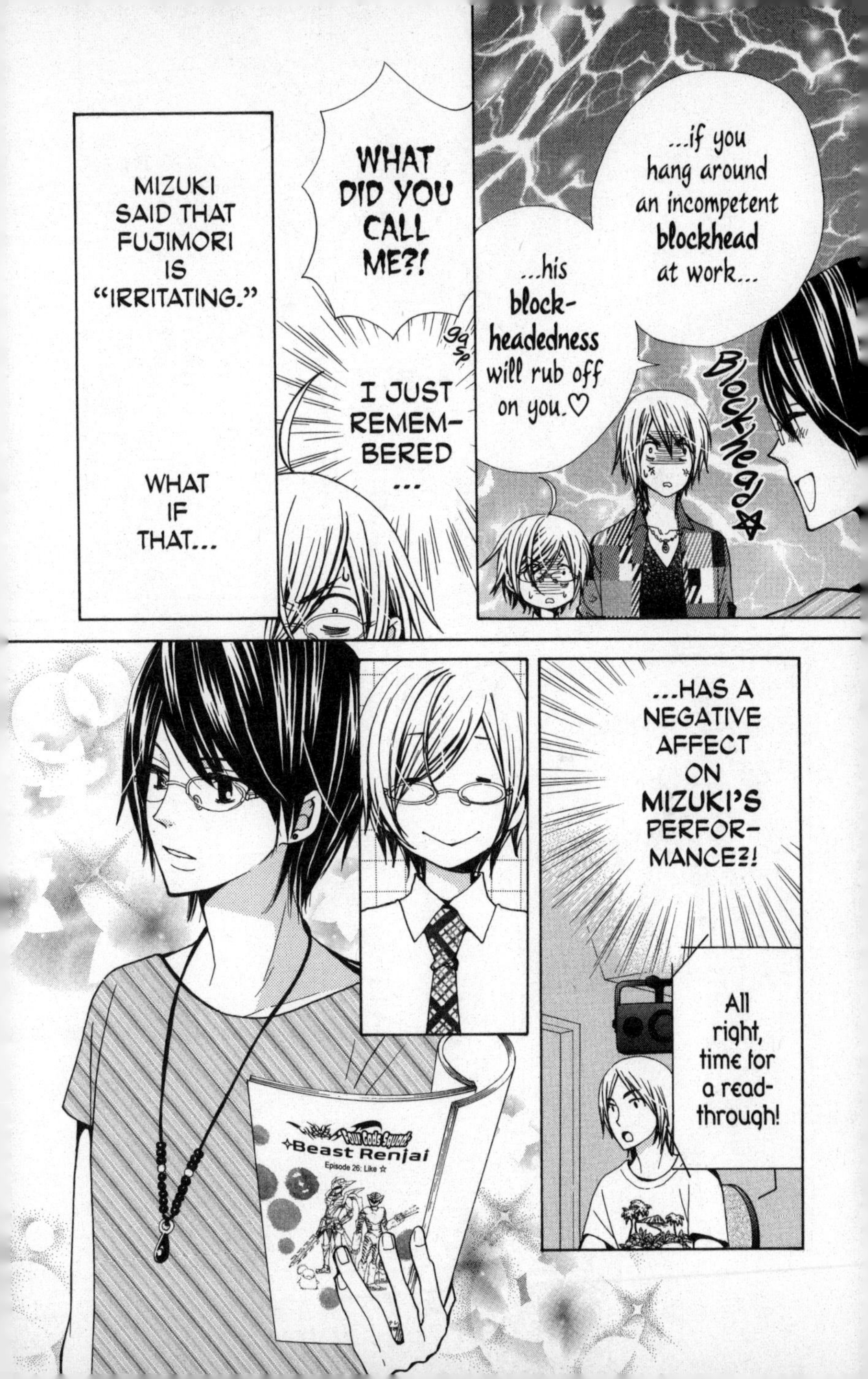
...if you hang around an incompetent blockhead at work...
...his block-headedness will rub off on you.♡
Blockhead☆
gasp
WHAT DID YOU CALL ME?!
I JUST REMEMBERED...
MIZUKI SAID THAT FUJIMORI IS "IRRITATING."
WHAT IF THAT...
...HAS A NEGATIVE AFFECT ON MIZUKI'S PERFORMANCE?!
All right, time for a read-through!
Four Gods Squad
Beast Renjai
Episode 26: Like ☆

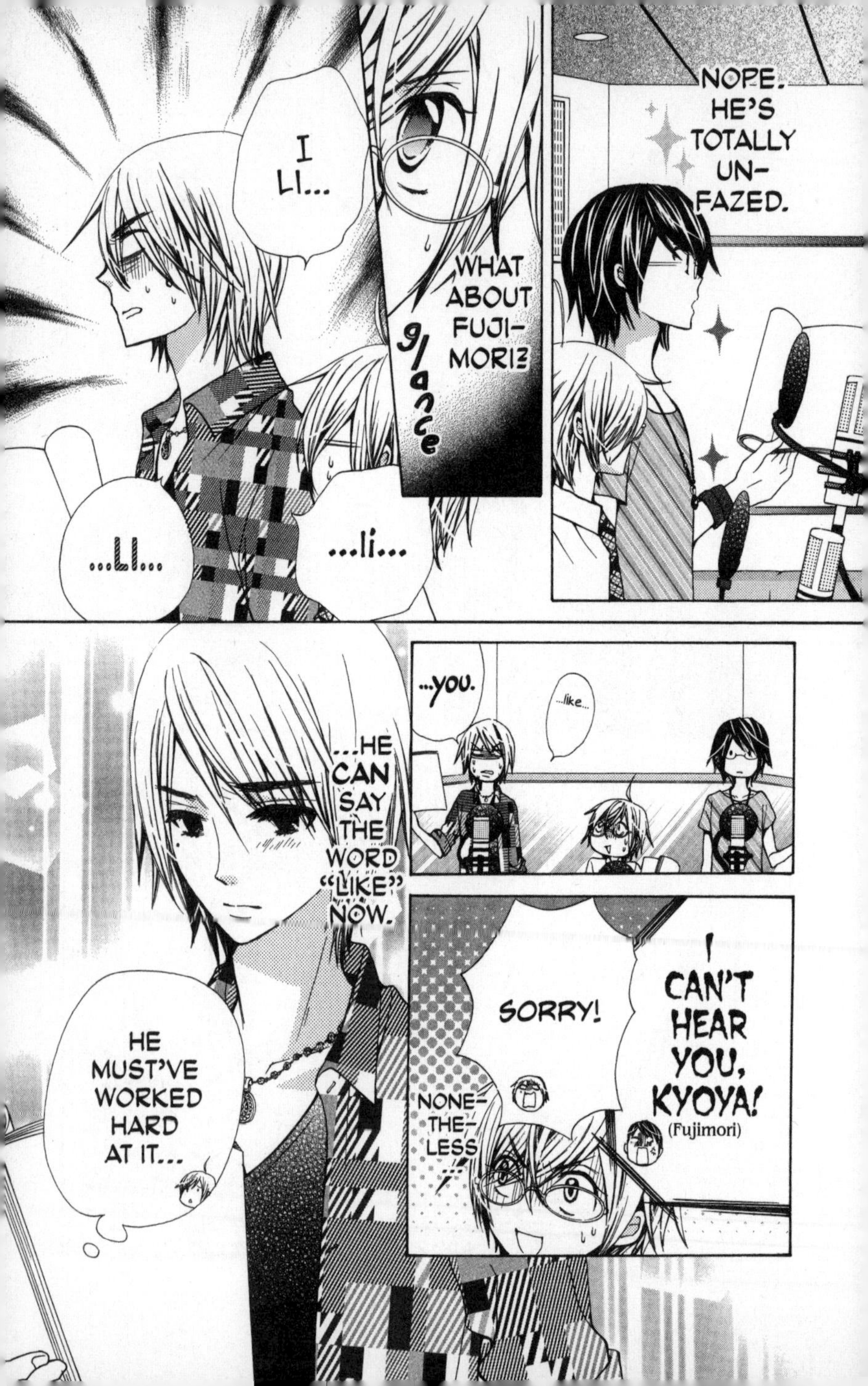

NOPE. HE'S TOTALLY UN-FAZED.
WHAT ABOUT FUJIMORI?
glance
I LI...
...li...
...LI...
...like...
...you.
I CAN'T HEAR YOU, KYOYA!
(Fujimori)
SORRY!
NONE-THE-LESS...
...HE CAN SAY THE WORD "LIKE" NOW.
HE MUST'VE WORKED HARD AT IT...

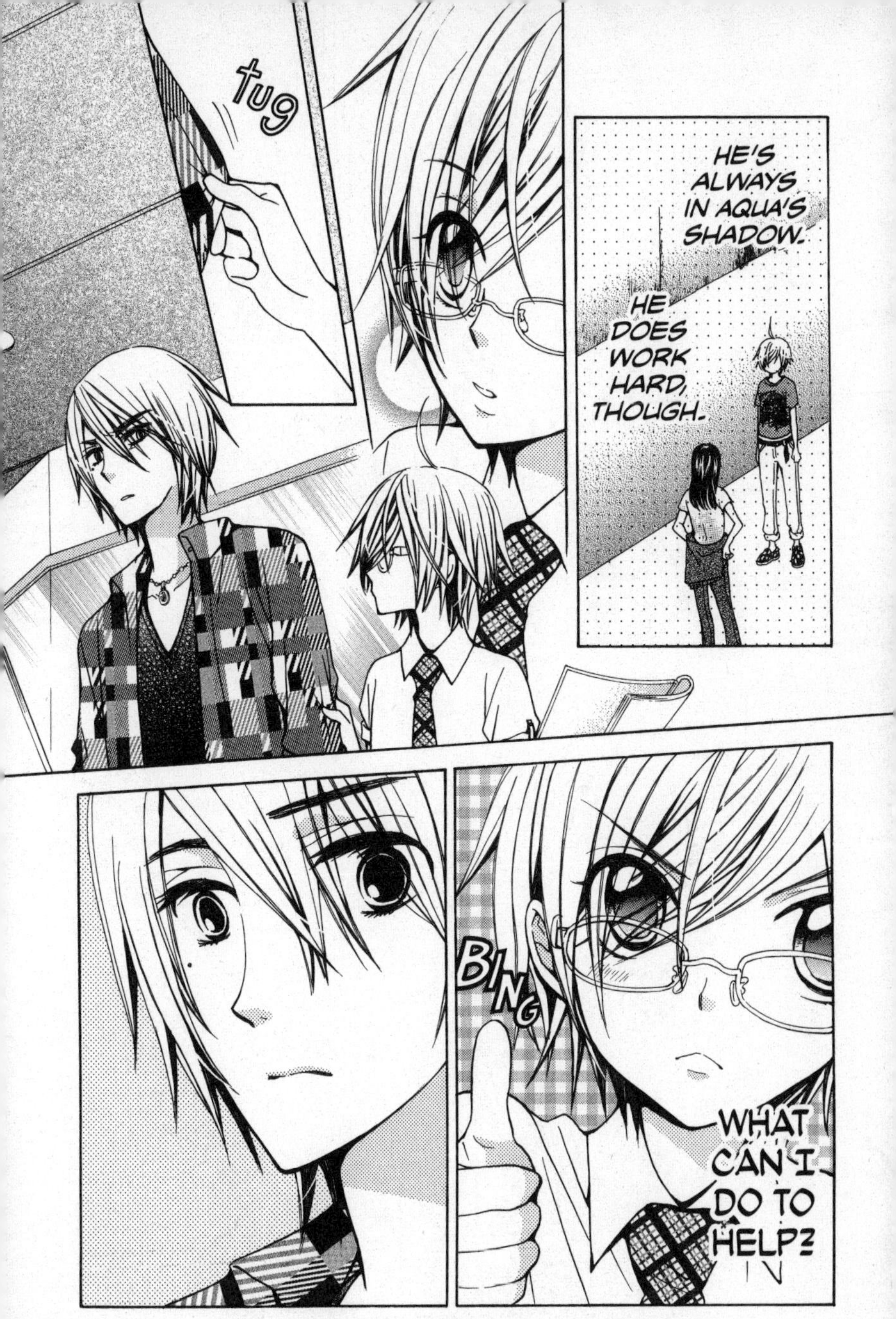
HE'S ALWAYS IN AQUA'S SHADOW.
HE DOES WORK HARD, THOUGH.
tug
BING
WHAT CAN I DO TO HELP?

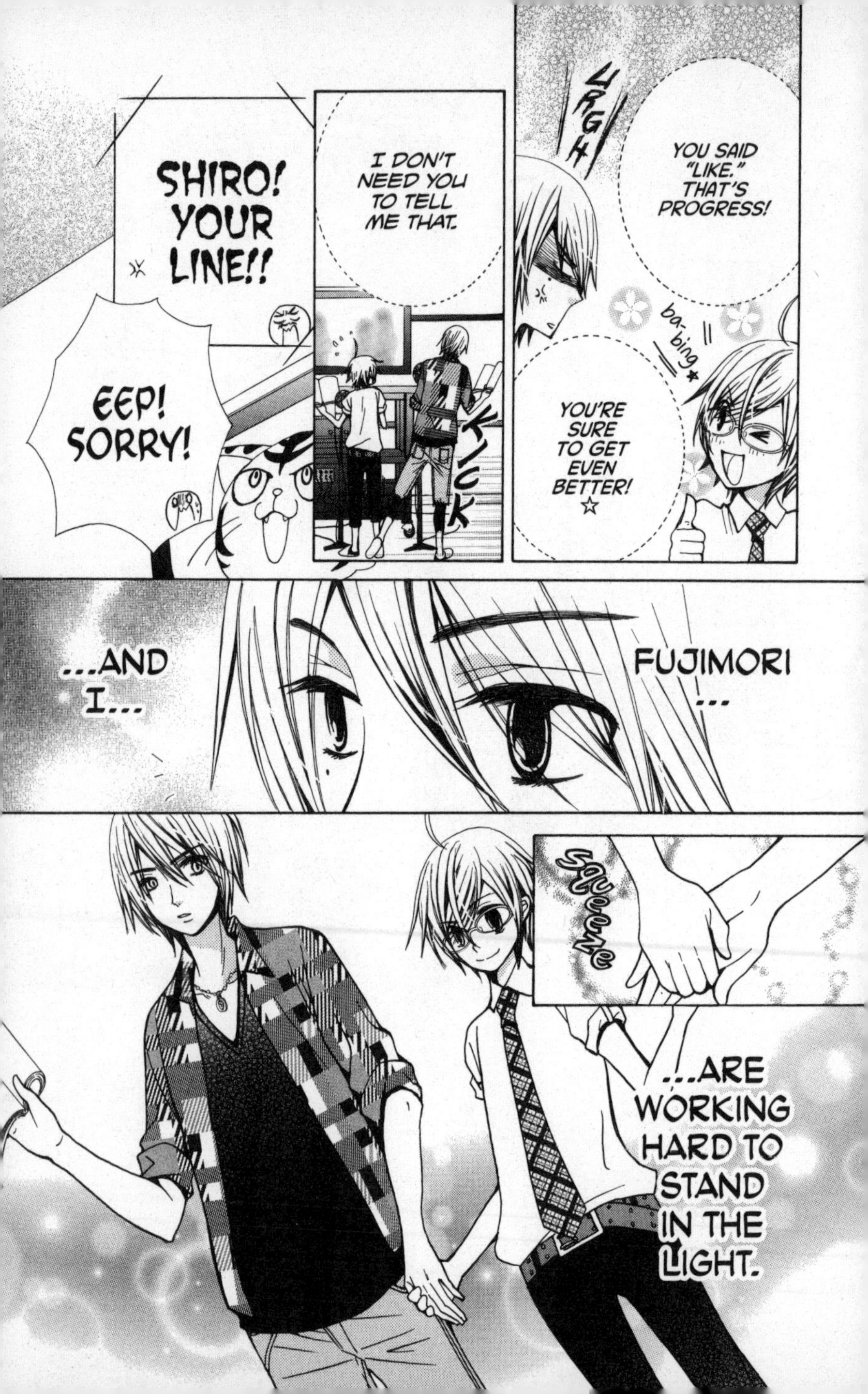
URGH
YOU SAID "LIKE." THAT'S PROGRESS!
ba-bing ★
YOU'RE SURE TO GET EVEN BETTER! ☆
I DON'T NEED YOU TO TELL ME THAT.
KICK
SHIRO! YOUR LINE!!
EEP! SORRY!
FUJIMORI ...
...AND I...
squeeze
...ARE WORKING HARD TO STAND IN THE LIGHT.

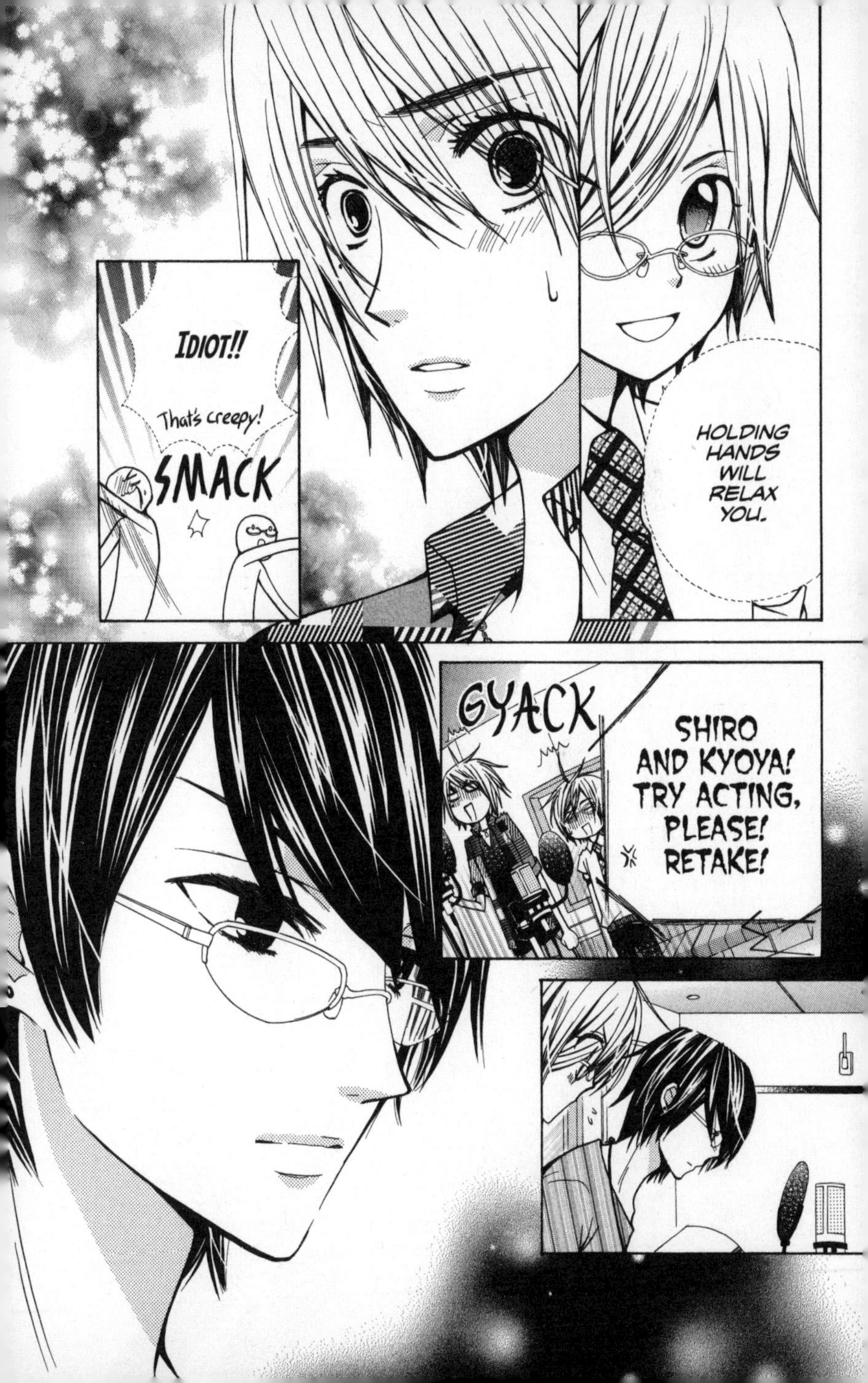
HOLDING HANDS WILL RELAX YOU.
IDIOT!!
That's creepy!
SMACK
SHIRO AND KYOYA! TRY ACTING, PLEASE! RETAKE!
GYACK

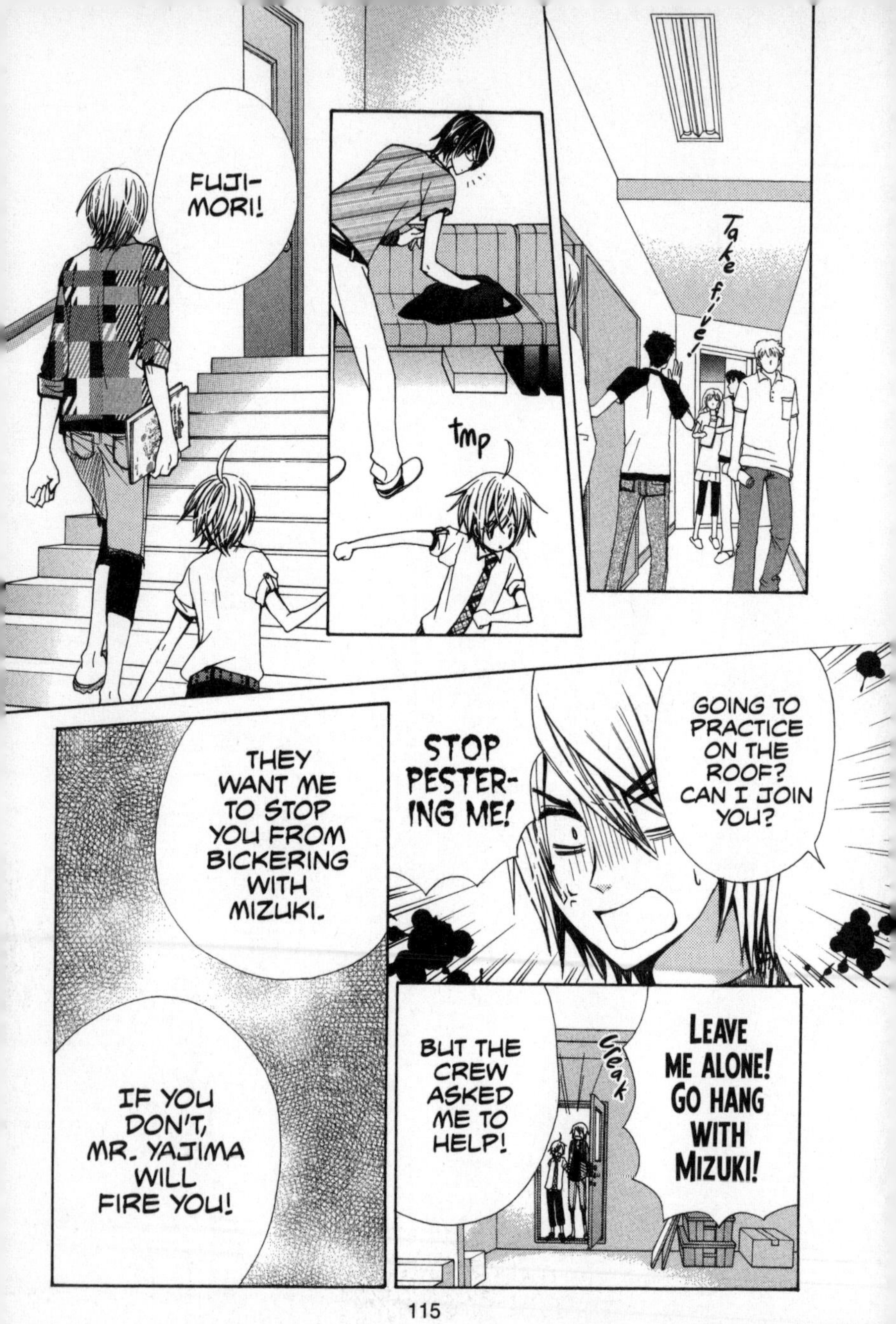
Take five!
tmp
FUJI-MORI!
GOING TO PRACTICE ON THE ROOF? CAN I JOIN YOU?
STOP PESTER-ING ME!
LEAVE ME ALONE! GO HANG WITH MIZUKI!
Creak
BUT THE CREW ASKED ME TO HELP!
THEY WANT ME TO STOP YOU FROM BICKERING WITH MIZUKI.
IF YOU DON'T, MR. YAJIMA WILL FIRE YOU!

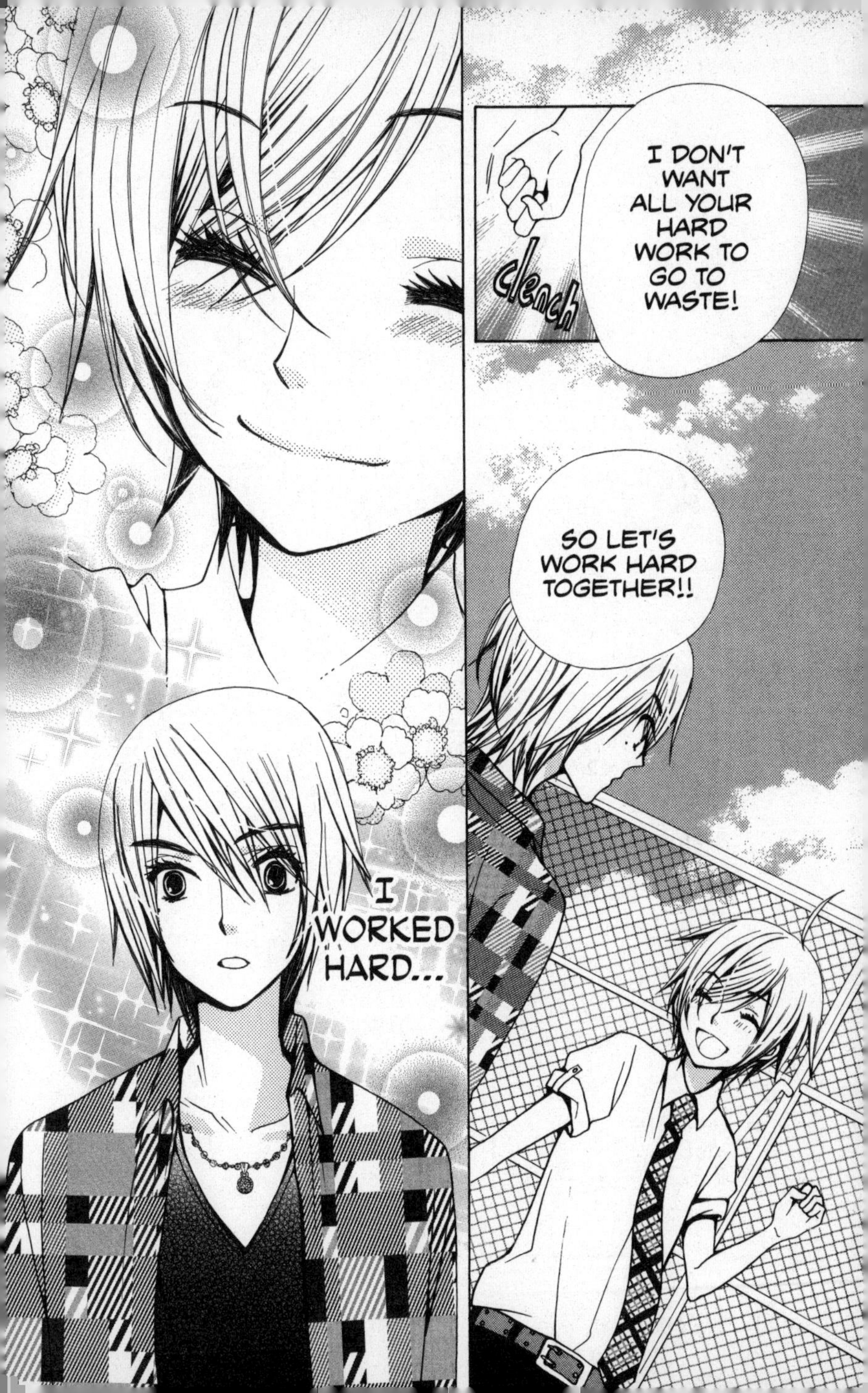
I DON'T WANT ALL YOUR HARD WORK TO GO TO WASTE!
clench
SO LET'S WORK HARD TOGETHER!!
I WORKED HARD...

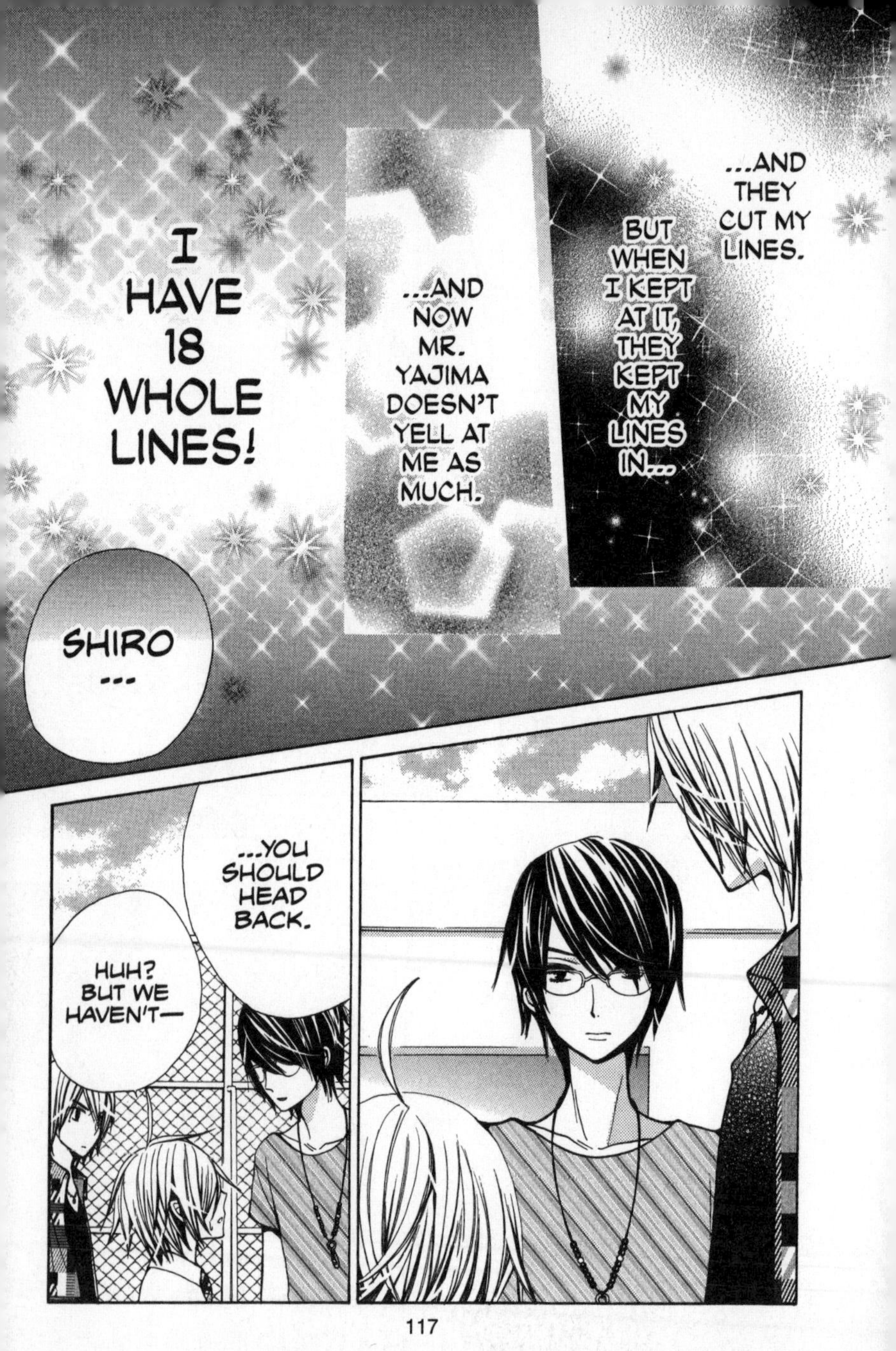
...AND THEY CUT MY LINES.
BUT WHEN I KEPT AT IT, THEY KEPT MY LINES IN...
...AND NOW MR. YAJIMA DOESN'T YELL AT ME AS MUCH.
I HAVE 18 WHOLE LINES!
SHIRO...
...YOU SHOULD HEAD BACK.
HUH? BUT WE HAVEN'T—

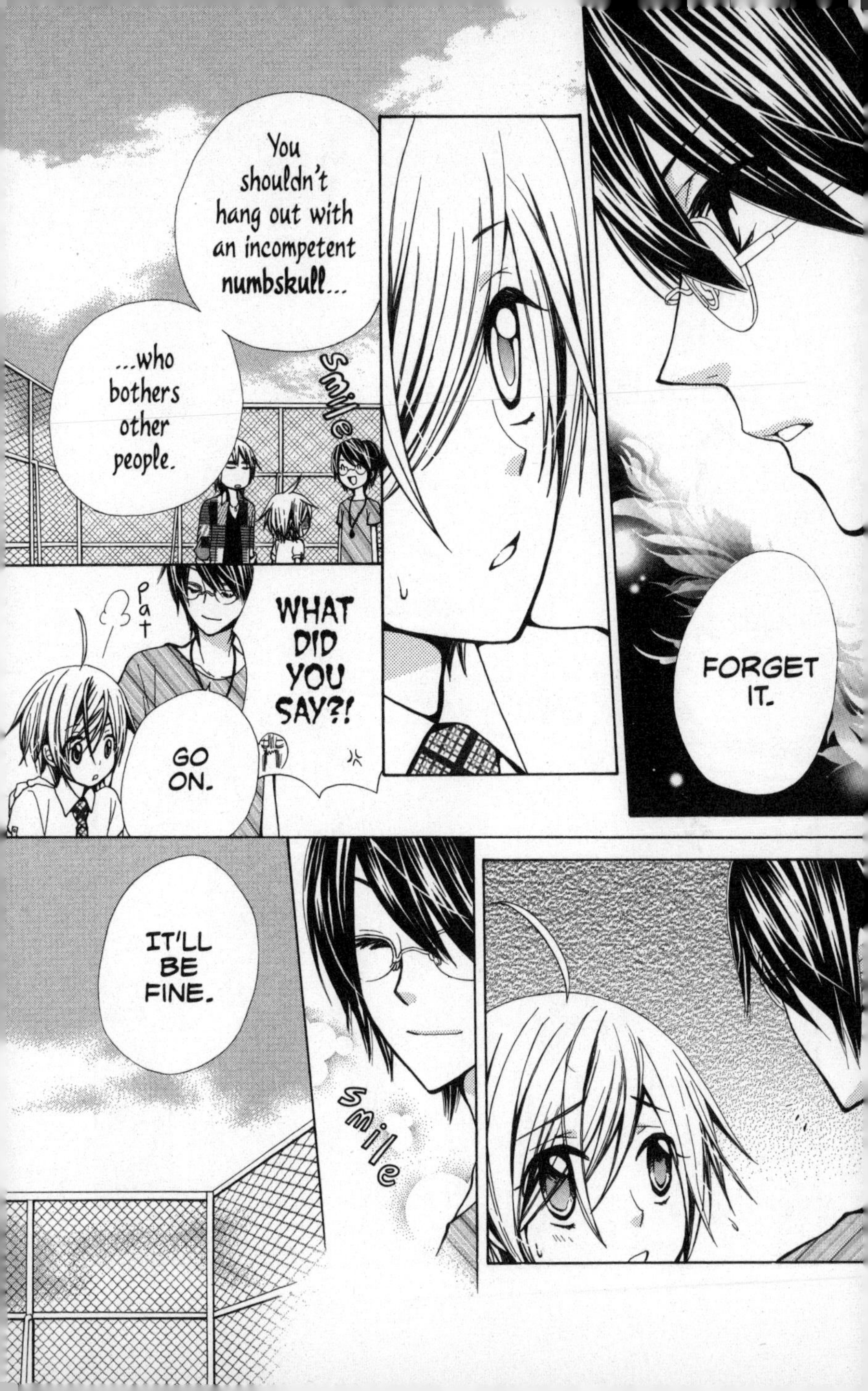
FORGET IT.
You shouldn't hang out with an incompetent numbskull...
...who bothers other people.
Smile
WHAT DID YOU SAY?!
Pat
GO ON.
IT'LL BE FINE.
Smile

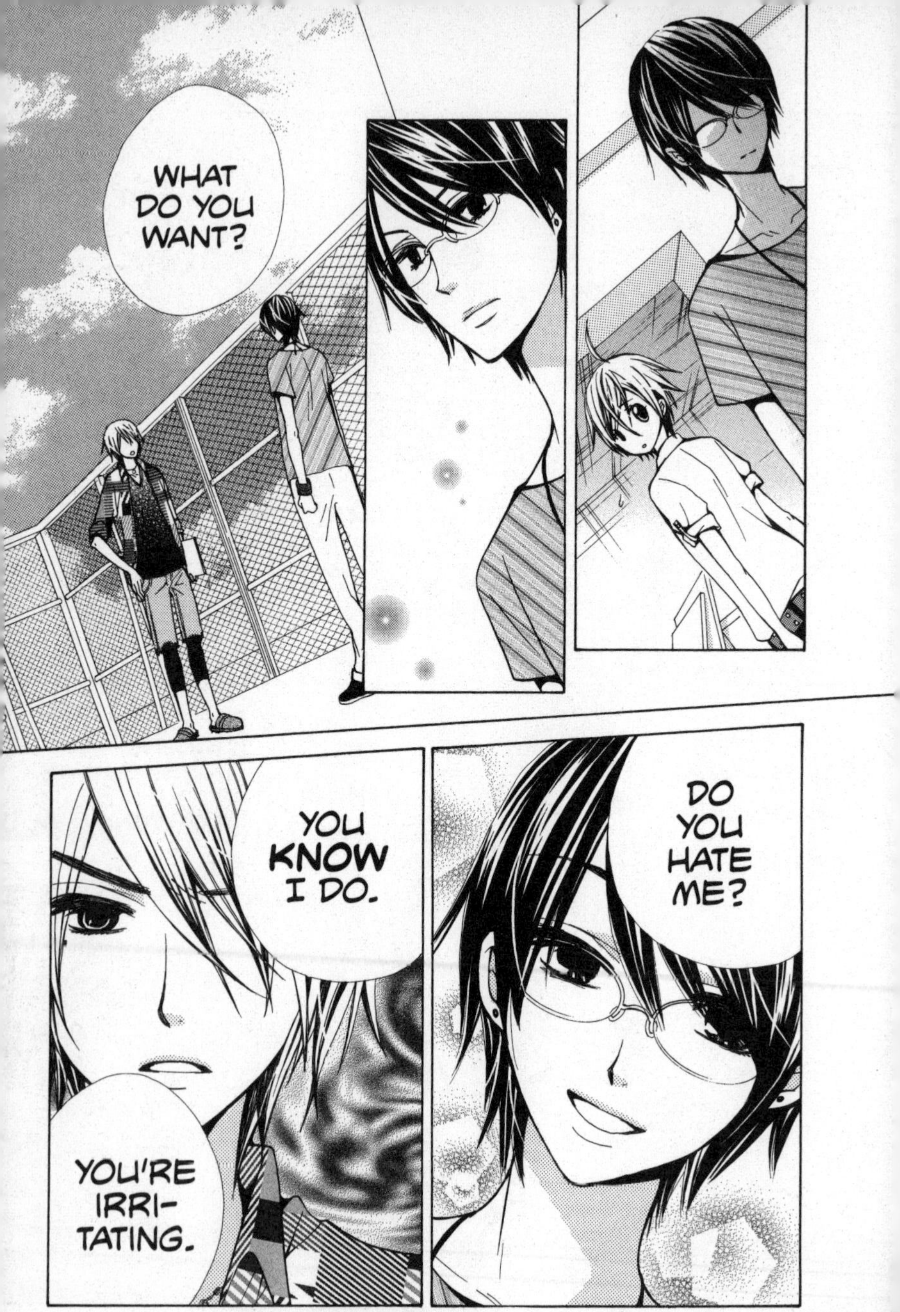
WHAT DO YOU WANT?
DO YOU HATE ME?
YOU KNOW I DO.
YOU'RE IRRI-TATING.

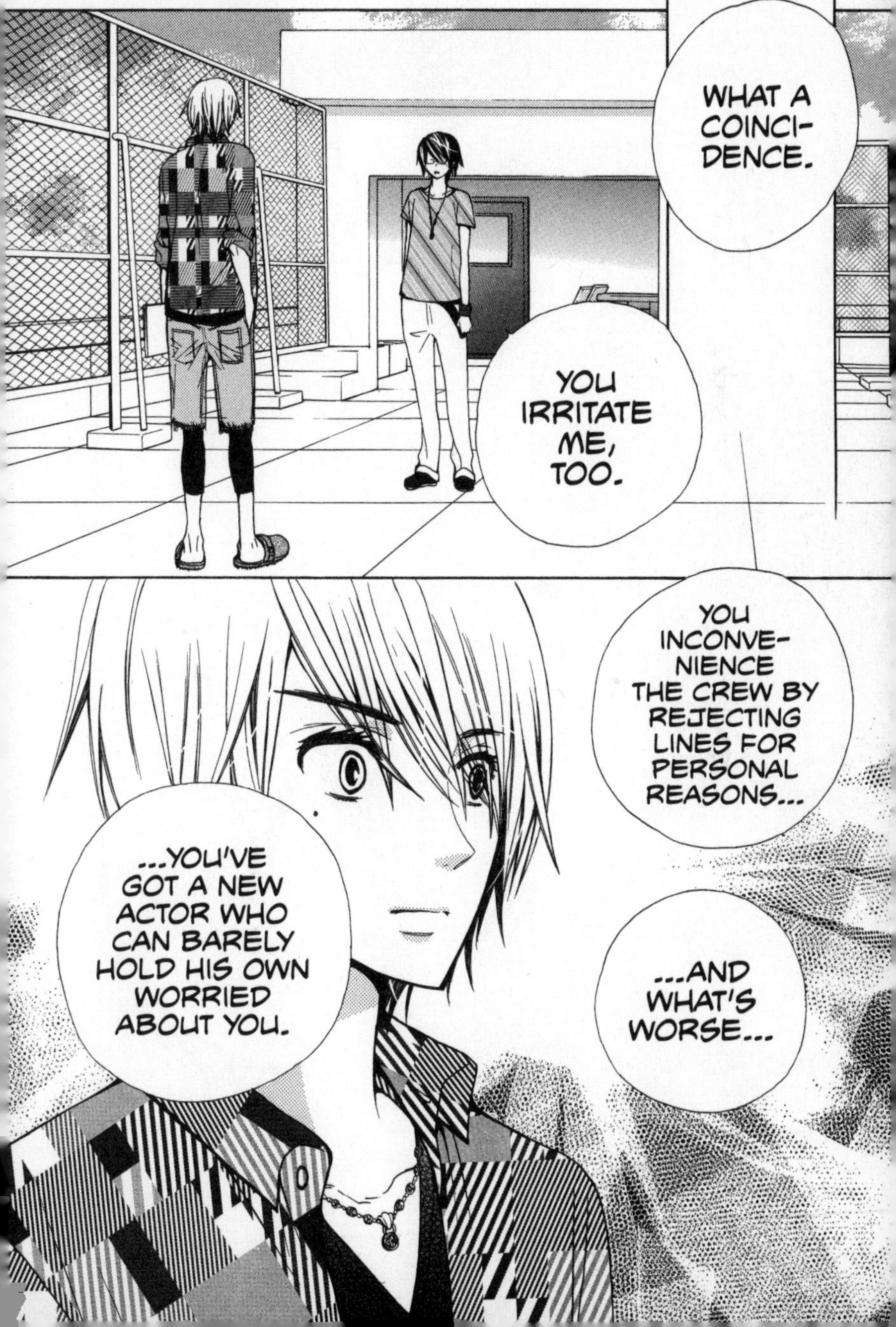
WHAT A COINCI-DENCE.
YOU IRRITATE ME, TOO.
YOU INCONVE-NIENCE THE CREW BY REJECTING LINES FOR PERSONAL REASONS...
...AND WHAT'S WORSE...
...YOU'VE GOT A NEW ACTOR WHO CAN BARELY HOLD HIS OWN WORRIED ABOUT YOU.

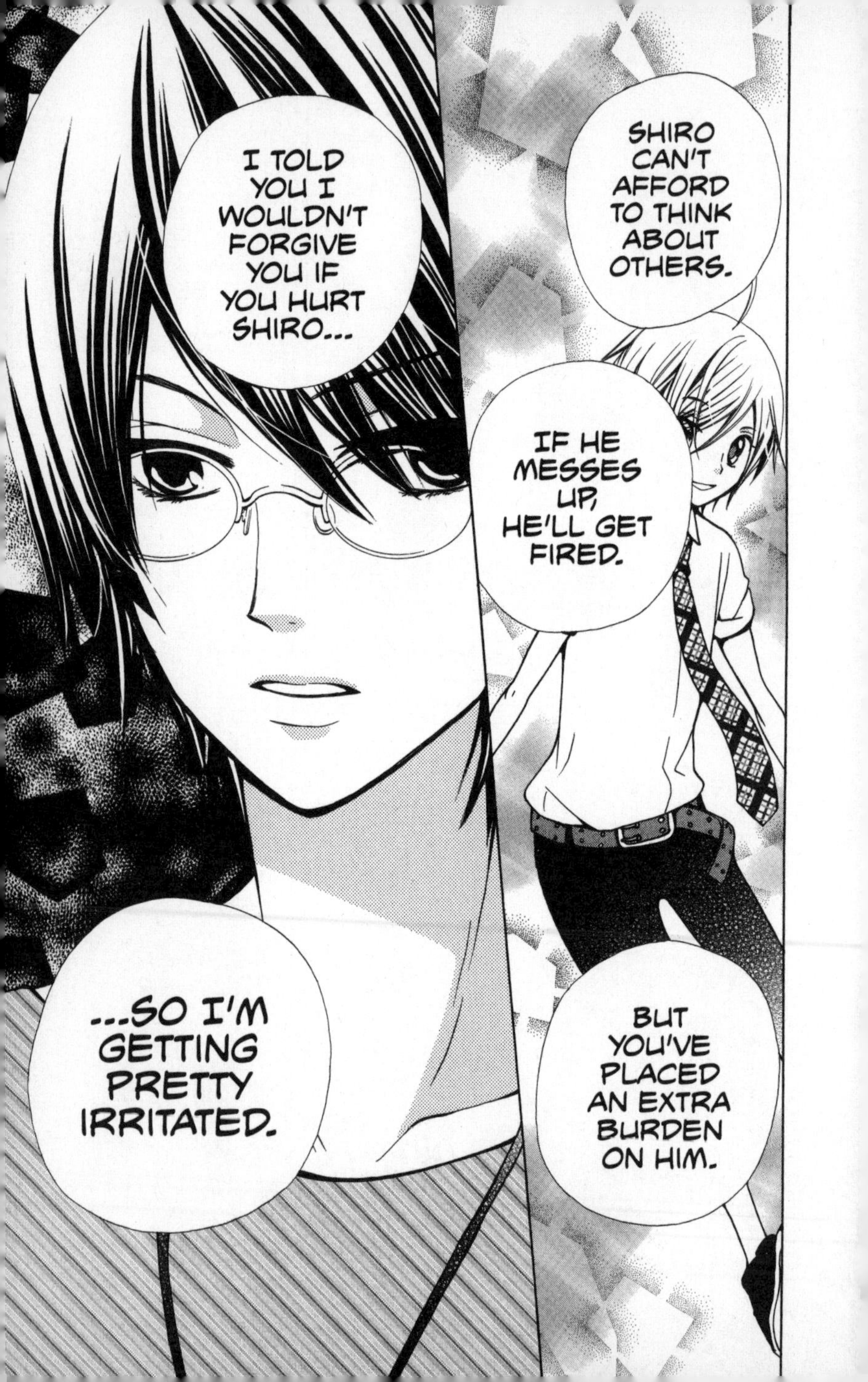
SHIRO CAN'T AFFORD TO THINK ABOUT OTHERS.
IF HE MESSES UP, HE'LL GET FIRED.
BUT YOU'VE PLACED AN EXTRA BURDEN ON HIM.
I TOLD YOU I WOULDN'T FORGIVE YOU IF YOU HURT SHIRO...
...SO I'M GETTING PRETTY IRRITATED.

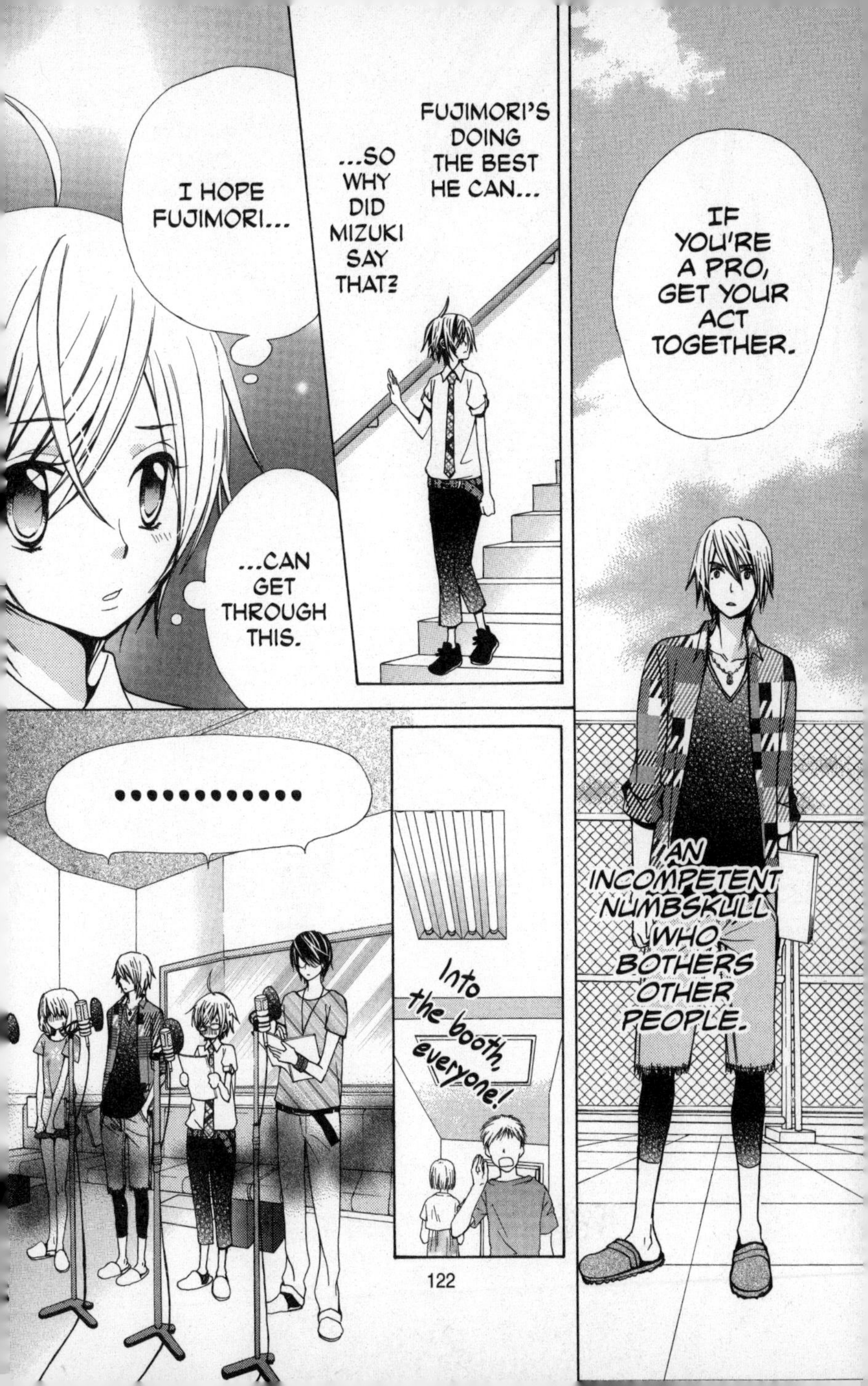
IF YOU'RE A PRO, GET YOUR ACT TOGETHER.
AN INCOMPETENT NUMBSKULL WHO BOTHERS OTHER PEOPLE.
FUJIMORI'S DOING THE BEST HE CAN...
...SO WHY DID MIZUKI SAY THAT?
I HOPE FUJIMORI...
...CAN GET THROUGH THIS.
Into the booth, everyone!
....

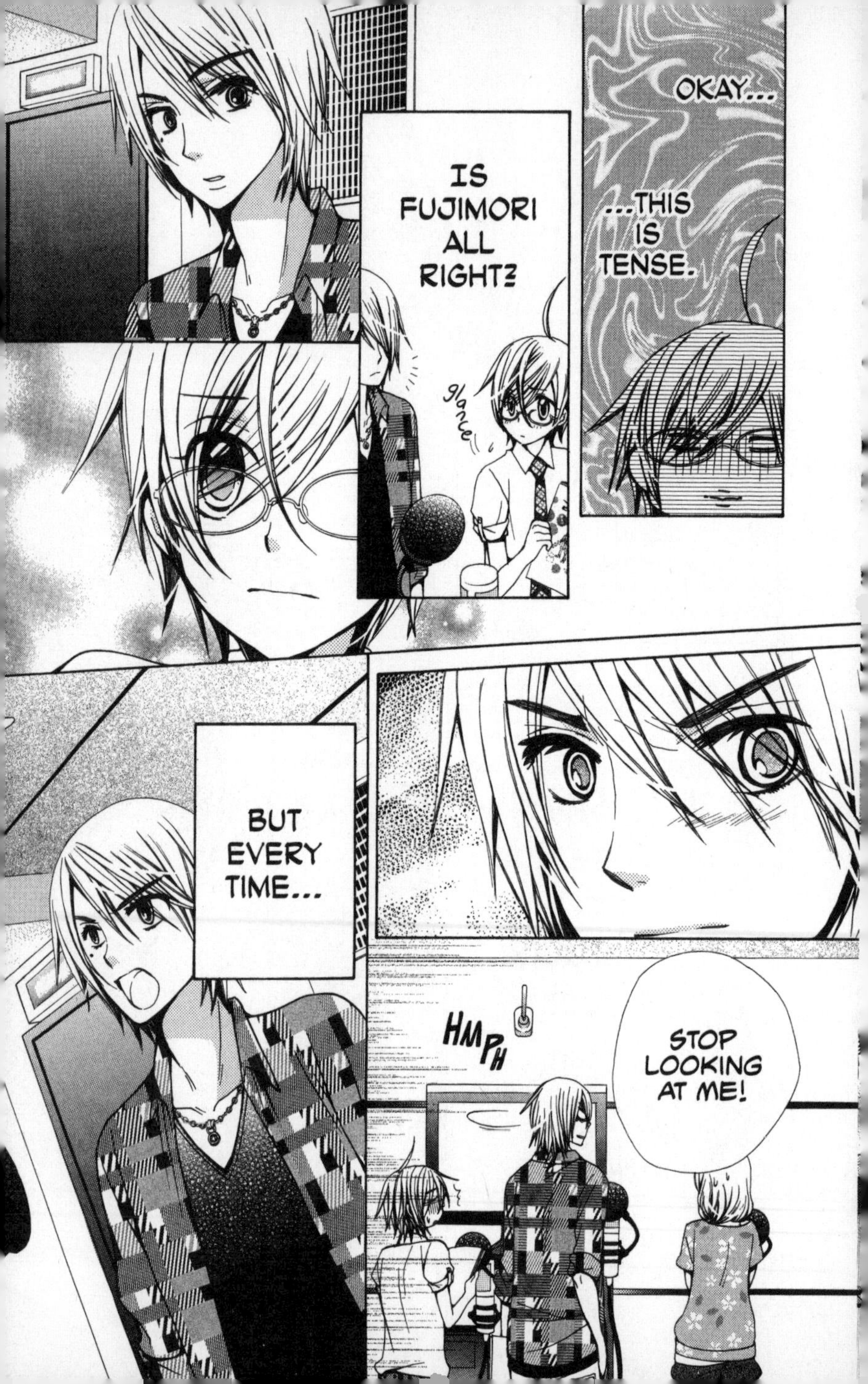
OKAY...
...THIS IS TENSE.
IS FUJIMORI ALL RIGHT?
glance
STOP LOOKING AT ME!
HMPH
BUT EVERY TIME...

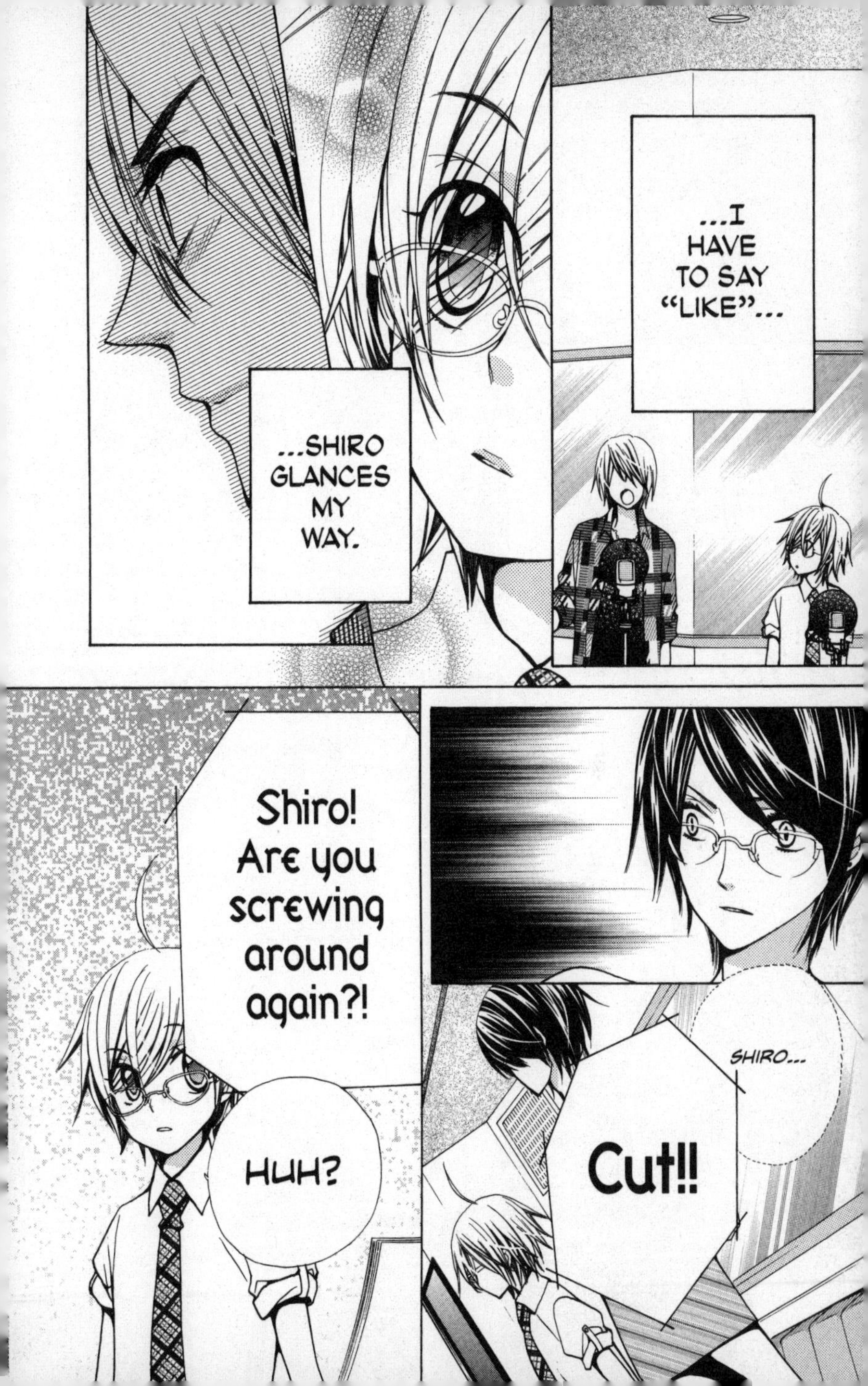
...I HAVE TO SAY "LIKE"...
...SHIRO GLANCES MY WAY.
SHIRO...
Cut!!
Shiro! Are you screwing around again?!
HUH?

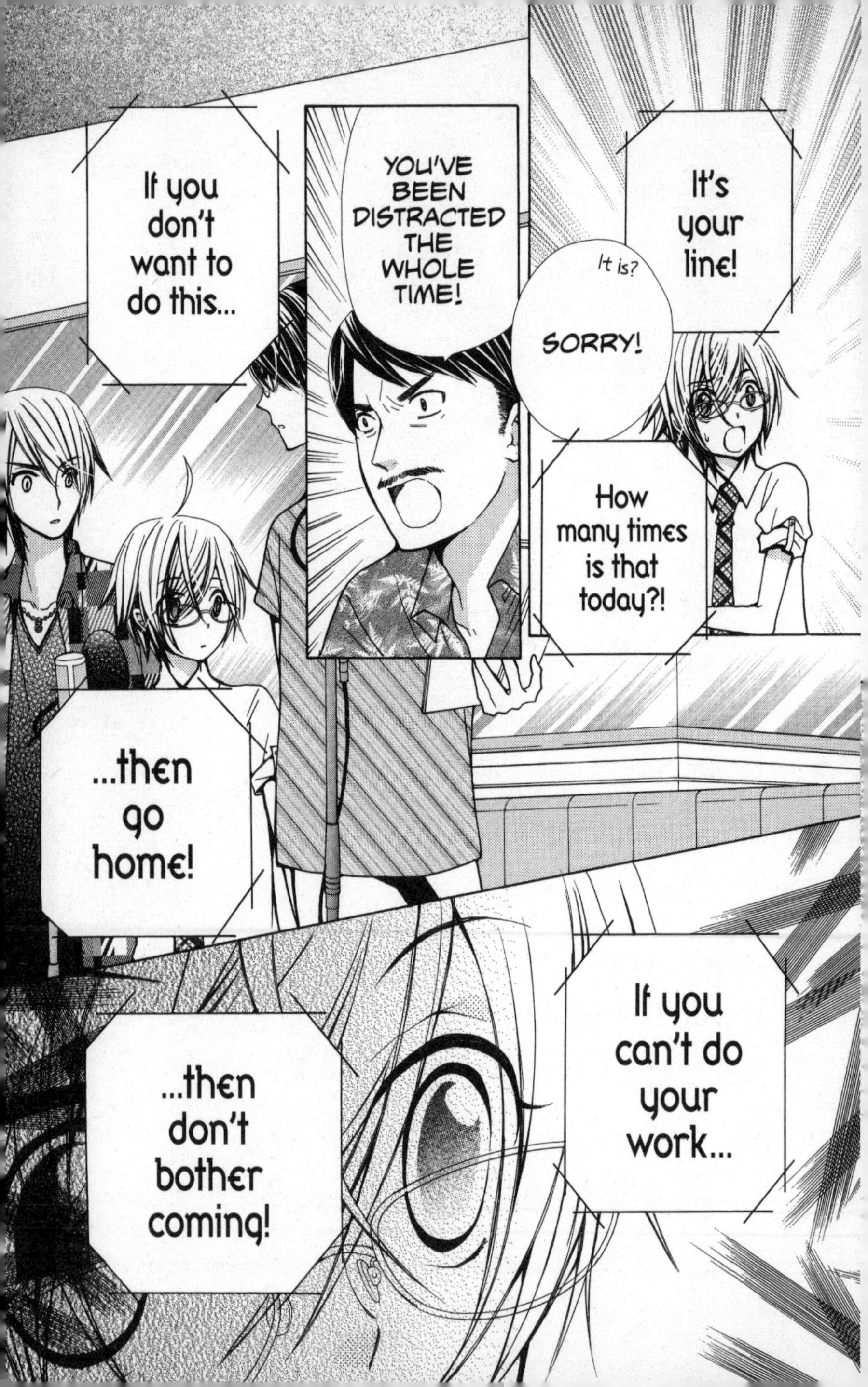
It's your line!
It is?
SORRY!
How many times is that today?!
YOU'VE BEEN DISTRACTED THE WHOLE TIME!
If you don't want to do this...
...then go home!
If you can't do your work...
...then don't bother coming!

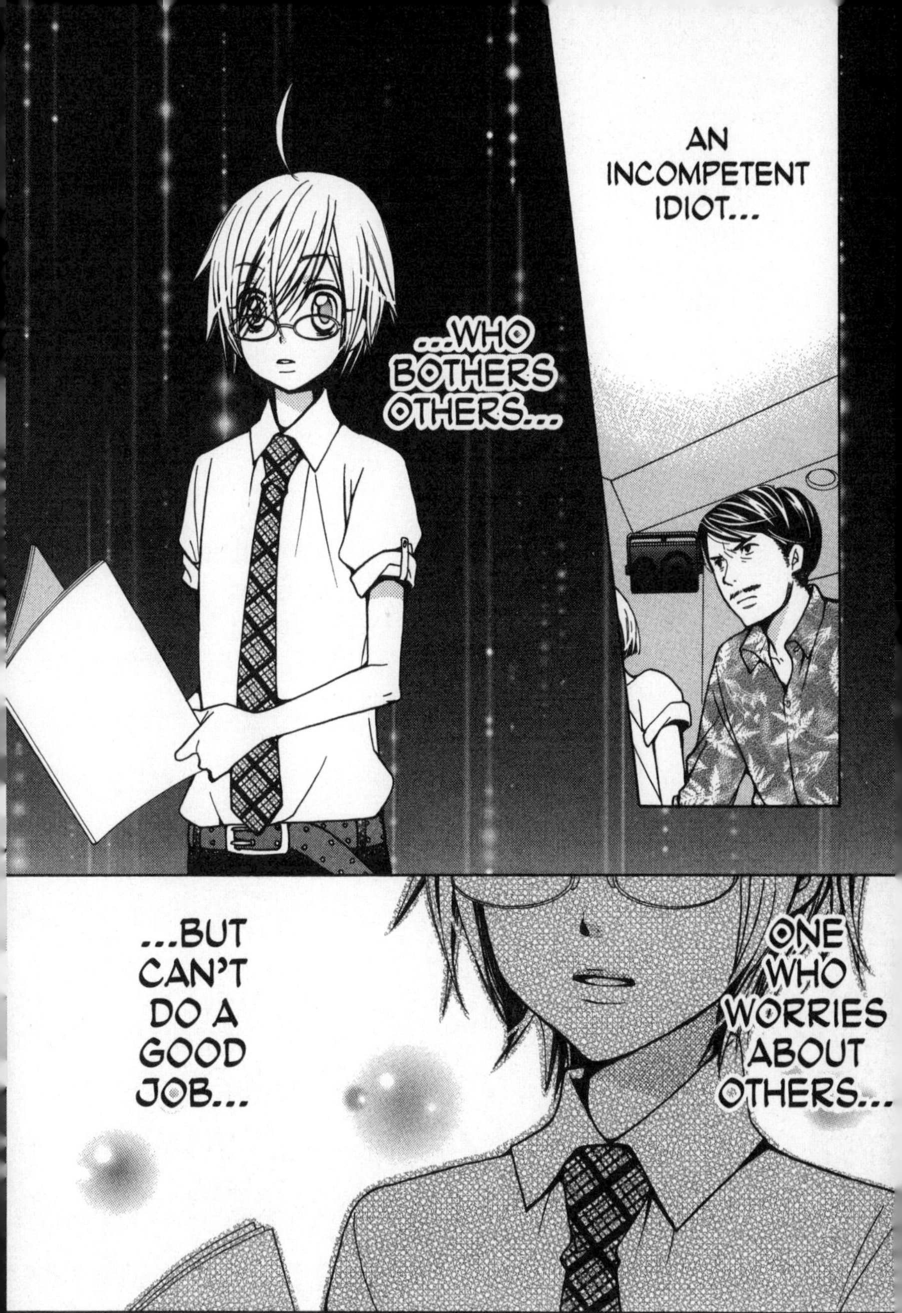
AN INCOMPETENT IDIOT...
...WHO BOTHERS OTHERS...
ONE WHO WORRIES ABOUT OTHERS...
...BUT CAN'T DO A GOOD JOB...

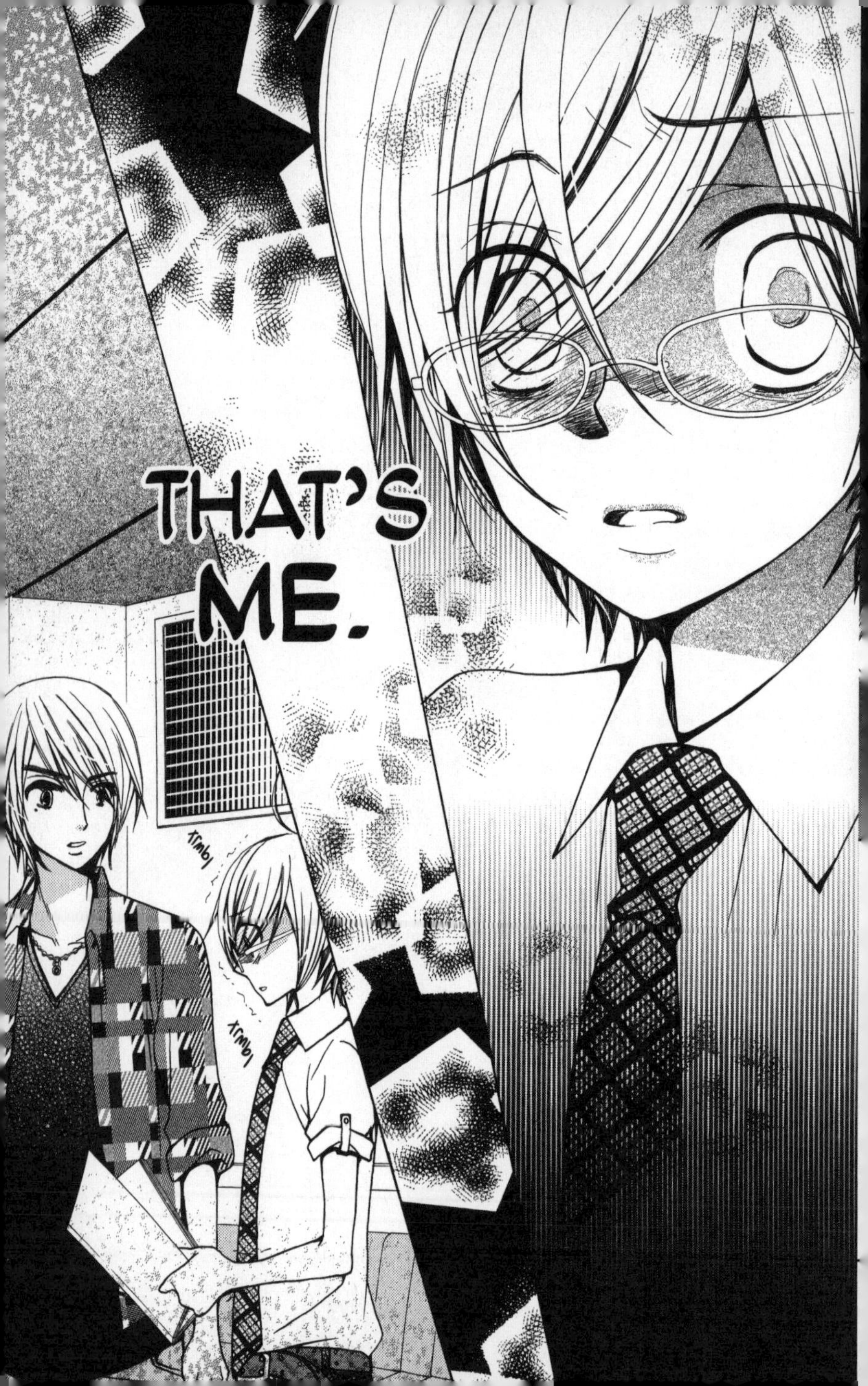
THAT'S ME.
trmbl
trmbl

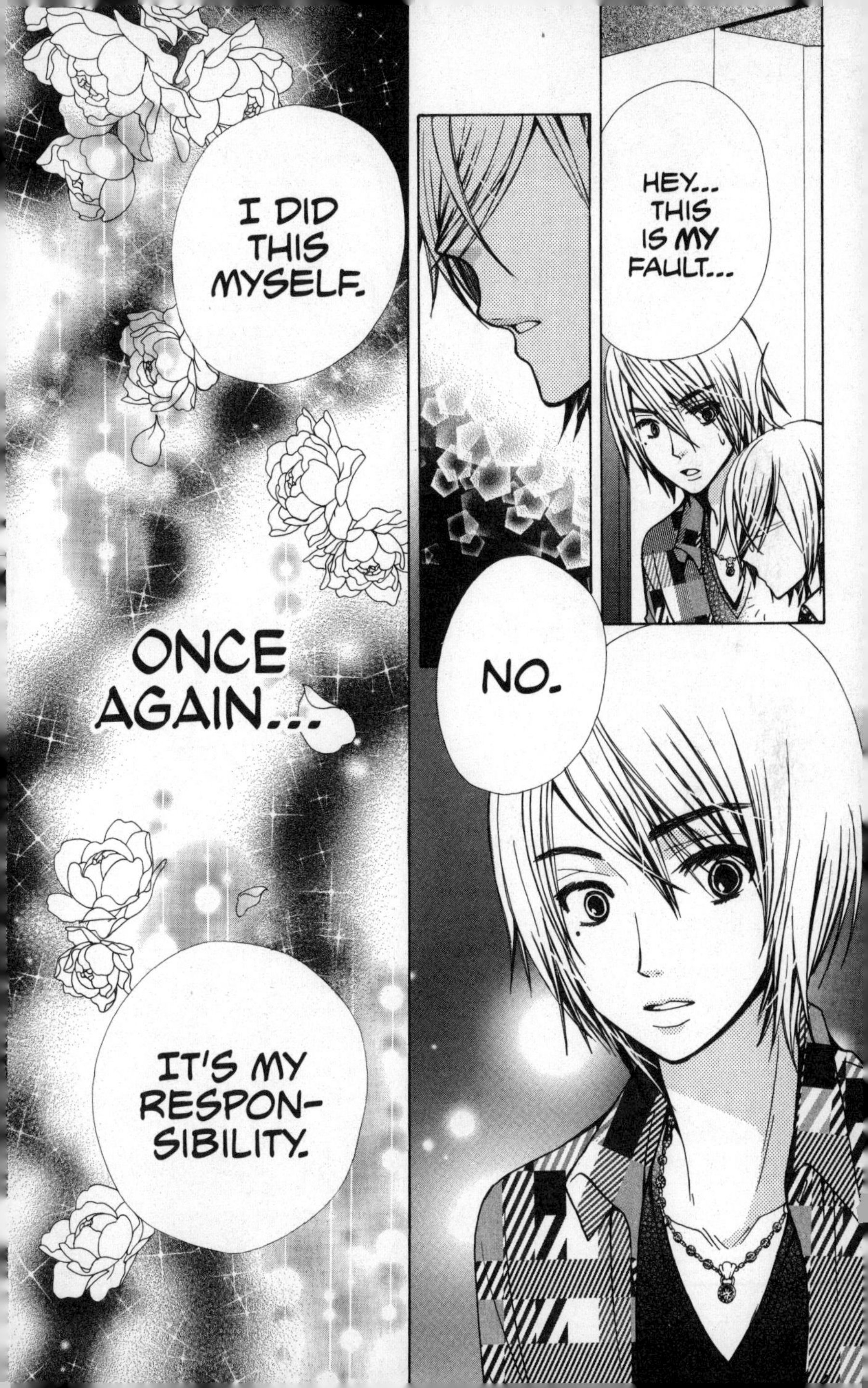
HEY... THIS IS MY FAULT...
NO.
I DID THIS MYSELF.
ONCE AGAIN...
IT'S MY RESPON- SIBILITY.

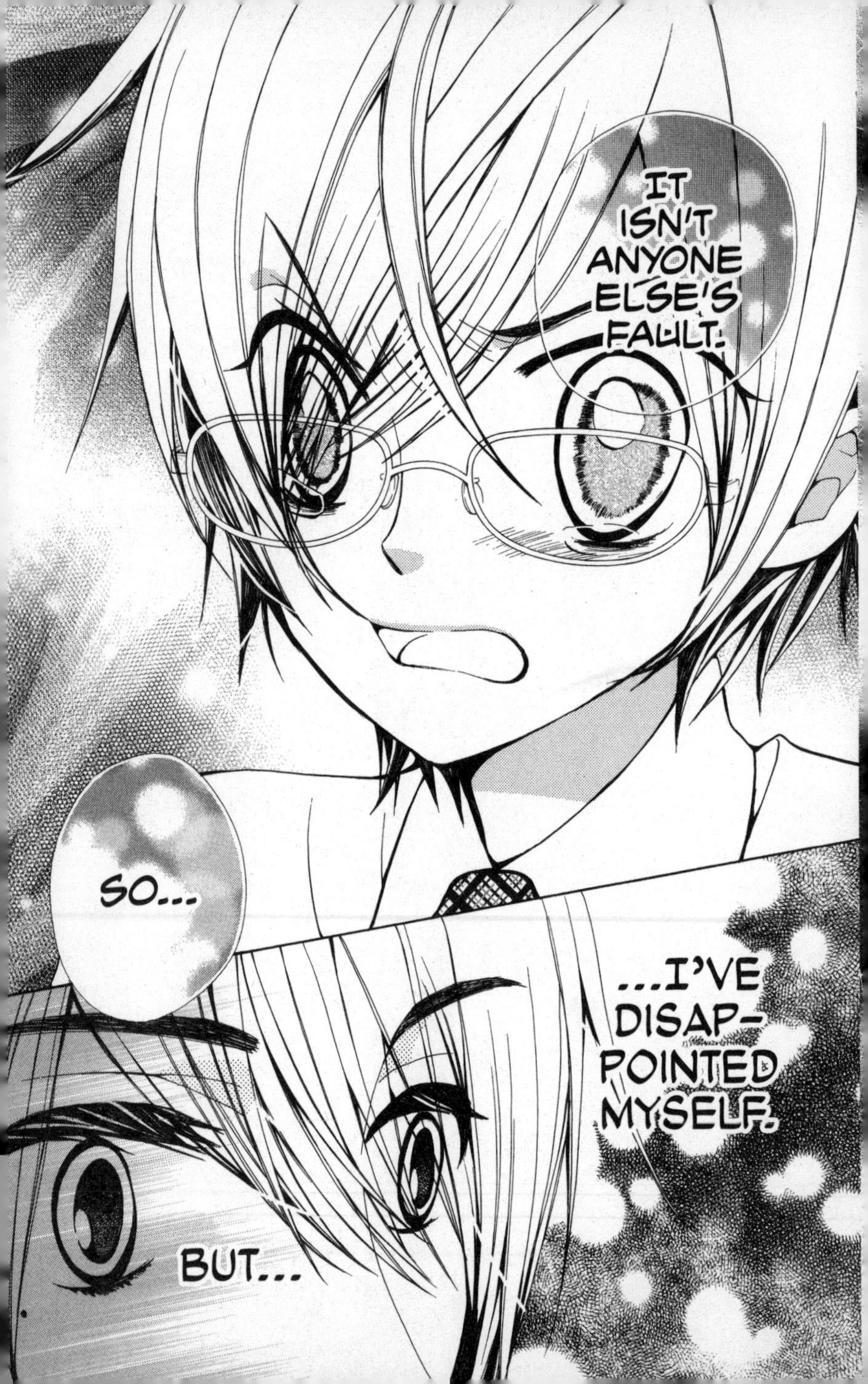
IT ISN'T ANYONE ELSE'S FAULT.
SO...
...I'VE DISAP-POINTED MYSELF.
BUT...

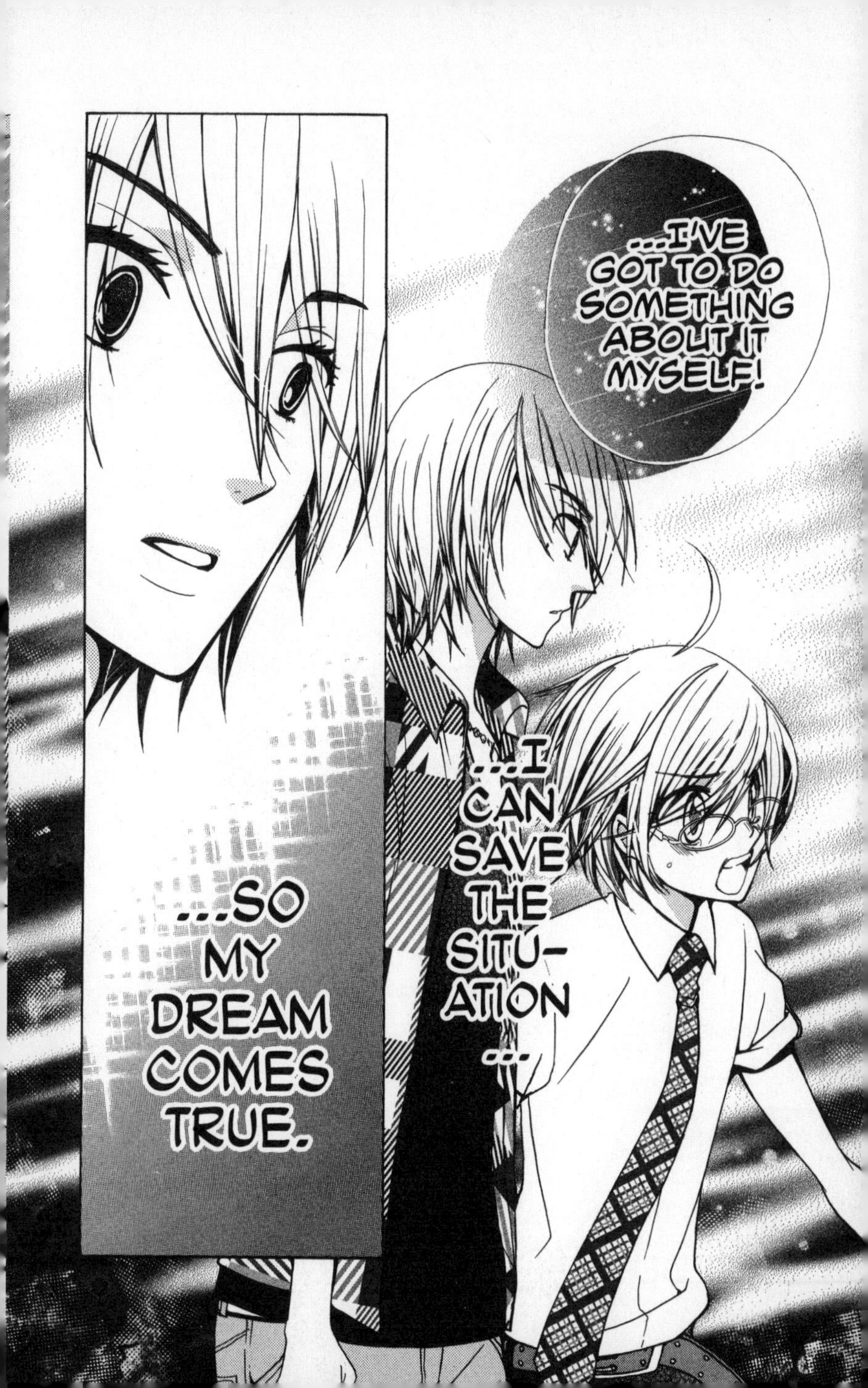
...I'VE GOT TO DO SOMETHING ABOUT IT MYSELF!
...I CAN SAVE THE SITU-ATION ...
...SO MY DREAM COMES TRUE.

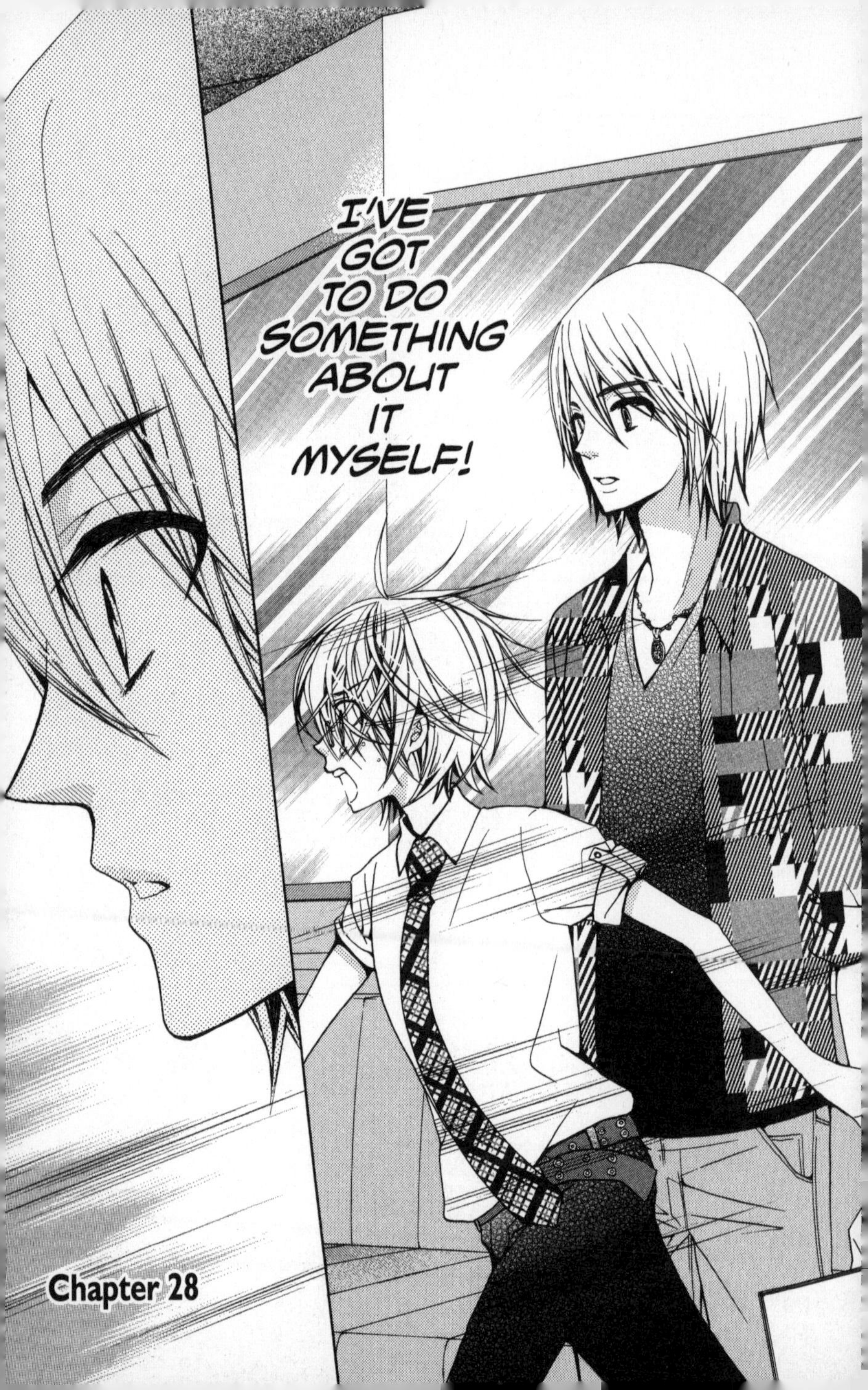
I'VE GOT TO DO SOMETHING ABOUT IT MYSELF!

Chapter 28

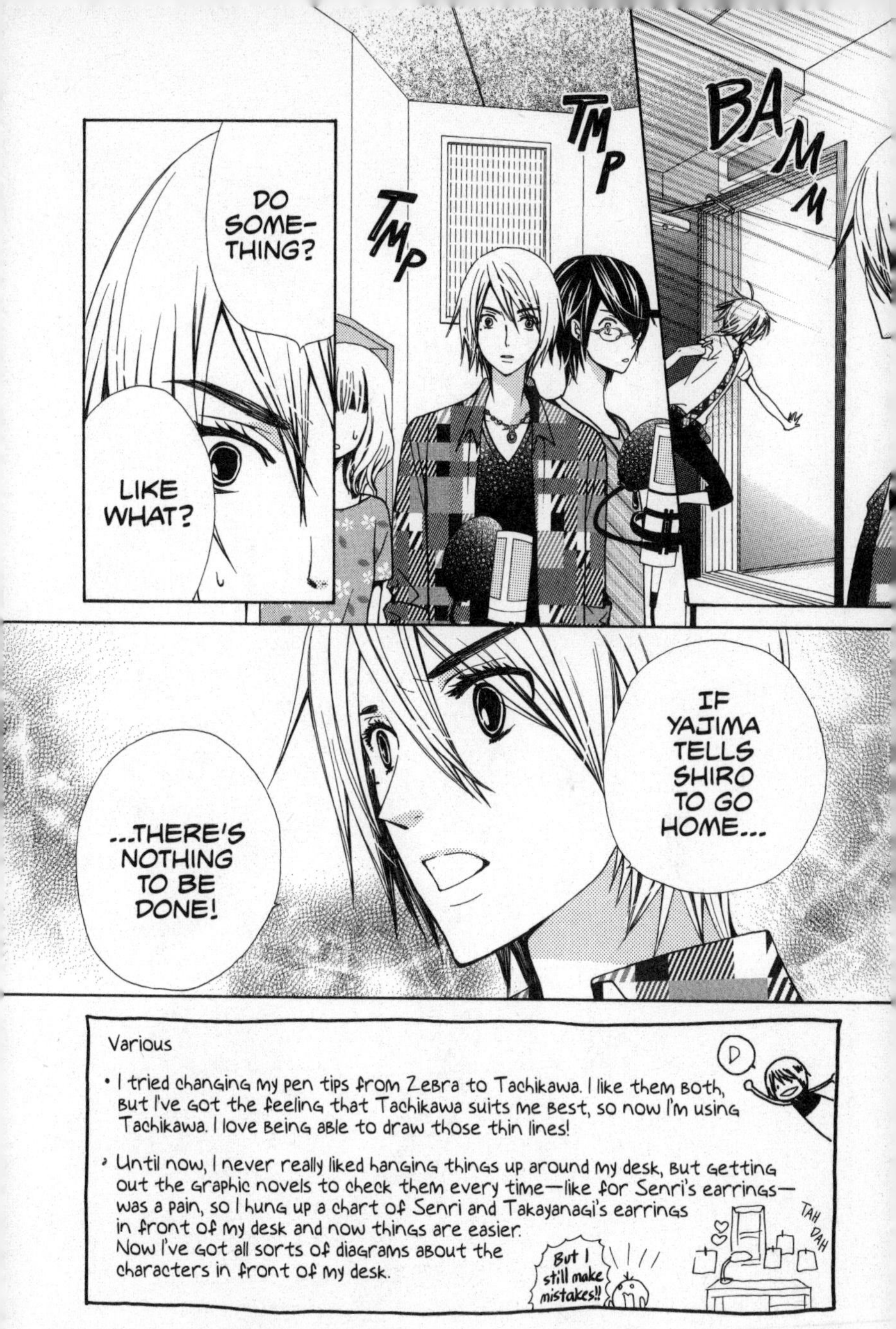
BAMM
TMP
TMP
DO SOMETHING?
LIKE WHAT?
IF YAJIMA TELLS SHIRO TO GO HOME...
...THERE'S NOTHING TO BE DONE!

Various

D

- I tried changing my pen tips from Zebra to Tachikawa. I like them both, but I've got the feeling that Tachikawa suits me best, so now I'm using Tachikawa. I love being able to draw those thin lines!
- Until now, I never really liked hanging things up around my desk, but getting out the graphic novels to check them every time—like for Senri's earrings—was a pain, so I hung up a chart of Senri and Takayanagi's earrings in front of my desk and now things are easier. Now I've got all sorts of diagrams about the characters in front of my desk.

TAH DAH

But I still make mistakes!!

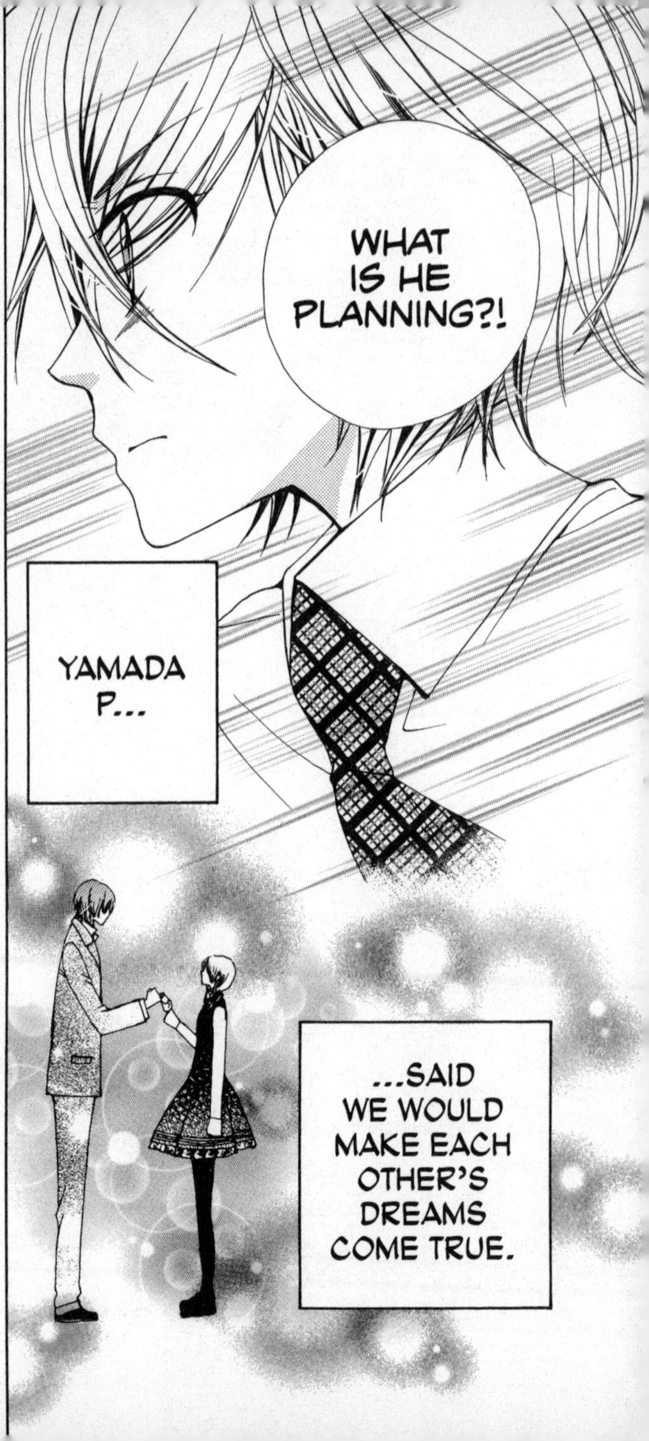
WHAT IS HE PLANNING?!
YAMADA P...
...SAID WE WOULD MAKE EACH OTHER'S DREAMS COME TRUE.

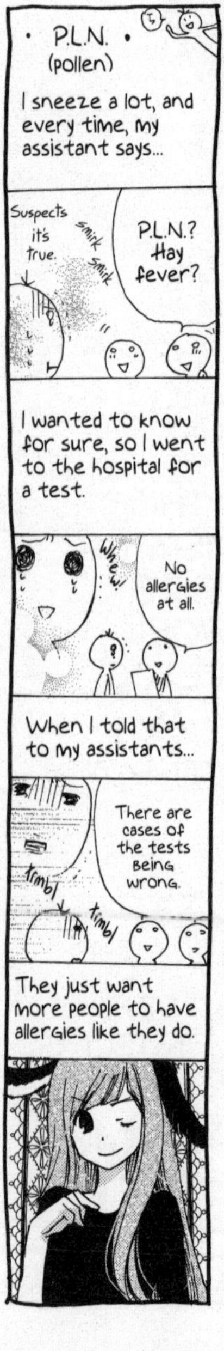
• P.L.N. •
(pollen)
I sneeze a lot, and every time, my assistant says...
P.L.N.? Hay fever?
smirk smirk
Suspects it's true.
I wanted to know for sure, so I went to the hospital for a test.
No allergies at all.
Whew!
When I told that to my assistants...
There are cases of the tests being wrong.
trimbl trimbl
They just want more people to have allergies like they do.

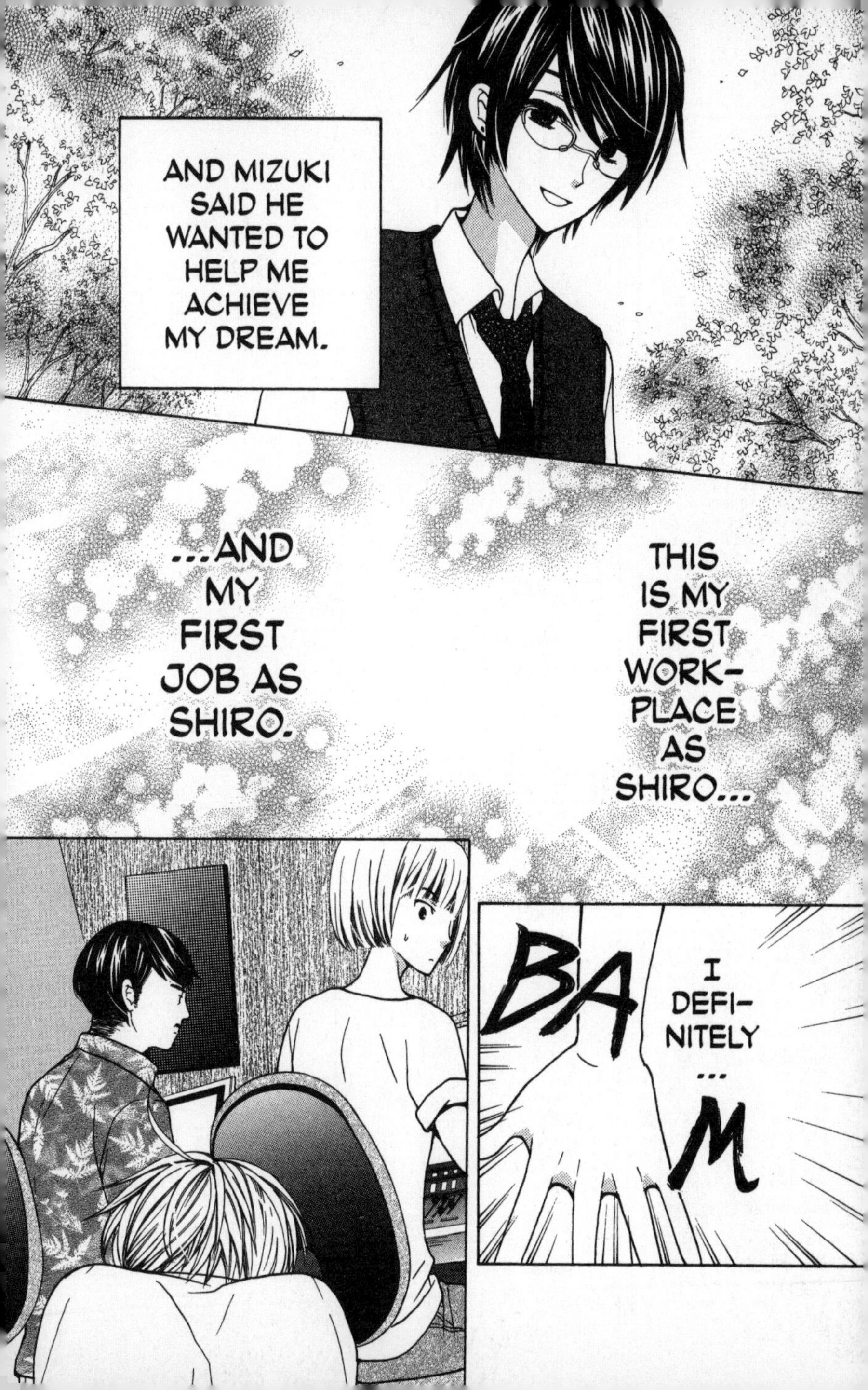
AND MIZUKI SAID HE WANTED TO HELP ME ACHIEVE MY DREAM.
THIS IS MY FIRST WORK-PLACE AS SHIRO...
...AND MY FIRST JOB AS SHIRO.
BAM
I DEFI-NITELY...

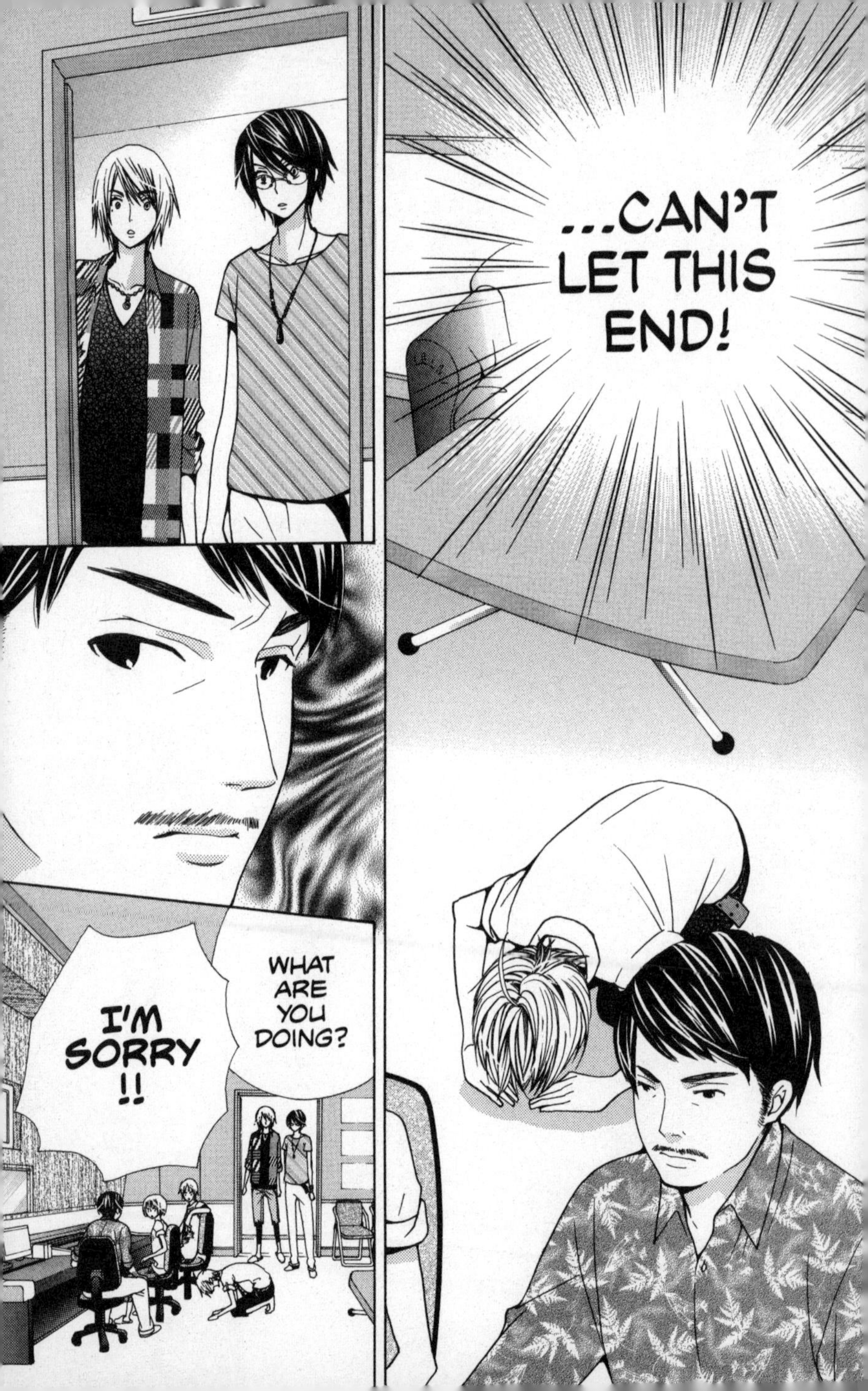
...CAN'T LET THIS END!
WHAT ARE YOU DOING?
I'M SORRY!!

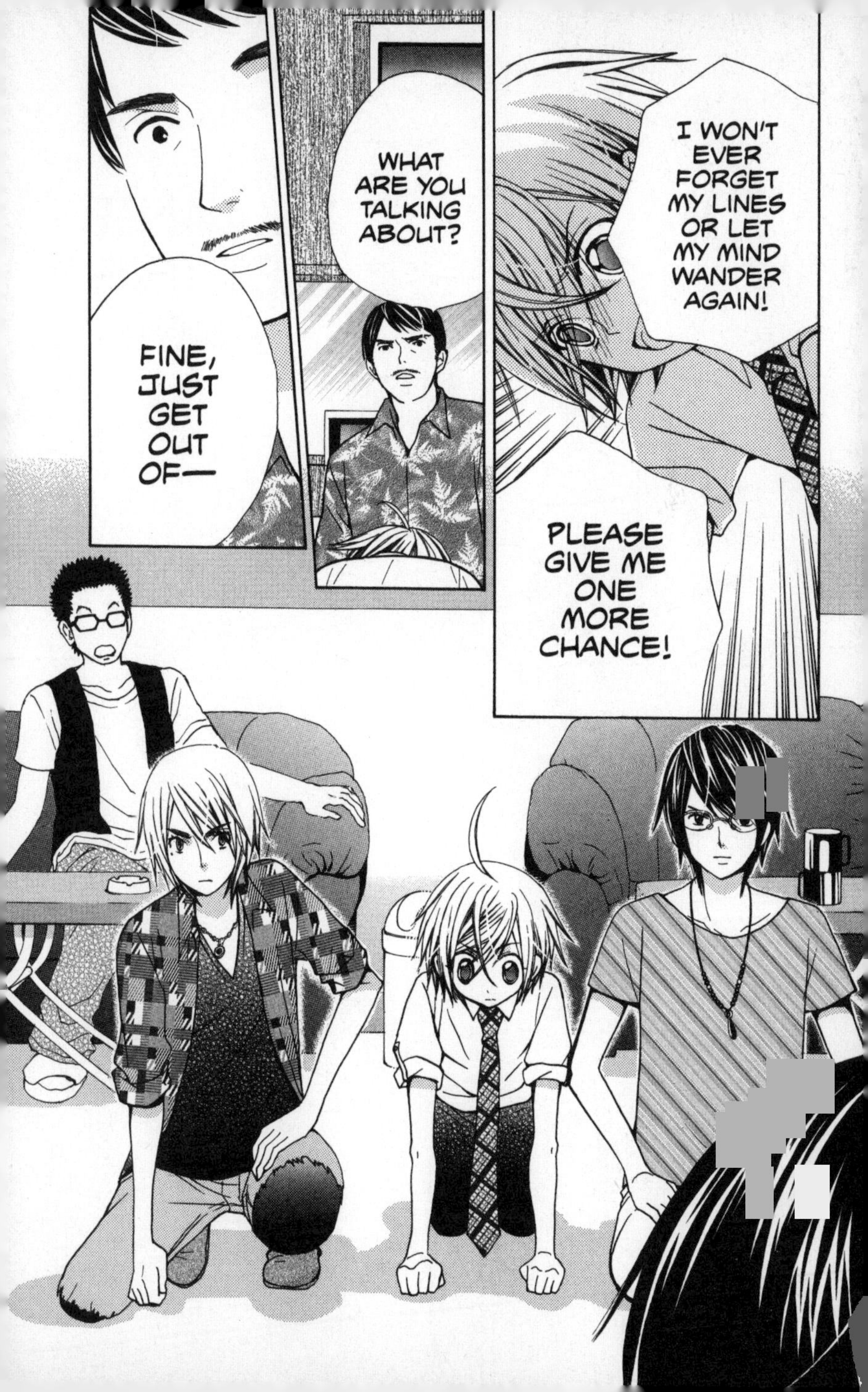
I WON'T EVER FORGET MY LINES OR LET MY MIND WANDER AGAIN!
PLEASE GIVE ME ONE MORE CHANCE!
WHAT ARE YOU TALKING ABOUT?
FINE, JUST GET OUT OF—

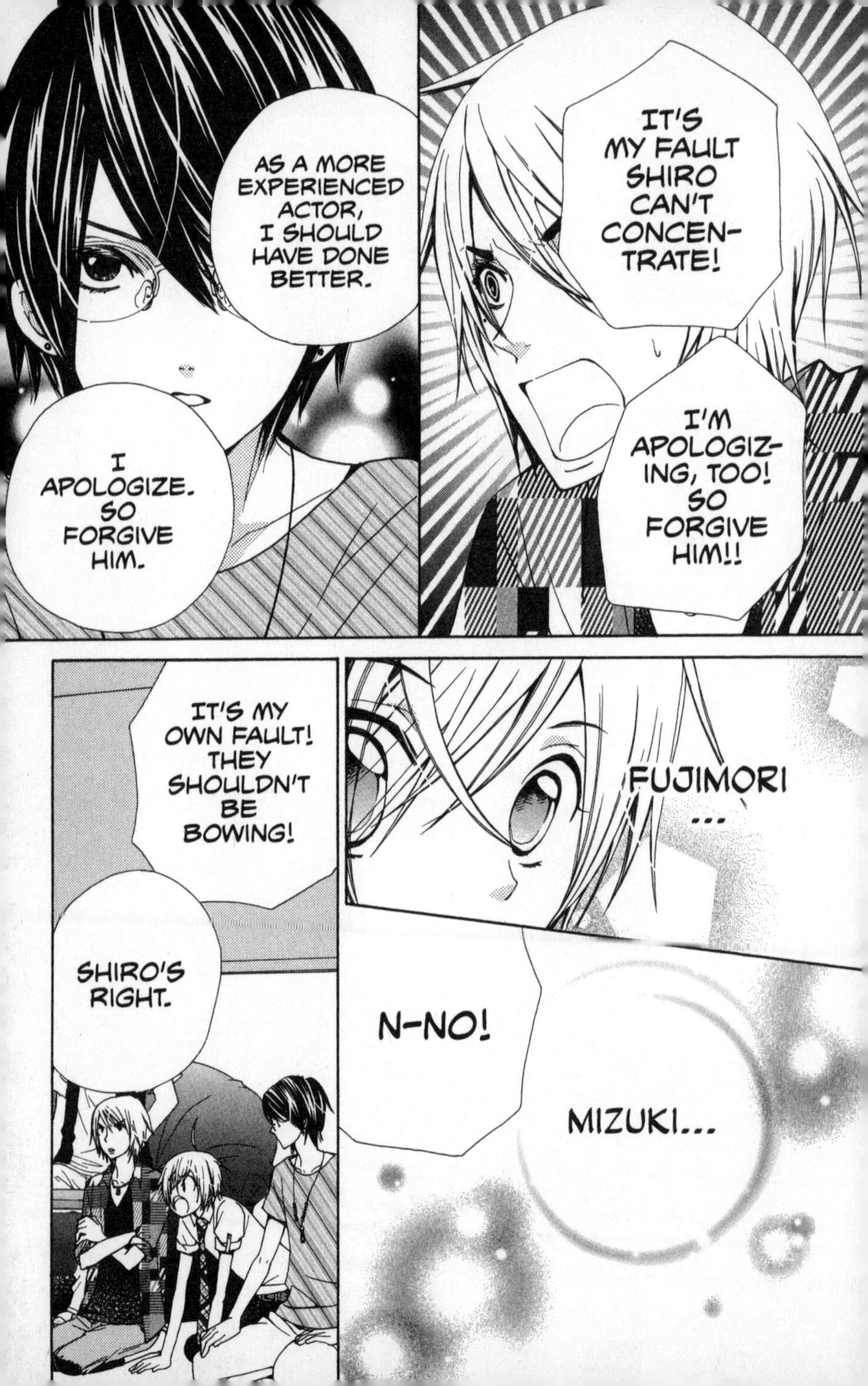
IT'S MY FAULT SHIRO CAN'T CONCEN-TRATE!
I'M APOLOGIZ-ING, TOO! SO FORGIVE HIM!!
AS A MORE EXPERIENCED ACTOR, I SHOULD HAVE DONE BETTER.
I APOLOGIZE. SO FORGIVE HIM.
FUJIMORI ...
MIZUKI...
N-NO!
IT'S MY OWN FAULT! THEY SHOULDN'T BE BOWING!
SHIRO'S RIGHT.

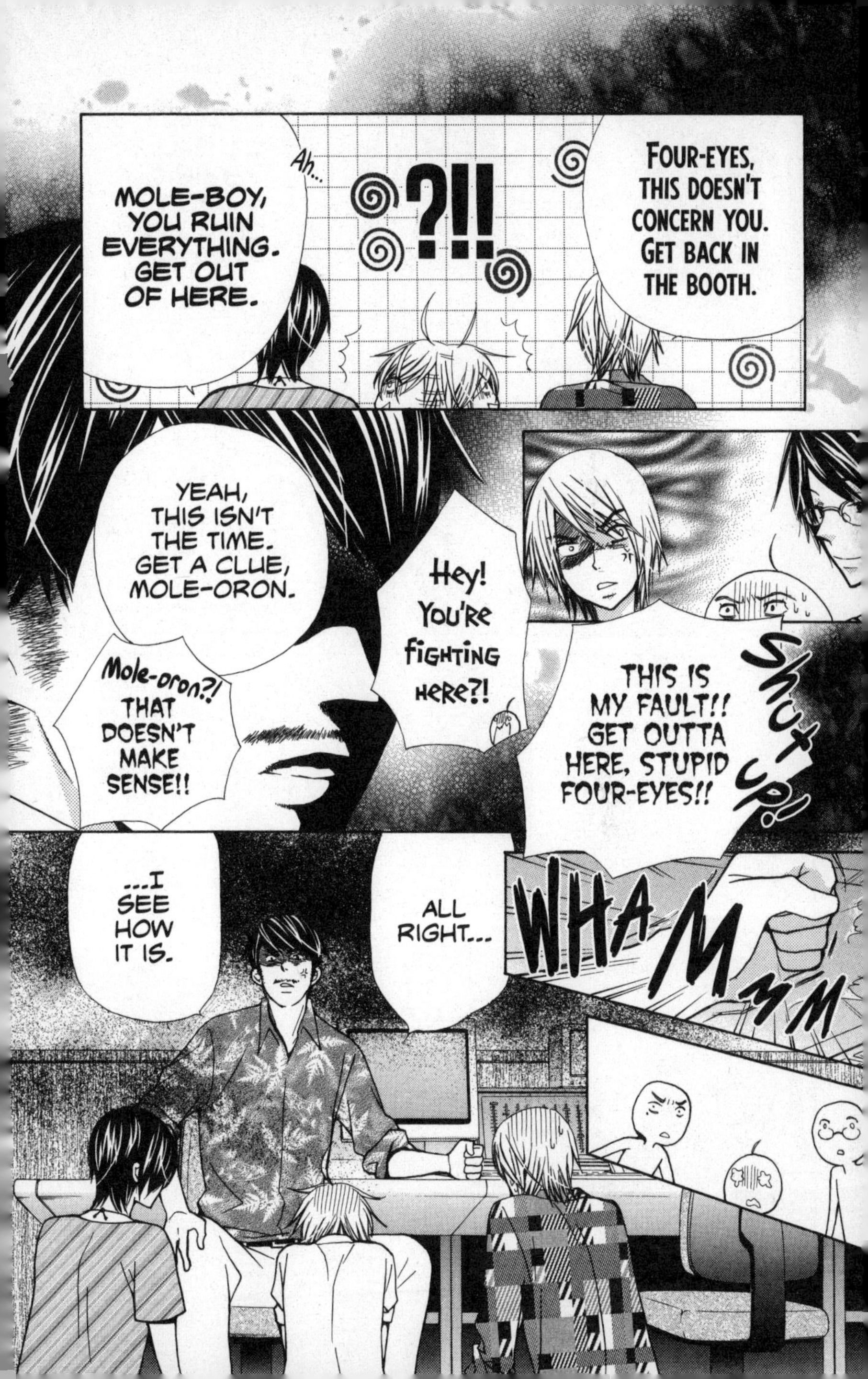
FOUR-EYES, THIS DOESN'T CONCERN YOU. GET BACK IN THE BOOTH.
?!!
Ah...
MOLE-BOY, YOU RUIN EVERYTHING. GET OUT OF HERE.
YEAH, THIS ISN'T THE TIME. GET A CLUE, MOLE-ORON.
Hey! You're fighting here?!
SHUT UP!!
THIS IS MY FAULT!! GET OUTTA HERE, STUPID FOUR-EYES!!
Mole-oron?! THAT DOESN'T MAKE SENSE!!
WHAMMM
ALL RIGHT...
...I SEE HOW IT IS.

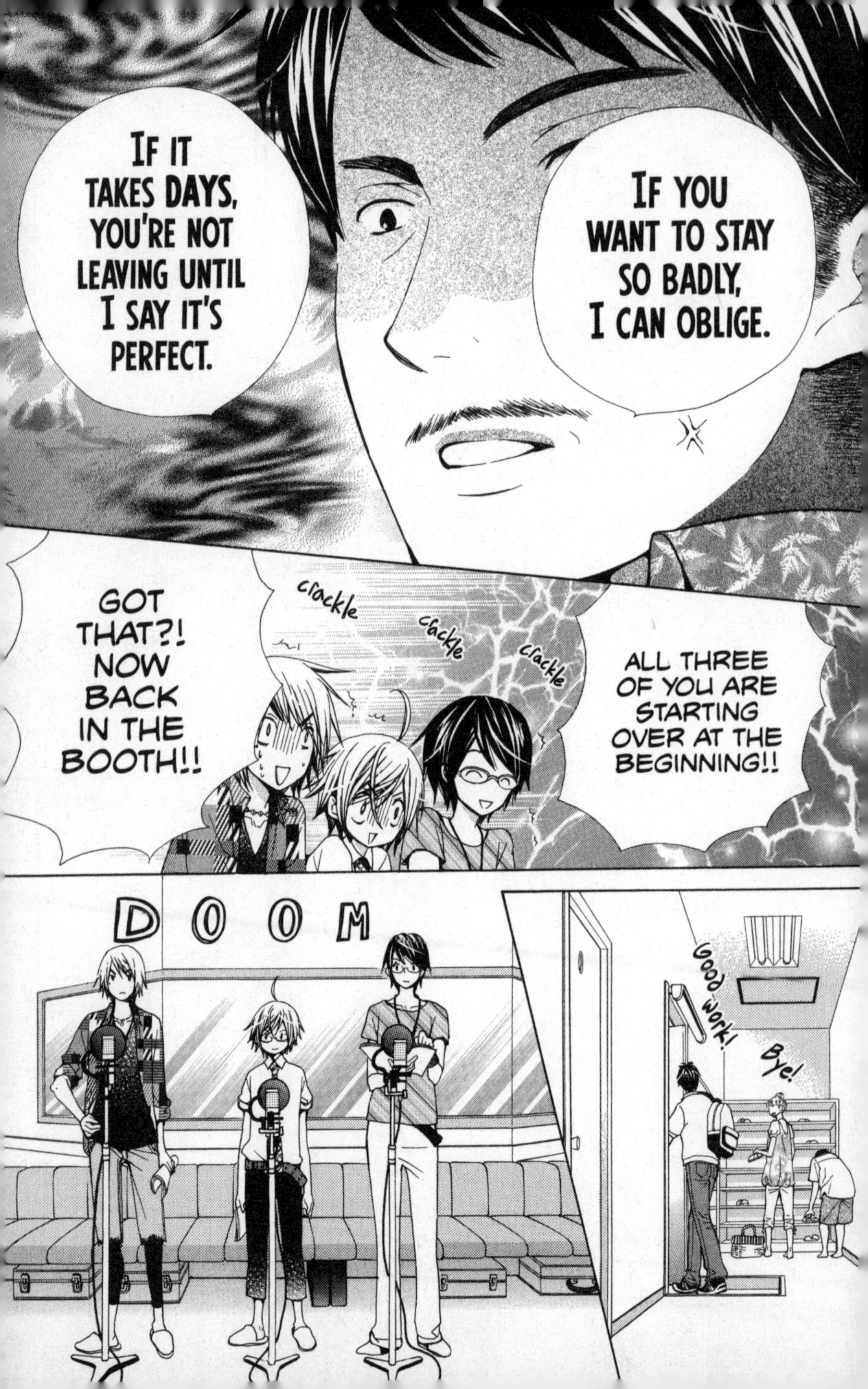
IF YOU WANT TO STAY SO BADLY, I CAN OBLIGE.
IF IT TAKES DAYS, YOU'RE NOT LEAVING UNTIL I SAY IT'S PERFECT.
ALL THREE OF YOU ARE STARTING OVER AT THE BEGINNING!!
crackle
crackle
crackle
GOT THAT?! NOW BACK IN THE BOOTH!!
Good work!
Bye!
DOOM

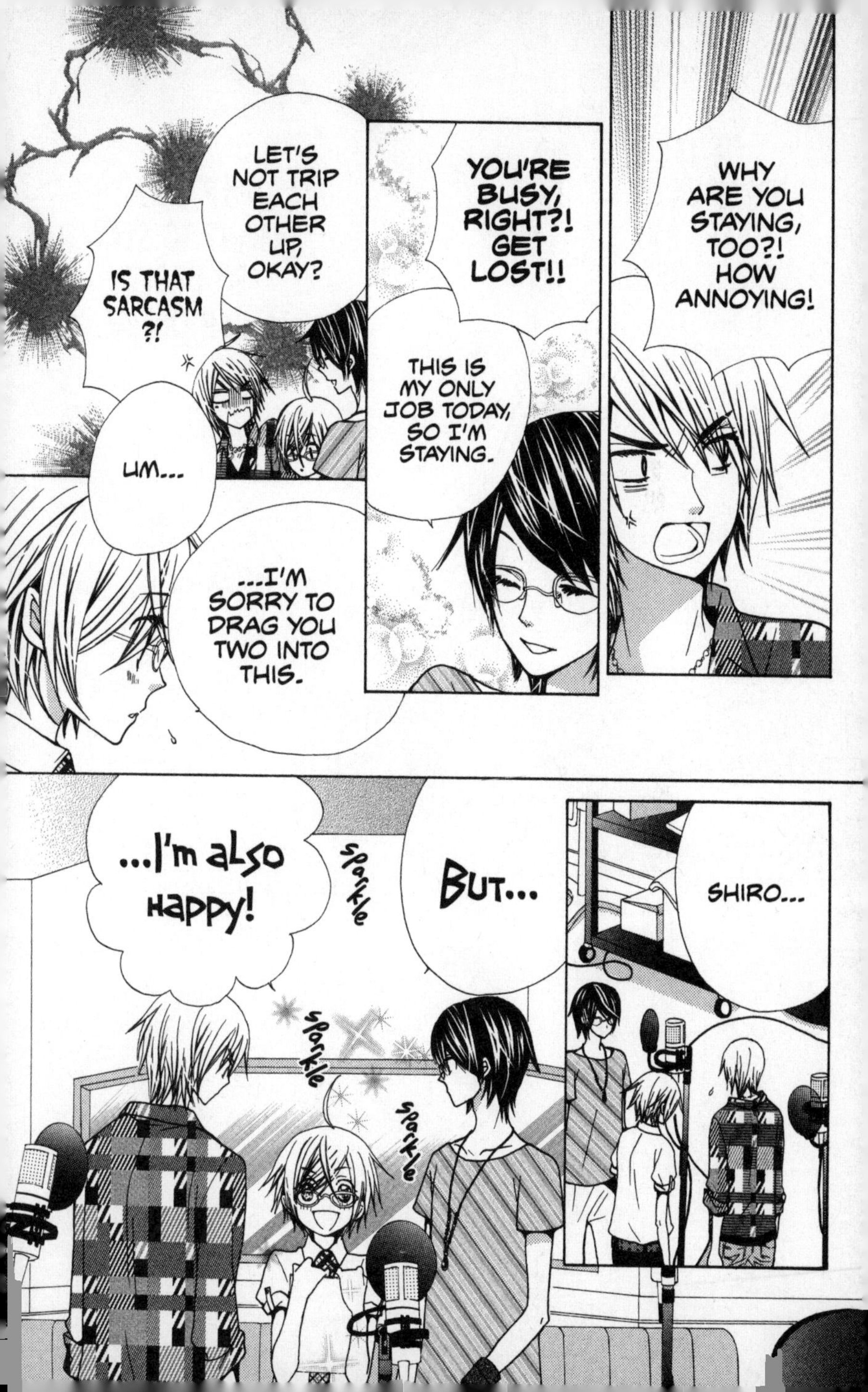
WHY ARE YOU STAYING, TOO?! HOW ANNOYING!
YOU'RE BUSY, RIGHT?! GET LOST!!
THIS IS MY ONLY JOB TODAY, SO I'M STAYING.
LET'S NOT TRIP EACH OTHER UP, OKAY?
IS THAT SARCASM ?!
UM...
...I'M SORRY TO DRAG YOU TWO INTO THIS.
SHIRO...
BUT...
sparkle
...I'm also happy!
sparkle
sparkle

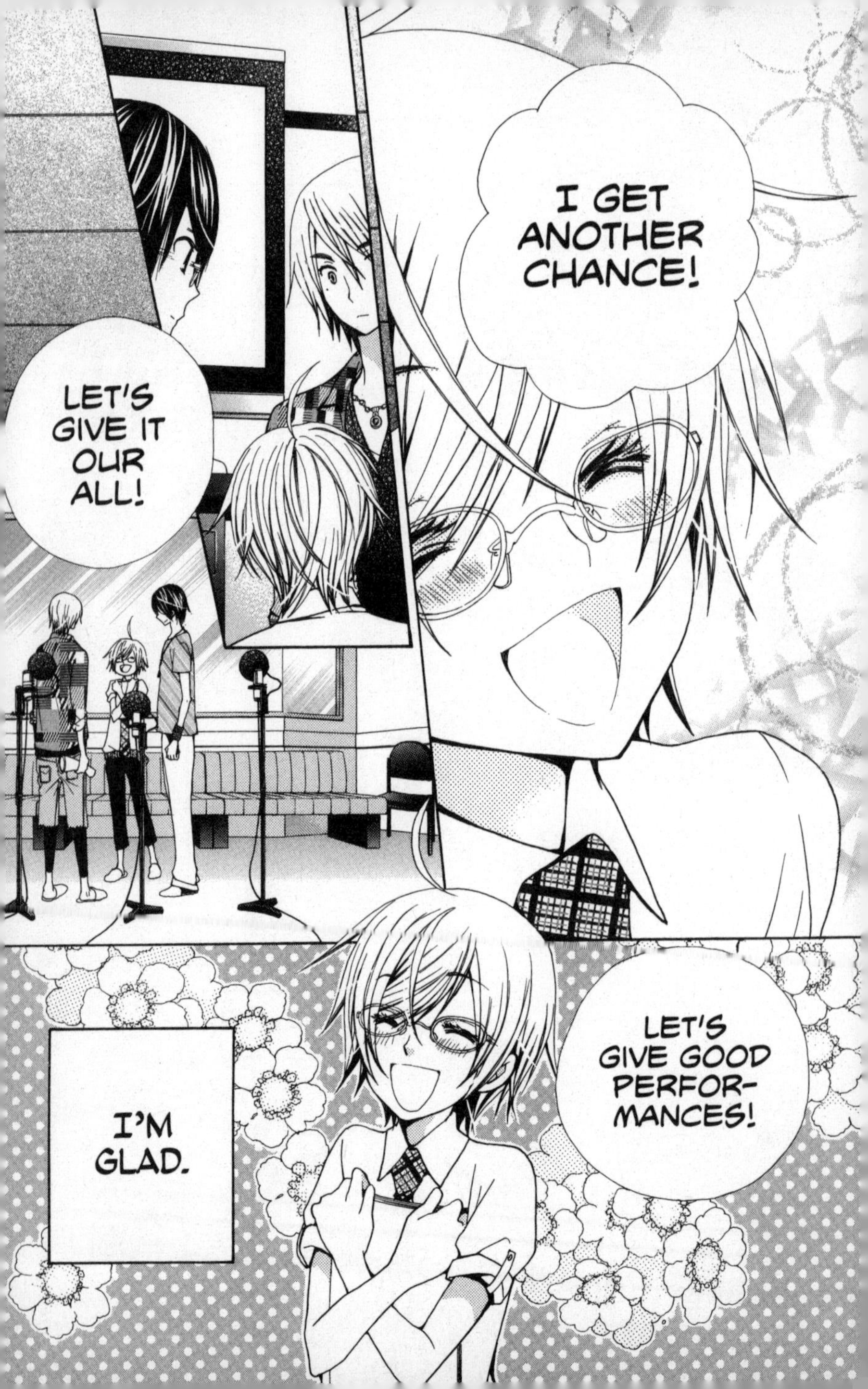
I GET ANOTHER CHANCE!
LET'S GIVE IT OUR ALL!
LET'S GIVE GOOD PERFOR-MANCES!
I'M GLAD.

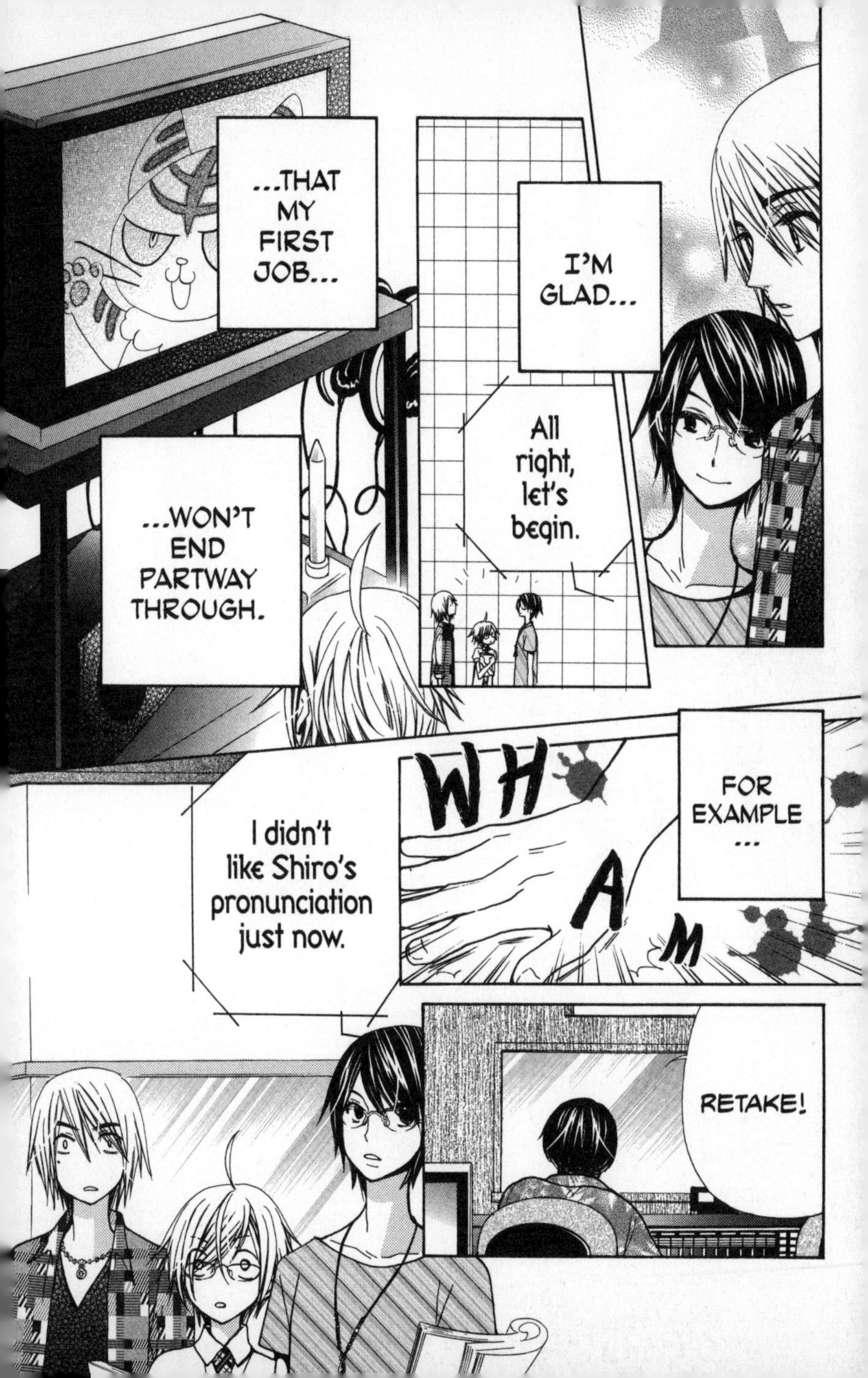
I'M GLAD...
All right, let's begin.
...THAT MY FIRST JOB...
...WON'T END PARTWAY THROUGH.
FOR EXAMPLE ...
WHAM
I didn't like Shiro's pronunciation just now.
RETAKE!

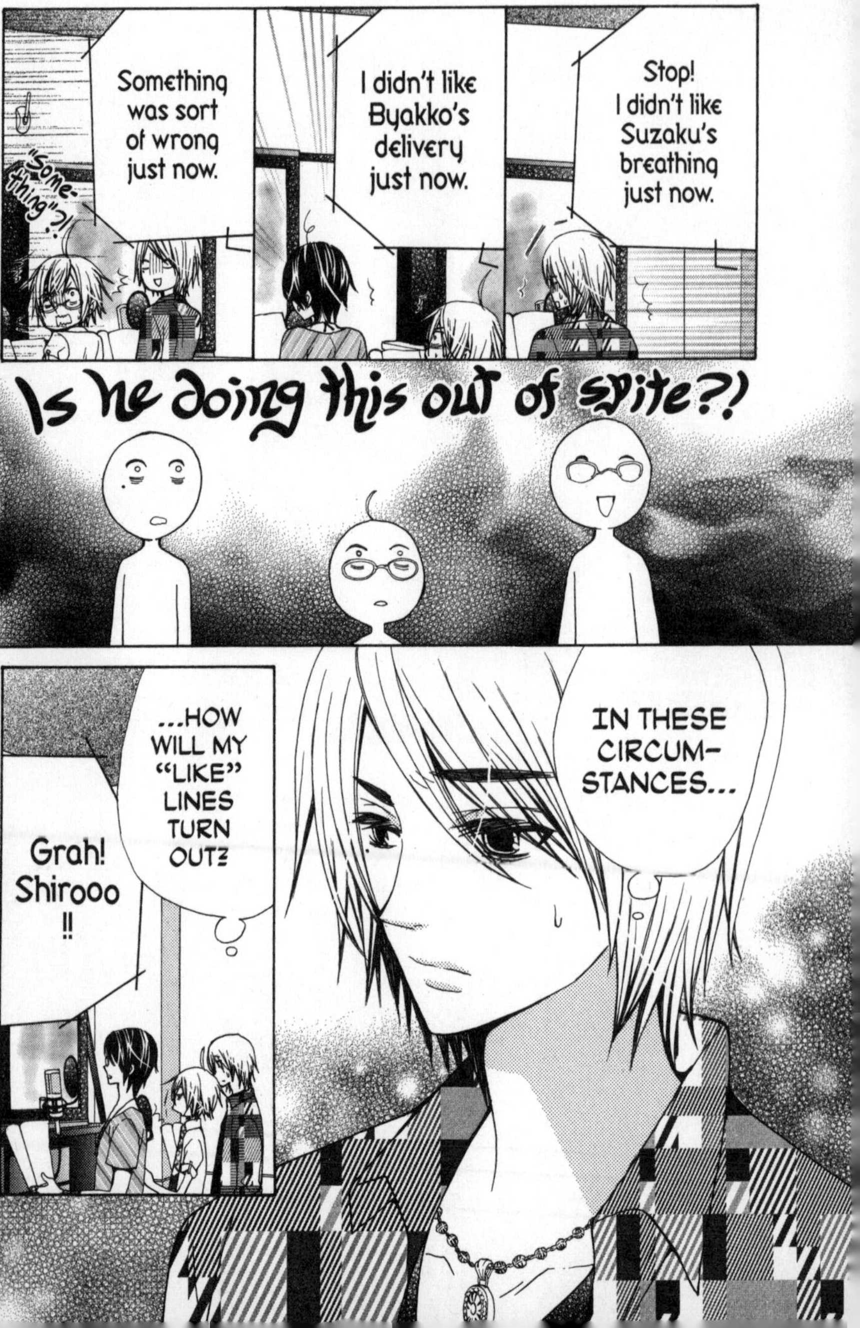
Stop! I didn't like Suzaku's breathing just now.
I didn't like Byakko's delivery just now.
Something was sort of wrong just now.
"Some-thing"?!
Is he doing this out of spite?!
IN THESE CIRCUM-STANCES...
...HOW WILL MY "LIKE" LINES TURN OUT?
Grah! Shirooo!!

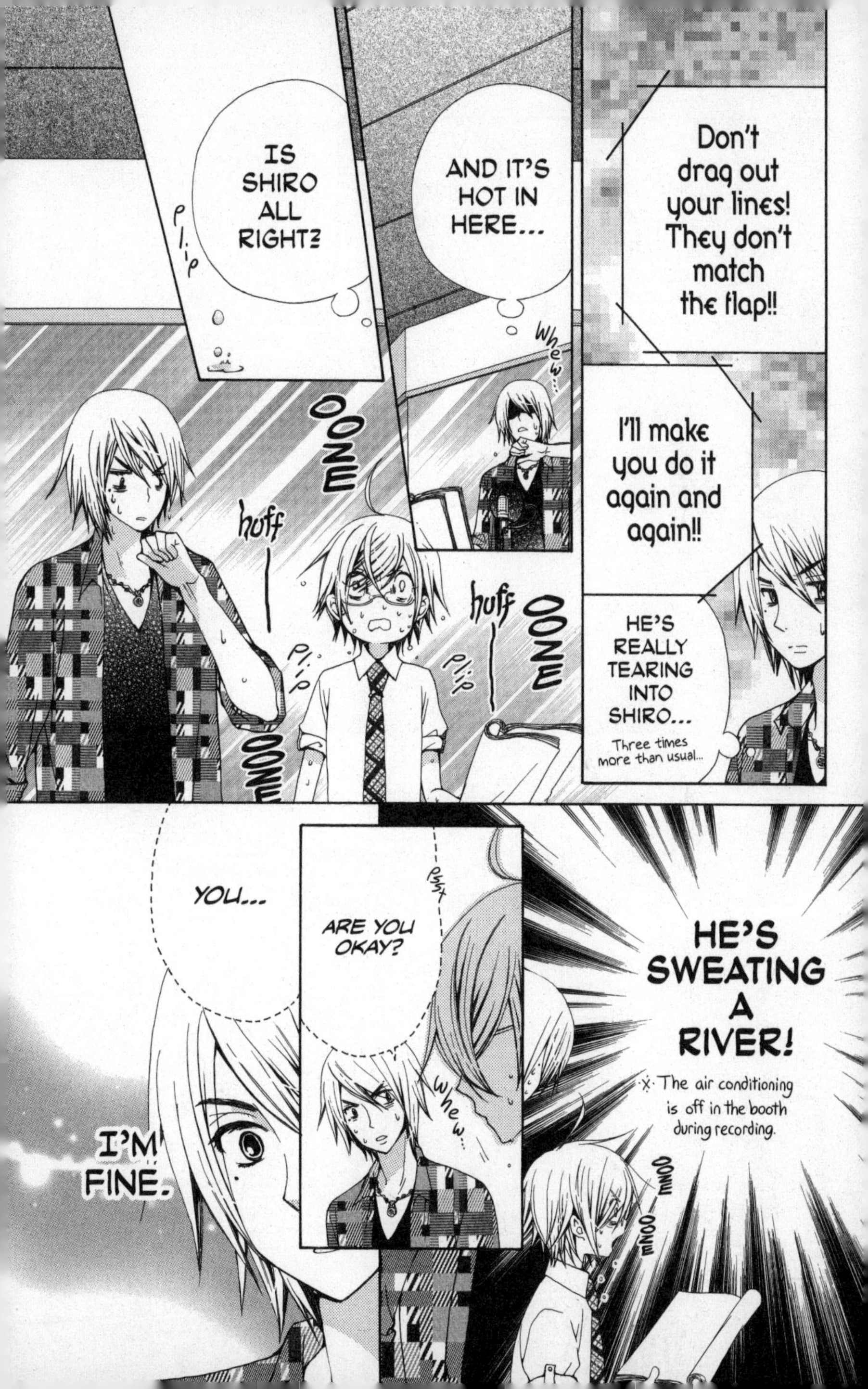
Don't drag out your lines! They don't match the flap!!
I'll make you do it again and again!!
HE'S REALLY TEARING INTO SHIRO...
Three times more than usual...
AND IT'S HOT IN HERE...
Whew...
IS SHIRO ALL RIGHT?
plip
OOZE
huff
huff
OOZE
plip
plip
OOZE
HE'S SWEATING A RIVER!
※ The air conditioning is off in the booth during recording.
OOZE
OOZE
Psst
ARE YOU OKAY?
Whew...
YOU...
I'M FINE.

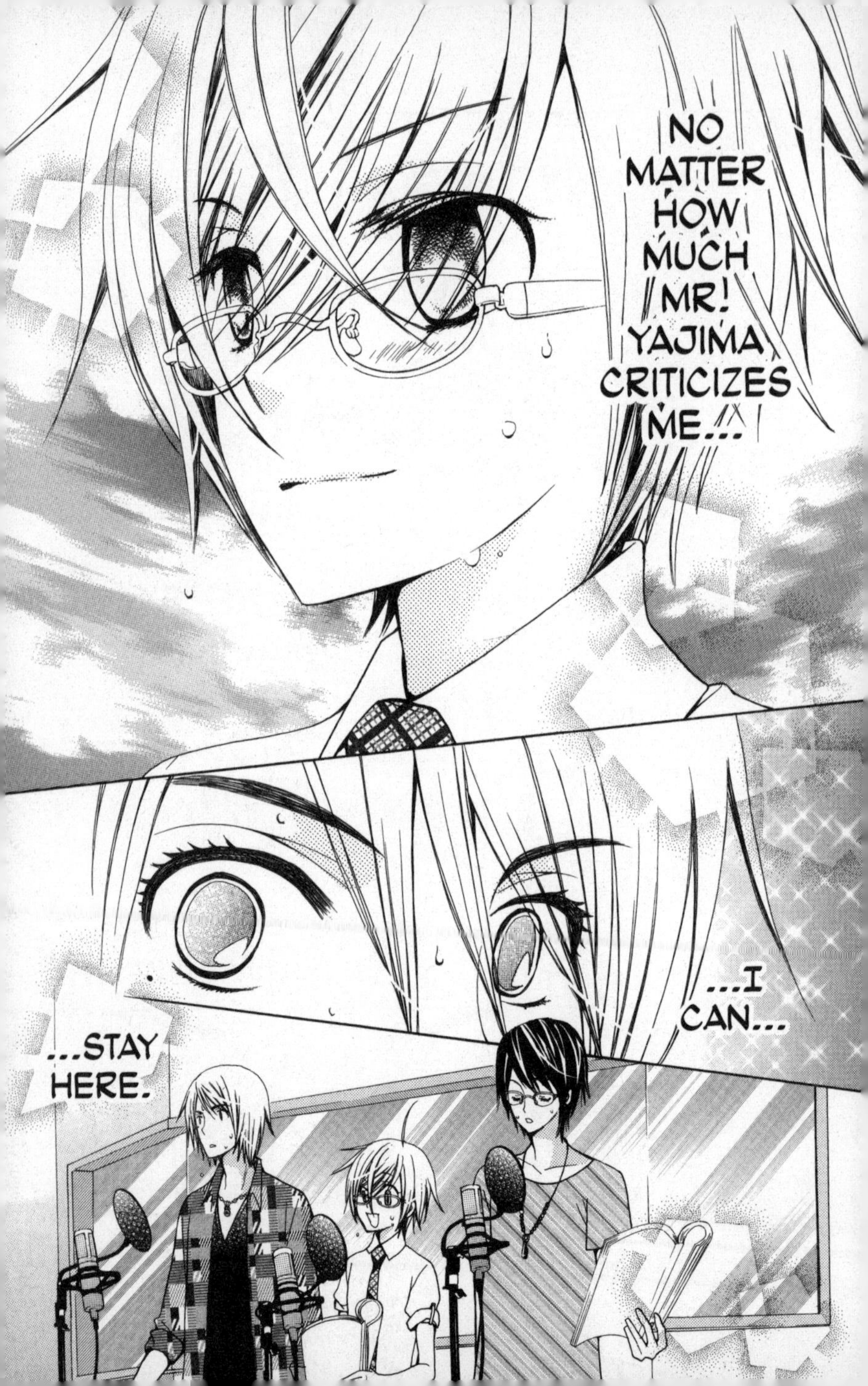
NO MATTER HOW MUCH MR. YAJIMA CRITICIZES ME...!!
...I CAN...
...STAY HERE.

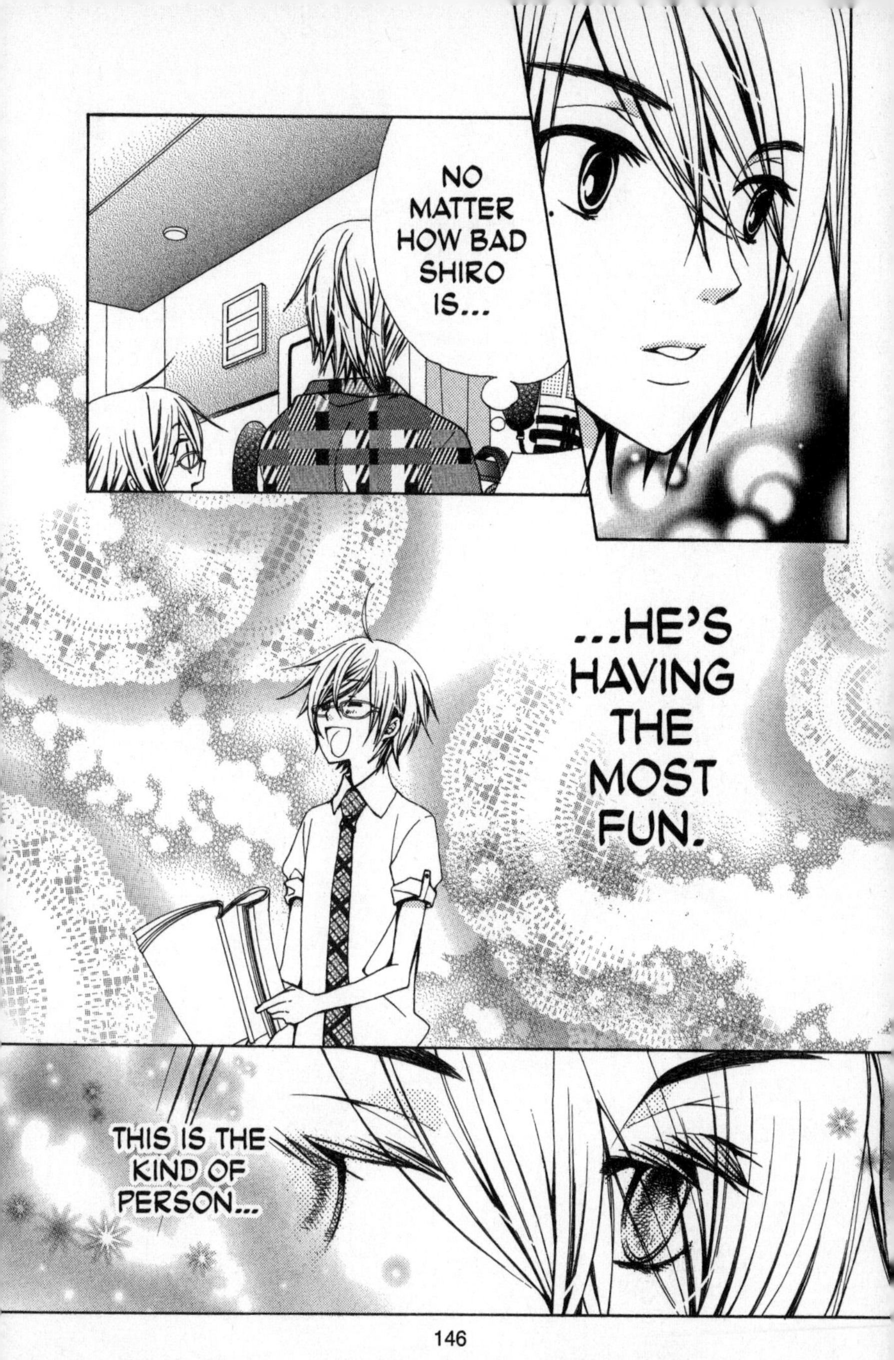
NO MATTER HOW BAD SHIRO IS...
...HE'S HAVING THE MOST FUN.
THIS IS THE KIND OF PERSON...

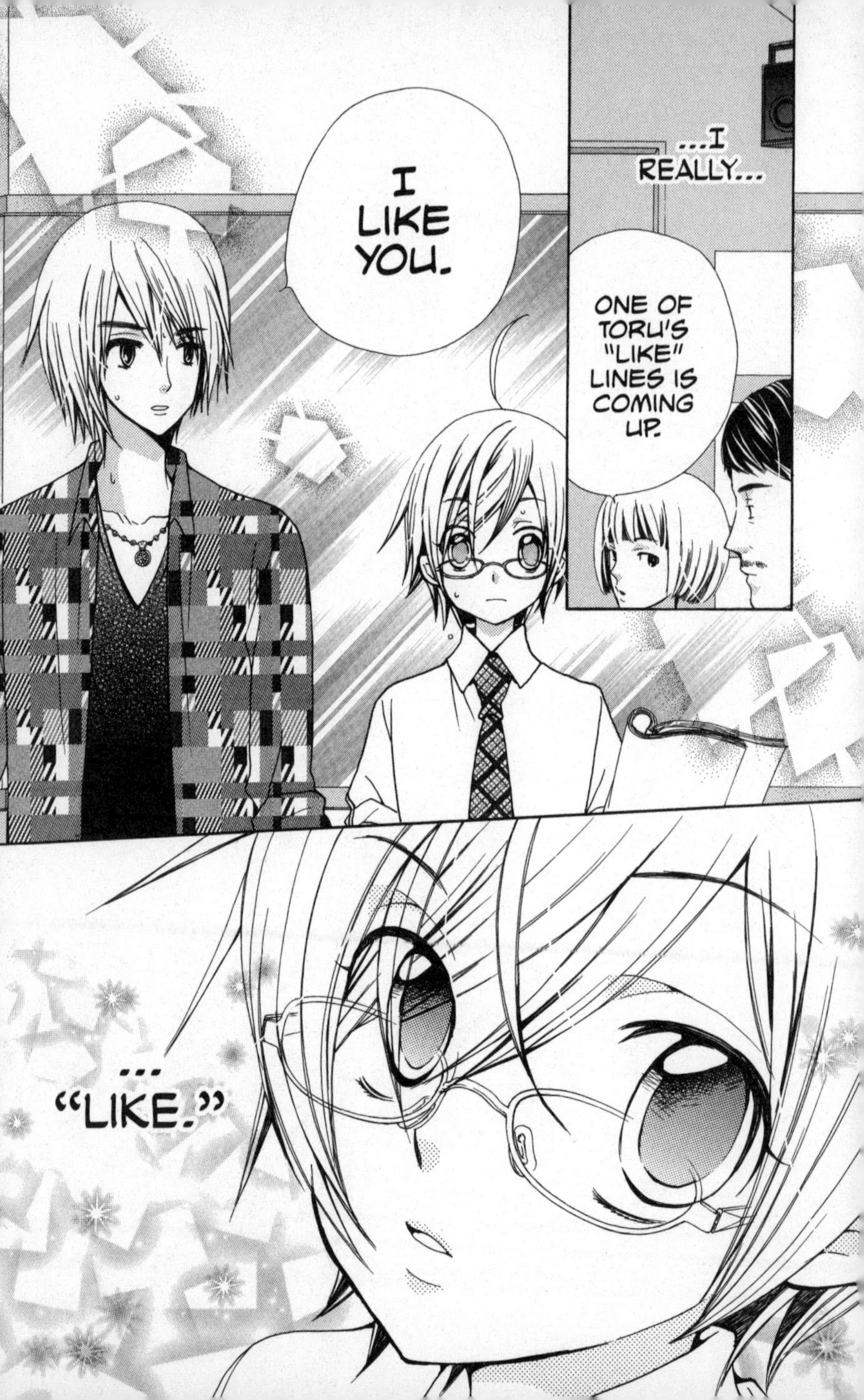
...I REALLY...
ONE OF TORU'S "LIKE" LINES IS COMING UP.
I LIKE YOU.
... "LIKE."

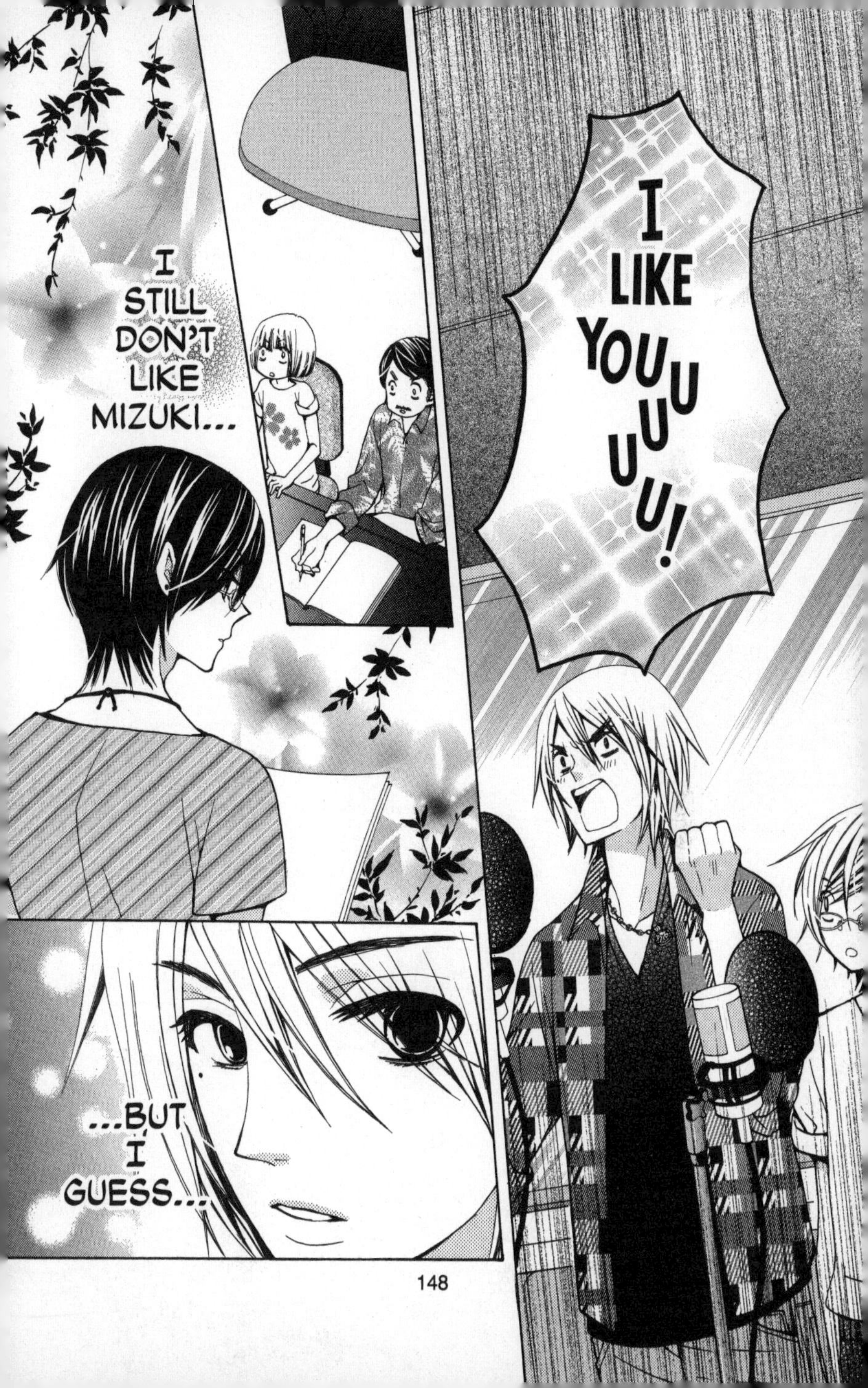
I LIKE YOUUUUUU!
I STILL DON'T LIKE MIZUKI...
...BUT I GUESS...

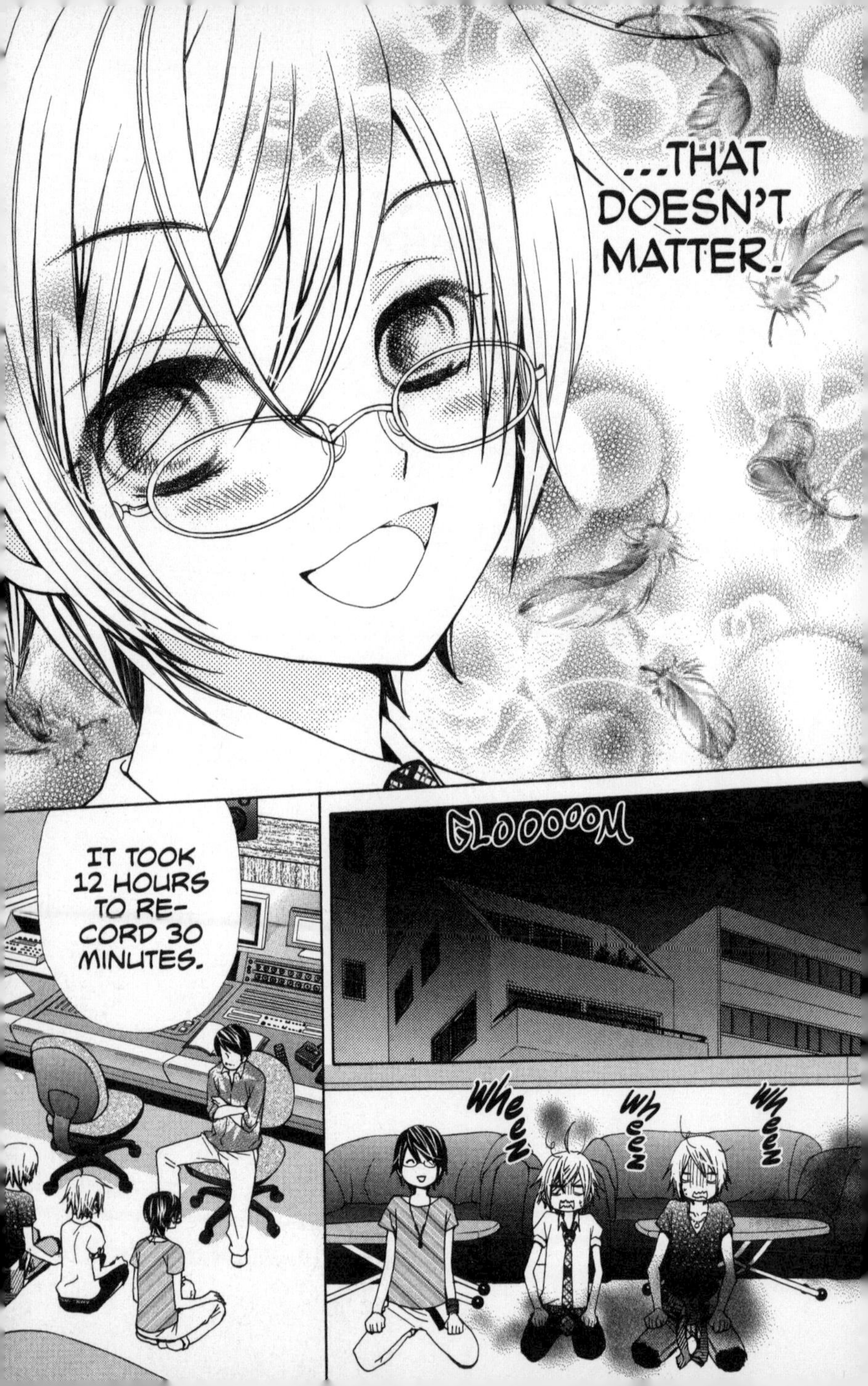
...THAT DOESN'T MATTER.
GLOOOOOM
wheeen
wheeen
wheeen
IT TOOK 12 HOURS TO RE-CORD 30 MINUTES.

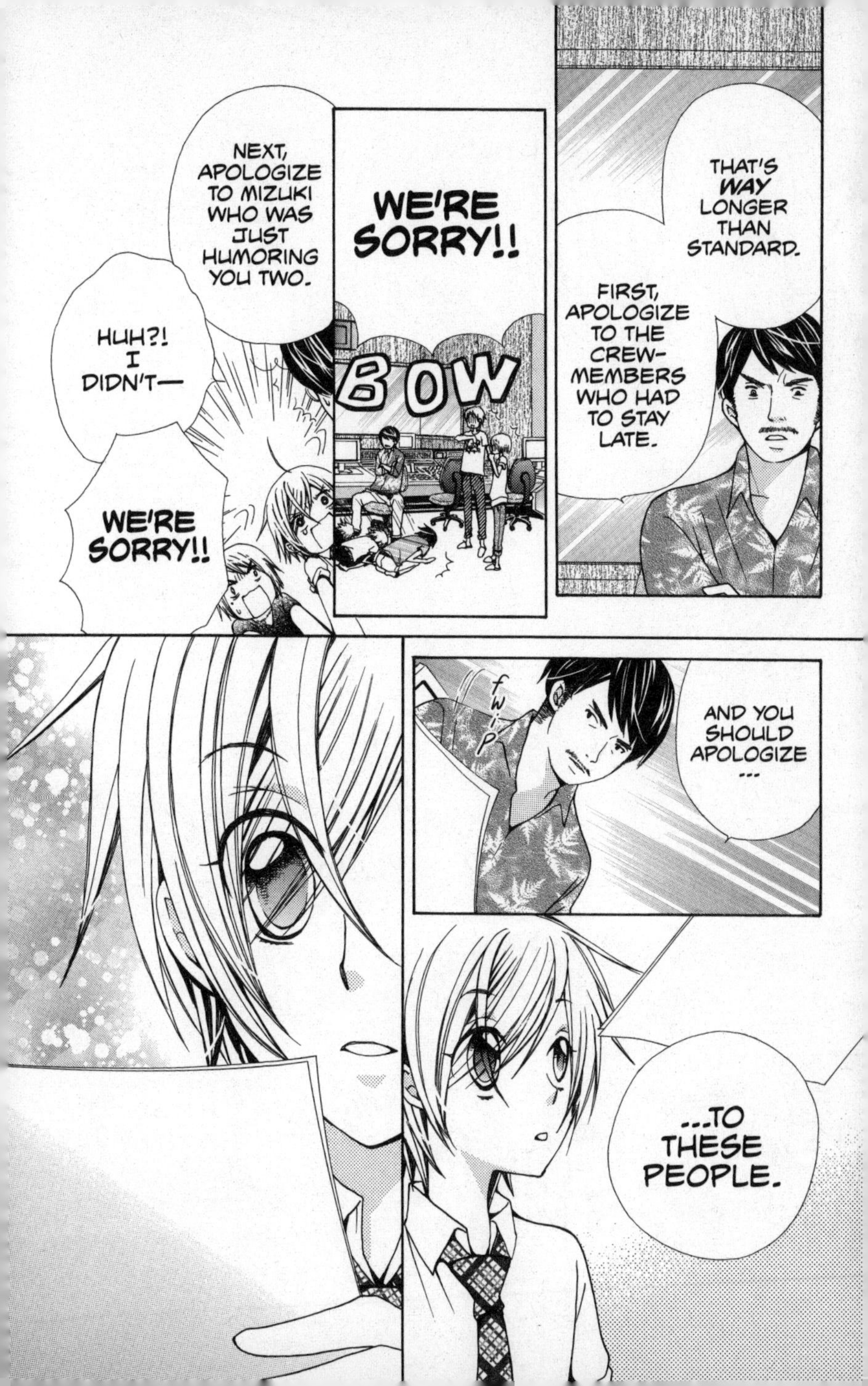
THAT'S WAY LONGER THAN STANDARD.
FIRST, APOLOGIZE TO THE CREW-MEMBERS WHO HAD TO STAY LATE.
WE'RE SORRY!!
BOW
NEXT, APOLOGIZE TO MIZUKI WHO WAS JUST HUMORING YOU TWO.
HUH?! I DIDN'T—
WE'RE SORRY!!
FWIP
AND YOU SHOULD APOLOGIZE ...
...TO THESE PEOPLE.

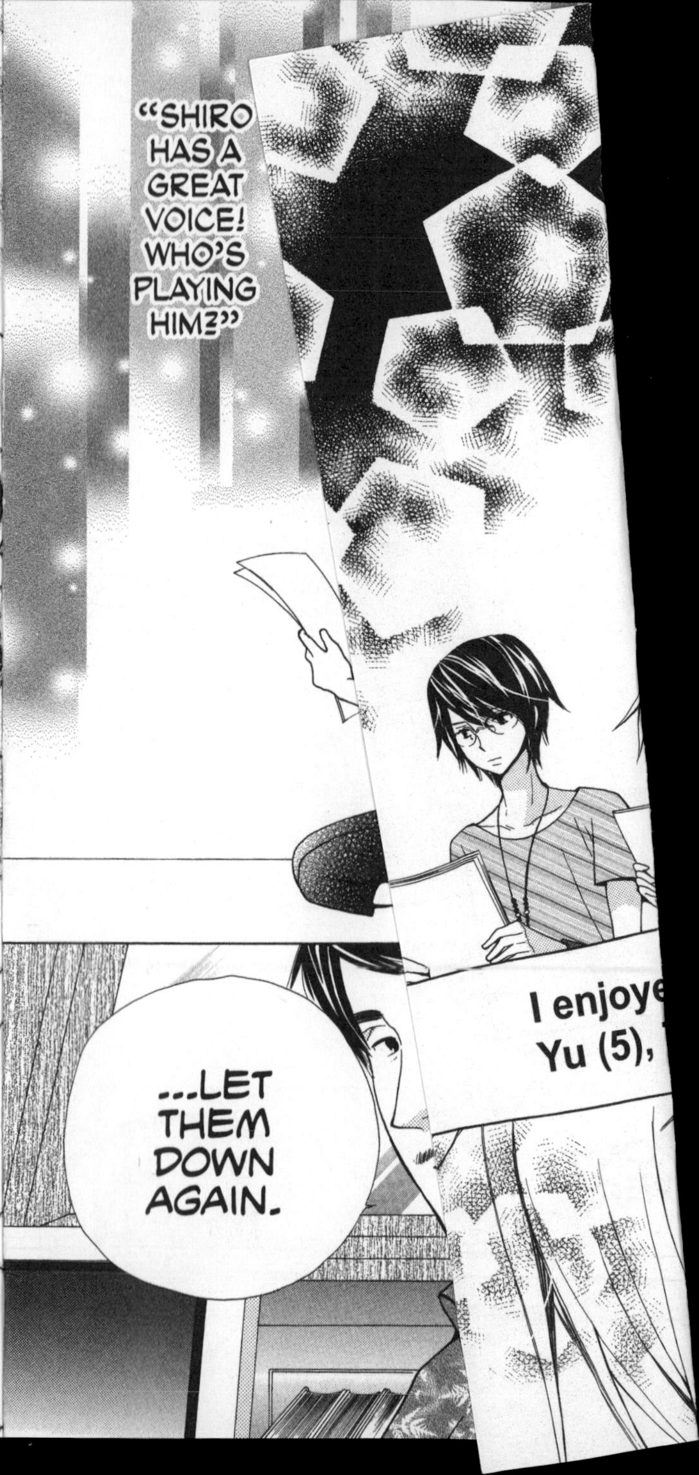
"SHIRO HAS A GREAT VOICE! WHO'S PLAYING HIM?"
I enjoye
Yu (5),
...LET THEM DOWN AGAIN.

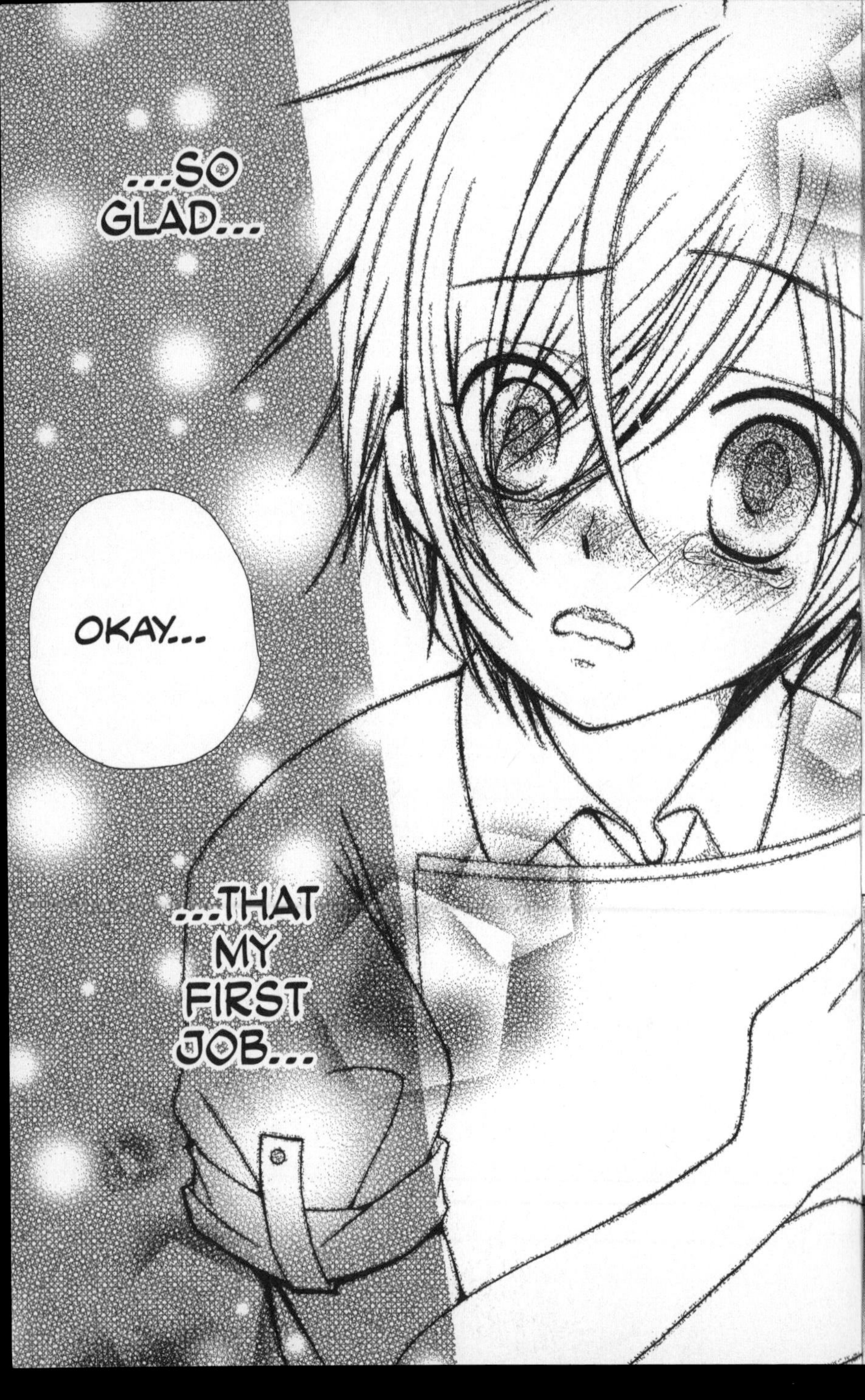
...SO GLAD...
OKAY...
...THAT MY FIRST JOB...

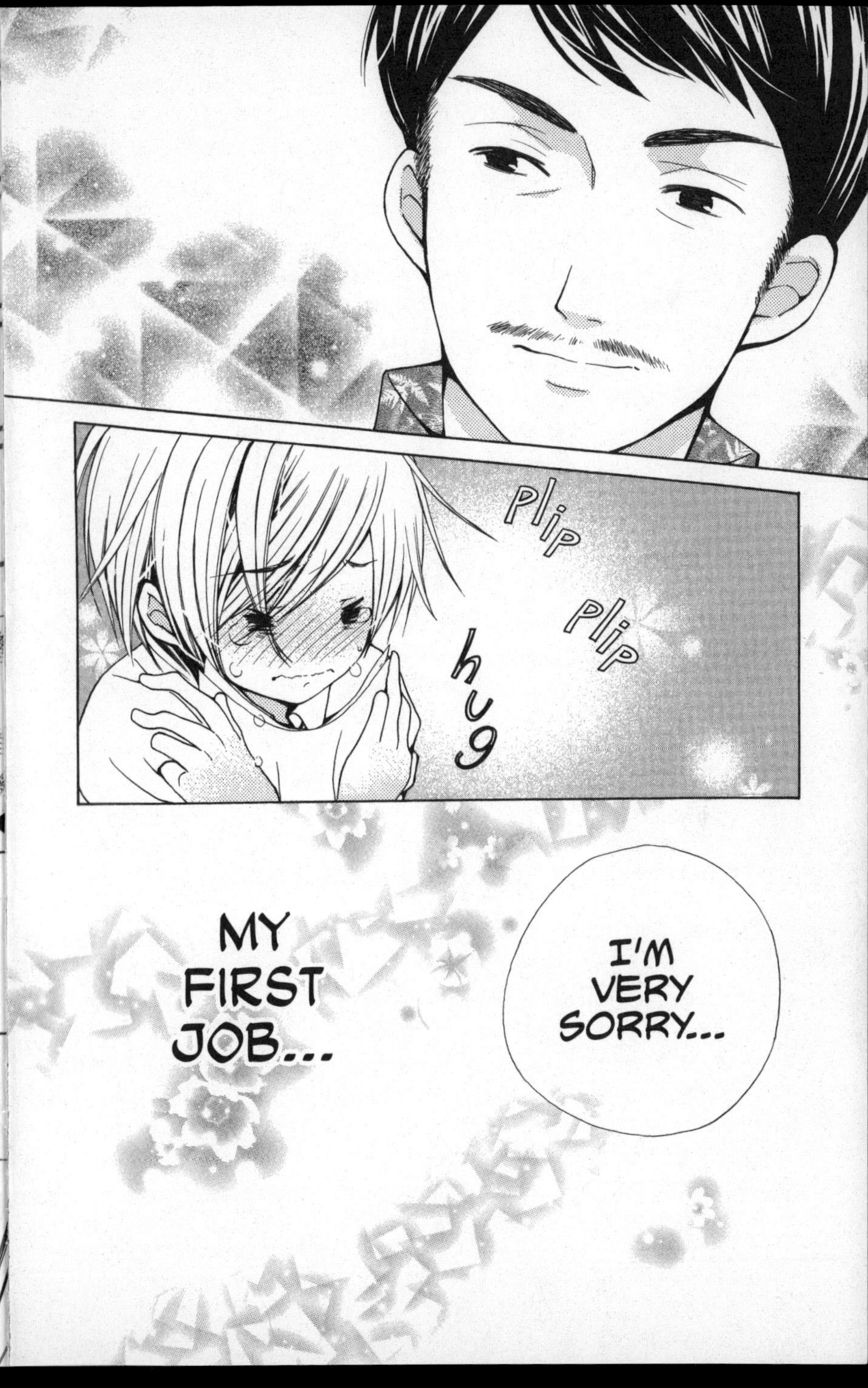
plip
plip
hug
I'M VERY SORRY...
MY FIRST JOB...

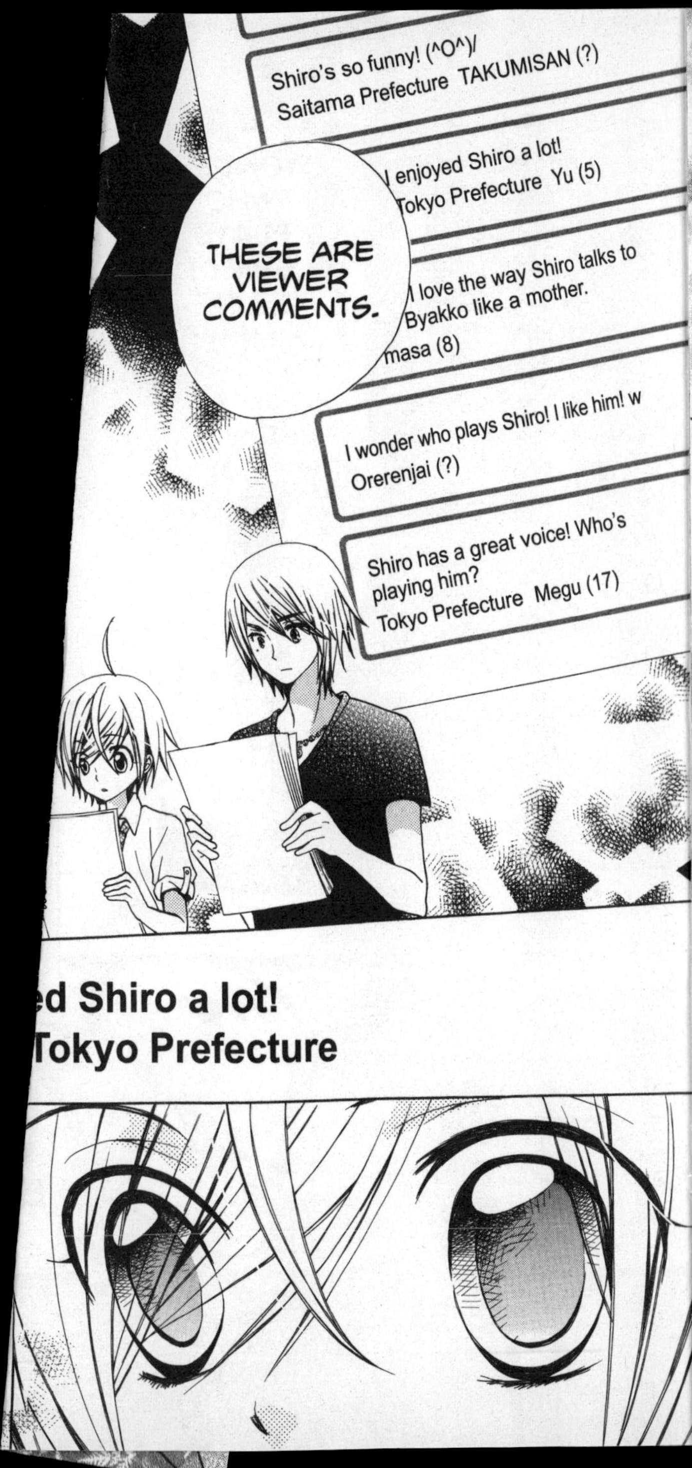
Shiro's so funny! (^O^)/
Saitama Prefecture TAKUMISAN (?)
I enjoyed Shiro a lot!
Tokyo Prefecture Yu (5)
I love the way Shiro talks to
Byakko like a mother.
masa (8)
I wonder who plays Shiro! I like him! w
Orerenjai (?)
Shiro has a great voice! Who's
playing him?
Tokyo Prefecture Megu (17)
THESE ARE VIEWER COMMENTS.
ed Shiro a lot!
Tokyo Prefecture

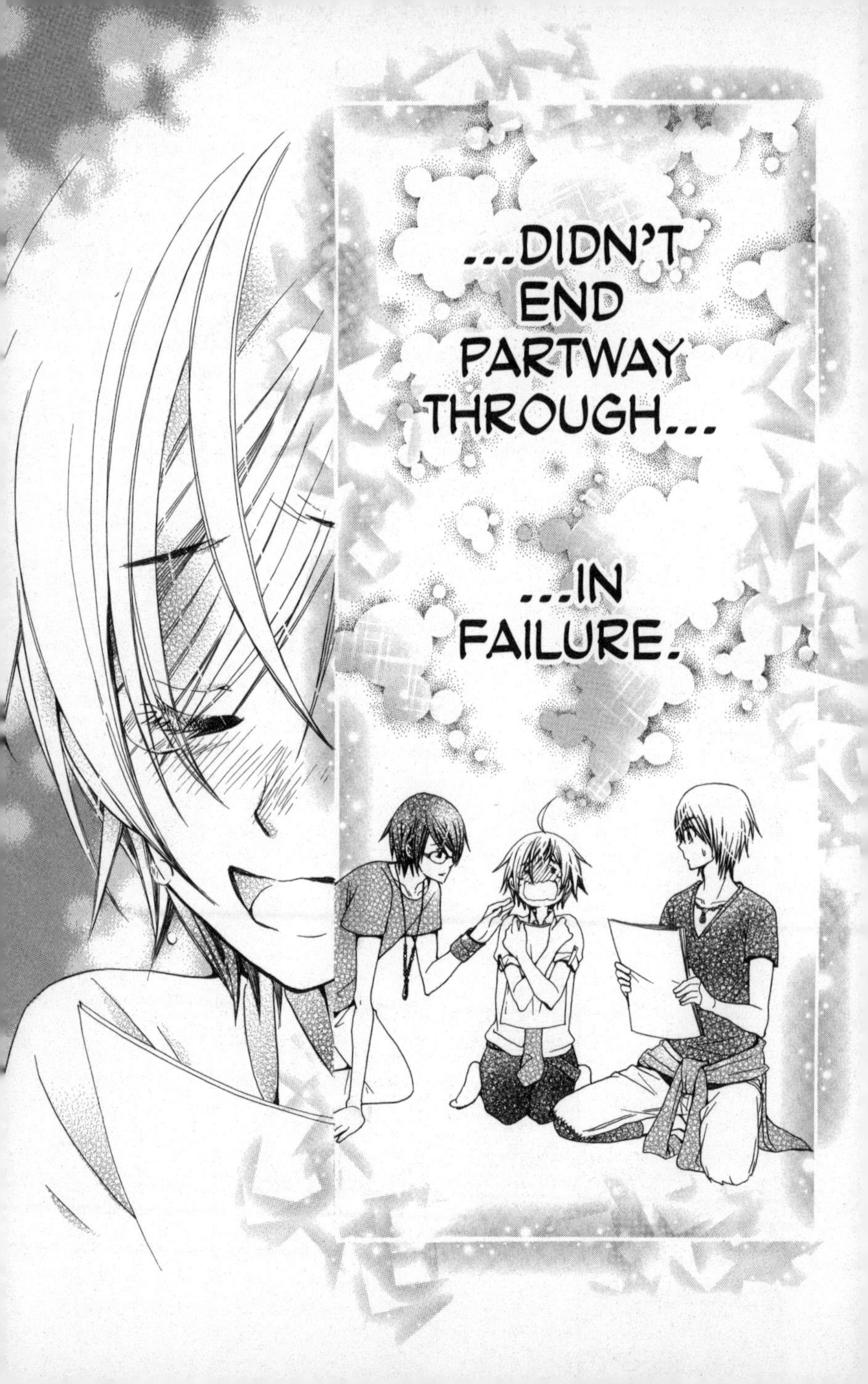
...DIDN'T END PARTWAY THROUGH...
...IN FAILURE.

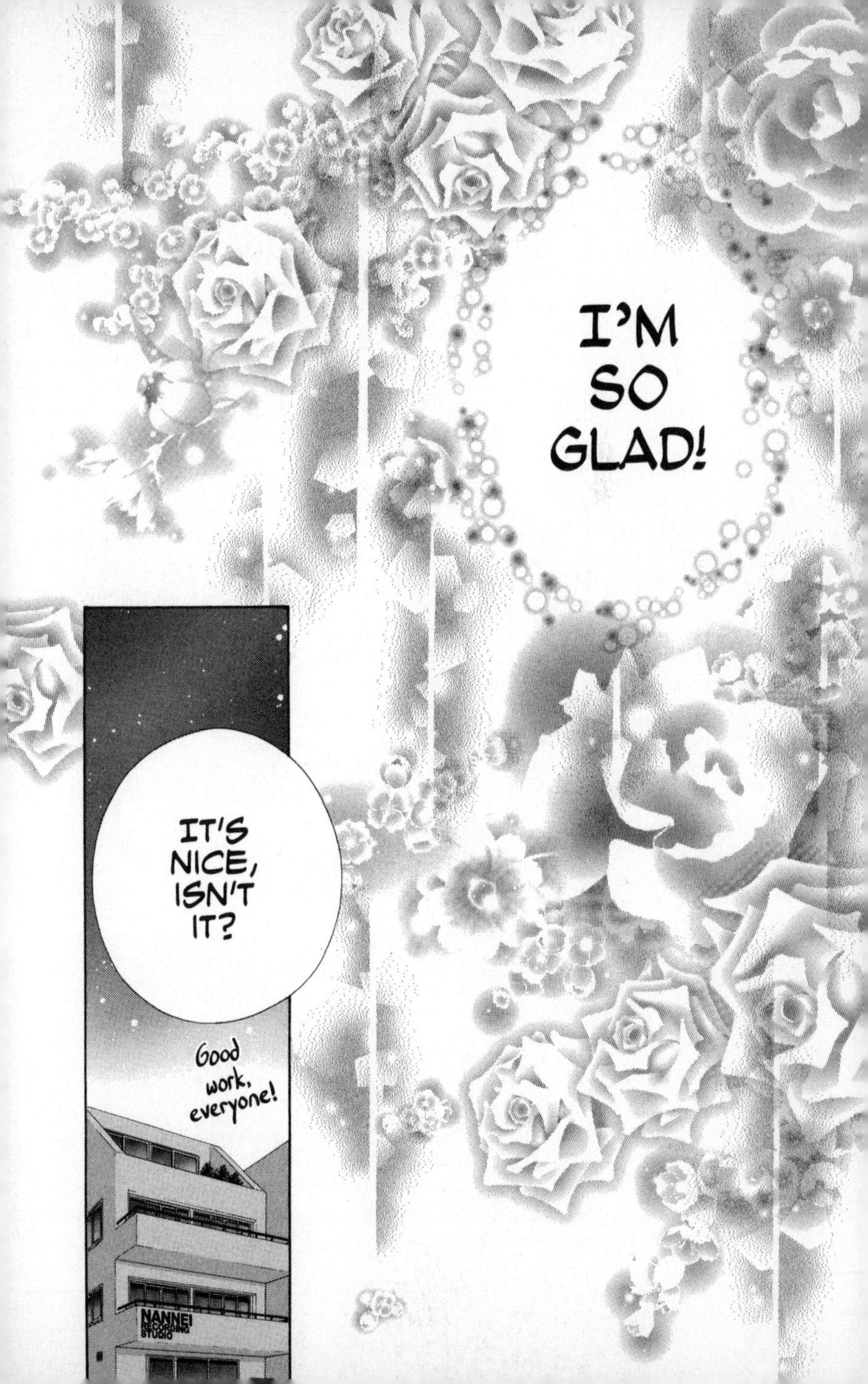
I'M SO GLAD!
IT'S NICE, ISN'T IT?
Good work, everyone!
NANNEI RECORDING STUDIO

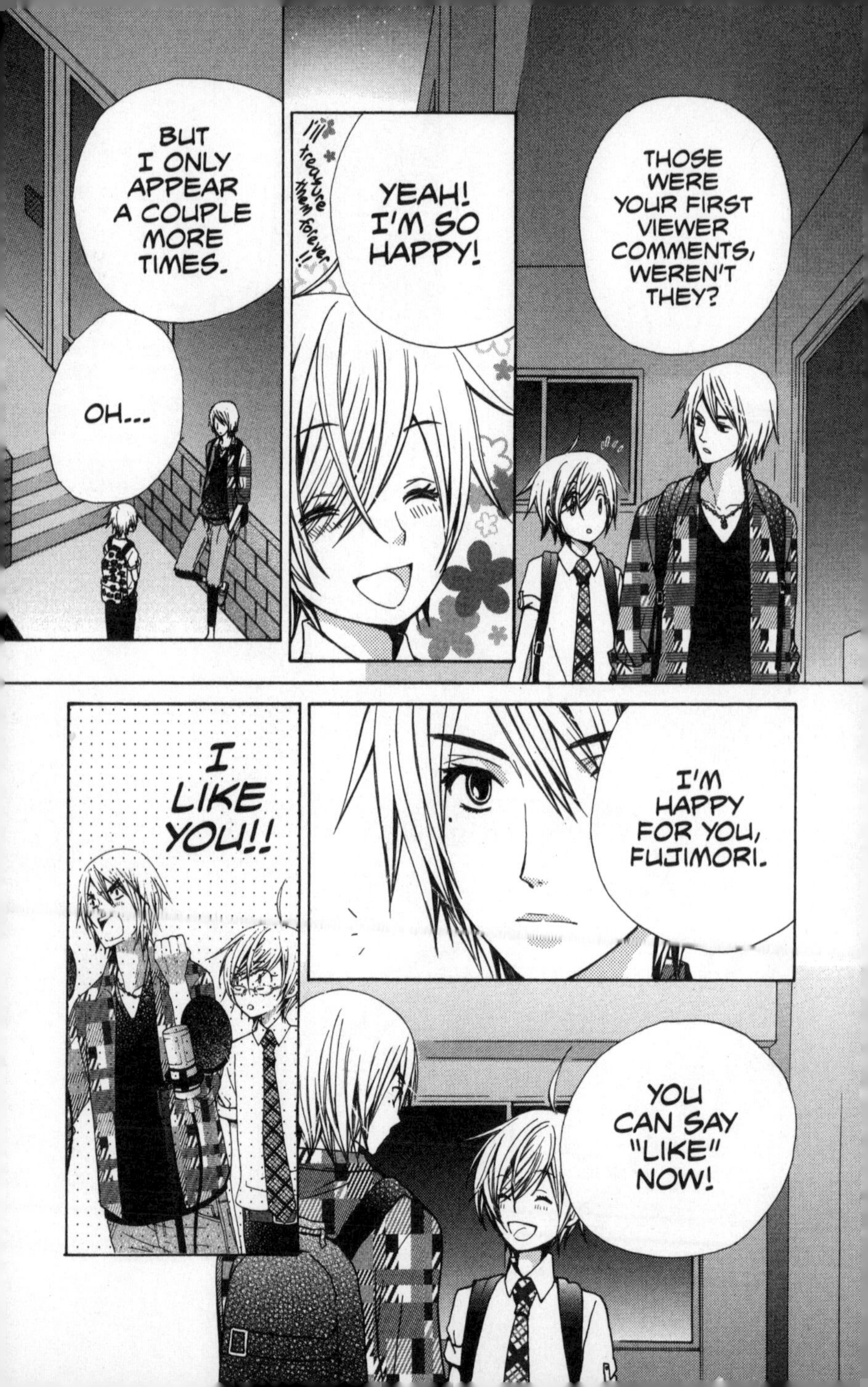
THOSE WERE YOUR FIRST VIEWER COMMENTS, WEREN'T THEY?
YEAH! I'M SO HAPPY!
I'll treasure them forever!!
BUT I ONLY APPEAR A COUPLE MORE TIMES.
OH...
I'M HAPPY FOR YOU, FUJIMORI.
YOU CAN SAY "LIKE" NOW!
I LIKE YOU!!

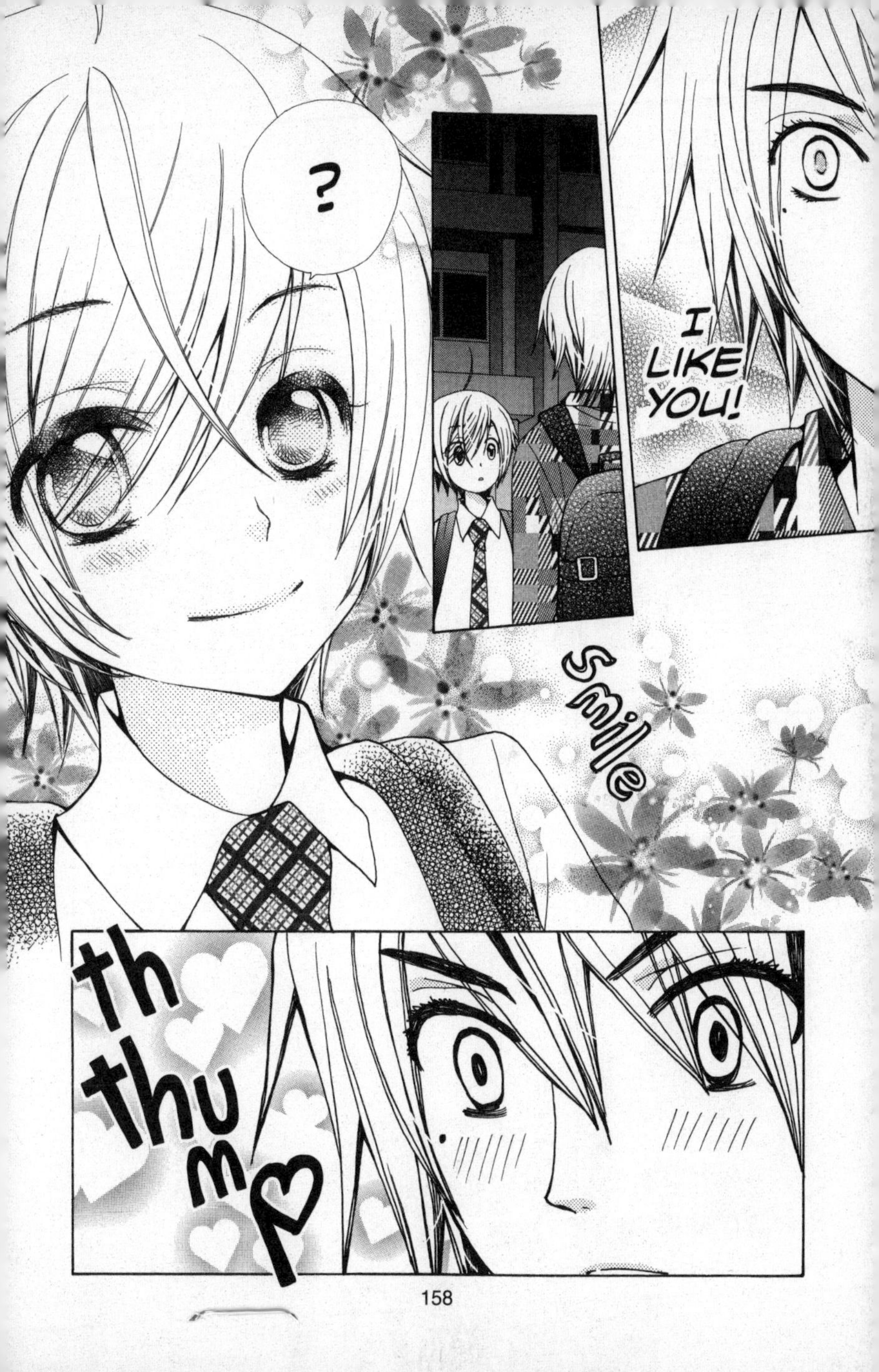
I LIKE YOU!
?
Smile
th thu mp

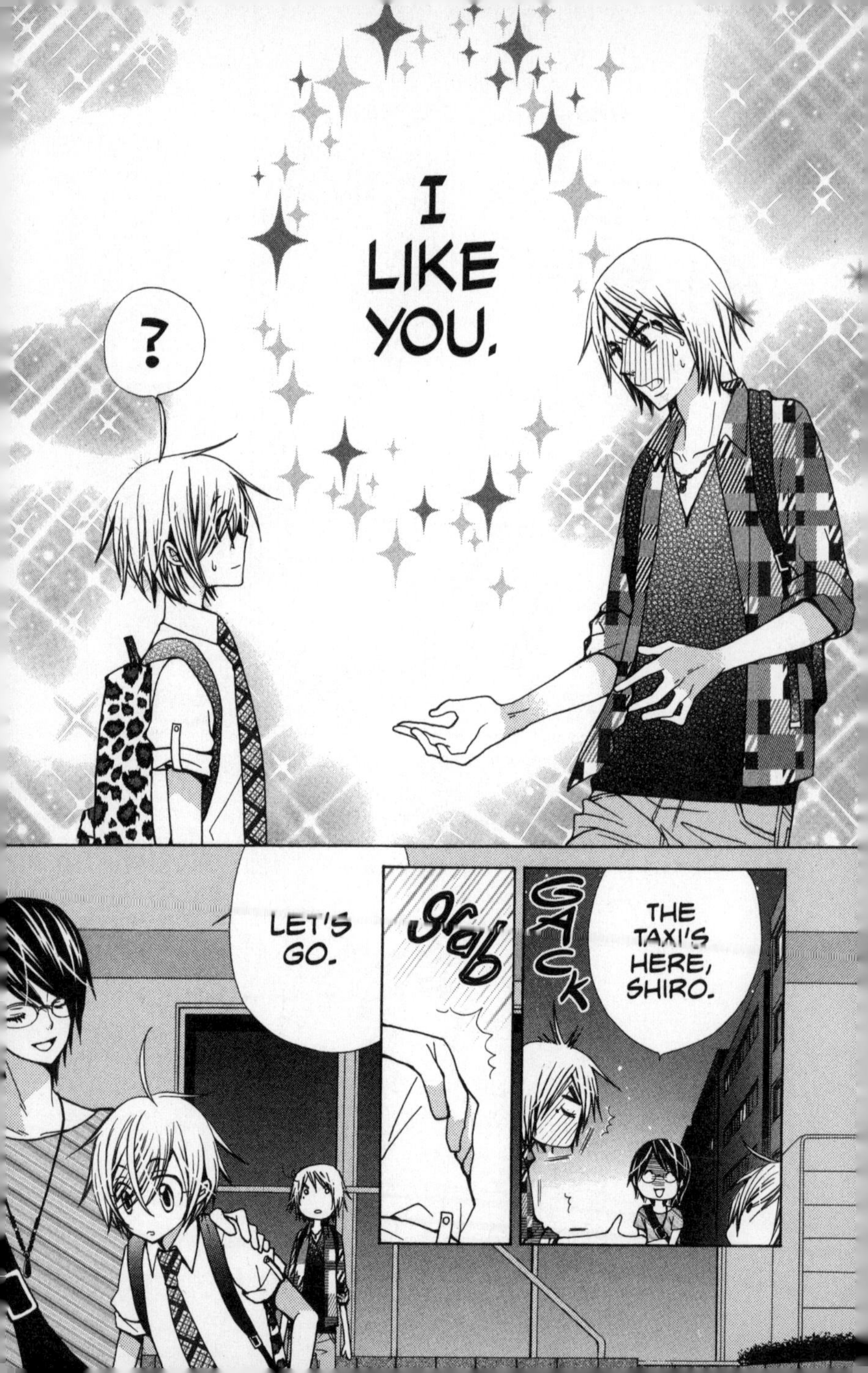
I LIKE YOU.
?
THE TAXI'S HERE, SHIRO.
GACK
grab
LET'S GO.

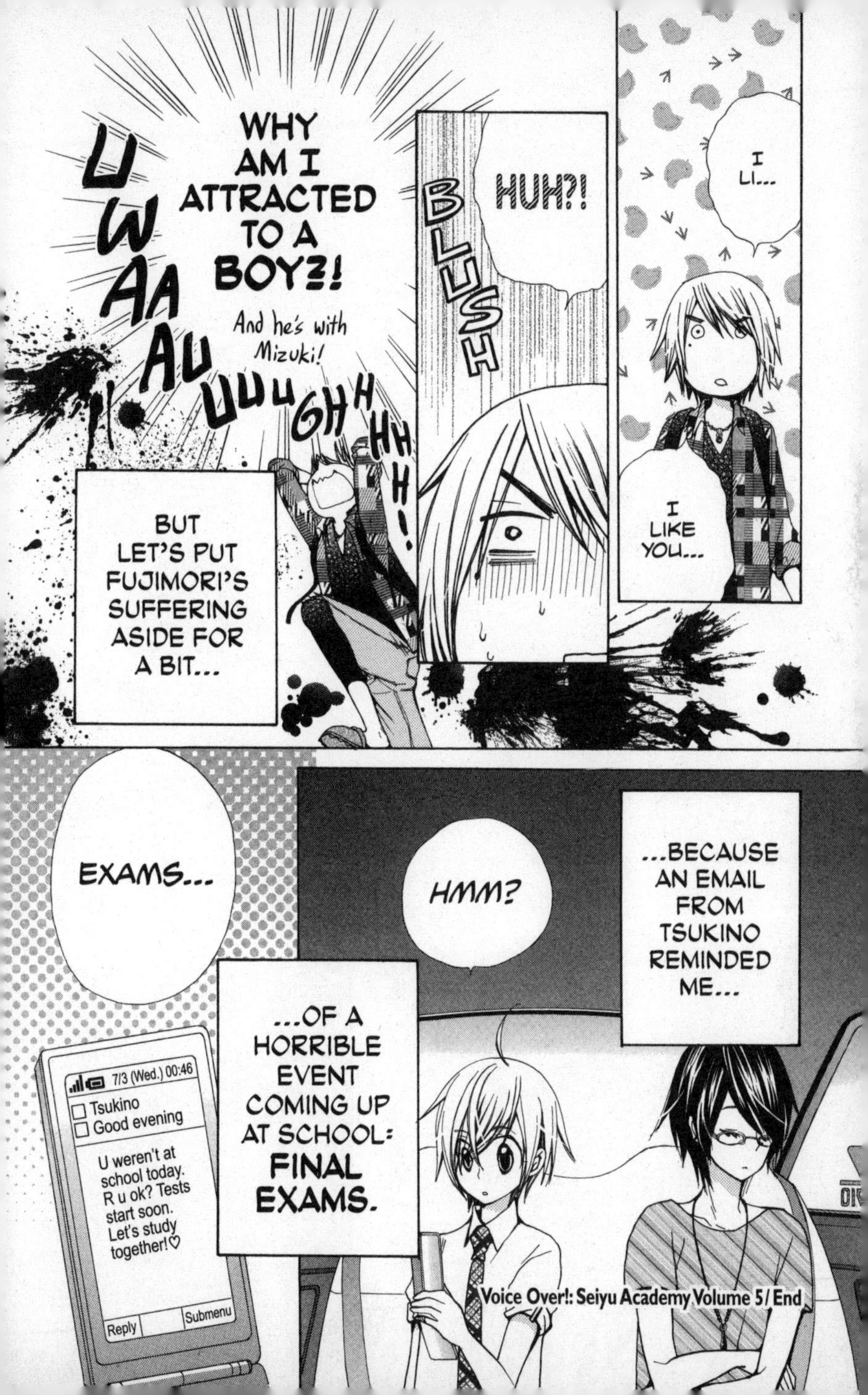

I LI...
I LIKE YOU...
HUH?!
BLUSH
WHY AM I ATTRACTED TO A BOY?!
UWAAAAUUUUGHHHHHH!
And he's with Mizuki!
BUT LET'S PUT FUJIMORI'S SUFFERING ASIDE FOR A BIT...
...BECAUSE AN EMAIL FROM TSUKINO REMINDED ME...
HMM?
...OF A HORRIBLE EVENT COMING UP AT SCHOOL: FINAL EXAMS.
Voice Over!: Seiyu Academy Volume 5/ End
EXAMS...
7/3 (Wed.) 00:46
Tsukino
Good evening
U weren't at school today. R u ok? Tests start soon. Let's study together!♡
Reply
Submenu

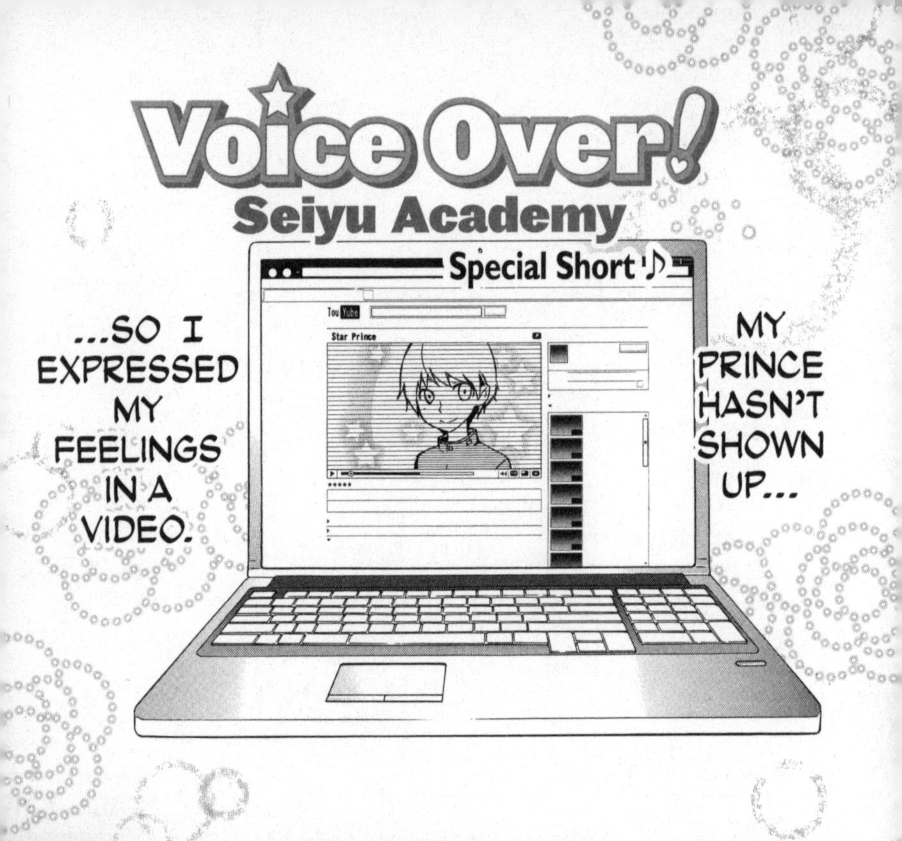
Voice Over!
Seiyu Academy
Special Short ♪
Star Prince
MY PRINCE HASN'T SHOWN UP...
...SO I EXPRESSED MY FEELINGS IN A VIDEO.
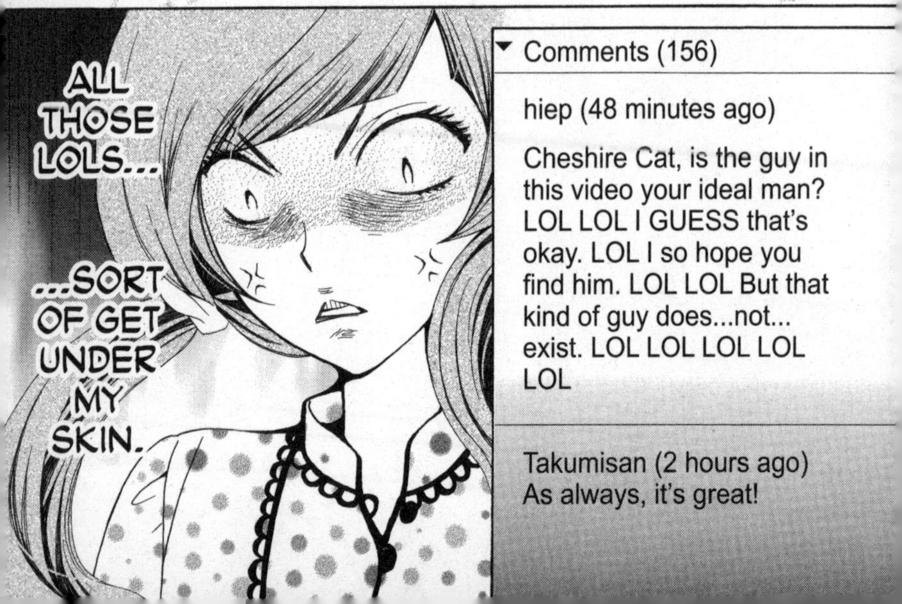
▼ Comments (156)
hiep (48 minutes ago)
Cheshire Cat, is the guy in this video your ideal man? LOL LOL I GUESS that's okay. LOL I so hope you find him. LOL LOL But that kind of guy does...not... exist. LOL LOL LOL LOL LOL
Takumisan (2 hours ago)
As always, it's great!
ALL THOSE LOLS...
...SORT OF GET UNDER MY SKIN.

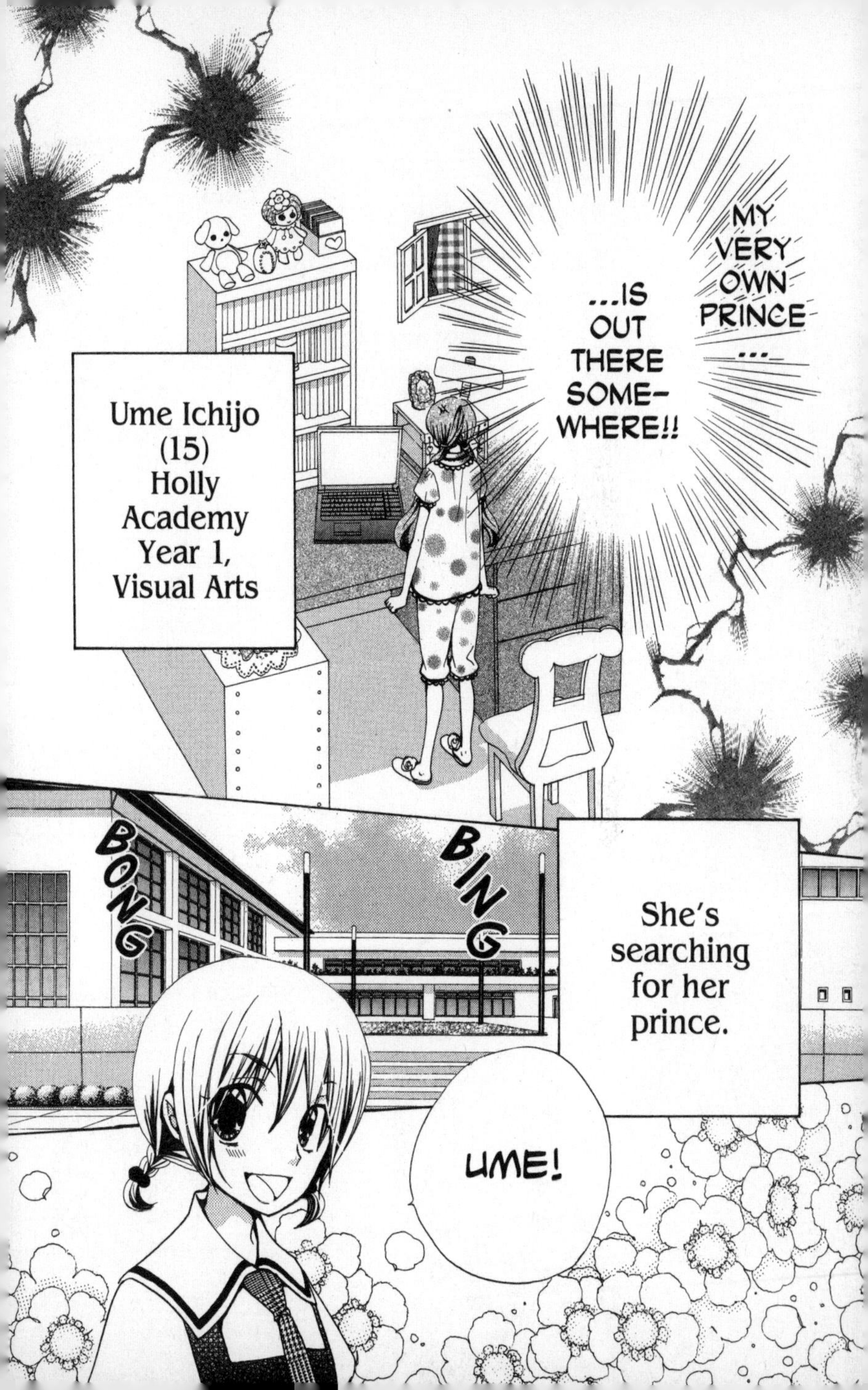
MY VERY OWN PRINCE...
...IS OUT THERE SOME-WHERE!!
Ume Ichijo (15) Holly Academy Year 1, Visual Arts
She's searching for her prince.
BING
BONG
UME!

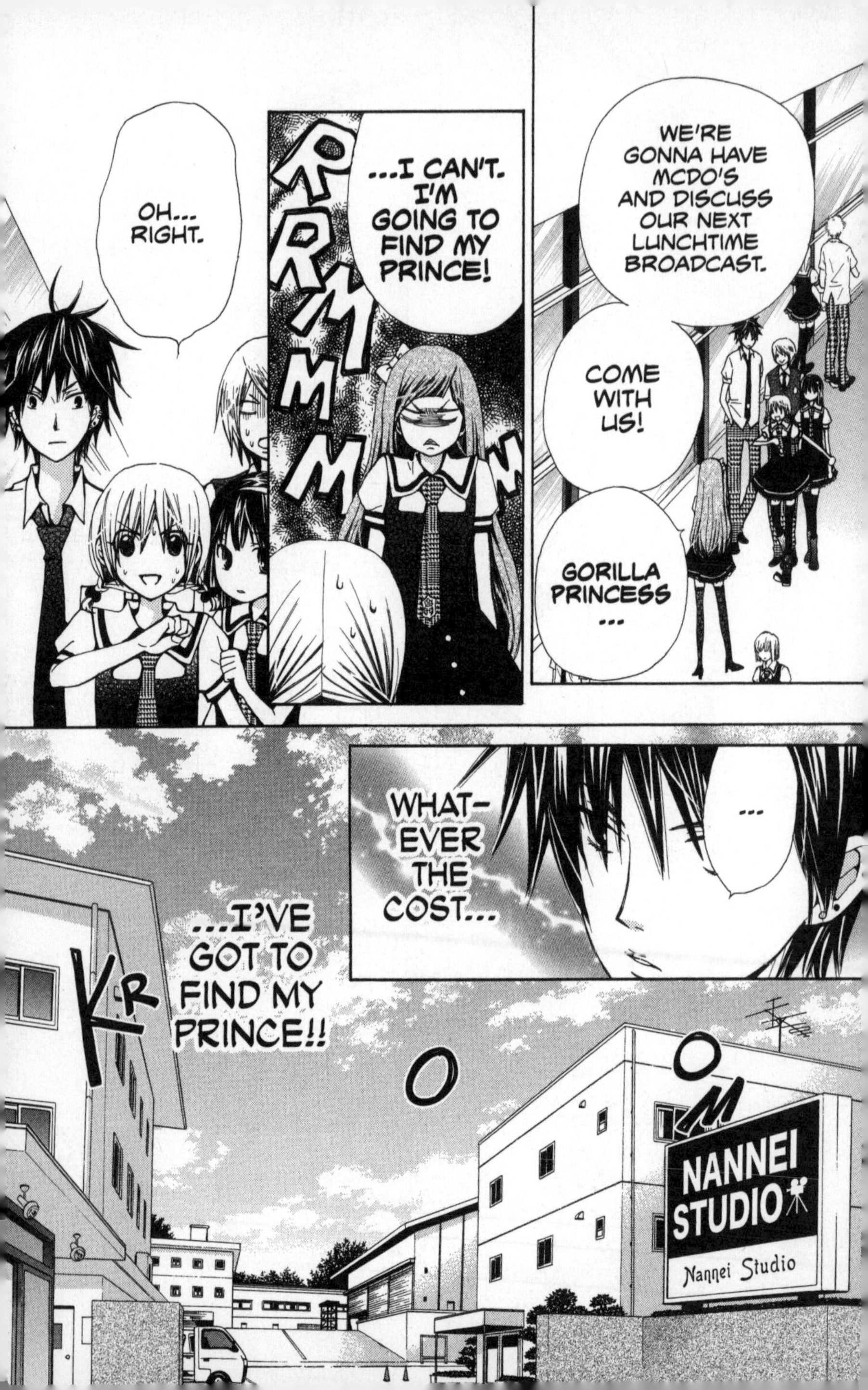
WE'RE GONNA HAVE MCDO'S AND DISCUSS OUR NEXT LUNCHTIME BROADCAST.
COME WITH US!
GORILLA PRINCESS...
RRMMMM
...I CAN'T. I'M GOING TO FIND MY PRINCE!
OH... RIGHT.
...
WHAT-EVER THE COST...
...I'VE GOT TO FIND MY PRINCE!!
KI-R
OMM
NANNEI STUDIO
Nannei Studio

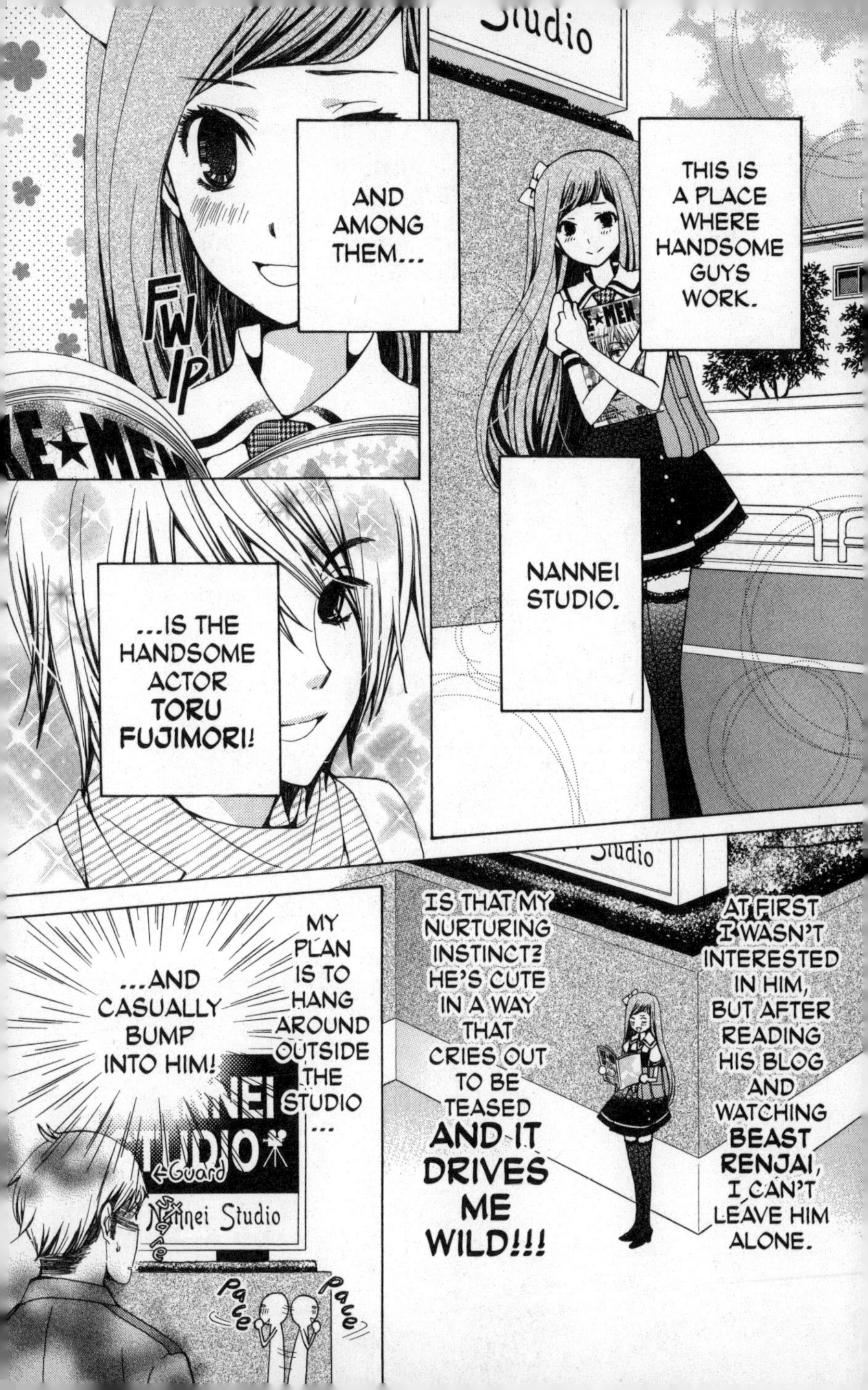
Studio
THIS IS A PLACE WHERE HANDSOME GUYS WORK.
E★MEN
NANNEI STUDIO.
AND AMONG THEM...
FWIP
E★MEN
...IS THE HANDSOME ACTOR TORU FUJIMORI!
Studio
AT FIRST I WASN'T INTERESTED IN HIM, BUT AFTER READING HIS BLOG AND WATCHING BEAST RENJAI, I CAN'T LEAVE HIM ALONE.
IS THAT MY NURTURING INSTINCT? HE'S CUTE IN A WAY THAT CRIES OUT TO BE TEASED AND IT DRIVES ME WILD!!!
MY PLAN IS TO HANG AROUND OUTSIDE THE STUDIO...
...AND CASUALLY BUMP INTO HIM!
NEI STUDIO
←Guard
Nannei Studio
Stare
Pace
Pace

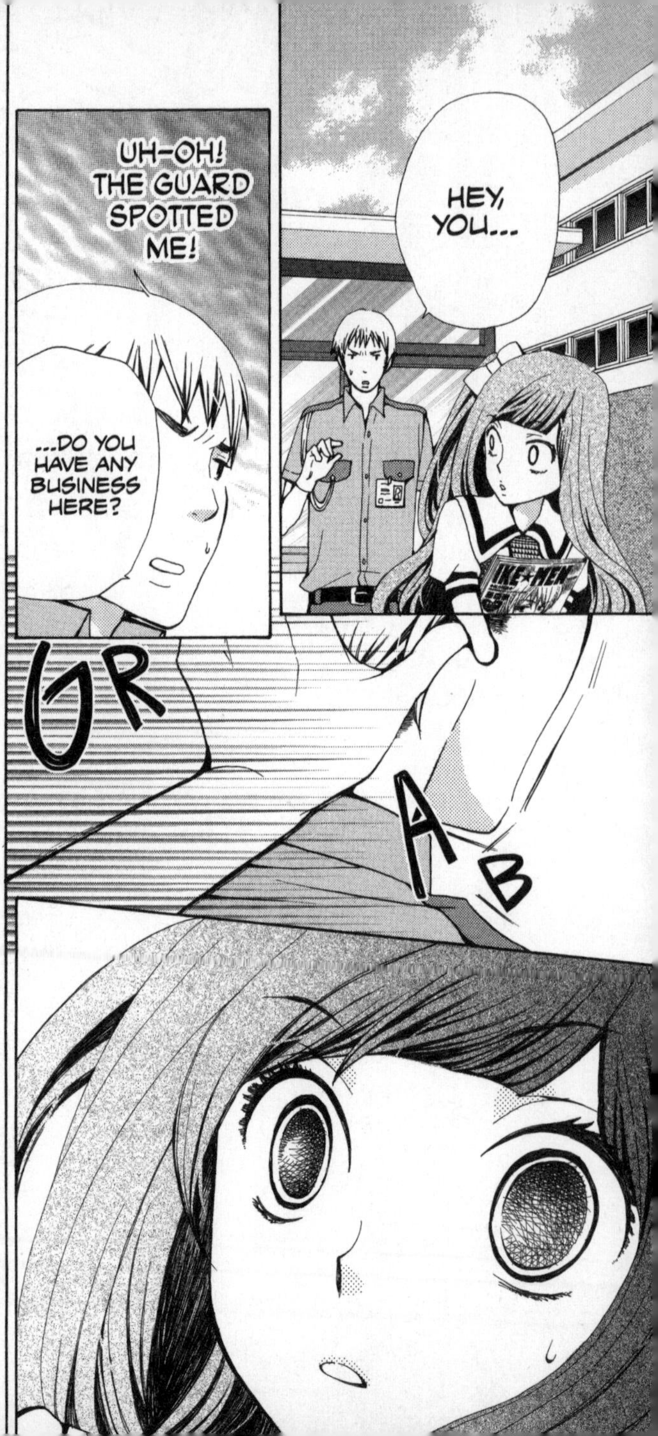
HEY, YOU...
UH-OH! THE GUARD SPOTTED ME!
...DO YOU HAVE ANY BUSINESS HERE?
GRAB

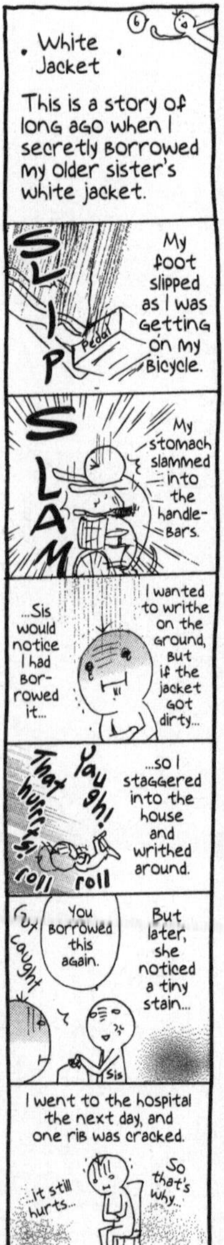
6
White Jacket
This is a story of long ago when I secretly borrowed my older sister's white jacket.
SLIP
My foot slipped as I was getting on my bicycle.
Pedal
SLAM
My stomach slammed into the handlebars.
...Sis would notice I had borrowed it...
I wanted to writhe on the ground, but if the jacket got dirty...
That hurrrts!
Yaugh!
roll roll
...so I staggered into the house and writhed around.
Gulp
caught
You borrowed this again.
But later, she noticed a tiny stain...
Sis
I went to the hospital the next day, and one rib was cracked.
...it still hurts...
So that's why...
I got what I deserved...

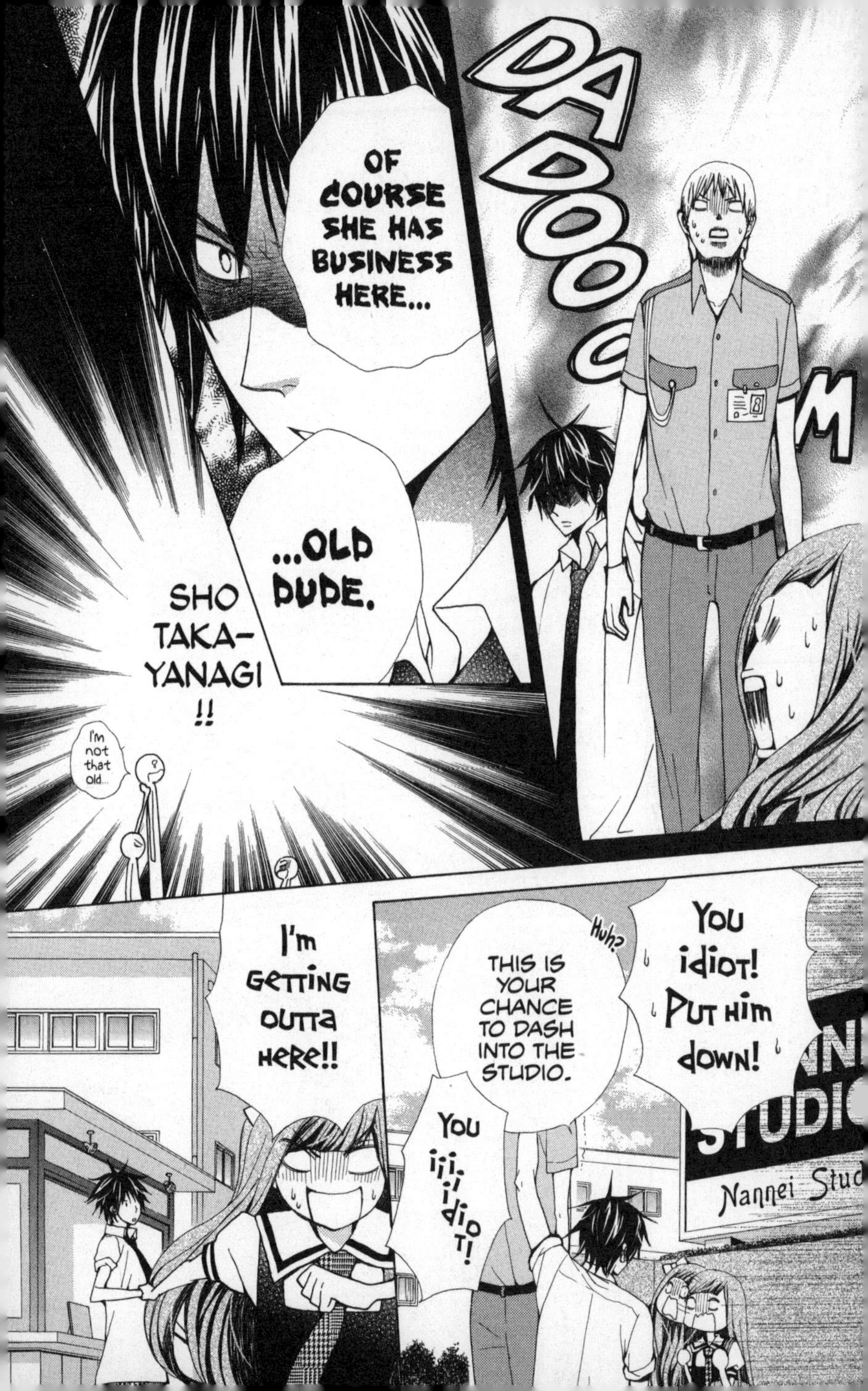
DADOOOOM
OF COURSE SHE HAS BUSINESS HERE...
...OLD DUDE.
SHO TAKA-YANAGI !!
I'm not that old...
You idiot! Put him down!
Huh?
THIS IS YOUR CHANCE TO DASH INTO THE STUDIO.
You iiiiidiot!
STUDIO
Nannei Stud
I'm getting outta here!!

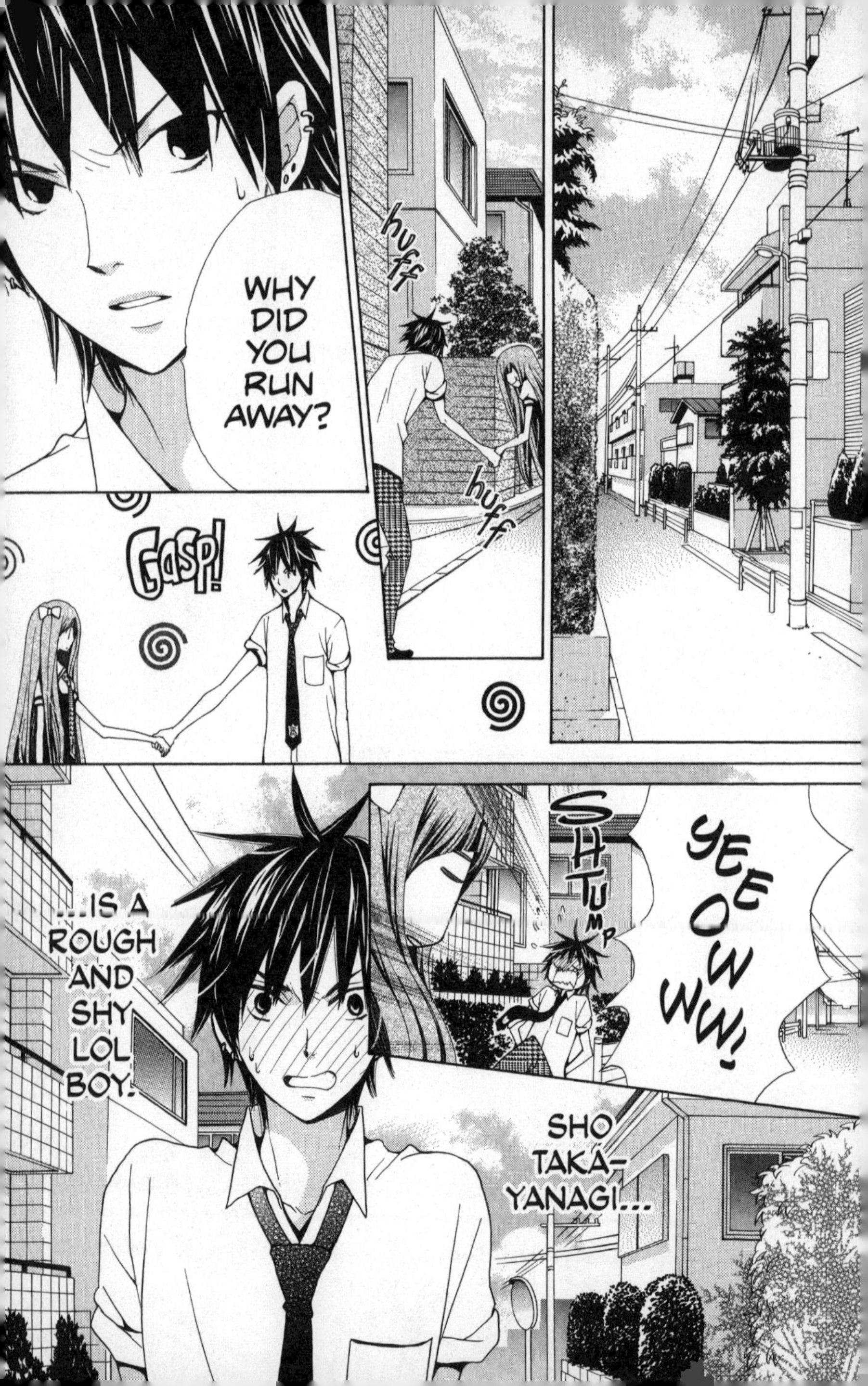
huff
huff
WHY DID YOU RUN AWAY?
GASP!
YEEOWWW!
SHTUMP
SHO TAKAYANAGI...
...IS A ROUGH AND SHY LOL BOY.

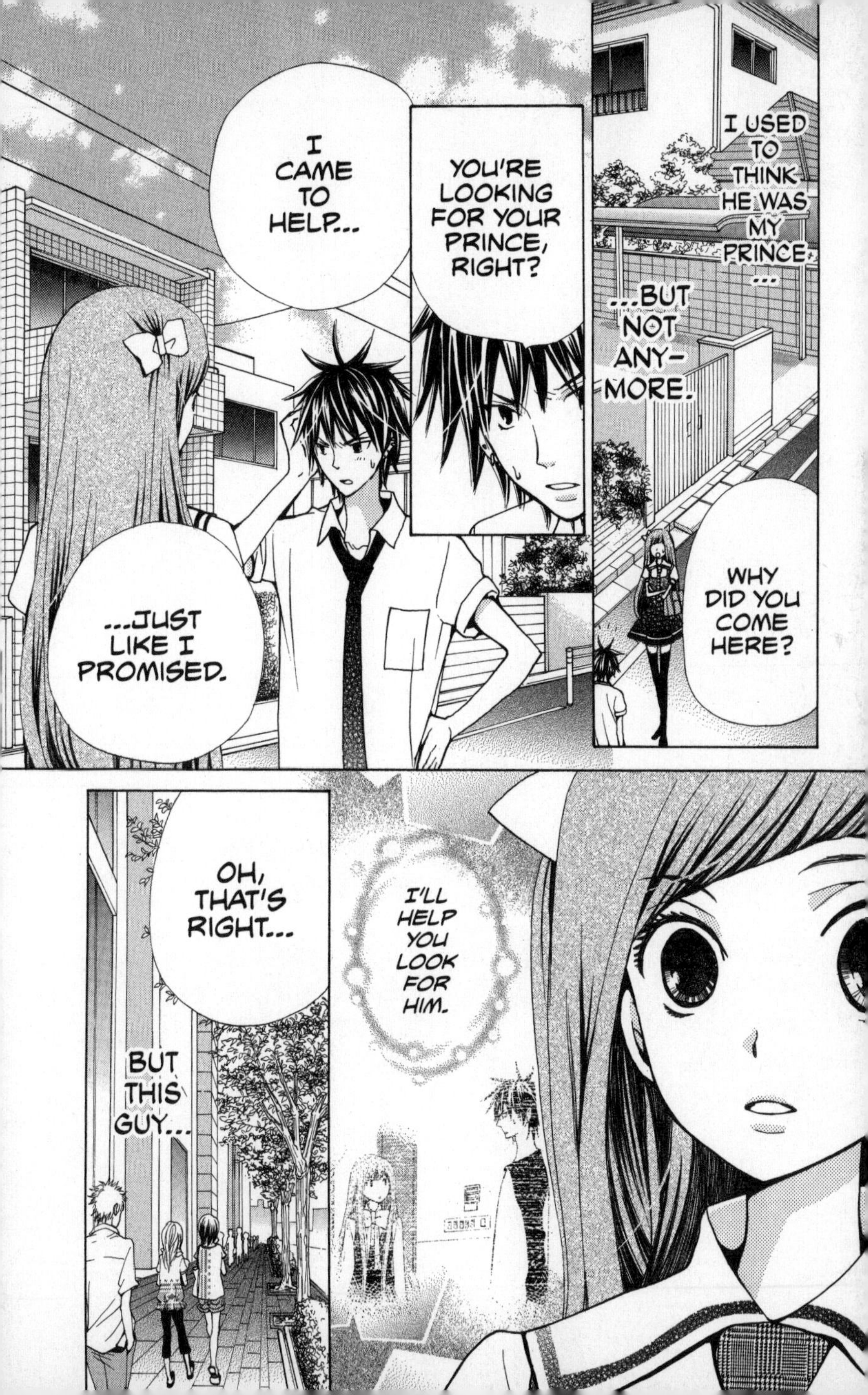
I USED TO THINK HE WAS MY PRINCE...
...BUT NOT ANYMORE.
WHY DID YOU COME HERE?
YOU'RE LOOKING FOR YOUR PRINCE, RIGHT?
I CAME TO HELP...
...JUST LIKE I PROMISED.
I'LL HELP YOU LOOK FOR HIM.
OH, THAT'S RIGHT...
BUT THIS GUY...

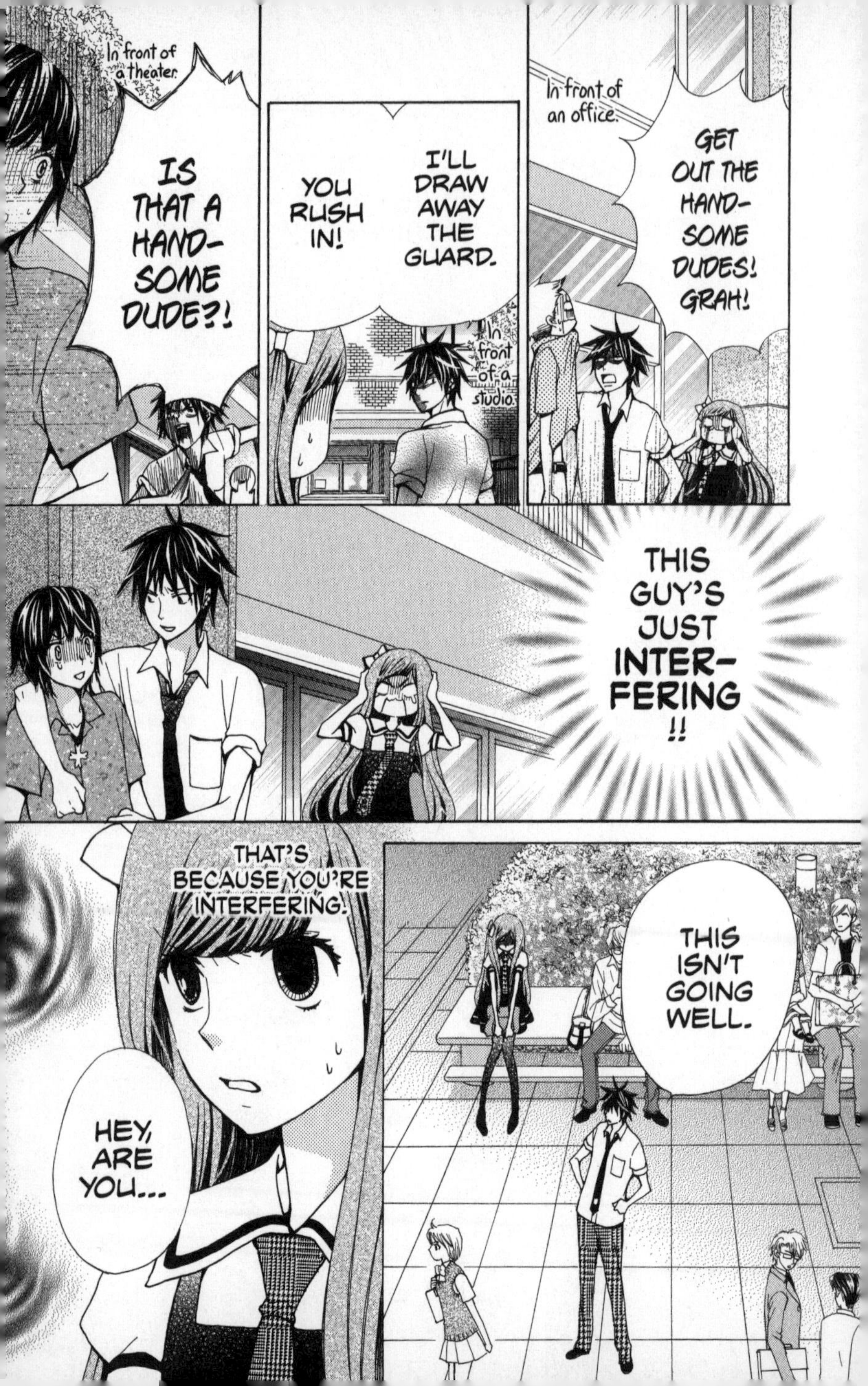
In front of an office.
GET OUT THE HAND-SOME DUDES! GRAH!
In front of a studio.
I'LL DRAW AWAY THE GUARD.
YOU RUSH IN!
In front of a theater.
IS THAT A HAND-SOME DUDE?!
THIS GUY'S JUST INTER-FERING !!
THIS ISN'T GOING WELL.
THAT'S BECAUSE YOU'RE INTERFERING!
HEY, ARE YOU...

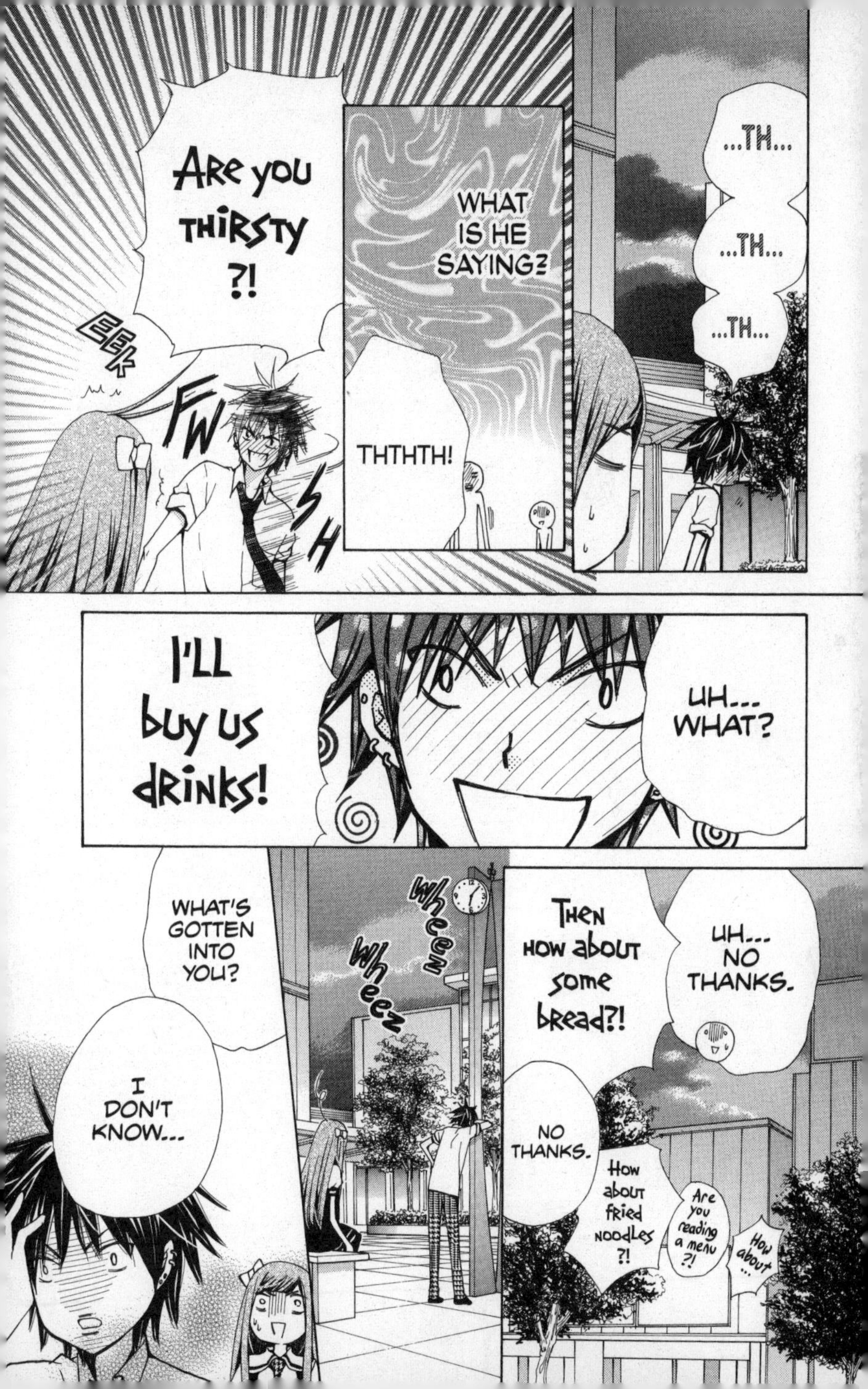
...TH...
...TH...
...TH...
WHAT IS HE SAYING?
THTHTH!
Are you THIRSTY ?!
EEK
FWSH
UH... WHAT?
I'LL buy us drinks!
UH... NO THANKS.
Then how about some bread?!
NO THANKS.
How about...
Are you reading a menu ?!
How about fried noodles ?!
wheez
wheez
WHAT'S GOTTEN INTO YOU?
I DON'T KNOW...

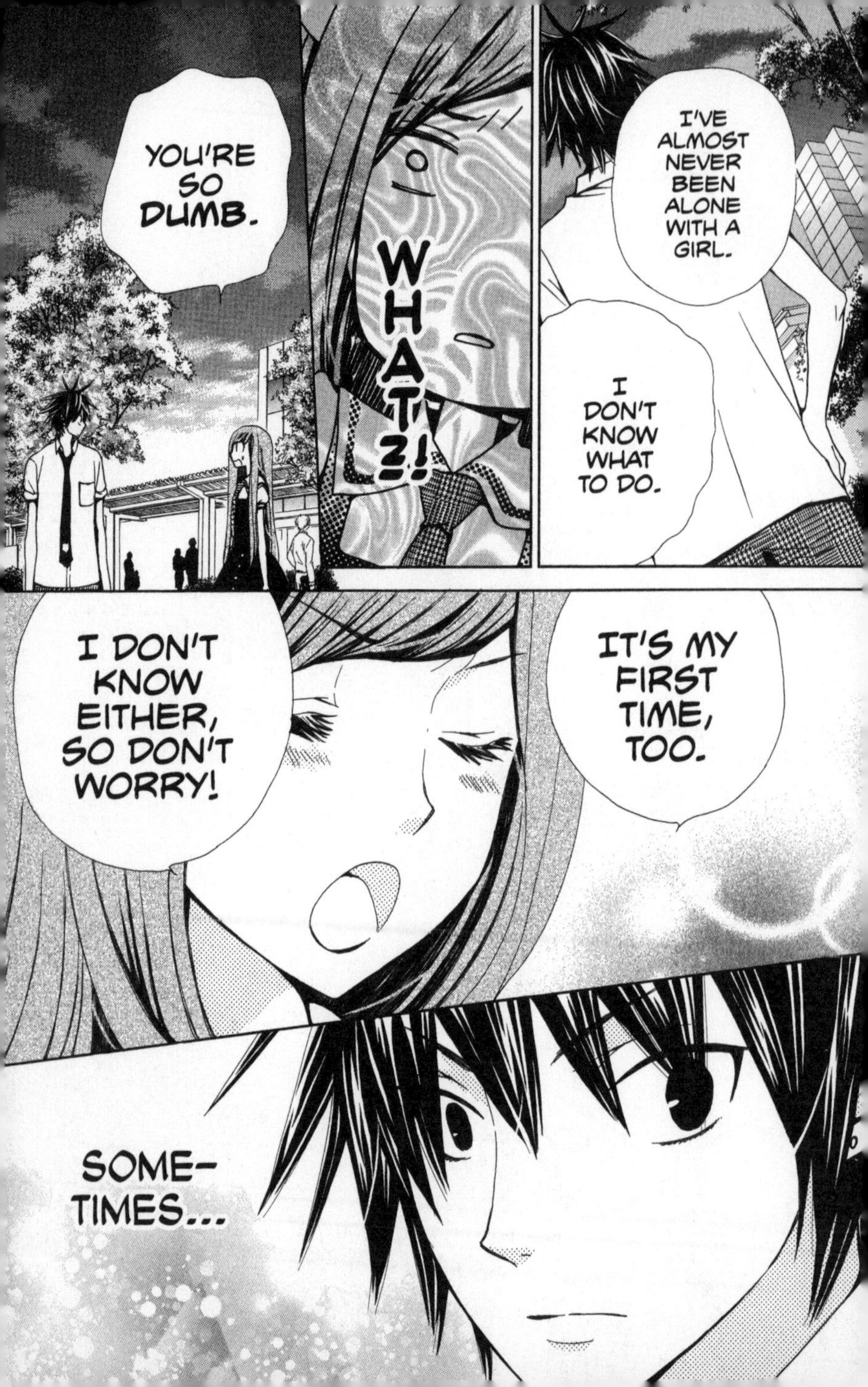
I'VE ALMOST NEVER BEEN ALONE WITH A GIRL.
I DON'T KNOW WHAT TO DO.
WHAT?!
YOU'RE SO DUMB.
IT'S MY FIRST TIME, TOO.
I DON'T KNOW EITHER, SO DON'T WORRY!
SOME-TIMES...

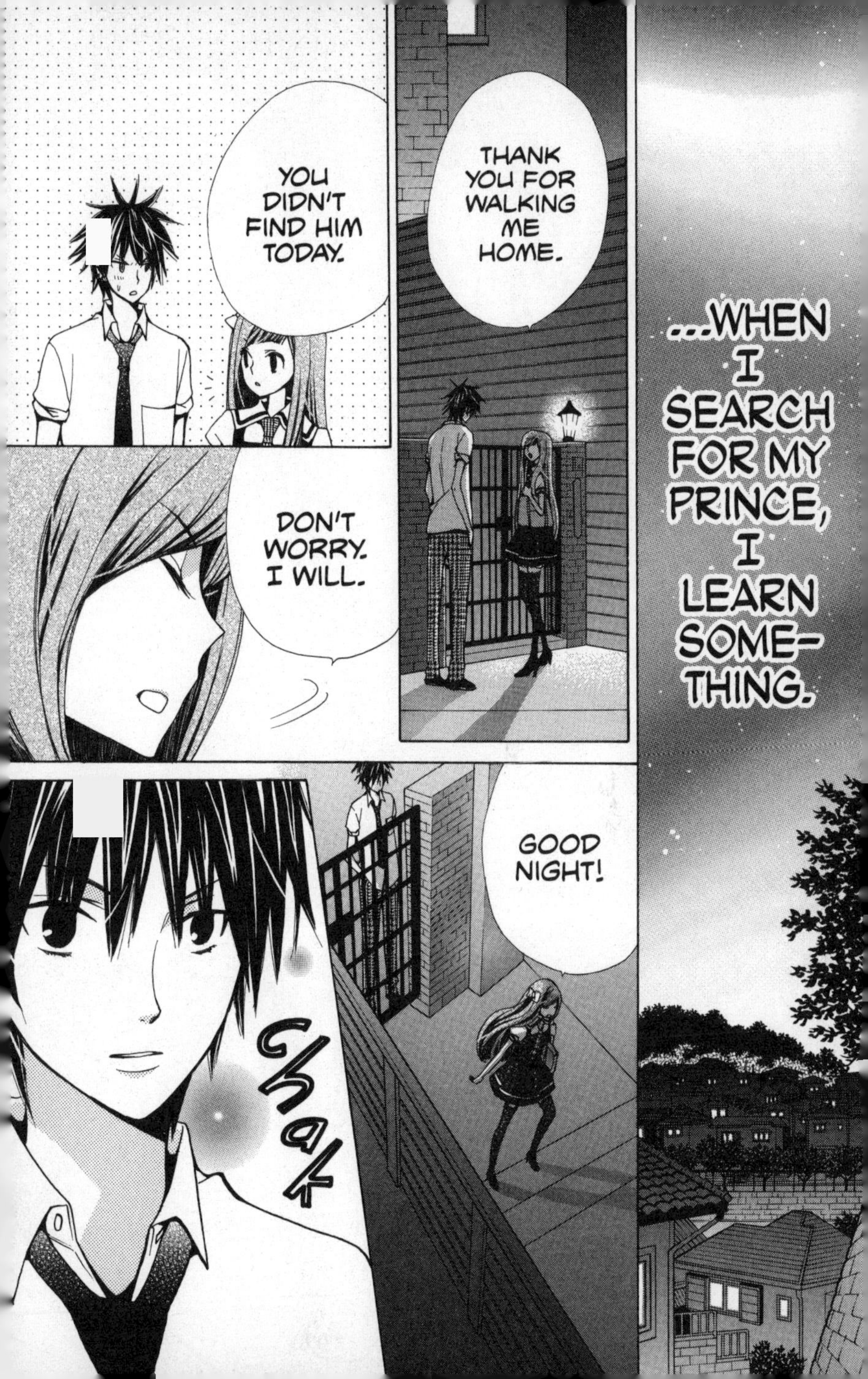
...WHEN I SEARCH FOR MY PRINCE, I LEARN SOME-THING.
THANK YOU FOR WALKING ME HOME.
YOU DIDN'T FIND HIM TODAY.
DON'T WORRY. I WILL.
GOOD NIGHT!
Chak

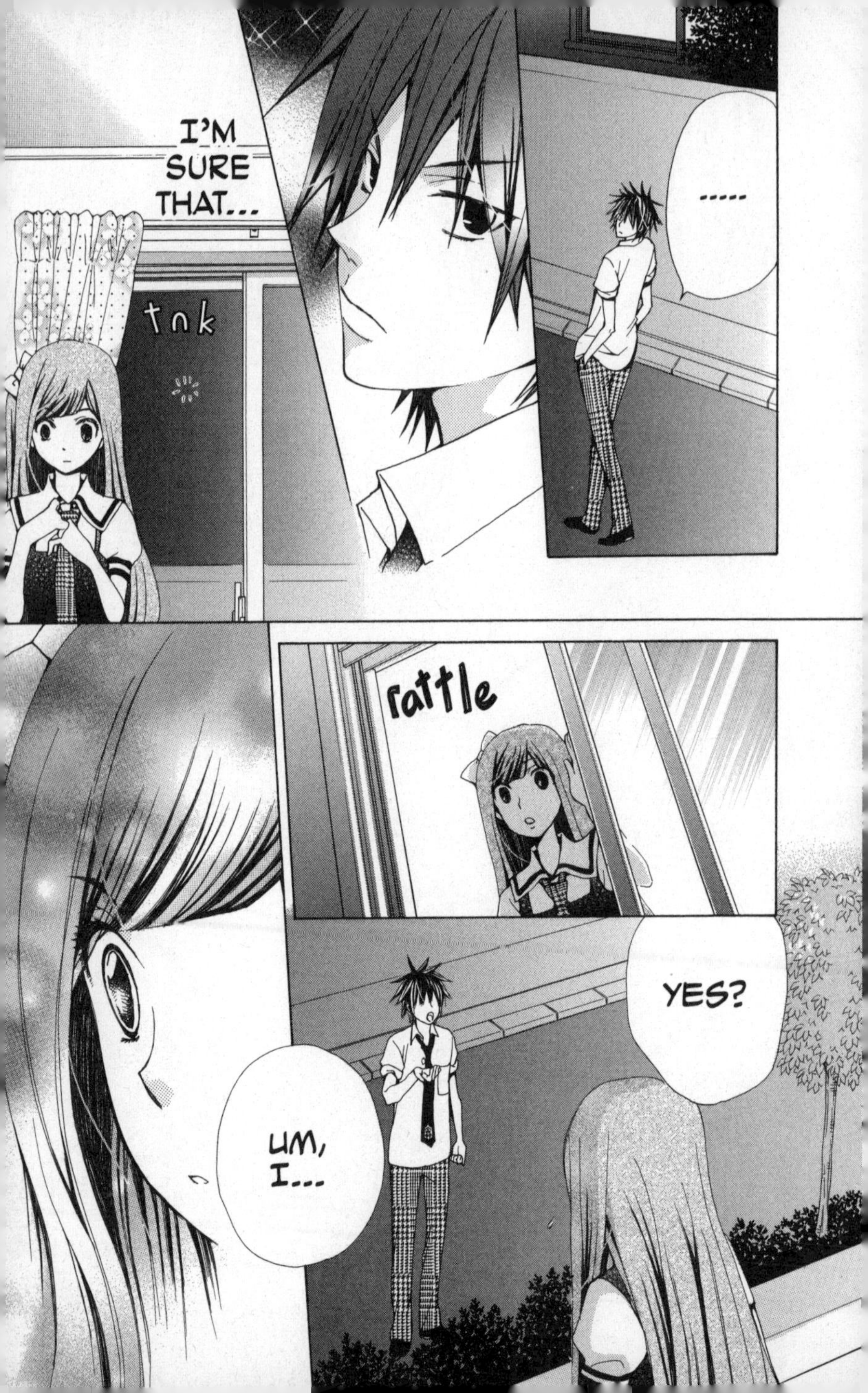
.....
I'M SURE THAT...
tnk
rattle
YES?
UM, I...

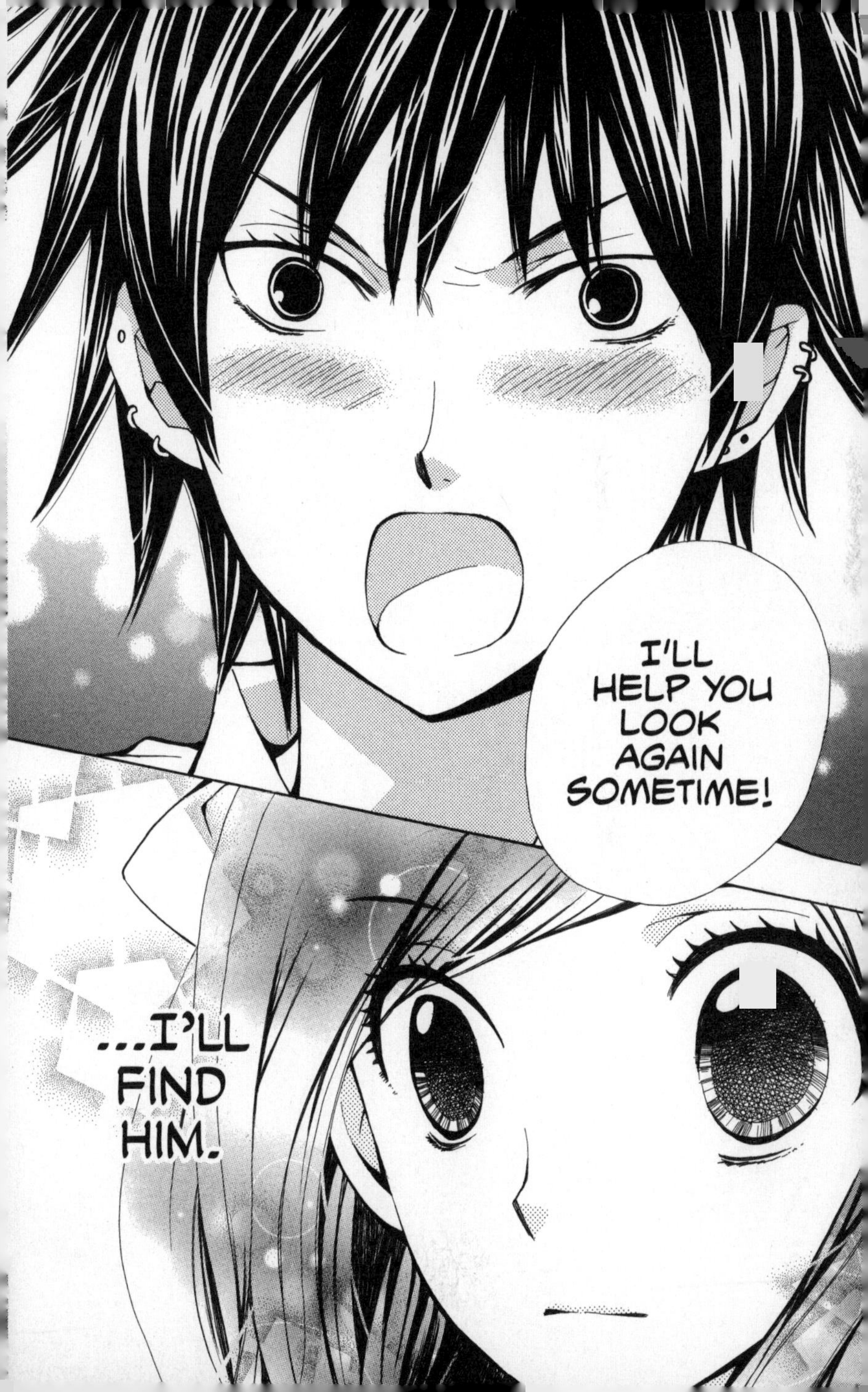
I'LL HELP YOU LOOK AGAIN SOMETIME!
...I'LL FIND HIM.

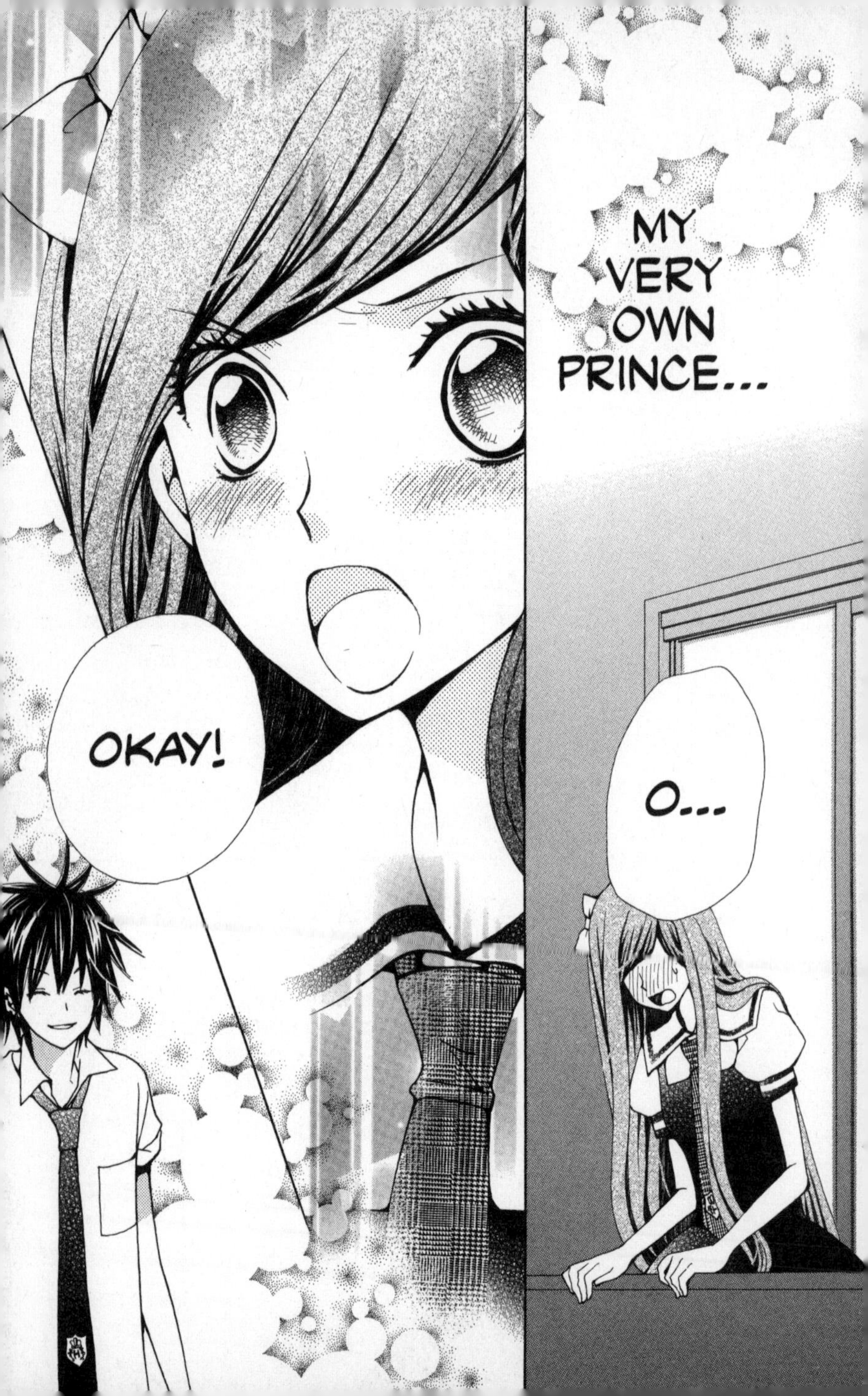
MY VERY OWN PRINCE...
O...
OKAY!

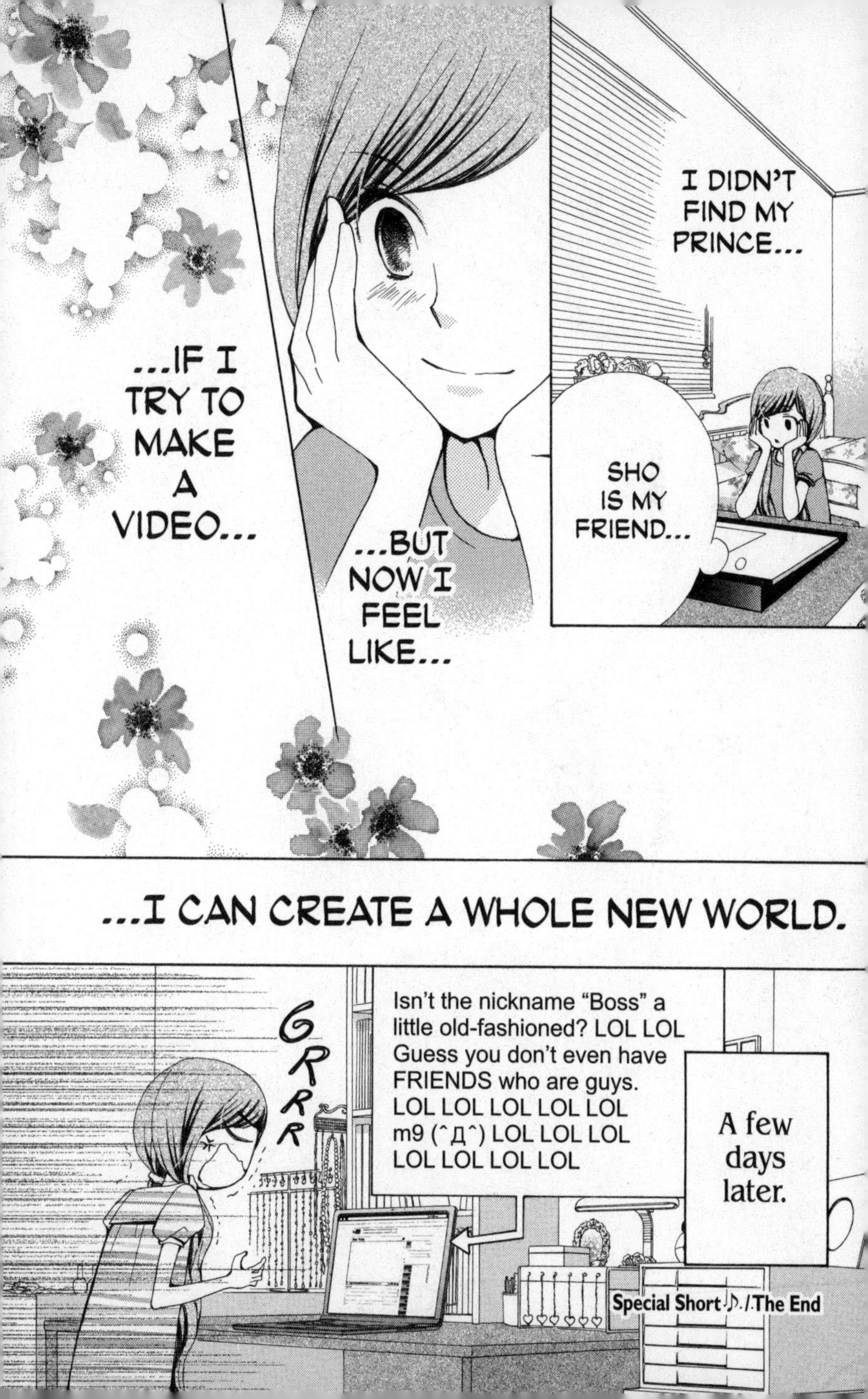
I DIDN'T FIND MY PRINCE...
SHO IS MY FRIEND...
...BUT NOW I FEEL LIKE...
...IF I TRY TO MAKE A VIDEO...
...I CAN CREATE A WHOLE NEW WORLD.
A few days later.
Isn't the nickname "Boss" a little old-fashioned? LOL LOL Guess you don't even have FRIENDS who are guys. LOL LOL LOL LOL LOL m9 (^Д^) LOL LOL LOL LOL LOL LOL LOL
GRRR
Special Short ♪ / The End

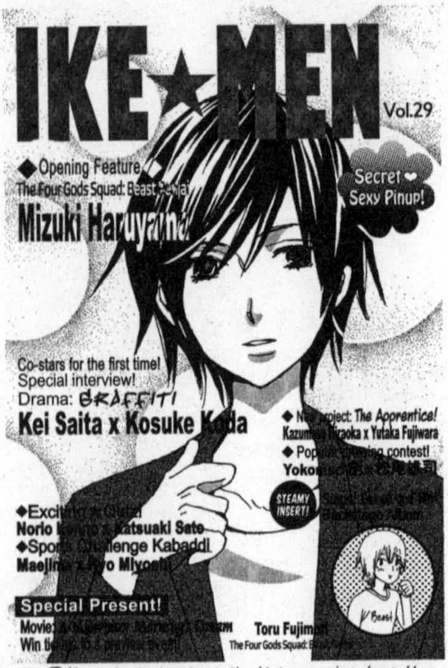
IKE★MEN
Vol.29
◆Opening Feature
Secret❤ Sexy Pinup!
Co-stars for the first time!
Special interview!
Drama: GRAFFITI
Kei Saita x Kosuke
STEAMY INSERT!
Special Present!

① If you look closely at the idol magazine *Ike★Men*, Fujimori is there, but really small. The headlines are really detailed.

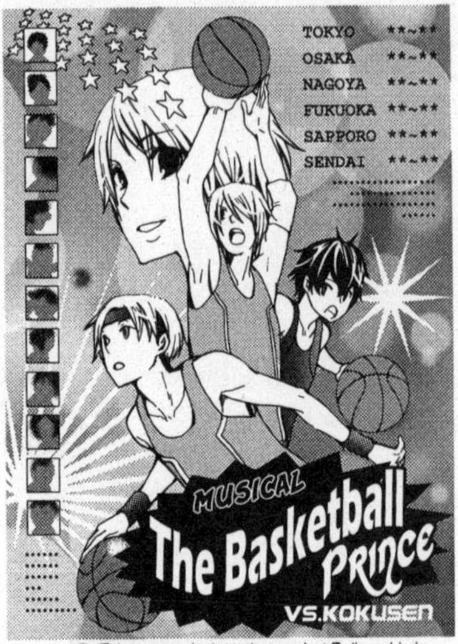
TOKYO **~**
OSAKA **~**
NAGOYA **~**
FUKUOKA **~**
SAPPORO **~**
SENDAI **~**
MUSICAL
The Basketball PRINCE
VS.KOKUSEN

② This poster is for the musical Fujimori is in. The photos of the cast on the left are incredible. huff huff

Sudden Bonus Content Corner!!

Introducing posters from *Voice Over!!* My assistant I-san made them. They're awesome!!

③ This poster is for an AQUA event. If you zoom in, you can tell the art is rough.

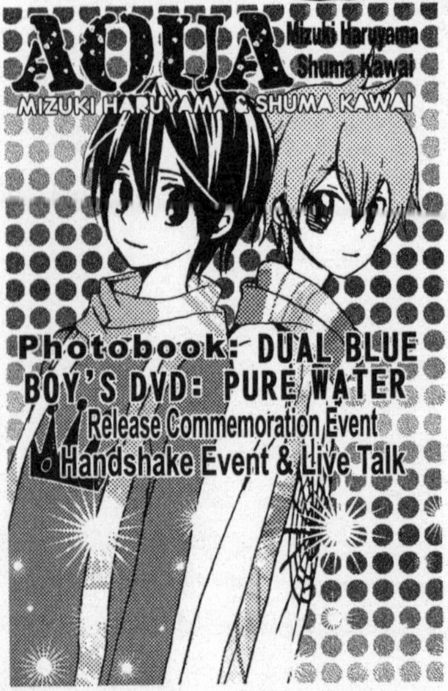
AQUA
Mizuki Haruyama
Shuma Kawai
MIZUKI HARUYAMA & SHUMA KAWAI
Photobook: DUAL BLUE
BOY'S DVD: PURE WATER
Release Commemoration Event
Handshake Event & Live Talk

④ This is an event poster for Toru Fujimori. Thanks to I-san for dressing up my weak illustration.

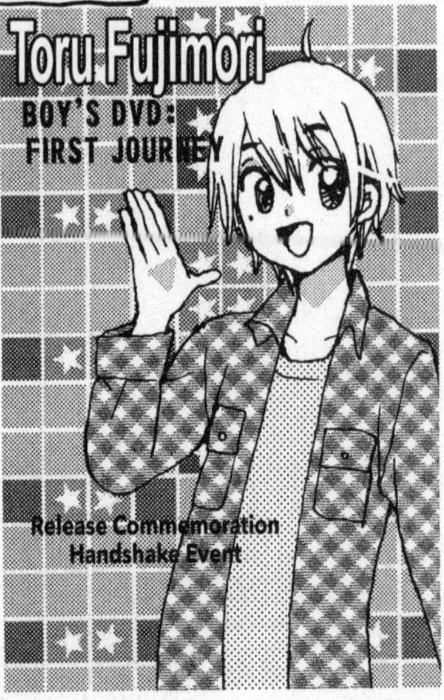
Toru Fujimori
BOY'S DVD:
FIRST JOURNEY
Release Commemoration
Handshake Event

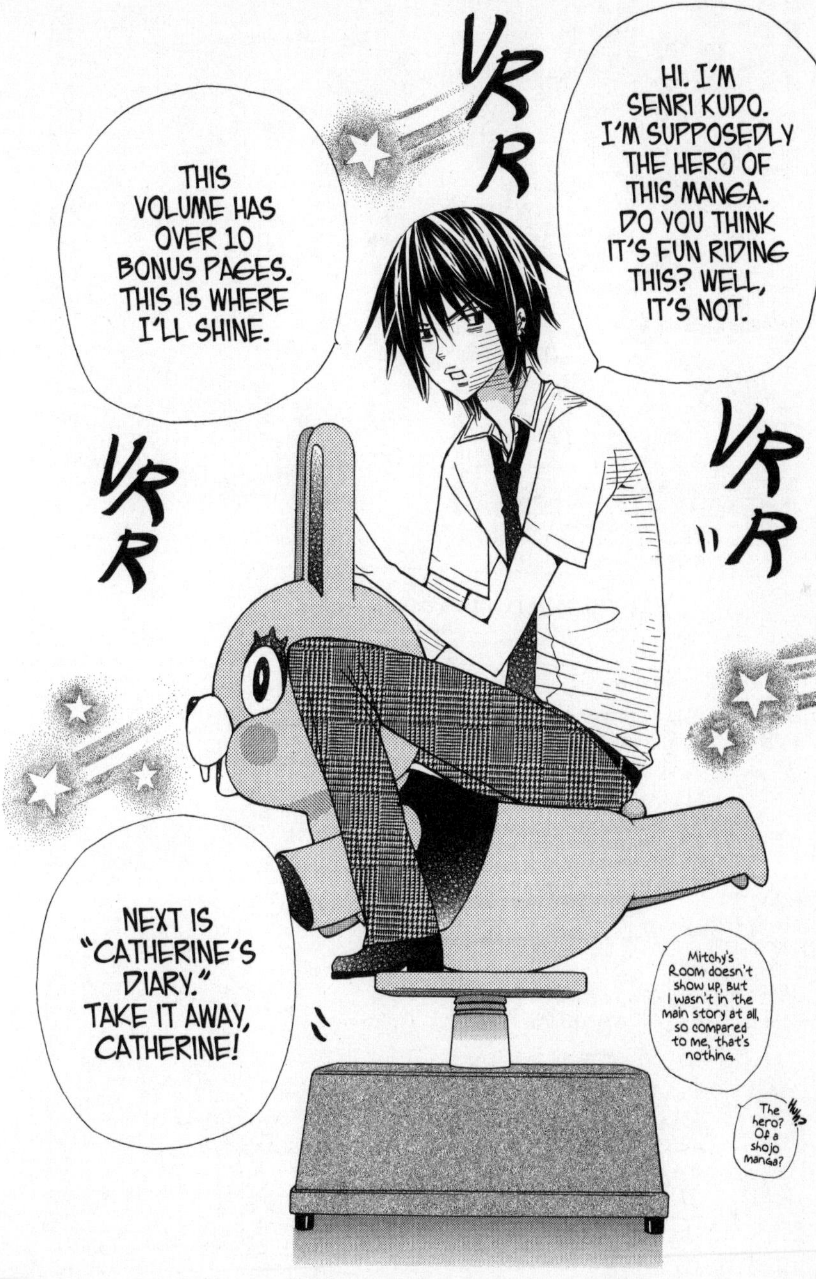
HI. I'M SENRI KUDO. I'M SUPPOSEDLY THE HERO OF THIS MANGA. DO YOU THINK IT'S FUN RIDING THIS? WELL, IT'S NOT.
VRR
THIS VOLUME HAS OVER 10 BONUS PAGES. THIS IS WHERE I'LL SHINE.
VRR
VRR
Mitchy's Room doesn't show up, but I wasn't in the main story at all, so compared to me, that's nothing.
NEXT IS "CATHERINE'S DIARY." TAKE IT AWAY, CATHERINE!
HUH?
The hero? Of a shojo manga?

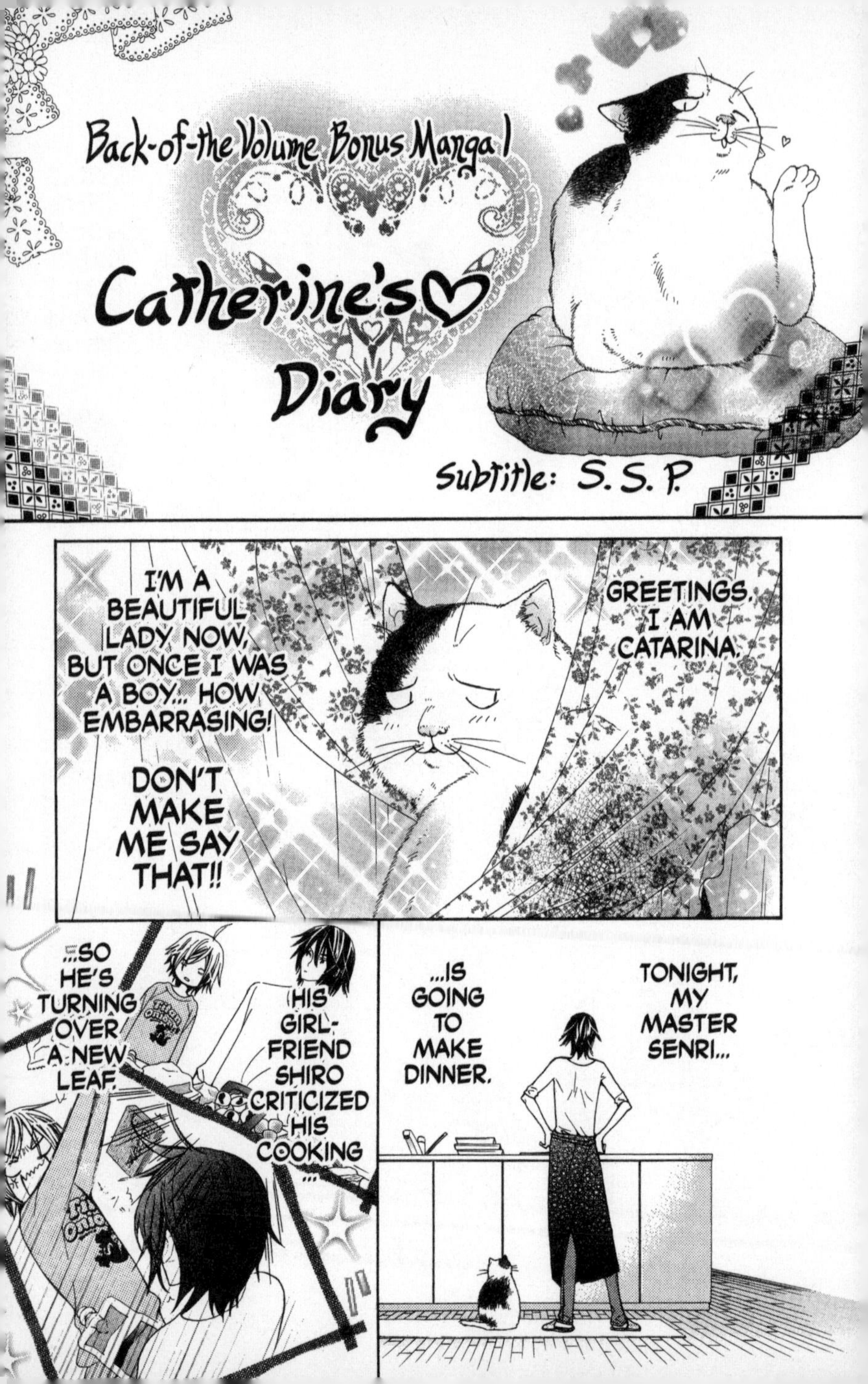
Back-of-the Volume Bonus Manga 1
Catherine's Diary
Subtitle: S.S.P.
GREETINGS. I AM CATARINA.
I'M A BEAUTIFUL LADY NOW, BUT ONCE I WAS A BOY... HOW EMBARRASING!
DON'T MAKE ME SAY THAT!!
TONIGHT, MY MASTER SENRI...
...IS GOING TO MAKE DINNER.
HIS GIRL-FRIEND SHIRO CRITICIZED HIS COOKING...
...SO HE'S TURNING OVER A NEW LEAF.

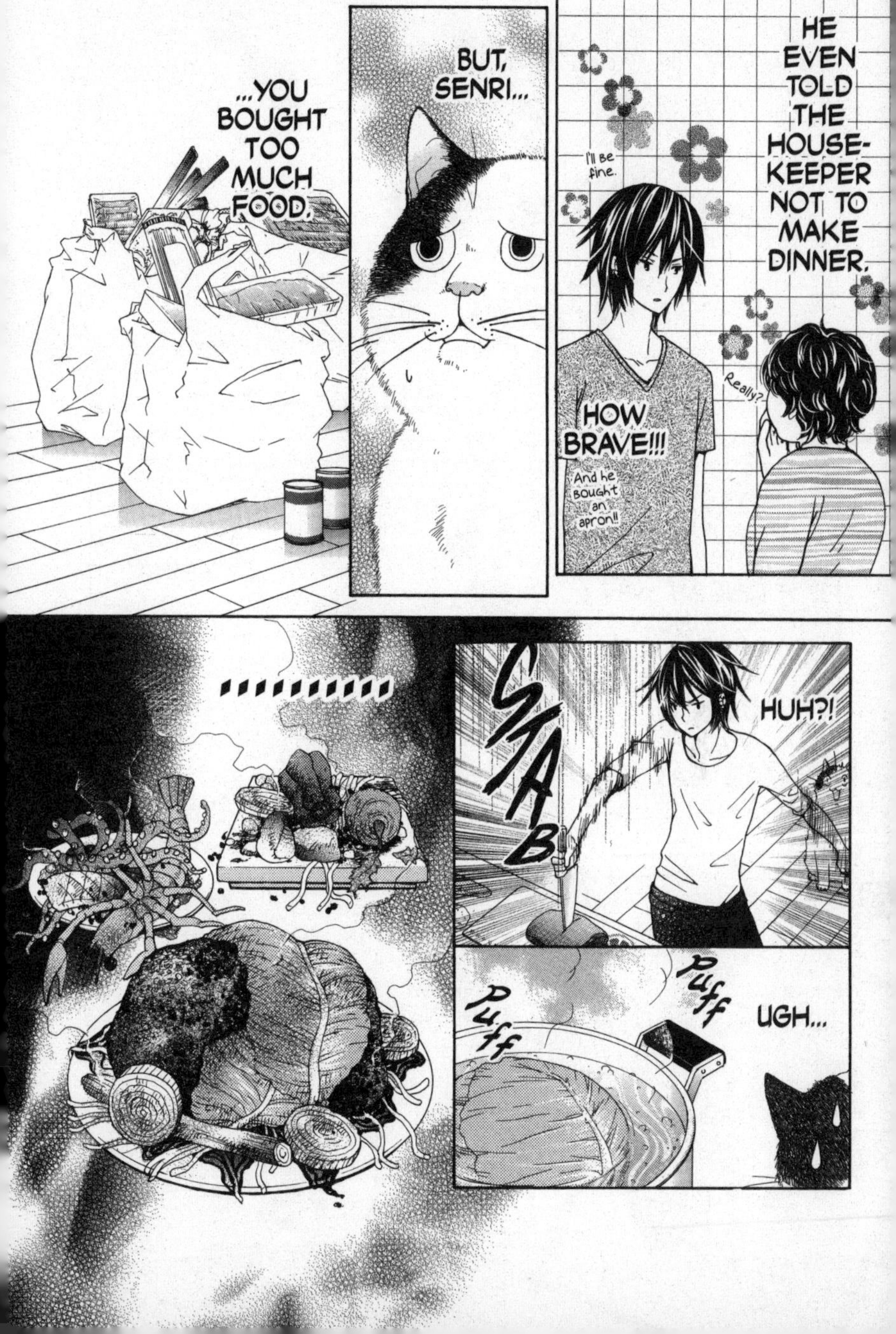
HE EVEN TOLD THE HOUSE-KEEPER NOT TO MAKE DINNER.
I'll be fine.
Really?
HOW BRAVE!!!
And he bought an apron!!
BUT, SENRI...
...YOU BOUGHT TOO MUCH FOOD.
HUH?!
STAB
Puff
Puff
UGH...
....

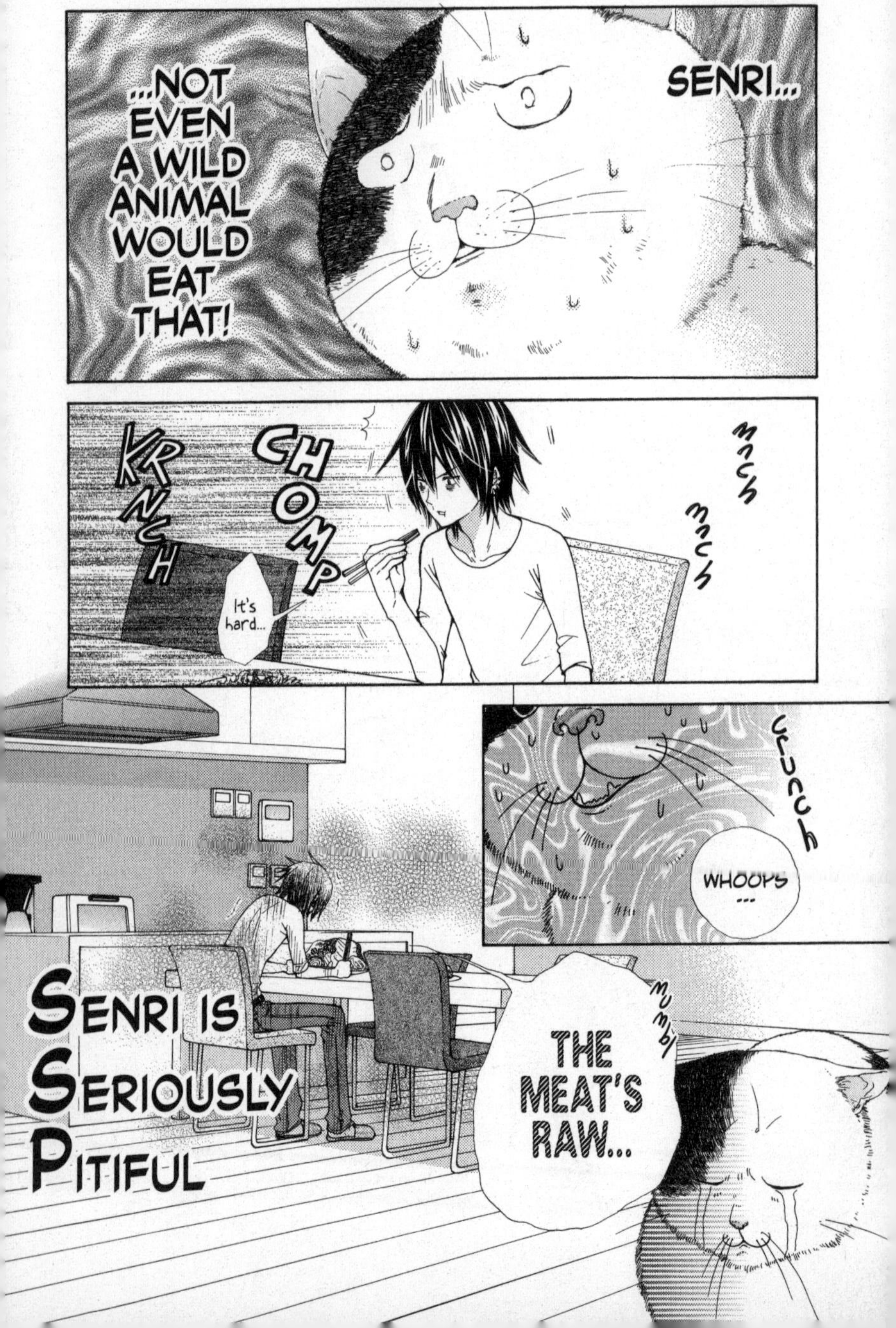
SENRI...
...NOT EVEN A WILD ANIMAL WOULD EAT THAT!
mnch
mnch
CHOMP
KRNCH
It's hard...
UGUUGH
WHOOPS ...
MUMBL
THE MEAT'S RAW...
SENRI IS SERIOUSLY PITIFUL

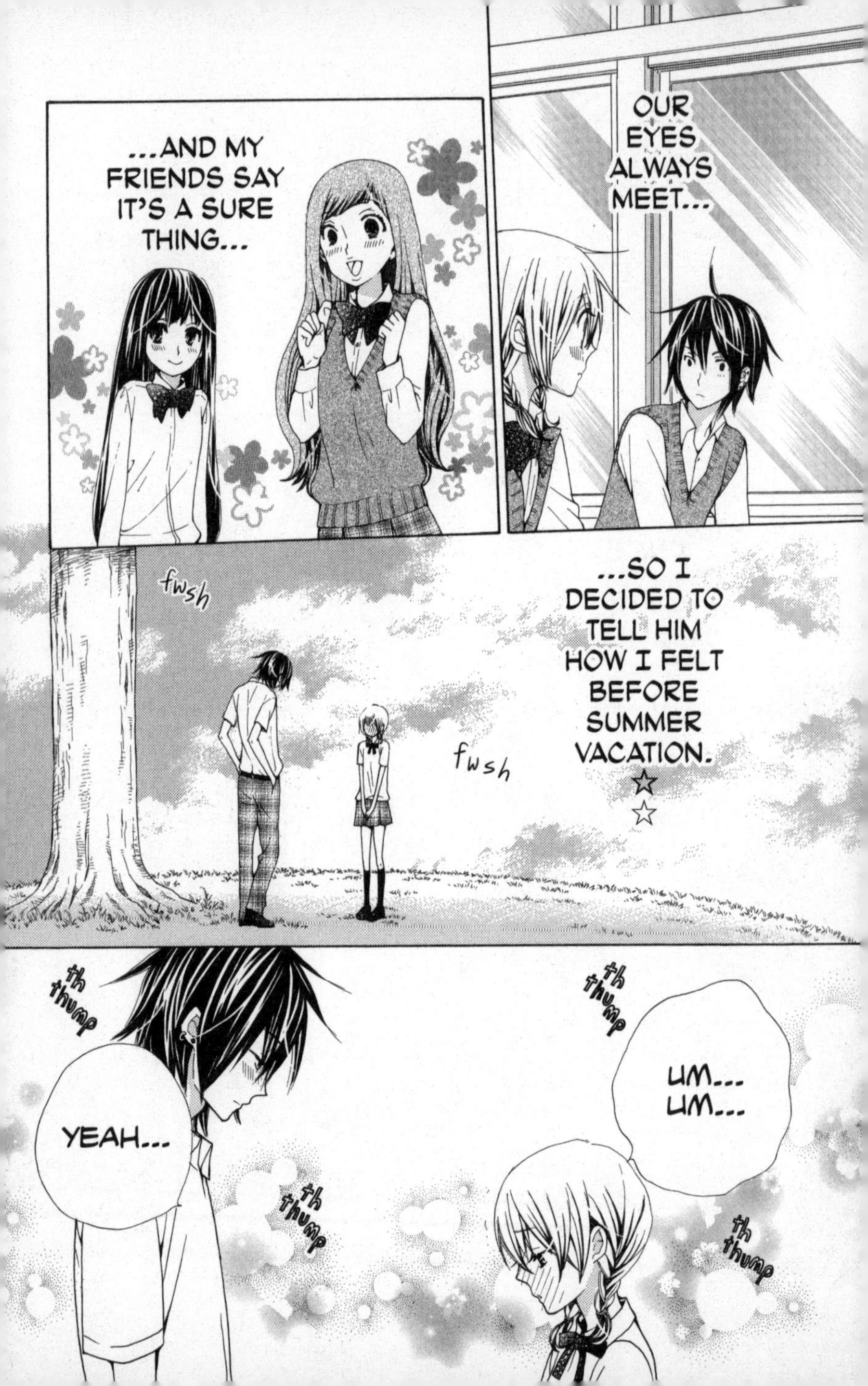
OUR EYES ALWAYS MEET...
...AND MY FRIENDS SAY IT'S A SURE THING...
...SO I DECIDED TO TELL HIM HOW I FELT BEFORE SUMMER VACATION. ☆ ☆
fwsh
fwsh
th thump
th thump
UM... UM...
th thump
YEAH...
th thump

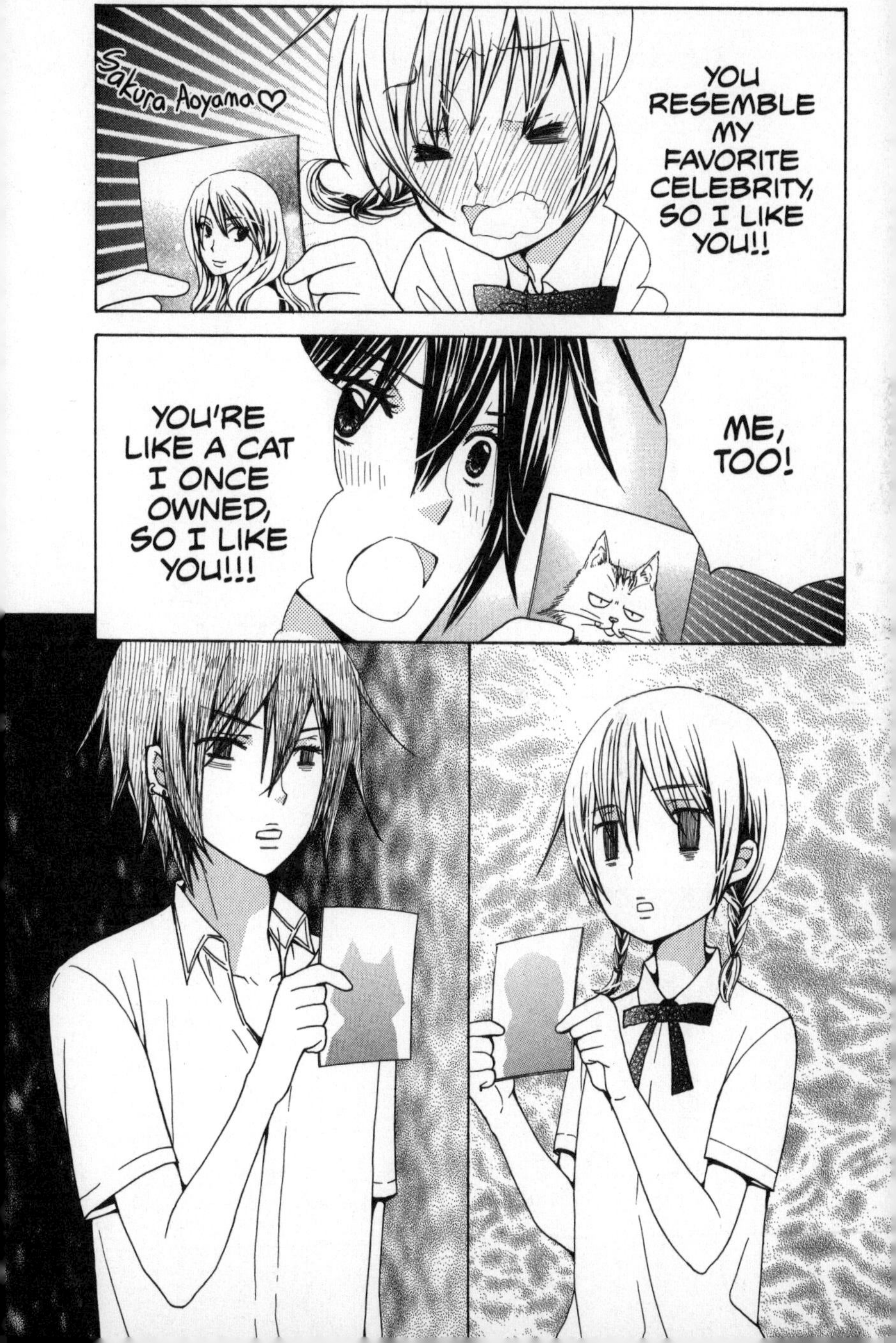
YOU RESEMBLE MY FAVORITE CELEBRITY, SO I LIKE YOU!!
Sakura Aoyama♡
ME, TOO!
YOU'RE LIKE A CAT I ONCE OWNED, SO I LIKE YOU!!!

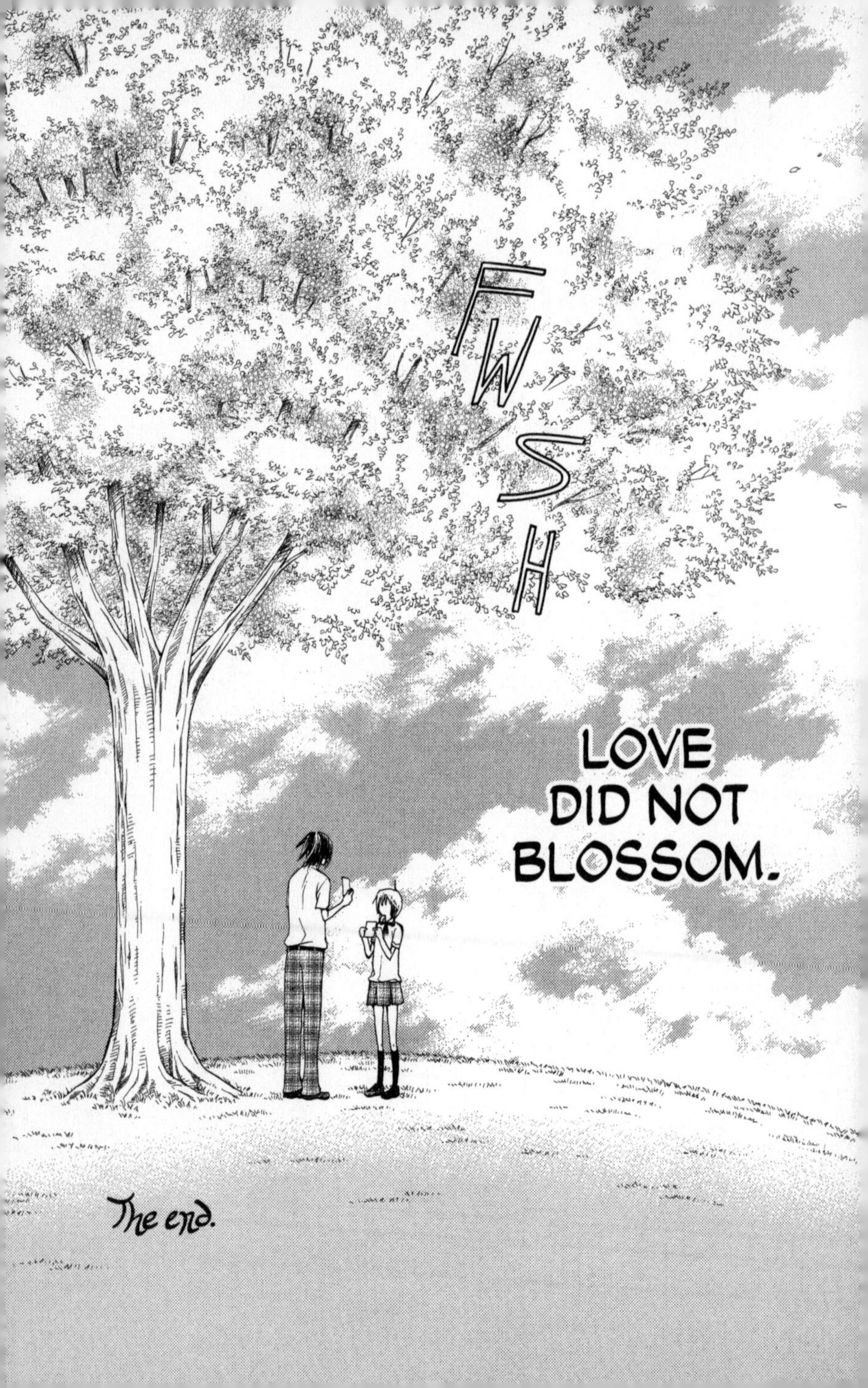
FWSH
LOVE DID NOT BLOSSOM.
The end.

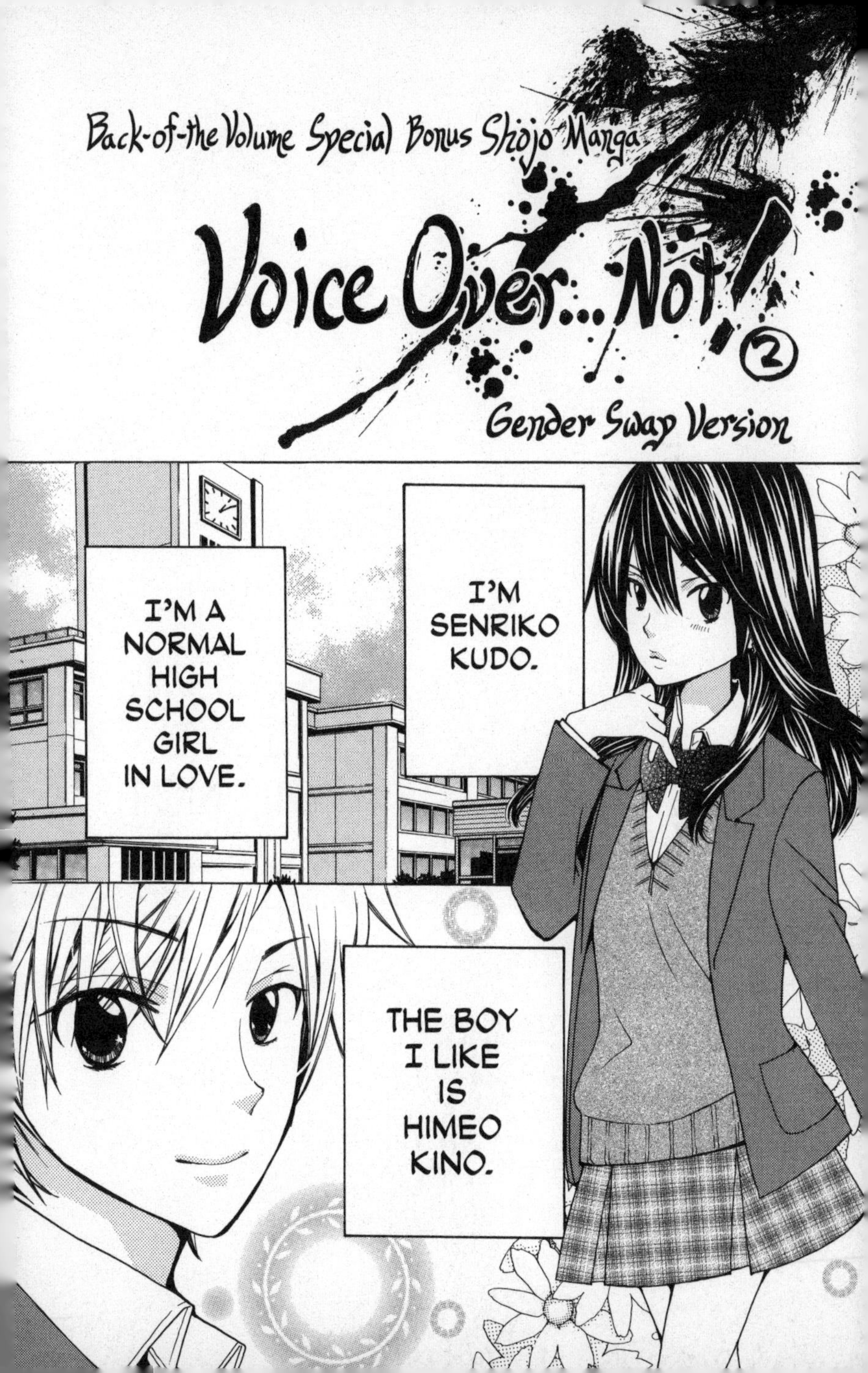
Back-of-the Volume Special Bonus Shojo Manga
Voice Over...Not! 2
Gender Swap Version
I'M SENRIKO KUDO.
I'M A NORMAL HIGH SCHOOL GIRL IN LOVE.
THE BOY I LIKE IS HIMEO KINO.

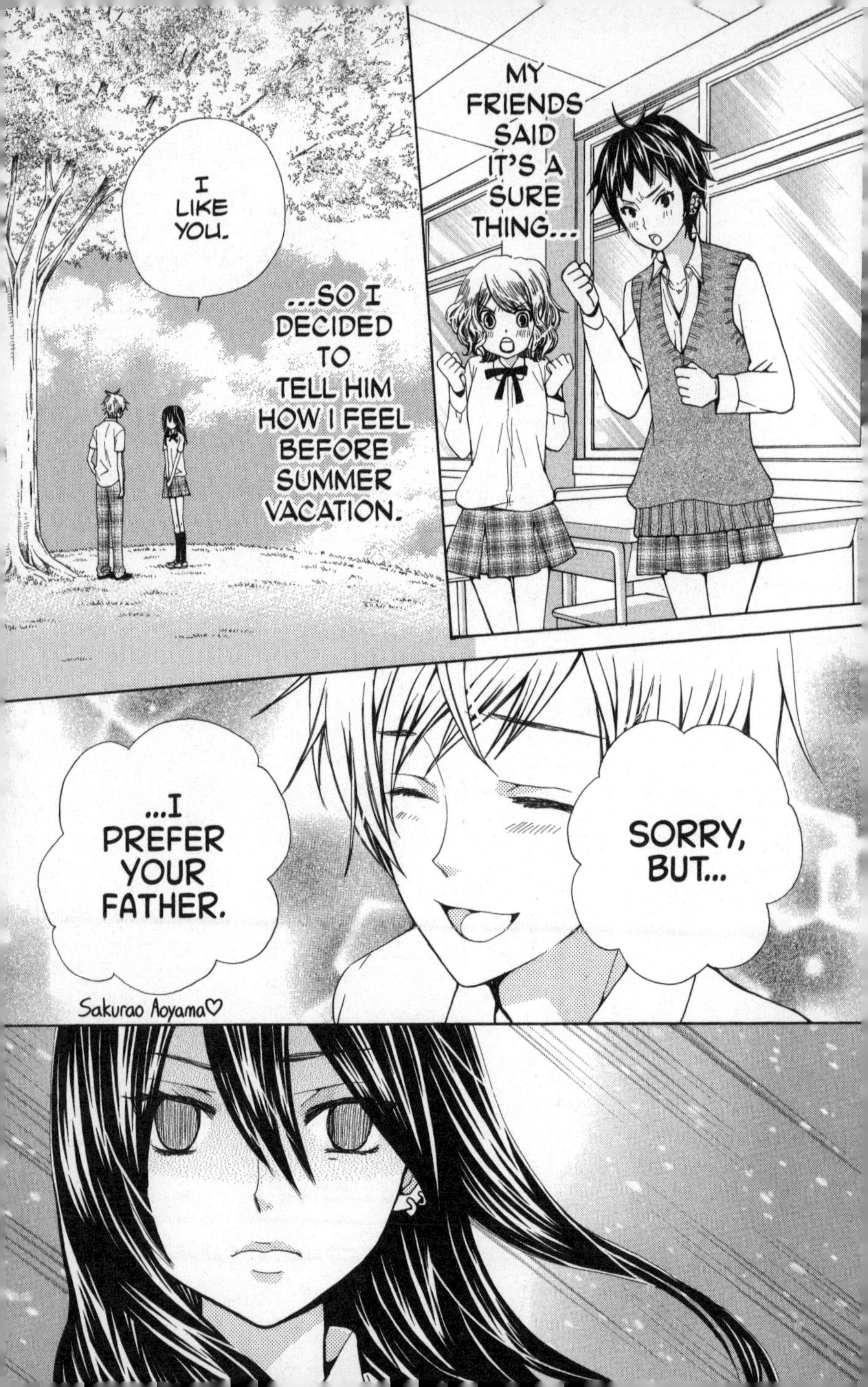
MY FRIENDS SAID IT'S A SURE THING...
...SO I DECIDED TO TELL HIM HOW I FEEL BEFORE SUMMER VACATION.
I LIKE YOU.
SORRY, BUT...
...I PREFER YOUR FATHER.
Sakurao Aoyama♡

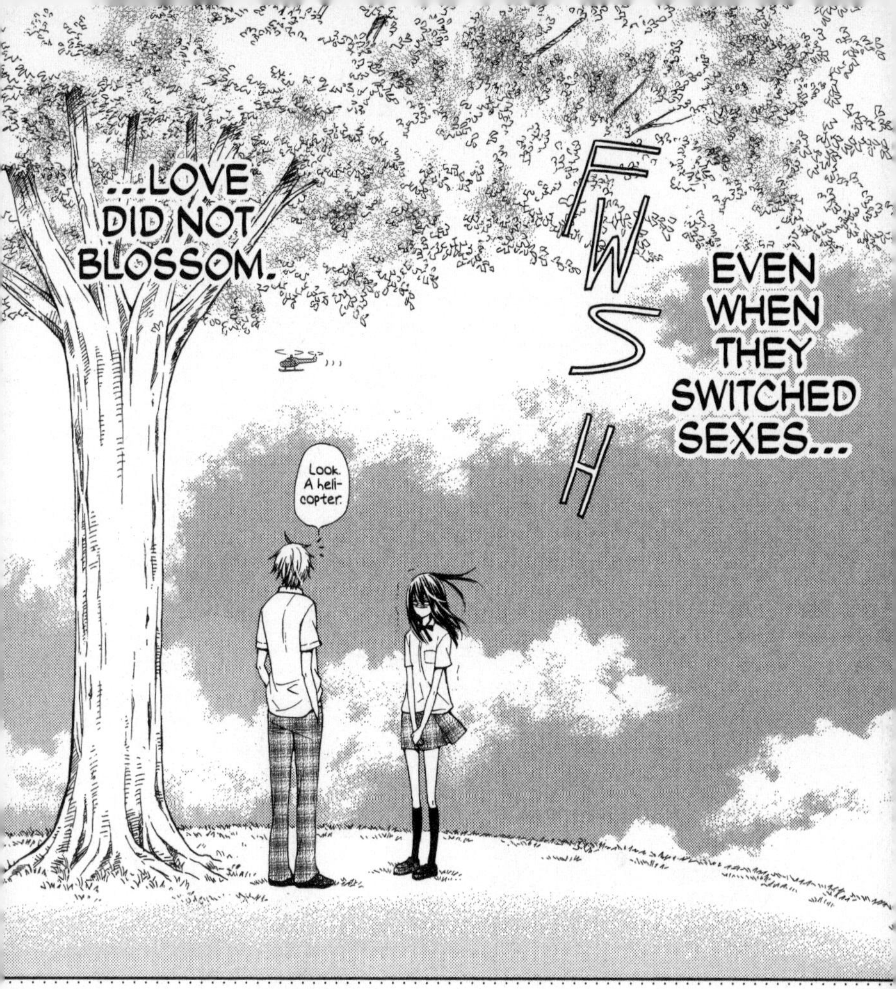
EVEN WHEN THEY SWITCHED SEXES...
FWSH
...LOVE DID NOT BLOSSOM.
Look. A heli-copter.
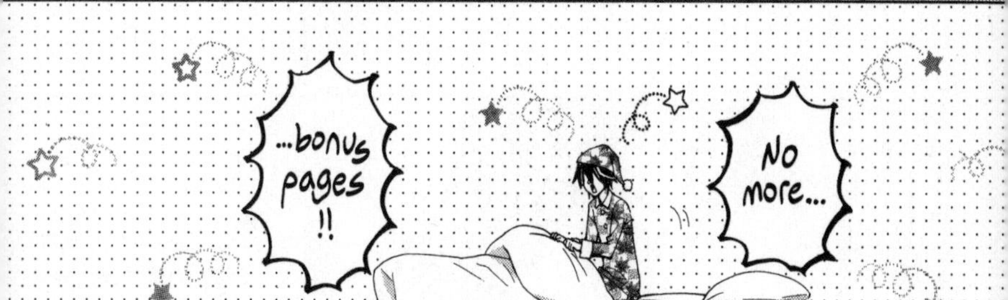
No more...
...bonus pages!!

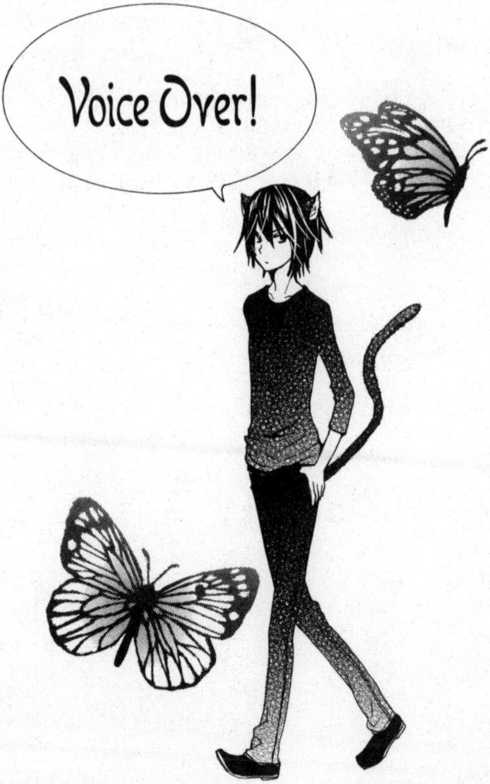
Voice Over!

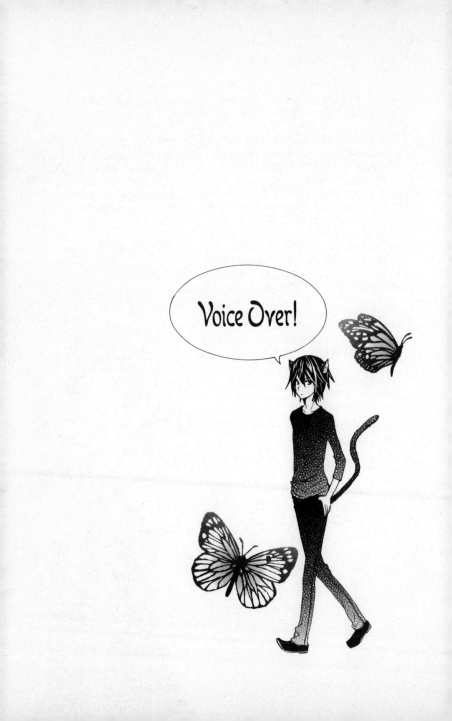

☆ Afterword ☆

- Thank you for reading!! I suddenly got two extra pages, so I get to write an afterword here.

- The requested illustrations this time were the ones with animal ears—with specific requests for Senri & Yamada P to wear cat ears!! Thanks for the requests!! Let me know if you have any more ideas!
And thank you very much for all the heartwarming letters!! I read every word of every last one. Sorry I'm so slow to reply.

- And much thanks to everyone who read this volume, everyone who helped with composition, everyone who helped with research, my editor, the graphic novel editor, my assistants, my friends and my family!!

- A lot of people are going through a hard time right now after the earthquake, but I sincerely hope that everyone can find something to smile about!

- See you in Volume 6!!

♡ If you want, let me hear your thoughts! ♡

Maki Minami c/o
Shojo Beat
P.O. Box 77010
San Francisco, CA
94107

Maki Minami
南マキ

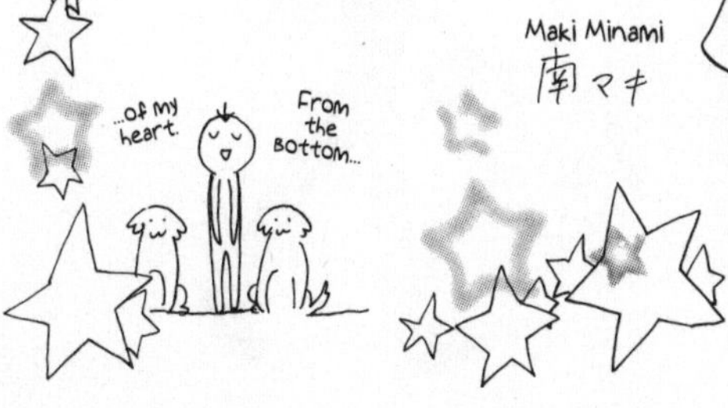

From the bottom...
...of my heart.

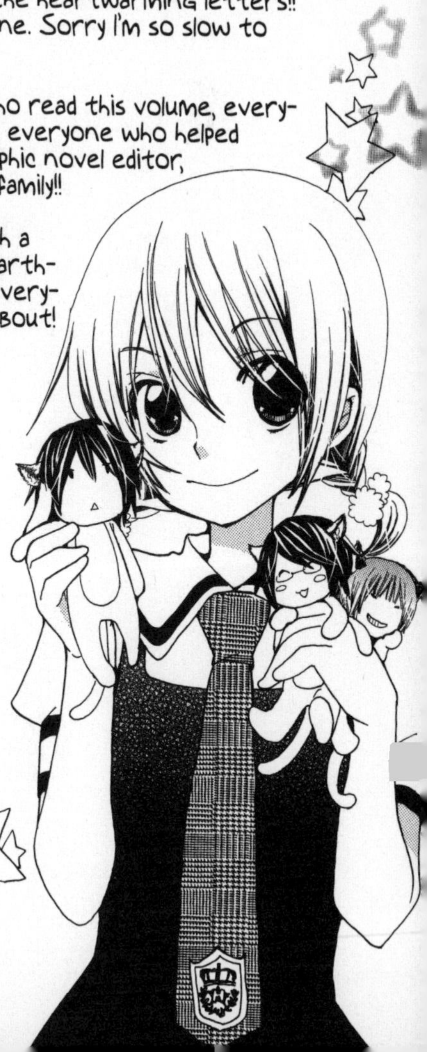

Voice Over! Seiyu Academy

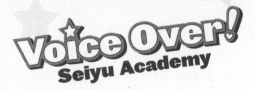

End Notes

Page 14, panel 1: Nikuta
In the original Japanese, the Nikuta was spelled 29太 (*ni ku ta*).

Page 14, panel 5: Power spots, ryuuketsu
Power spots are places with strong mystical or spiritual power. *Ryuuketsu* (dragon holes) are a type of power spot.

Page 70, panel 3: Geinou
Geinou (spelled with different kanji than used in the original) refer to entertainment and the entertainment world.

Maki Minami is from Saitama Prefecture in Japan. She debuted in 2001 with *Kanata no Ao* (Faraway Blue). Her other works include *Kimi wa Girlfriend* (You're My Girlfriend), *Mainichi ga Takaramono* (Every Day Is a Treasure), *Yuki Atataka* (Warm Winter) and *S•A*, which was published in English by VIZ Media.